The Mystery of the Trinity
in the Theological Thought
of Pope John Paul II

American University Studies

Series VII
Theology and Religion

Vol. 211

PETER LANG
New York • Washington, D.C./Baltimore • Boston • Bern
Frankfurt am Main • Berlin • Brussels • Vienna • Canterbury

Antoine E. Nachef, B.S.O.

The Mystery of the Trinity in the Theological Thought of Pope John Paul II

Preface by His Eminence Bernard Cardinal Law

PETER LANG
New York Washington, D.C./Baltimore Boston Bern
Frankfurt am Main Berlin Brussels Vienna Canterbury

Library of Congress Cataloging-in-Publication Data

Nachef, Antoine E.
The mystery of the Trinity in the theological thought of Pope John Paul II /
Antoine E. Nachef, B.S.O.; preface by His Eminence Bernard Cardinal Law.
p. cm. — (American university studies. Series VII:
Theology and religion; vol. 211)
Includes bibliographical references.
1. John Paul II, Pope, 1920– —Contributions in doctrine of the Trinity. 2. Trinity—History of
doctrines—20th century. 3. Catholic Church—Doctrines—History—20th century. I. Title.
BT109.N33   231'.044—dc21   99-17572
ISBN 0-8204-4524-X
ISSN 0740-0446

Die Deutsche Bibliothek-CIP-Einheitsaufnahme

Nachef, Antoine E.:
The mystery of the trinity in the theological thought of Pope John Paul II /
Antoine E. Nachef, B.S.O.; preface by His Eminence Bernard Cardinal Law.
–New York; Washington, D.C./Baltimore; Boston; Bern;
Frankfurt am Main; Berlin; Brussels; Vienna; Canterbury: Lang.
(American university studies: Ser. 7; theology and religion; Vol. 211)
ISBN 0-8204-4524-X

Cover design by Nona Reuter

The paper in this book meets the guidelines for permanence and durability
of the Committee on Production Guidelines for Book Longevity
of the Council of Library Resources.

ACKNOWLEDGMENTS

In his intimate life, God "is love," the essential love shared by the three divine Persons: personal love is the Holy Spirit as the Spirit of the Father and the Son. Therefore he "searches even the depths of God," as *uncreated Love–Gift*. It can be said that in the Holy Spirit the intimate life of the Triune God becomes totally gift, an exchange of mutual love between the divine Persons and that through the Holy Spirit God exists in the mode of gift. It is the Holy Spirit who is the *personal expression* of this self-giving, of this being–love. He is Person–Love. He is Person–Gift. Here we have an inexhaustible treasure of the reality and an inexpressible deepening of the concept of *person* in God, which only divine revelation makes known to us.

Pope John Paul II, *Dominum et Vivificantem*, 10

Glory Be To The Name Of Jesus The Savior !
To Jesus Through Mary

+

In Gratitude To
Almighty God For All His Blessings
And For His Dedicated Servants
Mike And Nancy Jean
Donna Munroe
Mark And Alice Carney

+

In Recognition Of
Father Frederick J. Collins, Pastor Of Saint Mary Church In Georgetown, Massachusetts

+

Dedicated To The Ministry Of My Salvatorian Brothers
Father J. P. Martin A. Hyatt, B.S.O.
Father Larry Tuminelli, B.S.O.

TABLE OF CONTENTS

PREFACE

Nothing is more important than living ever more profoundly our baptism into the mystery of Christ's life, death, and resurrection with His awe-inspiring friendship with the Father in the Holy Spirit. It is the greatest grace and joy of our Catholic and Christian faith that we are called into this Trinitarian love and friendship.

Fr. Antoine E. Nachef's study of the mystery of the Trinity in the work of Pope John Paul II introduces us to the theological reflections of our Holy Father on this central mystery of our faith. It is a most helpful guide in appreciating how the mystery of the most Holy Trinity is at the very heart of the life and work of Pope John Paul II.

One cannot appreciate fully the tireless apostolic ministry and many pastoral initiatives of this great Pope unless one sees how they flow from his own deep faith and life of prayerful communion with the Father, Son and Holy Spirit.

His Eminence Bernard Cardinal Law
Archbishop of Boston

CHAPTER ONE

INTRODUCTION

The theology of Pope John Paul II had a great influence on my theological formation since the first years of my studies at the Gregorian University in Rome. As I begin to prepare this volume on the trinitarian theology of the Pope, many of his talks come to mind, especially the first time at Mass in 1987 at the Basilica of St. Peter when I heard him speaking about the Holy Spirit. Now, after twelve years of a much closer look at the sermon volumes of John Paul II, I find the time fitting to take a careful tour through his writings from a trinitarian perspective.

Philosophical, moral, social, and theological treatises of all kinds have plumbed the depths of the thought of John Paul II. Among the mass of literature written on John Paul II there has not yet been a systematic presentation of his thought on the Trinity. A deep and creative thinking such as his should be carefully studied and located within the framework of other contemporary trinitarian theology.

For the last twenty years, St. Peter's 263rd successor, Pope John Paul II, has been exercising a vast influence upon the Catholic Church and the world with incomparable theological thinking.[1] This first–in–history Slavic Pope has already effected epoch–making changes in world history.[2] Those who have

---

[1]See André Frossard, *Portrait of John Paul II*, San Francisco: Ignatius Press, 1990, 15–19 and 50–52; Yves Calvez, "Extremely Self–Righteous," *30 Days* April, 1988, 42–43; J. Bryan Hehir, "Taking on the Super–Rivals: Reactions to the Pope's Latest Encyclical," in *Commonweal* 115 (1988): 170; Habiger Matthew, "Situating *Sollicitudo Rei Socialis* in Catholic Social Teaching," in *Social Justice Review* 79 (1988): 138; Peter Hebblethwaite, *Pope John Paul II and the Church*, Kansas City: Sheed and Ward, 1995, 7; Jan Cardinal Willebrands, "John Paul II and the search for full unity among Christians," in *John Paul II. A Panorama of his Teachings*, New York: New City Press, 1989, 48; Josef Cardinal Tomko, "Mission and dialogue in the teaching of John Paul II," in *John Paul II. A Panorama of his Teachings*, New York: New City Press, 1989, 91.

[2]See Pope John Paul II, *Gift and Mystery. On the Fiftieth Anniversary of my Priestly Ordination*, New York: Doubleday, 1996, 66; *The Thought of Pope John Paul II*, Edited by John M. McDermott, Rome: Gregorian University Press, 1993, XI; Daniel Callam, "The Gospel of Life," in *The Canadian Catholic Review* 13 (June 1995): 2; Carl Bernstein and Marco Politi, *His Holiness John Paul II and*

worked with him are aware of his immense intellect and appreciate that this is one of the finest minds they have ever met. A man of knowledge, he commands world–wide attention when he publishes a document because, as faithful as he is to the Tradition of the Church, he still presents that Tradition in a very accessible way to all contemporary readers.[3] The exercise of his office and his personal charism join together to produce a noticeable depth in his thinking about God and man.[4] Whether he is reformulating the faith of the Church or meditating on her identity and role in the modern world, he manifests a profound intellectual vitality. Hans Urs von Balthasar describes in short lines a noteworthy summary of Pope John Paul II's extraordinary talents:

> After all, we could have an entirely different Pope, who might not be a philosopher, and yet could state the tenets of our faith in quite a simple manner. To what degree is the personal philosophy and theology of the Holy Father authoritative for the universal Church? I think his teachings expressly contain theses which are central to the understanding of our faith; the body, for instance, the human person, the community, and the wonderful things he has to say on human labor and divine mercy. What is developed here is rooted directly in revelation, and should be pondered by every Christian, not in order to construct a closed system with his encyclicals, but to obtain from his great intuitions a point of departure from which new reflections on divine revelation may emerge.[5]

---

the Hidden History of our Time, New York: Doubleday, 1996, 1–13.

[3]See Pope John Paul II, *Gift and Mystery. On the Fiftieth Anniversary of my Priestly Ordination*, New York: Doubleday, 1996, 95; Tad Szulc, *Pope John Paul II. The Biography*, New York: Scribner, 1995, 55; Robert F. Morneau, "Redemptor Hominis: Themes and Theses." *Review for Religious*, 39 (1980), 247; J. Honoré, "Christ the Redeemer, Core of John Paul's Teaching," in *John Paul II. A Panorama of his Teachings*, New York: New City Press, 1989, 12; Joseph Cardinal Cordeiro, "The religious sense of man," in *John Paul II. A Panorama of his Teachings*, New York: New City Press, 1989, 75; Peter Hebblethwaite, *Pope John Paul II and the Church*, Kansas City: Sheed and Ward, 1995, 11; "A coup for the Pope," Editorial. *The Tablet* 247 (1993): 1251.

[4]See Karol Wojtyla, "The Task of Christian Philosophy Today," in *Proceedings of the American Catholic Philosophical Association* 53 (1979): 3–4; Anselm K. Min, "John Paul II's Anthropology of Concrete Totality," in *Proceedings of the American Catholic Philosophical Association* 58 (1984): 120; Roger M. Mahony, "Perspectives for Viewing the Social Concerns Encyclical," *Origins* 18 (1988): 69; *The Encyclicals of John Paul II*, Ed. J. Michael Miller, Indiana: Our Sunday Visitor Publishing Division, Our Sunday Visitor, Inc., 1996, 23; Joseph Cardinal Cordeiro, "The religious sense of man," in *John Paul II. A Panorama of his Teachings*, New York: New City Press, 1989, 73; Daniel Callam, "The Gospel of Life," in *The Canadian Catholic Review* 13 (June 1995): 2; Peter Hebblethwaite, *Pope John Paul II and the Church*, Kansas City: Sheed and Ward, 1995, 3–8.

[5]Hans Urs von Balthasar, *Test Everything: Hold Fast to What is Good*. An interview with Hans Urs von Balthasar by Angelo Scola, English Translation, San Francisco, 1989, 65.

Prerequisites for the study of John Paul II's Trinitarian Theology

If one takes into consideration the multitude of factors involved in publishing a papal document coming from John Paul II, one discovers that extreme care is necessary for studying the theological content of that specific document. Several elements that constantly emerge in the background of the trinitarian theology of the Pope constitute a body of prerequisites for the understanding of his thought. They could be summarized in seven points:

1. *Pastores Dabo Vobis* witnesses to John Paul II's constant intention to give reason for the hope and the faith of the Church (1 Pt 3:15). The importance of reasoning the faith results from his understanding of the concept of truth. The truth, being a gift of the Supreme Truth, cannot be created and measured by man. Yet, man is invited to reach the objective and universal truth relating to God and human existence, despite the difficulties and the limitations that are imposed on the intellect of man: "...faith itself cannot do without reason and the effort of 'thinking through' its contents, as that great mind Augustine bore witness: 'I wished to see with my mind what I have believed, and I have argued and labored greatly.' " If St. Augustine's words reflect the Pope's reasoning of the Church's faith, on the other hand, Aquinas provided him with the axiom that faith is and will always be the *habitus* of theology. Faith constitutes the permanent principle of theological operation, because the whole of theology is ordered to nourishing the faith of the Church.[6]

2. The abundant literary activity of John Paul II displays the thought of a man who is very well acquainted with social, political, philosophical, moral, and theological trends.[7] His writings show a blend of interests, but do not confuse the distinctive realms of inquiry. His *Letter to Families* (1994) displays his awareness of the multitude of currents that are invading even

---

[6]See St. Thomas Aquinas, "Fides, quae est quasi habitus theologiae": *In Lib. Boethii de Trinitate*, V, 4 ad 8; *In I Sentent. Prolog.*, q. I, a. 1–5; Pope John Paul II, *Pastores Dabo Vobis*, 53; *Fides et Ratio*, 43–44.

[7]See Pope John Paul II, *Catechesi Tradendae*, 60; *Fides et Ratio*, 36–48; Anna–Teresa Tymieniecka, "The Origins of the Philosophy of John Paul II," in *Proceedings of the American Catholic Philosophical Association* 53 (1979): 18; Gerald A. McCool, "The Theology of John Paul II," in *The Thought of Pope John Paul II*, John M. McDermott (ed.), Rome: Gregorian University Press, 1993, 29; Herbert McCabe, "Redemptor Hominis," in *New Blackfriars* 60 (1979), 146; James Schall, "Redemptoris Mater: The Amazement of God," in *Homiletic and Pastoral Review* 80 (October 1979): 12; Donal Dorr, "The New Social Encyclical," in *The Furrow* 32 (1981): 700–701; Mary Craig, *Man from a Far Country. A Portrait of Pope John Paul II*, London: Hodder and Stoughton, 1982, 64; Roger M. Mahony, "Perspectives for Viewing the Social Concerns Encyclical," *Origins* 18 (1988): 69; J. Honoré, "Christ the Redeemer, Core of John Paul's Teaching," in *John Paul II. A Panorama of his Teachings*, New York: New City Press, 1989, 14; Joseph Cardinal Cordeiro, "The religious sense of man," in *John Paul II. A Panorama of his Teachings*, New York: New City Press, 1989, 75; Richard J. Taylor, "*Redemptoris Mater*: Pope John Paul II's Encyclical for the Marian Year: Some Reflections," in *Priest & People* 2 (1988): 134.

Catholic circles: "Who can deny that our age is one marked by a great crisis, which appears above all as a profound 'crisis of truth'? A crisis of truth means, in the first place, a crisis of concepts."[8] This statement does not imply a blind refusal of the richness resulting from different approaches to the truth, since many elements of truth and holiness also exist outside the visible boundaries of the Catholic Church. That statement does not imply a monopolization of truth either. The Pope is inviting all theologians to serve the truth as Christ handed it down to the Apostles and as transmitted and interpreted by the Magisterium. Theology, if separated from service to the Magisterium, could become a sterile system of well–ordered ideas.

3. Beside the fact that the Pope himself constantly refers to the Divine Persons, one should detect what kind of influence his philosophical anthropology has had on his understanding of the notion of Divine Person. What imprint does his pre–papal philosophical formation on the human person leave on his Encyclicals, Apostolic Exhortations, Letters, Apostolic Letters and Post–Synodal Apostolic Exhortations? In the writings of John Paul, one does not find just the categories of traditional Thomistic orthodoxy that dominated Catholic theology in the century before Vatican II, although Thomism explains the intrinsic connection between his theological writings, his pastoral teaching, and his philosophical reflection.[9] The traditional Thomism that was taught to him at the Angelicum in Rome by the famous Garrigou–Lagrange[10] will always be a point of reference in all the disciplines developed by John Paul II. Buttiglione rightly states that the choice of the theme of St. John of the Cross for Wojtyla's first dissertation betrays an evident influence on the part of Garrigou–Lagrange, who was himself a devotee of St. John of the Cross.[11] John

[8]Pope John Paul II, *Letter to Families from Pope John Paul II*, 13; *Fides et Ratio*, 47. Already in 1979, Wojtyla expressed the deep crisis of concepts that is invading not only the theology of the Church but its philosophy and anthropology [See Karol Wojtyla, "The Task of Christian Philosophy Today," in *Proceedings of the American Catholic Philosophical Association* 53 (1979): 3; Anselm K. Min, "John Paul II's Anthropology of Concrete Totality," in *Proceedings of the American Catholic Philosophical Association* 58 (1984): 120].

[9]See Gerald A. McCool, "The Theology of John Paul II," in *The Thought of Pope John Paul II*, John M. McDermott (ed.), Rome: Gregorian University Press, 1993, 31; Roger Duncan, "On Reading *Laborem Exercens*," *Homiletic ans Pastoral Review* 86 (July 1986): 11; Pope John Paul II, *Fides et Ratio*, 43–44.

[10]See Rocco Buttiglione, Karol Wojtyla. *The Thought of the Man who became Pope John Paul II*, trans. Paolo Guietti and Francesca Murphy, Grand Rapids/Cambridge: William B. Eerdmans Publishing Company, 1997, 44–45; Tad Szulc, *Pope John Paul II. The Biography*, New York: Scribner, 1995, 143; Peter Hebblethwaite, *Pope John Paul II and the Church*, Kansas City: Sheed and Ward, 1995, 5–6.

[11]See Rocco Buttiglione, *Karol Wojtyla. The Thought of the Man who became Pope John Paul II*, trans. Paolo Guietti and Francesca Murphy, Grand Rapids/Cambridge: William B. Eerdmans

Paul, however, has clearly been rethought by a very perceptive mind in touch with the concrete reality of faith, fascinated by the experience of mystics,[12] and trained in a personalist philosophy.[13] The Pope does not follow blindly the two–step method of neoscholastic analysis, according to which a question is studied from the point of view of natural reason (philosophy) and then evaluated from the viewpoint of revelation (theology). Instead of the method that was current in the Church documents of the first half of the present century, he "intertwines the philosophical and theological perspectives in a study of problems rooted in the fundamental framework of anthropology."[14] Often in his Encyclicals and writings John Paul II employs a phenomenological method of description to analyze the structures of reality. The phenomenology of the *person* is an abundant source of the terms and categories that were applied to his theology, thus reproducing an incomparable newness to many aspects of the Church's theology and tradition.

4. One should not be surprised to find a very skillful blending of St. Augustine and St. Thomas Aquinas. John Paul II is not a man who can be imprisoned in the box of an exclusive and defined system of thinking. As the prime teacher in the Catholic Church, he acknowledges the richness of Tradition and seeks the truth above all things. Buttiglione states that in John Paul II "the thought of St. Thomas is thus not schematically opposed to that of Augustine." One will notice in the investigation of the trinitarian thought of John Paul the synthesis between the Aristotelian elements and the

---

Publishing Company, 1997, 45; Réginald Garrigou–Lagrange, *Les trois âges de la vie intérieur, prélude de celle du ciel,* 2 vols., Paris: Cerf, 1938; Ibid., *Perfection chrétienne et contemplation selon St. Thomas d'Aquin et St. Jean de la Croix,* 2 vols, Saint Maximin, 1923; Ibid., *Les trois conversions et les trois voies,* Paris: Cerf, 1933.

[12]It should not be forgotten that before he began his doctoral studies at Lublin, Wojtyla had already earned his Doctorate in theology under the direction of the same Garrigou–Lagrange. His dissertation entitled *Faith according to Saint John of the Cross,* explains the efficacious influence of mysticism on his personal spiritual life and theology (see Karol Wojtyla, *Faith According to Saint John of the Cross,* San Francisco: Ignatius Press, 1981; John Paul II, *Be Not Afraid! Interviews with A. Frossard,* Garden City, N.Y.: Doubleday–Image, 1985, 16–18; Tad Szulc, *Pope John Paul II. The Biography,* New York: Scribner, 1995, 54).

[13]See *The Thought of Pope John Paul II,* Edited by John M. McDermott, Rome: Gregorian University Press, 1993, XIII; Roger Duncan, "On Reading *Laborem Exercens,*" *Homiletic and Pastoral Review* 86 (July 1986): 12; Peter Hebblethwaite, *Pope John Paul II and the Church,* Kansas City: Sheed and Ward, 1995, 6; Pope John Paul II, *Fides et Ratio,* 46.

[14]John J. Conley, "The philosophical foundations of the thought of John Paul II. A Response," in *The Thought of Pope John Paul II,* John M. McDermott (ed.), Rome: Gregorian University Press, 1993, 25–26. See also Pope John Paul II, *Fides et Ratio,* 36–48.

Platonic–Augustinian elements.[15]

5. One must first become aware of John Paul II's perception of the present historical moment. As he himself asserted in *Tertio Millennio Adveniente*, 23, "the year 2000 has become as it were a hermeneutical key of my Pontificate." With this awareness of the historical moment he intends not to introduce any form of a new millenarianism, but to increase the "sensitivity to all that the Spirit is saying to the Church and to the Churches (cf. Rev 2:7ff)..."[16] We are standing at the close of the Second Millennium with a Pope who grew visibly with the Second Vatican Council and is naturally very well acquainted with its history and its theology.[17] John Paul II took part in all four sessions of the Second Vatican Council, was on drafting committees for the "Constitution on the Church in the Modern World" and the marriage session of "The Church in the World Today." Moreover, he also took part in every synod from the first in 1967 to the one immediately held before his election to the papacy in 1977. He constantly watches and interprets the signs of time and, therefore, makes his own the wish of Pope John XXIII to make the Church enjoy a maximum visibility and presence in the world. This desire of Pope John XXIII inspired the Second Vatican Council's Pastoral Constitution *Gaudium et Spes* and explains John Paul II's constant reference to *Gaudium et Spes* with his intimate attachment to its theology and its spirituality.[18]

---

[15]Rocco Buttiglione, Karol Wojtyla. *The Thought of the Man who became Pope John Paul II*, trans. Paolo Guietti and Francesca Murphy, Grand Rapids/Cambridge: William B. Eerdmans Publishing Company, 1997, 75.

[16]Pope John Paul II, *Tertio Millennio Adveniente*, 23. See also Ibid., *Dominicae Cenae*, 13; *Pastores Dabo Vobis*, 82; *Ut Unum Sint*, 1; Thomas H. Stahel, "Redemptoris Mater," in *America* 156 (1987): 353; J. Honoré, "Christ the Redeemer, Core of John Paul's Teaching," in *John Paul II. A Panorama of his Teachings*, New York: New City Press, 1989, 25.

[17]See Pope John Paul II, *Tertio Millennio Adveniente*, 18–19; Gerald M. McCool, "The Theology of John Paul II," in *The Thought of Pope John Paul II*, John M. McDermott (ed.), Rome: Gregorian University Press, 1993, 30–31; Basil Hume, "Foreword to the British Edition," in Karol Wojtyla, *Sign of Contradiction*, 1979, p. X; Mary Craig, *Man from a Far Country. A Portrait of Pope John Paul II*, London: Hodder And Stoughton, 1982, 64; Peter Hebblethwaite, *Pope John Paul II and the Church*, Kansas City: Sheed and Ward, 1995, 3; Hans Cardinal Groër, "The Church Sacrament of Salvation," in *John Paul II. A Panorama of his Teachings*, New York: New City Press, 1989, 28–29; Jan Cardinal Willebrands, "John Paul II and the search for full unity among Christians," in *John Paul II. A Panorama of his Teachings*, New York: New City Press, 1989, 49–51; Richard J. Taylor, "*Redemptoris Mater*: Pope John Paul II's Encyclical for the Marian Year: Some Reflections," in *Priest & People* 2 (1988): 133.

[18]See Karol Wojtyla, "The Task of Christian Philosophy Today," in *Proceedings of the American Catholic Philosophical Association* 53 (1979): 3–4; Pope John Paul II, *Duodecimum Saeculum*, 12; *Centesimus Annus*, 1–3; *Dominicae Cenae*, 13; *The Freedom of Conscience and of Religion*, 3; *Redemptionis Donum*, 1; *Mulieris Dignitatem*, 1; *Pastores Dabo Vobis*, 8; *Letter to Families from Pope John Paul II*, 3; *Vita Consecrata*, 53; *The Encyclicals of John Paul II*, Ibid.,

6.The difficult time that the Church has been going through before and after the Second Vatican Council has efficaciously influenced Pope John Paul II.[19] In his first Encyclical, *Redemptor Hominis*, he explicitly describes the obstacles that Pope Paul VI faced in his Petrine ministry when trying to implement the teaching of Vatican II in the Church. Interior and exterior difficulties shaped the Pontificate of Paul VI. Tormented as he was by the crisis that the Church was experiencing, and convinced that "the split between the Gospel and culture is undoubtedly the tragedy of our time,"[20] Pope Paul VI, as Pope John Paul II describes him, "knew how to display *ad extra*, externally, the true countenance of the Church, in spite of the various internal weaknesses that affected her in the postconciliar period."[21] Especially did the theology of the Second Vatican Council and that of Pope Paul VI play a major role in the doctrinal underpinnings of Pope John Paul II.

7. It is true, Christ stands at the center of Pope John Paul II's theological thinking, but this is not as simple as it appears. His first Encyclical, *Redemptor Hominis*, reveals the main lines of his Pontificate's program as far as theology is concerned. But Christ, as a Divine Person, is part of the Blessed Trinity which constitutes for the Pope the core of the Christian Revelation.[22] He is convinced that Christology and trinitarian theology are two intimately interrelated disciplines.[23] The publishing of *Celebrate 2000! Reflections on*

24; Edna Mcdonagh, "Redemptor Hominis and Ireland," in *The Furrow* 30 (1979): 625; Josef Cardinal Tomko, "Mission and dialogue in the teaching of John Paul II," in *John Paul II. A Panorama of his Teachings*, New York: New City Press, 1989, 83; Carl Bernstein and Marco Politi, *His Holiness John Paul II and the Hidden History of our Time*, New York: Doubleday, 1996, 8–10.

[19]See Pope John Paul II, *Redemptor Hominis*, 11; *Celebrate 2000! Reflections on Jesus, the Holy Spirit, and the Father*, Ann Arbor, Michigan: Servant Publications, 1996, 52–53; *Gift and Mystery. On the Fiftieth Anniversary of my Priestly Ordination*, New York: Doubleday, 1996, 66; André Frossard, *Portrait of John Paul II*, San Francisco: Ignatius Press, 1990, 20–22; *The Thought of Pope John Paul II*, Edited by John M. McDermott, Rome: Gregorian University Press, 1993, XIII; Tad Szulc, *Pope John Paul II. The Biography*, New York: Scribner, 1995, 316–317; Jan Cardinal Willebrands, "John Paul II and the search for full unity among Christians," in *John Paul II. A Panorama of his Teachings*, New York: New City Press, 1989, 48–53.

[20]Pope Paul VI, *Evangelii Nuntiandi*, 20.

[21]*Redemptor Hominis*, 4. See also Pope Paul VI, *Lumen Ecclesiae*, 8; Pope John Paul II, *Fides et Ratio*, 43.

[22]See Pope John Paul II, *Redemptor Hominis*, 11; *Vita Consecrata*, 15.

[23]See Pope John Paul II, *Vita Consecrata*, 14 and 21; John Saward, *Christ is the Answer. The Christ–Centered teaching of Pope John Paul II*, New York: Alba House, 1995, 21–26.

Jesus, the Holy Spirit, and the Father[24] situates John Paul's Christology in the overall context of his thinking about the Trinity. In *Tertio Millennio Adveniente*, he explains that the thematic structure over the span of three years, from 1997 to 1999, "centered on Christ, the Son of God made man, must necessarily be theological, and therefore Trinitarian."[25]

Certainly it is difficult to investigate all the aspects of John Paul's trinitarian theology in the present research. My purpose is limited to shed light on the Pope's understanding of the mystery of the Trinity: how he envisions the *intra–trinitarian life* of the Father, the Son and the Holy Spirit; how he understands the role of the Divine Persons in *creation*, in *redemption* and in *eschatology*.

Theological Content and Method of Analysis

As a first step, the origins of John Paul II's philosophical and theological thinking will be investigated, especially in their relationship with the Second Vatican Council, Thomism, the philosophy of Max Scheler, and the various resources he came in contact with before and after his election to the papacy. To delve into philosophy would not be necessary in the present work if the Christian personalism of John Paul II were not a major factor for understanding the notion of *person* in the trinitarian context. The philosophical notion of *person*, then, will be studied in terms of its function in his trinitarian theology as it appears in papal documents. Whether it is Thomism or Schelerian phenomenology that stands at the roots of John Paul II's philosophical approach to the person, makes a big difference in his presentation of a Trinity of Persons in God. The influence of philosophical personalism on his understanding of the economy of the Son will be a constant theme. Whether it is theology of creation (chapter three), theology of redemption (chapter four), or christology (chapter five), the reference of John Paul to his philosophical notion of person is very noticeable. The same is also valid in the remaining chapters on the theology of the Holy Spirit.

Prior to his election to the See of St. Peter, Karol Wojtyla has already considered the truths of Divine Revelation in their proper ordering: *Creation, Incarnation, Redemption*, and finally the *Sending of the Holy Spirit*. These truths must be viewed from the center of the 'Christ–event' and understood as

---

[24]See *Celebrate 2000! Reflections on Jesus, the Holy Spirit, and the Father*, Ann Arbor, Michigan: Servant Publications, 1996.

[25]Pope John Paul II, *Tertio Millennio Adveniente*, 39.

a unity.[26] Many of Pope John Paul II's writings and speeches betray the fact that he thinks he is tackling what he considers to be an inadequate theology of the Trinity. Nevertheless, he avoids explicit debates and controversies with post–conciliar christologies and theologies. In the midst of innumerable books and articles studying the thought of the Pope, the present work systematically presents his specific approach to the Divine Persons. It is not an easy task to present a systematic teaching on the Holy Trinity of a Pope who constantly and from many different points of view theologizes on the Persons of the Father and the Son and the Holy Spirit.

John Paul II has produced massive documentation: pastoral, moral–pastoral, theological, theologico–pastoral, spiritual, poetic, and philosophical. With such a multiplicity of references, the Pope's logical *akolouthia* becomes very hard to follow: it is too complex, too sophisticated to be grasped easily.[27] The earliest documents of his Pontificate illustrate an interdisciplinary method. In meditating upon any theological discipline, John Paul II interweaves trinitarian, christological, ecclesiological, anthropological, soteriological, sacramental, mariological, and social categories of analysis. Whereas academicians are accustomed to a strict separation of the disciplines and their respective methods, the Pope, as John J. Conley describes him, "shifts methodically from one perspective to another in order to provide multiple viewpoints on a given issue..."[28] I think this method shows the originality of John Paul's thinking, since all theological disciplines are ultimately united in the single science of theology. Therefore, in order to be fair to the trinitarian and christological thought of Pope John Paul II, the present work, with no claim of being exhaustive, proposes to penetrate into his trinitarian thought as it is displayed in *all his writings without exception*.

---

[26]See Karol Wojtyla, *Sources of Renewal: The Implementation of the Second Vatican Council,* San Francisco: Harper and Row, 1980, 35–41; Lothar Roos, "On a theology and Ethics of Work," in *Communio* 11 (1984): 103; J. Honoré, "Christ the Redeemer, Core of John Paul's Teaching," in *John Paul II. A Panorama of his Teachings,* New York: New City Press, 1989, 113–14; Tad Szulc, *Pope John Paul II. The Biography,* New York: Scribner, 1995, 317.

[27]See J. Honoré, "Christ the Redeemer, Core of John Paul's Teaching," in *John Paul II. A Panorama of his Teachings,* New York: New City Press, 1989, 14; Peter Hebblethwaite, *Pope John Paul II and the Church,* Kansas City: Sheed and Ward, 1995, 52–53; Anna–Teresa Tymieniecka, "The Origins of the Philosophy of John Paul II," in *Proceedings of the American Catholic Philosophical Association* 53 (1979): 16.

[28]John J. Conley, "The philosophical foundations of the thought of John Paul II," in *The Thought of Pope John Paul II,* John M. McDermott (ed.), Rome: Gregorian University Press, 1993, 26; Giacomo Cardinal Biffi, "The Action of the Holy Spirit in the Church and in the World," in *John Paul II. A Panorama of his Teachings,* New York: New City Press, 1989, 38; Raymond T. Gawronski, "Redemptor Hominis," in *The Thought of Pope John Paul II,* Rome: Gregorian University, 1993, 221.

The development of the trinitarian theology of John Paul II entangles itself in a tricky framework: some aspects that are merely mentioned in a certain document, are more extensively explored in others. I hope that my method of presenting John Paul's theology does not give the reader the impression of an anachronistic study. One should not conclude that the historical development is in any way neglected in the trinitarian theology of the Pope when the present work simultaneously refers to many different papal documents for the purpose of analyzing a certain specific theological idea. The thought of Pope John Paul II has evolved since the beginning of his Pontificate in 1978, yet all of his writings are still interconnected and, therefore, should be studied as one piece. What the Pope starts to present in a certain document, he looks at it in another document from another point of view and for more depth and understanding.

The extensive analysis of a key text pertaining to a certain document helps to single out the main ideas of the Pope's trinitarian theology that are configurated in that specific text. Often, what a key text contains is also spread throughout the same document and even present in many other writings. This method of studying a key text by drawing parallels from the same and other papal documents, facilitates the research because it shows the different angles of the Pope's approach to that question and, at the same time, manifests the evolution of his thought.

CHAPTER TWO

THE PHILOSOPHICAL ANTHROPOLOGY OF POPE JOHN PAUL II AND ITS IMPLICATION ON HIS THEOLOGICAL NOTION OF PERSON

A Note on the Concept of Person in the Tradition of the Church

The traditional belief in God as "One God in Three Persons" is the result of a very complicated history.[1] Since the beginning of the Church's reflection on the identity of the Son and the Holy Spirit, there has been the constant problem of the nature of their relationships with the Father. A heavy theological debate concerning the nature of that relationship clearly reached its culminating point in the fourth century: *Modalism* emphasized the unity of the nature of God at the expense of a God who exists in Three self-subsistent Persons; *Subordinationism*, in the line of Hellenistic philosophical thinking, placed the Son and the Holy Spirit in a lesser degree of being than the Father.

The Council of Nicea (325) which confirmed the equality of nature between Son and Father through the use of the term *homoousios* did not terminate the theological debate concerning the Trinity. Before and after the Council, there were many confusions in theological circles concerning the definition of the concepts of *persona, hypostases, prosopon,* and *ousia*.[2] That confusion was worsened by the major differences in interpreting theological concepts between East and West. In the East, *Three Hypostases* were used to indicate the Three Divine Persons. However, since *Hypostases* was translated as *natura* in the West, the West accused Eastern trinitarian theology of having a Tritheistic tendency. The West employed the expression *Three prosopon* to indicate the Three Divine Persons. Since *Prosopon* was translated as *mask* in the East, Eastern Fathers accused the West of Sabellianic tendency in their outlook

---

[1] I agree with John O'Donnell when he says:"Uno sguardo alla storia della teologia cristiana rivela che la formula non è così chiara come può apparire e che il termine persona non ebbe un ingresso pacifico nella teologia." (*Il Mistero della Trinità*, Roma: Editrice Pontificia Università Gregoriana, Edizioni Piemme, 1989, 101).

[2] See Yves Congar, *Credo nello Spirito Santo*, Vol. III, Brescia: Queriniana, 1987, 7.

about God.[3] This is how St. Gregory Nazianzen describes the confusing differences between East and West:

> The Italians also mean the same thing, but owing to the scantiness of their vocabulary and its poverty of terms they are unable to distinguish between Essences and Hypostases and therefore introduce the term Persons...This slight difference of sound was taken to indicate a difference of faith. Then, Sabellianism was suspected in the doctrine of Three Persons, Arianism and that of Three Hypostases, both being the offspring of a contentious spirit. And then, from the gradual but constant growth of irritation (the unfailing result of contentiousness) there was a danger of the whole world being torn asunder in the strife about syllables. [4]

Stout defender of the orthodoxy of faith that he was, St. Athanasius sensed the difficulty of language and identified 'ousia' (essence) with 'hypostasis'.[5] Such terminology did not have an easy introduction even into the thought of the genius St. Jerome. Actually, the question was still presenting its problems up to the middle ages.[6] The problem of terminology as it was treated by both East and West from the very beginning created a difference in understanding the concept of nature and person, a difference that would influence both theologies for many generations. Whereas the trinitarian doctrine in the West found itself at home emphasizing the divine unity of the three Divine Persons, in the East where the intellectual atmosphere was impregnated with neoplatonic tendencies towards the hierarchy of being, the question was treated easier with the notion of person at its center.[7] That difference in approach led to the fact that Latin Scholasticism and Orthodox dogmatic theology analyze the problem differently. This difference, as De Régnon observed, is still very

---

[3]See Yves Congar, *Credo nello Spirito Santo*, vol. III, 2nd ed., Brescia: Editrice Queriniana, 1987, 43 and 47; E. Bailleux, "Le personnalisme trinitaire des Pères grecs." *MSR* 27 (1970): 7–10. R. Arnou, "Unité numérique et unité de nature chez les Pères, après le Concile de Nicée." *Greg* 15 (1934): 254; B. Otis, "Gregory of Nyssa and the Cappadocian Conception of Time." In *Studia Patristica XIV*, Part III, Berlin: Akademie–Verlag, 1976, 338; my own work on the Mariology of the Cappadocian Fathers: "Mary Virgin Mother in the Theological Thought of St. Basil the Great, St. Gregory Nazianzen, and St. Gregory of Nyssa," doctoral diss., International Marian Research Institute, Dayton, Ohio, Fairview Park: Anderson Print and Copy, 1997, 2–4.

[4]Gregory Nazianzen, *Oratio XXI*: 35, PG 35: 1124 D– 1125 B.

[5]See G. Bardy, *Dictionnaire de Théologie Catholique*, Vol. XV, col. 1666–67; S. Ephiphanius, *Haer.* 69: 72.

[6]See Yves Congar, *Credo nello Spirito Santo*, Vol. III, Brescia: Queriniana, 1987, 7; G.–L. Prestige, *Dieu dans la Pensée Patristique*, Paris, 1955, 163: Th. De Régnon, *Etudes de Théologie positive sur la Sainte Trinité*, Vol. I, 216; St. Anselm, *Epist. de Incarnatione Verbi*, XXI, (t. II, 35); St. Thomas Aquinas, *C. Err. Graec.*, I, prol.

[7]See J. N. D. Kelly, *Initiation à la doctrine des Pères de l'Eglise*, transl. C. Tunmer, Paris, 1968, 145.

obvious and relevant in contemporary trinitarian theology as far as the ecumenical dialogue between Catholics and Orthodox is concerned.[8]

Beyond doubt, the Cappadocian Fathers have essentially contributed in determining the use and value of these terms for the formulation of trinitarian dogma.[9] In their long *Auseinandersetzung* with Eunomius, they have had to resort sometimes more to the resources of reason than the data of Divine Revelation. Eunomius defended a homogeneous and simplistic knowledge of God presenting Him as an object among others for our faculty of knowing. By not compromising the incomprehensibility of God, the Cappadocians gradually clarified the situation by proposing the formula: One *ousia*, Three *hypostases*. The expression *hypostases* guarantees the concrete objectivity of the Three divine Persons: God exists in three objectively different Persons. By suggesting the notion of *relation* as the way to distinguish the Three Persons, the Cappadocians opened the road for many Fathers and theologians who later articulated the concepts of *agennesia*, *genesia*, and *ekporeusis* to explain the difference between the Divine Persons.[10] St. Augustine, a contemporary of the Cappadocians, translated the term *hypostases* as *Persona* because the expression *substantia*, which is the original meaning of *hypostases*, sounded to him to be too tritheistic.[11]

In the medieval period, *Boethius'* definition of 'person' became fundamental: 'person' is *substantia individualis naturae rationalis* (an individual substance of a rational nature), an independent type of being among many beings, either angelic or human. Since Boethius remained in the category of substances, as Joseph Ratzinger confirms,[12] his definition of person "obscured the associated notions of freedom, action and relationship which are so clear in the literary scriptural understanding of person."[13] For *Richard of St. Victor* the person is *naturae rationalis incommunicabilis existentia* (an unshared existence of an intellectual nature). Like Boethius, Richard of St.

[8]See Th. De Régnon, *Etudes de Théologie Positive sur la Sainte Trinité*, Vol. I, 251–252.

[9]See Yves Congar, *Credo nello Spirito Santo*, Vol. III, Brescia: Queriniana, 1987, 10; my own work: "Mary Virgin Mother in the Theological Thought of St. Basil the Great, St. Gregory Nazianzen, and St. Gregory of Nyssa," doctoral diss., International Marian Research Institute, Dayton, Ohio, Fairview Park: Anderson Print and Copy, 1997, 3–4.

[10]See John O'Donnell, *Ibid.*, 102.

[11]See St. Augustine, *De Trinitate*, Liber V, 9.

[12]See Joseph Ratzinger, *Dogma e Predicazione*, Brescia: Queriniana, 1974, 183; Anselm K. Min, "John Paul II's Anthropology of Concrete Totality," in *Proceedings of the American Catholic Philosophical Association* 58 (1984): 122.

[13]Brian M. Nolan, "Person, Divine," in *The New Dictionary of Theology*, Editors Joseph A. Komonchak, Mary Collins, Dermot A. Lane, Delaware 1987, 758.

Victor emphasized the substance providing it, however, with the new aspect of relationality. In fact, the expression *existence* comes from the Latin *ex–sistere*: *sistere* indicates that the person has his or her being in themselves, not in others. *Ex* indicates the relation of origin that constitutes the person.[14]

St. Thomas Aquinas, genius thinker that he was, started to reflect on Boethius' definition but ended with focusing on the relationality within the Divine nature.[15] The Three Divine Persons are *subsistent relations*. The relations are *subsistent* because each Person enjoys the whole divine essence; each Person subsists in the divinity. On the other hand, each Divine Person is what it is because it stands in a relation to the other Two Persons; the Person can be defined only in its reference to the other Two. Therefore, as John O'Donnell concludes, in St. Thomas' theology 'person' has a double connotation: *esse in* and *esse ad*.[16] St. Thomas Aquinas' notion of person found favor in many theological circles. Since the Scholastic times, each Divine Person is identified as a subsistent relation of opposition: paternity, filiation and spiration constitute the Persons of the Father, the Son and the Holy Spirit within the one Divine Nature.

Karl Barth has advocated "three modes (or ways) of being in God":[17] the one and the same personal God exists in the mode of the Father, in the mode of the Son and in the mode of the Holy Spirit. Barth does not claim to have offered a definitive solution to the problem because, ultimately he considers the Trinity a mystery. There are Three in God, but we do not know how.[18] *Karl Rahner*, in his philosophical anthropology, proposes that the human subject, in the same act in which he is aware of his limitations, becomes aware of the infinite being of God. God is the ultimate I, perfect self–conscience, pure subjectivity. In God there are "three distinct ways of being there (in the economy of salvation) and three different ways of subsistence (immanently)".[19] For Rahner there is one Divine conscience that exists in triple mode.

Joseph Cardinal Ratzinger criticizes both Barth and Rahner: we cannot think of God as an absolute *I* neglecting the dimension of *We*. Although conserving the Monotheism of the Old Testament, the Church has always considered the Absolute as a communion. Within the Oneness there is always

---

[14]See John O'Donnell, *Ibid.*, 102.

[15]See *Summa Theologica*, I, q. 29, art. 1; Brian M. Nolan, "Person, Divine," *Ibid.*, 758.

[16]John O'Donnell, *Ibid.*, 103.

[17]Karl Barth, *Church Dogmatics* I, Edinburgh: T. And T. Clark, 1975, 359.

[18]See John O'Donnell, *Ibid.*, 104.

[19]See Karl Rahner, "Il Dio trino come fondamento originario e trascendente della storia della salvezza," *Mysterium Salutis*, 3, (a curà) J. Feiner and M. Löhrer, Brescia: Queriniana, 1969, 492.

multiplicity when one thinks of God:

> The Christian concept of God gave, from the very beginning, an identic dignity to the multiplicity as well as to the oneness. Whereas for the ancients multiplicity appears only as a dissolution of the oneness, for the Christian faith, that rationalize in trinitarian terms, multiplicity possesses *a priori* the same dignity as the oneness.[20]

H. U. von Balthasar looks at the person from the point of view of mission. There is a difference between person and individual. An individual detaches himself or herself from the collective, and becomes human as human. Only when individuals embrace the particular mission that God has in store for them do they become what they are supposed to be, that is persons. Of course, this is realized in its perfect manner in the God–man Jesus Christ who gives each human person a share in his mission through a special charism.[21] *Garrigou–Lagrange* understood person as a substantial mode terminating an essence. In the same way that a point terminates a line rendering it ready to receive its act of existence, so the person terminates the human essence and grants it the act of existence.[22] *Maritain*, leaning more to the existential understanding of person, looked at the person as that which possesses and exercises an act of existence.[23]

Max Scheler

In the Introduction to *The Acting Person*, Karol Cardinal Wojtyla himself asserted the dependency of his thought on the phenomenology of Max Scheler. A quick presentation of the main thought of Scheler would seem beneficial for understanding John Paul's philosophical anthropology and, consequently, his theological notion of the human person.[24]

The major work of Max Scheler (1874–1928), *Formalism in Ethics and the*

---

[20]Joseph Ratzinger, *Dogma e Predicazione*, Brescia: Queriniana, 1974, 188.

[21]See H.U. von Balthasar, *Theodramatik 2/2, Die Personen in Christus*, Einsiedeln: Johannes Verlag, 1978; Johann G. Roten, "Im Zeichen der Ellipse. Hans Urs von Balthasars theologische Anthropologie," in *Marian Library Studies*, New Series 24 (1992–95): 62–63.

[22]See R. Garrigou–Lagrange, *De Christo Salvatore*, Torino: Marietti, 1949, 115–124.

[23]See J. Maritain, *Degrees of Knowledge*, New York: Scribner's, 1959, 430–444.

[24]See Pope John Paul II, *The Acting Person*, viii; Rocco Buttiglione, *Karol Wojtyla. The Thought of the Man who became Pope John Paul II*, Grand Rapids: Eerdmans Publishing Company, 1997, 117–123; Anna–Teresa Tymienieckia, "The Origins of the Philosophy of John Paul II," in *Proceedings of the American Catholic Philosophical Association* 53 (1979): 18; Robert F. Harvanek, "The philosophical foundations of the thought of John Paul II," in *The Thought of Pope John Paul II*, Rome: Gregorian University Press, 1993, 1–2.

Non–Formal Ethics of Values,[25] displays the main lines of his philosophical thought. In his time Scheler was not fully accepted in Catholic circles because he was not a Thomist or scholastic. Actually, he was spoken about as *Augustinus Redivivus* for his affinity with the theology of St. Augustine. The development of his own phenomenology places him more within the Augustinian tradition than in anything else.[26]

Scheler set his focus on philosophical anthropology when he switched to philosophy under Dilthey in Berlin. This latter has built an anti–Cartesian reaction to conceiving the human being as a union of spirit and matter.[27] Descartes denied the existence of life in plants, animals and everything except beings endowed with a spirit. Dilthey's main theme focused on transferring vitalism to the level of reality: life is a primary category.

Edmund Husserl is another phenomenologist contemporary with Max Scheler. It is very hard to establish what kind of influence Husserl had on Scheler, but he surely influenced Karol Wojtyla along with Scheler. It remains clear, according to Buttiglione, that meeting one Roman Ingarden, a disciple of Husserl and a dominant figure in the cultural milieu of Cracow, was a decisive factor in Wojtyla's interest in phenomenology.[28] For sure, however, Scheler did not study under Husserl. In Robert F. Harvanek's opinion, Scheler "may have been influenced by and also influenced the Munich phenomenologists...who were disciples of Husserl's first period and critics of his later transcendental phenomenology period."[29] These disciples may have left Husserl because his transcendental phenomenology showed him to be more a follower of Kant's *apriorism* than a recuperator of the objective philosophy of essences. Scheler's *Formalism* accepts Kant's thesis that ethics must be founded in the immediacy of the noumenal self and cannot, therefore, be

[25]Max Scheler, *Formalism in Ethics and Non–Formal Ethics of Values*, Evanston: Northwestern U., 1973. See also Anna–Teresa Tymieniecka, "The Origins of the Philosophy of John Paul II," in *Proceedings of the American Catholic Philosophical Association* 53 (1979): 18–19.

[26]See Robert F. Harvanek, "The philosophical foundations of the thought of John Paul II," in *The Thought of Pope John Paul II*, Rome: Gregorian University Press, 1993, 2–3.

[27]See Robert F. Harvanek, "The philosophical foundations of the thought of John Paul II," in *The Thought of Pope John Paul II*, Rome: Gregorian University Press, 1993, 3.

[28]See Rocco Buttiglione, *Karol Wojtyla. The Thought of the Man who became Pope John Paul II*, trans. Paolo Guietti and Francesca Murphy, Grand Rapids/Cambridge: William B. Eerdmans Publishing Company, 1997, 54.

[29]Robert F. Harvanek, "The philosophical foundations of the thought of John Paul II," in *The Thought of Pope John Paul II*, Rome: Gregorian University Press, 1993, 3–4; Rocco Buttiglione, *Karol Wojtyla. The Thought of the Man who became Pope John Paul II*, trans. Paolo Guietti and Francesca Murphy, Grand Rapids/Cambridge: William B. Eerdmans Publishing Company, 1997, 54–55.

theological. At the heart of his theory, Scheler draws a distinction between value and good: he makes values the autonomous sphere which governs the whole ethical realm. Whereas values are not things in themselves, goods are things that possess values. By the same token, Scheler rejects Kant's formalism of practical reason. Scheler argues that values are given in intentionality and have a content by which they are diversified.[30] Their objective content can be compared to Aquinas' theory of virtues. Values belong to the intentional order; their reality cannot be found either in the mind or in the essence of things. They are independent of perception in the same way that the physical world in Descartes is an extension that does not depend upon perception and in the same way that the scholastic universals exist in an absolute state of being abstracted from the concrete. Values can be objects for the mind without being already objectively experienced as a reality. Here, intentionality is the principle sphere of philosophizing.[31]

In developing his philosophy of the person, Scheler is not doing a metaphysical anthropology; rather, he is busy in phenomenology presenting the way reality faces the intentional mind of the human person. Differently from Pope John Paul II who tackled the Aristotelian metaphysics of substance, Scheler's theory is "anti–Cartesian in that it rejects the mechanization of life and refuses to reduce human nature to the dualism of mind and body."[32] The philosophical anthropology of Scheler, an aspect that was of a primary interest for him, explains Pope John Paul II's promotion of the philosophy of human nature as found in *The Acting Person.*

Scheler's philosophy of person is comparable to Aristotle's nous: life is a primary category that supplies the energy to be guided by the mind. This mind, however, is separate from the levels of life. In Harvanek's opinion, "this is what critics have referred to as the extreme dualism of Scheler, the distinction of spirit and human, or person and nature."[33] Whereas the scholastic notion of *person* brings to mind mainly Boethius' *substantia individualis naturae*

---

[30]See Anna–Teresa Tymieniecka, "The Origin of the Philosophy of John Paul II," in *Proceedings of the American Catholic Philosophical Association* 53 (1979):18–21; Rocco Buttiglione, *Karol Wojtyla. The Thought of the Man who became Pope John Paul II*, trans. Paolo Guietti and Francesca Murphy, Grand Rapids/Cambridge: William B. Eerdmans Publishing Company, 1997, 55.

[31]See Robert F. Harvanek, "The philosophical foundations of the Thought of John Paul II," in *The Thought of Pope John Paul II*, Rome: Gregorian University Press, 1993, 7–8; Anna–Teresa Tymieniecka, "The Origins of the Philosophy of John Paul II," in *Proceedings of the American Catholic Philosophical Association* 53 (1979): 19.

[32]Robert F. Harvanek, *Ibid.*, 9. See also Anna–Teresa Tymieniecka, "The Origins of the Philosophy of John Paul II," in *Proceedings of the American Catholic Philosophical Association* 53 (1979): 18.

[33]Robert F. Harvanek., *Ibid.*, 9.

rationalis, this notion assumes a completely different form in the philosophy of Scheler. This latter considers person not as an individual substance, but as an act or, more specifically, a moral act. The switching of the understanding of person from ontological to dynamic suggests the absence of person until all the necessary functions that make up the moral act are present. This kind of person stands in relationship with other persons not merely when he encounters them in a social context; rather, this relationship is part of the very constitution of the person. To Boethius' definition of a person as an individual substance of a rational nature, John Paul II added the incommunicability which prevented it from being possessed by anyone else.[34]

The Notion of Person in the Philosophical and Theological Thought of Pope John Paul II

The study by Pope John Paul II of the philosophical and theological principles of the notion of person is not an innovation. Even before the Council of Chalcedon in 451 A.D., Christian thinking had already started to investigate the meaning of personhood. One can say that the notion of person is more or less the invention of Christianity. Christianity views person as a particular entity which God wanted man to have beyond and different from all entities that belong to the other constitutive elements of the cosmos. The unity of the self was looked upon by non–Christian religions differently. The unity of the self was located in a purely spiritual dimension and ultimately at the level of universal being held in common by all creatures. The idea of a particular entity that is destined to an eternity apart from all creatures of the cosmos is peculiar to Christian thinking.[35]

Although a theologian and philosopher, Pope John Paul II taught ethics at the University of Lublin. Lublin was the only independent university in Poland at that time and a center of Thomism. Besides his doctoral dissertation on St. John of the Cross presented at the Angelicum in Rome under Garrigou–Lagrange, John Paul earned a second doctorate in the ethics of Max Scheler which had a dominant influence on his famous philosophical work, *The Acting Person*.[36] Several questions arise immediately: Is the philosophical background of Pope John Paul II more that of a Lublin Thomist or a Schelerian

---

[34]See Karol Wojtyla, *Amore e Responsabilità*, 2nd ed., tr. A. Milanoli, Torino: Marietti, 1978, 12, 14, 86, 113; Anselm Min, "John Paul II's Anthropology of Concrete Totality," in *Proceedings of the American Catholic Philosophical Association* 58 (1984): 121–124; John M. McDermott, "The Theology of John Paul II. A Response," in *The Thought of Pope John Paul II*, John M. McDermott (ed.), Rome: Gregorian University Press, 1993, 57.

[35]See Stratford Caldecott, "Cosmology, Eschatology, Ecology: Some Reflections on *Sollicitudo Rei Socialis*," in *Communio* 15 (1988): 307–308.

[36]K. Wojtyla, *The Acting Person*, Boston: Reidel Publishing Company, 1979.

phenomenologist? Is Pope John Paul II's thought fundamentally phenomenological while borrowing some elements from Thomism, or is it metaphysical and greatly expanding Thomism with insights from phenomenology? What changes did the notion of person undergo as Wojtyla succeeded St. Peter as Pontiff? What kind of influence did the Second Vatican Council exercise on his philosophical anthropology?[37] Obviously, the answers are not that simple. Only during the course of the present work and after investigating the philosophical categories used in theology does it become possible to discover what proportions of the two philosophical schools are present in the Pope's thinking.

It is necessary, as a first step, to summarize Wojtyla's philosophy in relation to the concept of person. His book, *The Acting Person,*[38] as well as "The Person: Subject and Community,"[39] and many other philosophical articles of Wojtyla provide the material needed for our analysis.

Experience, Conscience, and the Efficient Causality of the Person[40]

In experience man encounters reality that is made up of things and, most importantly, of other people. The experience of man, an expression that presents much ambiguity in itself, indicates the experience of which man is the subject and also the object. All men experience themselves as existing and acting, but I experience myself as existing and acting differently from the way I experience all others. Each of us has an experience of humanity as manifested in his "I." There is also an experience of himself which results from the reflection on his own being and action as being performed among other human persons. The constitutive elements of subjectivity are given more clearly when the object of man's experience is his own self. There exists, therefore, in man a sphere of internal experience and a sphere of external experience. As complicated as it looks, "human experience is profoundly unitary because the different acts of experience converge in that object which is man and they nourish the knowledge of man."[41] The external experience of other persons

---

[37]See Pope John Paul II, *Spiritus Domini,* 3.

[38]*The Acting Person* has been published as Vol. 10 of Analecta Husserliana, with Anna–Teresa Tymieniecka as Editor (Dordrecht, Holland: D. Reidel Publishing Company).

[39]See K. Wojtyla, "The Person: Subject and Community," in *The Review of Metaphysics* 33 (1979): 273–308.

[40]See Rocco Buttiglione, *Karol Wojtyla. The Thought of the Man who became Pope John Paul II,* trans. Paolo Guietti and Francesca Murphy, Grand Rapids/Cambridge: William B. Eerdmans Publishing Company, 1997, 123–141.

[41]See Rocco Buttiglione, *Karol Wojtyla. The Thought of the Man who became Pope John Paul II,* trans. Paolo Guietti and Francesca Murphy, Grand Rapids/Cambridge: William B. Eerdmans

enlightens the internal experience of myself and is also enlightened by it.

This leads us to a study of the consciousness, which is "the source of moral decisions"[42] and the experience of a subject in action or the experience of efficacy. For John Paul, experience itself, through the process of cognition, excludes a pure subjective consciousness because the subject is necessarily and essentially involved in every experience: "he who experiences is man, and he, whom the subject of the experience experiences, is also man; he is both the subject and the object." Analyses of human subjectivity in all its forms has categorical limits because it is connected to the objectivity of experience. Such an objectivity affords us the opportunity to explain human subjectivity. Therefore, as soon as 'pure consciousness' is accepted, one falls into a misinterpretation of the real subjectivity of man.[43] In giving a definition of subject (*suppositum*), Wojtyla says:

> In saying that man—whether others or myself—is given in experience as a subject we are stating that the whole experience of man, which reveals him as one who is, exists, and acts, forces us to think of man as the subject of his own existence and action. This is precisely the meaning of the concept 'subject,' which states man's subjectivity in its metaphysical sense."[44]

By 'metaphysical' is meant not so much the 'extraphenomenal' as 'transphenomenal': The manifestations which are the factors of man's experience constitute his totality as he exists and acts.[45] Without being a 'subject' man undergoes the danger of loosing his identity, because his existence and actions which are given in experience stop being his 'existence' and his 'actions.' Metaphysical subjectivity as expressed in man's experience

---

Publishing Company, 1997, 124; Avery Dulles, "John Paul II and the Truth about Freedom," in *First Things* 55 (1995): 37; Joseph Fuchs, "Good Acts and Good Persons," in *The Tablet* 247 (1993): 1444; Damian P. Fedoryka, "The Gift of Veritatis Splendor," in *Social Justice Review* 85 (1994): 140; Alasdair MacIntyre, "How Can We Learn What *Veritatis Splendor* Has To Teach?" in *The Thomist* 58 (1994): 174–175.

[42]Pope John Paul II, *Sollicitudo Rei Socialis*, 9; *Evangelium Vitae*, 4.

[43]See K. Wojtyla, "The Person: Subject and Community," in *The Review of Metaphysics* 33 (1979): 273–274; Rocco Buttiglione, *Karol Wojtyla. The Thought of the Man who became Pope John Paul II*, trans. Paolo Guietti and Francesca Murphy, Grand Rapids/Cambridge: William B. Eerdmans Publishing Company, 1997, 129–141; Avery Dulles, "John Paul II and the Truth about Freedom," in *First Things* 55 (1995): 37; Alasdair MacIntyre, "How Can We Learn What *Veritatis Splendor* Has To Teach?" in *The Thomist* 58 (1994): 174–175; Michaël Devaux, "The Truth of Love, the Lie of Death," in *Communio* 23 (1996): 114.

[44]See K. Wojtyla, "The Person: Subject and Community," in *The Review of Metaphysics* 33 (1979): 274–275; Pope John Paul II, *Evangelium Vitae*, 19.

[45]See Romanus Cessario, "Moral Absolutes in the Civilization of Love," in *Crisis* 13 (May 1995): 19.

guarantees his identity in existence and in action.

Man's subjectivity in the metaphysical sense opens a fundamental approach to the relation between existence and action. *Operari sequitur esse*, as The Thomistic philosophical principle according to which the act follows upon being, assumes a double direction in Wojtyla's philosophy. Beyond a unilateral relation of causal dependence of action on existence, there is also "an opposite gnoseological relation between the two." The act not only results from being and from the fact that man is the subject of that act, but also provides the most correct approach to knowledge of that being and of who man is as the subject of his own action. Beyond the metaphysical sense concerned with here is the subject including everything complex and differentiated that makes man a personal subject. One is able to show an overall picture of human subjectivity if one analyzes man's dynamics including everything that occurs in him.[46]

As far as the *human act* is concerned, scholastic tradition has analyzed it from the point of view of its character as free (*voluntarium*).[47] Freedom of action is the result of understanding because the will (*voluntas*) is the intellectual appetite (*appetitus intellectivus*) expressed in free choice (*liber arbitrium*). The consciousness of subjectivity that should be present in every act was, in Wojtyla's opinion, absent from the scholastic tradition: it is time to return to the concept of conscious being, not in the sense that the being is constituted in and by consciousness, but in the sense that "it constitutes consciousness and the reality of human action as conscious."[48] Consciousness is always rooted in the human subject: "The person and act, that is, my own self existing and acting is constituted in consciousness which consequently reflects the existence and the action of the self."[49] For Wojtyla, this manner of considering consciousness is at the basis of transcendental philosophy. This philosophy "examines acts of cognition as intentional acts of consciousness directed to trans–subjective matter and, therefore, to what is objective or to

---

[46]See K. Wojtyla, *The Acting Person*, 189–258; "The Person: Subject and Community," in *The Review of Metaphysics* 33 (1979): 274–275; Pope John Paul II, *Evangelium Vitae*, 24; Avery Dulles, "John Paul II and the Truth about Freedom," in *First Things* 55 (1995): 37; Daniel Callam, "The Gospel of Life," in *The Canadian Catholic Review* 13 (June 1995): 3.

[47]See K. Wojtyla, "The Person: Subject and Community," in *The Review of Metaphysics* 33 (1979): 277–278.

[48]See K. Wojtyla, "The Person: Subject and Community," in *The Review of Metaphysics* 33 (1979): 278; Pope John Paul II, *Evangelium Vitae*, 4, 21 and 24; Joseph Fuchs, "Good Acts and Good Persons," in *The Tablet* 247 (1993): 1444; Jack Healy, "*Veritatis Splendor* and the Human Person," in *The Linacre Quarterly* 61 (November 1994): 19–20.

[49]See K. Wojtyla, "The Person: Subject and Community," in *The Review of Metaphysics* 33 (1979): 278.

phenomena."[50] Such a philosophical approach should not become, however, a philosophy of reality itself, or the reality of the human person. The function of the consciousness is not exclusively cognitive in the same sense as are acts of human knowledge. Human acts of knowledge or self–knowledge are not generated by consciousness, although consciousness reflects what has been objectivized by man: consciousness constitutes the subjective dimension proper to man and "interiorizes everything man recognizes, together with what he knows by acts of self–knowledge; it makes all this the content of the subject's experience."[51]

For Wojtyla, to be a subject is different from living one's own self as a subject. The consciousness is what makes the human subject become a human self. It reveals human subjectivity to itself as a self. Without being reduced to consciousness, the self "is constituted by the self–consciousness in the human subject only by means of all the existence and action proper to the subject."[52] Consciousness presupposes that man lives his own self as a subject because only then he is a subject. Living one's own self as a subject requires a relation between the concrete, conscious human act and the particular self. Every conscious act is attributed to that self as its author: "In such an agency there appears the factor of will, and therefore of liberty, and hence that of moral responsibility. This brings us to what is essential in man's personal subjectivity."[53]

Self–determination and The Transcendence of the Person in Action

Pope John Paul II's *second discussion* in *The Acting Person* is concerned with the human person's self–determination. Actions determine the human person and give shape to his or her being according to those actions: Self–determination is the deeper and more fundamental dimension of the

[50]See K. Wojtyla, "The Person: Subject and Community," in *The Review of Metaphysics* 33 (1979): 278.

[51]See K. Wojtyla, *The Acting Person*, 25–59; "The Person: Subject and Community," in *The Review of Metaphysics* 33 (1979): 279; Jack Healy, *"Veritatis Splendor* and the Human Person," in *The Linacre Quarterly* 61 (November 1994): 19–20.

[52]See K. Wojtyla, "The Person: Subject and Community," in *The Review of Metaphysics* 33 (1979): 279; Pope John Paul II, *Evangelium Vitae*, 24; Daniel Callam, "The Gospel of Life," in *The Canadian Catholic Review* 13 (June 1995): 3.

[53]See K. Wojtyla, "The Person: Subject and Community," in *The Review of Metaphysics* 33 (1979): 280; "The Task of Christian Philosophy Today," in *Proceedings of the American Catholic Philosophical Association* 53 (1979): 3; Anna–Teresa Tymieniecka, "The Origins of the Philosophy of John Paul II," in *Proceedings of the American Catholic Philosophical Association* 53 (1979): 21; Jack Healy, *"Veritatis Splendor* and the Human Person," in *The Linacre Quarterly* 61 (November 1994): 19–20.

causality of the human self.[54] Thus, because of the continual changing condition of the human person in the world, actions influence the ontological reality of the acting person who, consequently, moves forward in shaping his existence. Every subject who through his human action turns towards various aims and objects, turns at the same time towards his own self as a goal. He becomes an object for himself as well as a subject every time he chooses values because through them he is necessarily determining himself. Hence the autoteleological dimension is something inherent in the structure of the human act: "Self–determination contained in acts, that is, in authentic human agency, indicates a different dimension of auto–teleology connected ultimately with truth and goodness in their absolute and disinterested meaning (*bonum honestum*)." For Wojtyla, since the self–determination is constantly taking place through human acts, these acts reveal the transcendence "which is to a certain extent another name for the person."[55] Since the conscious actions which are at the root of self–determination make one's subjectivity become a human self, subjectivity is revealed through self–determination because "self–determination expresses the transcendental dimension of essentially human action." But this transcendental dimension remains with the person as a subject without being able to go beyond. The human person is the reason for its existence: "Ultimately, therefore, the causality of the person enhances his proper subjectivity in each and every act, choice, or decision."[56]

The transcendence of the human person,[57] a term that indicates the

---

[54]See K. Wojtyla, "The Person: Subject and Community," in *The Review of Metaphysics* 33 (1979): 281; Avery Dulles, "John Paul II and the Truth about Freedom," in *First Things* 55 (1995): 37; Alasdair MacIntyre, "How Can We Learn What *Veritatis Splendor* Has To Teach?" in *The Thomist* 58 (1994): 173; Daniel Callam, "The Gospel of Life," in *The Canadian Catholic Review* 13 (June 1995): 3.

[55]See K. Wojtyla, "The Person: Subject and Community," in *The Review of Metaphysics* 33 (1979): 282; Romanus Cessario, "Moral Absolutes in the Civilization of Love," in *Crisis* 13 (May 1995): 20; Daniel Callam, "The Gospel of Life," in *The Canadian Catholic Review* 13 (June 1995): 3.

[56]See K. Wojtyla, "The Person: Subject and Community," in *The Review of Metaphysics* 33 (1979): 282; "The Task of Christian Philosophy Today," in *Proceedings of the American Catholic Philosophical Association* 53 (1979): 3–4; Joseph Fuchs, "Good Acts and Good Persons," in *The Tablet* 247 (1993): 1444; Romanus Cessario, "Moral Absolutes in the Civilization of Love," in *Crisis* 13 (May 1995): 20; Avery Dulles, "John Paul II and the Truth about Freedom," in *First Things* 55 (1995): 37.

[57]See also Pope John Paul II, *Redemptionis Donum*, 4; *Mulieris Dignitatem*, 18; *Pastores Dabo Vobis*, 45; Roger Duncan, "On Reading *Laborem Exercens*," *Homiletic and Pastoral Review* 86 (July 1986): 17; Joseph Cardinal Cordeiro, "The religious sense of man," in *John Paul II. A Panorama of his Teachings*, New York: New City Press, 1989, 67.

"independence of the person from subjectivity and determinism,"[58] lies in the dynamic function of created human freedom. Although limited in its essence, the human nature cannot capture the subjectivity of the human person in a closed circle: the human individual is constantly open to the absolute. The person stands free of nature in an order of transcendence. In *Laborem Exercens*, Pope John Paul provides an extensive investigation of the human person's transcendence from the point of view of his relationship with human work.[59] In this document one finds such expressions as: "Man has to subdue the earth and dominate it, because as the 'image of God' he is a person, that is to say, a subjective being capable of acting in a planned and rational way, capable of deciding about himself, and with a tendency of self–realization."[60] Again, the human person is "a conscious and free subject, that is to say, a subject that decides about himself."[61] "Being a person," John Paul affirms again in *Mulieris Dignitatem*, 7, "means striving towards a self–realization [the Council text (*Gaudium et Spes*, 24) speaks of self–discovery], which can only be achieved 'through a sincere gift of self.' "

For Wojtyla, through this agency called self–determination the personal subject of man is not only revealed to our cognition, "but really constituted in itself as a specific reality, essentially different from all other subjects encountered in the surrounding world."[62] This human subject that is constituted and constitutes itself through acts of self–determination, is the *self*. The full dimension of the human self is constituted and conditioned by consciousness, although it can never be reduced to consciousness. The self–consciousness of the human person is an indispensable requirement for the constitution of the self and is due principally to acts of self–determination: "In them is revealed the structure proper to man and the profile of his self–possession and

---

[58]See Robert F. Harvanek, *Ibid.*, 12; Pope John Paul II, *General Audience*, January 7, 1979; Romanus Cessario, "Moral Absolutes in the Civilization of Love," in *Crisis* 13 (May 1995): 20; Joseph Fuchs, "Good Acts and Good Persons," in *The Tablet* 247 (1993): 1444; Joseph Cardinal Cordeiro, "The religious sense of man," in *John Paul II. A Panorama of his Teachings*, New York: New City Press, 1989, 67.

[59]See Roger Duncan, "On Reading *Laborem Exercens*," *Homiletic and Pastoral Review* 86 (July 1986): 17.

[60]Pope John Paul II, *Laborem Exercens*, 6; Daniel Callam, "The Gospel of Life," in *The Canadian Catholic Review* 13 (June 1995): 3; Romanus Cessario, "Moral Absolutes in the Civilization of Love," in *Crisis* 13 (May 1995): 20.

[61]Pope John Paul II, *Laborem Exercens*, 6; Joseph Fuchs, "Good Acts and Good Persons," in *The Tablet* 247 (1993): 1444; Romanus Cessario, "Moral Absolutes in the Civilization of Love," in *Crisis* 13 (May 1995): 20; Avery Dulles, "John Paul II and the Truth about Freedom," in *First Things* 55 (1995): 37.

[62]See K. Wojtyla, "The Person: Subject and Community," in *The Review of Metaphysics* 33 (1979): 282–283.

self–domination."[63] Every act of self–determination reveals the structure proper to man because that structure is realized anew through those acts. The concrete human self which cannot be reduced to self–consciousness, can be constituted only through the realization of the structure proper to man, the structure of self–possession and self–domination. In experiencing every act the human self identifies itself with self–possession and self–determination. These, again, are revealed in the dynamics of the personal causality which is self–determination: "This makes the close connection between the subject and the human self still more evident. Self is nothing other than the concrete human subject... Thus, the self is not only self–consciousness, but self–possession and self–domination which are proper to the concrete human subject and revealed most of all by act."[64] The self–consciousness is what constructs the bridge between the self and the personal subjectivity proper to man, because the full dimension of the human self is conditioned by self–consciousness, and both self–possession and self–domination belong to that dimension: "through its proper function of interiorization consciousness is essential to constituting subjectivity."[65]

Some theologians[66] think that, for Pope John II, the foundation of the human person's existence is the action: "I act, therefore I am." This conviction contradicts what has just been said: the experiencing of one's own personal subjectivity conditioned by the self–consciousness of self–possession and self–determination, "is nothing other than a full actualization of everything contained virtually in the human subject, in metaphysical subjectivity... This seems to be the philosophical sense of the old adage: to act follows upon being."[67] The human act serves to know the human person and, therefore,

[63]See K. Wojtyla, "The Person: Subject and Community," in *The Review of Metaphysics* 33 (1979): 282–283; Avery Dulles, "John Paul II and the Truth about Freedom," in *First Things* 55 (1995): 37; Romanus Cessario, "Moral Absolutes in the Civilization of Love," in *Crisis* 13 (May 1995): 20.

[64]See K. Wojtyla, "The Person: Subject and Community," in *The Review of Metaphysics* 33 (1979): 282–283.

[65]See K. Wojtyla, "The Person: Subject and Community," in *The Review of Metaphysics* 33 (1979): 282–283; "The Task of Christian Philosophy Today," in *Proceedings of the American Catholic Philosophical Association* 53 (1979): 3; Anna–Teresa Tymieniecka, "The Origins of the Philosophy of John Paul II," in *Proceedings of the American Catholic Philosophical Association* 53 (1979): 25.

[66]See Avery Dulles, "The Prophetic Humanism of John Paul II," *America*, 169 (1993):7; *The Encyclicals of John Paul II*, Ed. J. Michael Miller, Indiana: Our Sunday Visitor Publishing Division, Our Sunday Visitor, Inc., 1996, 28; Robert F. Harvanek, "The philosophical foundations of the thought of John Paul II," in *The Thought of Pope John Paul II*, Rome: Gregorian University Press, 1993, 12.

[67]See K. Wojtyla, "The Person: Subject and Community," in *The Review of Metaphysics* 33 (1979): 283–284; Damian P. Fedoryka, "The Gift of Veritatis Splendor," in *Social Justice Review*

should follow upon the being of that person.[68]

Self–fulfillment and Transcendence of the Human Person

If acting serves knowledge of the human person as it has been explained, "to what degree is the fulfillment of an act a fulfillment of one's self, that is, of the person who fulfills the act?"[69] At the root of the conscious human act there is the tendency to fulfill oneself, a tendency that belongs to the very structure of the subjectivity of the human person. This tendency, however, manifests in the subject two dimensions: contingency and autoteleology. On the one hand, the tendency to fulfill one's self clearly reveals the incompleteness of the self as a contingency of the being. At the same time this tendency challenges the human person to go beyond that incompleteness and to fulfill himself. But this becomes possible only through the self–consciousness of acts. "In these acts, through the moment of self–determination, the human self—is revealed to itself, not only as self–possession and self–domination, but also as tendency to self–fulfillment."[70] This tendency to self–fulfillment shows that personal subjectivity, self–consciousness, self–possession, or self–domination, cannot seal off man within his own subject, neither can they constitute a closed structure, because turning in toward self through consciousness and self–determination opens the subject towards reality: "In man as personal subject there is a close connection between self–fulfillment and transcendence." Transcendence, again, is another name for person: the transcendence of the human subject is manifested in various ways but ultimately flows from one source which, in the final analysis, proves that the human subject is of a spiritual nature.[71]

Later on, as Pope John Paul II develops the transcendence of the human person's subjectivity from a theological point of view, God as a communion

---

[68]See Karol Wojtyla, *The Acting Person*, 73, 82, 91, 113, 153, 265; John M. McDermott, "The Theology of John Paul II. A Response," in *The Thought of Pope John Paul II*, John M. McDermott (ed.), Rome: Gregorian University Press, 1993, 59.

[69]See K. Wojtyla, "The Person: Subject and Community," in *The Review of Metaphysics* 33 (1979): 284.

[70]See K. Wojtyla, "The Person: Subject and Community," in *The Review of Metaphysics* 33 (1979): 284; Pope John Paul II, *Ut Unum Sint*, 28; Romanus Cessario, "Moral Absolutes in the Civilization of Love," in *Crisis* 13 (May 1995): 20.

[71]See K. Wojtyla, *The Acting Person*, 103–186; "The Person: Subject and Community," in *The Review of Metaphysics* 33 (1979): 285; Romanus Cessario, "Moral Absolutes in the Civilization of Love," in *Crisis* 13 (May 1995): 20; Daniel Callam, "The Gospel of Life," in *The Canadian Catholic Review* 13 (June 1995): 3.

among Three different Divine Persons becomes the model for such an interpretation of the human person. This trinitarian communion is reflected in man created in the image and likeness of God. It is a fact, therefore, that every human person, because he is in the image of God, has a vocation, and it is only by responding and offering himself as a gift to others according to the demands of that vocation that the human person discovers and fulfills his own reality. In *Centesimus Annus*, John Paul says: "Indeed, it is through the free gift of self that one truly finds oneself. This gift is made possible by the human person's essential 'capacity for transcendence.' "[72]

Cognitive and Pragmatic Approach

The influence of Thomism in Pope John Paul II's *cognitive approach* to the act of the human person, is clear in many of his philosophical and theological positions.[73] The *pragmatic approach* would determine what is good and proceed to accomplish it, i.e. the human person would work from the good to the true.[74] For Wojtyla, however, the act of the human person enjoys a cognitional dimension, that is, a process of knowing or mental operation by which he becomes aware of his acts. This dimension opens the person to the order of truth: consciousness in act reveals the transcendence of the human person. In fact, in the inmost depth of the human conscience is where the truth makes itself heard as the source of moral duty and as the "condition which constitutes the liberty proper to act, where liberty reveals itself as the self–determination of the person."[75] Thus, since to be free not only means to will, but to choose and to decide, there should be a transcendent subordination

---

[72]Pope John Paul II, *Centesimus Annus*, 41. See also Ibid., *Sollicitudo Rei Socialis*, 29; General Audience, January 7, 1979; Damian P. Fedoryka, "The Gift of Veritatis Splendor," in *Social Justice Review* 85 (1994): 140; Joseph Cardinal Cordeiro, "The religious sense of man," in *John Paul II. A Panorama of his Teachings*, New York: New City Press, 1989, 67; Stratford Caldecott, "Cosmology, Eschatology, Ecology: Some Reflections on *Sollicitudo Rei Socialis*," in *Communio* 15 (1988): 307.

[73]See Pope John Paul II, *Evangelium Vitae*, 18, 20, 68 and 70; *Celebrate 2000! Reflections on Jesus, the Holy Spirit, and the Father*, Ann Arbor, Michigan: Servant Publications, 1996, 63; *Ut Unum Sint*, 28; Romanus Cessario, "Moral Absolutes in the Civilization of Love," in *Crisis* 13 (May 1995): 20; Rocco Buttiglione, *Karol Wojtyla. The Thought of the Man who became Pope John Paul II*, trans. Paolo Guietti and Francesca Murphy, Grand Rapids/Cambridge: William B. Eerdmans Publishing Company, 1997, 79–80. Pope Paul VI often had recourse to the cognitive method placing truth as the starting point to reach the good, linking and never separating the pedagogy of the Church from her doctrine (see Pope Paul VI, *Humanae Vitae*, 29).

[74]See Robert Harvanek, *Ibid.*, 13.

[75]See K. Wojtyla, "The Person: Subject and Community," in *The Review of Metaphysics* 33 (1979): 285–286; Daniel Callam, "The Gospel of Life," in *The Canadian Catholic Review* 13 (June 1995): 3; Terence P. Curley, "*Evangelium Vitae* and Our Culture," in *The Priest* 51 (October 1995): 18.

of good to truth in action and in act. But, "conscience alone is, so to speak, the proper place for this subordination."[76] The transcendence of the human person in his act owes to conscience the willing and the choosing of the true good because only through the conscience is the transcendence of truth revealed in the act and in its efficient subject. The basis of all human *praxis*, for Wojtyla, is man's constant transcendence of himself in conscience in the direction of the true good. Without this transcendence, the personal subject fails to fulfill himself and consequently would not be a complete self. "That is why," concludes Wojtyla, "we do not enhance the personal properties of man in analyzing his acts of knowledge or will and their connected world of values unless in so doing we bring to the surface the transcendence inherent in these acts. This is done through reference to truth and good as the true or honest, that is, as willed and chosen on the principle of truth."[77]

The cognitive approach moves from the truth to the good. Since truth is the correspondence between mind and reality, when the mind asserts what is actually the case, the truth is present. However, this truth cannot merely be a product of the natural reason because, ultimately, the eternal and divine law is the source of man's natural reason revealing to him the truth about God and himself.[78] Often, John Paul had recourse to anthropological, social, and cultural language in order to prove the absolute conformity that should exist between the Divine Revelation and the natural law. That conformity is based on the very nature of the human act that is performed in a specific context, namely moral theology which, by its very existence, is "a science which accepts and examines divine revelation while at the same time responding to the demands of human reason." Moral theology is 'morality' inasmuch as it is concerned with the good or the evil acts performed by the human person. It is also a 'theology' because "it acknowledges that the origin and end of moral action are found in the One who 'alone is good' and who, by giving himself to man in

[76]See K. Wojtyla, "The Person: Subject and Community," in *The Review of Metaphysics* 33 (1979): 286.

[77]See K. Wojtyla, "The Person: Subject and Community," in *The Review of Metaphysics* 33 (1979): 286; Rocco Buttiglione, *Karol Wojtyla. The Thought of the Man who became Pope John Paul II*, trans. Paolo Guietti and Francesca Murphy, Grand Rapids/Cambridge: William B. Eerdmans Publishing Company, 1997, 156; Alasdair MacIntyre, "How Can We Learn What *Veritatis Splendor* Has To Teach?" in *The Thomist* 58 (1994): 174–175.

[78]See Pope John Paul II, ; *Veritatis Splendor*, 29; *Familiaris Consortio*, 22; *Mulieris Dignitatem*, 1; *Christifideles Laici*, 50; *Pastores Dabo Vobis*, 52; *Ordinatio Sacerdotalis*, 2; J. Honoré, "Christ the Redeemer, Core of John Paul's Teaching," in *John Paul II. A Panorama of his Teachings*, New York: New City Press, 1989, 14; Daniel Callam, "The Gospel of Life," in *The Canadian Catholic Review* 13 (June 1995): 3.

Christ, offers him the happiness of divine life."[79] Both vertical and horizontal data strengthen the Pope's argument about the harmony between Divine Revelation and human reason.

The Pope uses the *cognitive dimension* of the human person's act in order to manifest the truth about man and God. That dimension guarantees the placement of truth as revealed by God at the very roots of moral order. Proceeding from the truth to the good becomes a regular format in his logic: "Since the moral order reveals and sets forth the plan of God the Creator, for this very reason it cannot be something that harms man, something impersonal."[80] In order to seek this truth, he often establishes propositions proving them and refuting the counter propositions. This makes the content of his theological and philosophical argument strictly Thomistic. *Veritatis Splendor*, 32, is an excellent illustration of the cognitive dimension of the Pope's approach:

> Once the idea of a universal truth about the good, knowable by human reason, is lost, inevitably the notion of conscience also changes. Conscience is no longer considered in its primordial reality as an act of a person's intelligence, the function of which is to apply the universal knowledge of the good in a specific situation and thus to express a judgement about the right conduct to be chosen here and now. Instead, there is a tendency to grant to the individual conscience the prerogative of independently determining the criteria of good and evil and then acting accordingly... Taken to its extreme consequences, this individualism leads to a denial of the very idea of human nature. [81]

The Integration of the Person in Action: Integration and the Body

In *the third part* of *The Acting Person*, Pope John Paul II considers the question of the integration of the person in the action: the unity of person and

---

[79]See Pope John Paul II, *Veritatis Splendor*, 29; *Familiaris Consortio*, 22 and 32; Alasdair MacIntyre, "How Can We Learn What *Veritatis Splendor* Has To Teach?" in *The Thomist* 58 (1994): 174–175.

[80]Pope John Paul II, *Familiaris Consortio*, 34; J. Honoré, "Christ the Redeemer, Core of John Paul's Teaching," in *John Paul II. A Panorama of his Teachings*, New York: New City Press, 1989, 14; Giacomo Cardinal Biffi, "The Action of the Holy Spirit in the Church and in the World," in *John Paul II. A Panorama of his Teachings*, New York: New City Press, 1989, 43; Russell Hittinger, "The Pope and the Theorists: The Oneness of Truth," in *Crisis* 11 (December 1993): 32–33; Jack Healy, "*Veritatis Splendor* and the Human Person," in *The Linacre Quarterly* 61 (November 1994): 17–18; Alasdair MacIntyre, "How Can We Learn What *Veritatis Splendor* Has To Teach?" in *The Thomist* 58 (1994): 174–175.

[81]See also Alasdair MacIntyre, "How Can We Learn What *Veritatis Splendor* Has To Teach?" in *The Thomist* 58 (1994): 174–175; Russell Hittinger, "The Pope and the Theorists: The Oneness of Truth," in *Crisis* 11 (December 1993): 32–33; Jack Healy, "*Veritatis Splendor* and the Human Person," in *The Linacre Quarterly* 61 (November 1994): 16–17.

nature, the correlate of transcendence. The classical distinction in the human being between body and soul discussed here takes an original direction in the thought of the Pope: the human person is still operating within the context of his own subjectivity, as a subject in action. The human person is acting with consciousness, including his consciousness of his body. Thus we introduce the term psychosomatic and *soma* in this section. The person cannot be reduced to the body and is not identical with the body, because it always transcends the body. In the process of action the body is never seen as a separate entity and by itself, but rather "as the complexity that is unified in action, and the passive element in action."[82] Therefore, as Harvanek states, "in the dynamic perspective of the acting person the dualism appears in tensions such as freedom and determinism rather than in ontic relationships of soul and body."[83] The body expresses the person and determines many of his features.

What does Pope John Paul II have to say of the relationship between the body and the soul? The unity of the body and the soul, as it has been developed during his Pontificate, assumes not only a philosophical but also a theological direction. John Paul II considers the human person as a "unified totality"[84] whose nature is both corporeal and spiritual. Both the spiritual and the material realms, invisible and visible, are brought together in the being of the human person who is a unity of rational soul and physical body. The human body is substantially united with a spiritual soul from the very moment of the person's conception in the womb of the mother. Because man is a person in the unity of his body and his spirit, the spirit is embodied and the body is spiritualized.[85] Man becomes for John Paul "an incarnate spirit, that is a soul which expresses itself in a body and a body informed by an immortal spirit..."[86] He looks at both body and soul as the constitutive elements of the human person. The specific nature of man "is a bodily and a spiritual nature, symbolized in the second creation account by the two elements: the earth, from which God forms man's

[82]Robert F. Harvanek, *Ibid.*, 15; Damian P. Fedoryka, "The Gift of Veritatis Splendor," in *Social Justice Review* 85 (1994): 140.

[83]Robert F. Harvanek, *Ibid.*, 15.

[84]Pope John Paul II, *Familiaris Consortio*, 11. See also Ibid., *The Acting Person*, preface; *Veritatis Splendor*, 13 and 50; Damian P. Fedoryka, "The Gift of Veritatis Splendor," in *Social Justice Review* 85 (1994): 140.

[85]See Congregation for the Doctrine of the Faith, *Donum Vitae* (Instruction on Bioethics), Introduction, 3; Pope John Paul II, *Letter to Families from Pope John Paul II*, 19; Damian P. Fedoryka, "The Gift of Veritatis Splendor," in *Social Justice Review* 85 (1994): 140.

[86]Pope John Paul II, *Familiaris Consortio*, 11; *Veritatis Splendor*, 50; *Evangelium Vitae*, 23; Darió Castrillón, "The family in the Magisterium of John Paul II," in *John Paul II. A Panorama of his Teachings*, New York: New City Press, 1989, 115.

body, and the breath of life which he breathes into man's nostrils (cf. 2:7)."[87]

Pope John Paul II develops a theology of the *human body* based on a non–syncretic combination of his exegesis of Scripture, especially the first chapter of Genesis, and his philosophy of the acting person. The body is the part through which the person manifests and expresses himself. The body is the most concrete expression of the human person because it is visible and tangible. Every human person, because of the possession of a body, becomes the nexus of all cosmic realities. Through the human body the entire material world is inserted into or comes in contact with the spiritual nature of the person.[88]

All actions of the human person involve somehow *the body that becomes necessarily a sharer in the spiritual actions of that person.* No part of the human person may be left behind or left out; all must be integrated and brought along in the action by which the person involves his unified totality.[89] The Pope forcefully affirms this at the 35th General Assembly of the World Medical Association (1983) when he says:

> Each human person, in his absolutely unique singularity, is constituted not only by his spirit, but by his body as well. Thus, in the body and through the body, one touches the person himself in his concrete reality. To respect the dignity of man consequently amounts to safeguarding this identity of the man *corpore et anima unus*, as the Second Vatican Council says (GS, 14). [90]

In looking at the concrete reality of the human person as a composite of body and soul, John Paul avoids the platonic approach that depreciates the body and exalts the soul. The positive outlook at the reality of the human body

---

[87]Pope John Paul II, *Sollicitudo Rei Socialis*, 29; Darió Castrillón, "The family in the Magisterium of John Paul II," in *John Paul II. A Panorama of his Teachings*, New York: New City Press, 1989, 115.

[88]See Pope John Paul II, *Celebrate 2000! Reflections on Jesus, the Holy Spirit, and the Father*, Ann Arbor, Michigan: Servant Publications, 1996, 77–78; Stratford Caldecott, "Cosmology Eschatology, Ecology: Some Reflections on *Sollicitudo Rei Socialis*," in *Communio* 15 (1988): 308; Damian P. Fedoryka, "The Gift of Veritatis Splendor," in *Social Justice Review* 85 (1994): 140.

[89]See Pope John Paul II, *Familiaris Consortio*, 11 and 80; Roger Duncan, "On Reading *Laborem Exercens*" in *Homiletic and Pastoral Review* 86 (July 1986): 17; Darió Castrillón, "The family in the Magisterium of John Paul II," in *John Paul II. A Panorama of his Teachings*, New York: New City Press, 1989, 115; Jack Healy, "*Veritatis Splendor* and the Human Person," in *The Linacre Quarterly* 61 (November 1994): 18. As to the involvement of the human person in all actions, Cardinal Law's recent letter quotes John Paul II's *Familiaris Consortio* in the context of marriage where "conjugal love involves a totality, in which all the elements of the person enter..." (See Bernard Cardinal Law, *Christian Marriage. A Covenant of Love and Life*, Boston: Daughters of St. Paul, 1998, 17–18)

[90]Pope John Paul II, *Discourse to the Members of the 35th General Assembly of the World Medical Association*, October 29, 1983: *AAS* 76 (1984), 393.

is based on theological and philosophical arguments.[91] In *Veritatis Splendor*, 48, John Paul argues against those moral theologians who envision human nature and body "as presuppositions or preambles, materially necessary, for freedom to make choice, yet extrinsic to the person, the subject and the human act." These theologians end up creating the response for the tension "between freedom and a nature conceived of in a reductive way" in terms of a division existing within man himself. John Paul emphasizes that the Church has always taught the unity of the human person, "whose rational soul is *per se et essentialiter* the form of his body. The spiritual and immortal soul is the principle of unity of the human being whereby it exists as a whole—*corpore et anima unus* (*Gaudium et Spes*, 14)—as a person."[92]

Besides the resurrection to glory that constitutes the ultimate destiny of the human body, human reason and free will are linked with all the bodily and sense faculties. Herein lies the person's dignity as a free subject who determines himself when acting: the act of the human person emanates from his one complex reality as a unity of body and spiritual soul. Therefore, as John Paul expresses this in *Veritatis Splendor*, 48, the whole person, including the body, "is entrusted to himself, and it is in the unity of body and soul that the person is the subject of his own moral acts." The body of the human person is a positive reality because it involves the whole person in every act that ultimately determines the value of that specific act and influences the destiny of the entire human person. Man's reason, which is inseparably linked to his bodily reality, grasps the specific moral value of those goods towards which he is naturally inclined and constantly invited to perform. The person, "by the light of reason and the support of virtue, discovers in the body anticipatory signs, the expression and the promise of the gift of self, in conformity with the wise plan of the Creator." For John Paul, the ultimate positivity of the human body is fundamentally based not only on the essential goodness that comes from the act of creation by God, but also on the impossibility of dissociating the moral act from the bodily dimension of the human person. In the human person as a whole, in the willing agent and in the deliberate act, body and soul are inseparable. They stand or fall together. In commenting on the words of St. Paul in Gal 5:16–17, "now the works of the flesh are plain: fornication, impurity, licentiousness...," John Paul affirms that "for the Apostle it is not a

---

[91]See Pope John Paul II, *Orientale Lumen*, 11; Damian P. Fedoryka, "The Gift of Veritatis Splendor," in *Social Justice Review* 85 (1994): 140.

[92]Pope John Paul II, *Veritatis Splendor*, 48; Ecumenical Council of Vienna, Constitution *Fidei Catholicae*: *DS* 902; Fifth Lateran Ecumenical Council, Bull *Apostolici Regiminis*: *DS* 1440; German Grisez, "Veritatis Splendor: Revealed Truth versus Dissent," in *Homiletic and Pastoral Review* 94 (March 1994): 10; Damian P. Fedoryka, "The Gift of Veritatis Splendor," in *Social Justice Review* 85 (1994): 140.

question of discriminating against and condemning the body, which with the spiritual soul constitutes man's nature and personal subjectivity."[93]

The Pope rejects the many atheistic approaches that reduce the human person to a mere complex of tissues, organs and functions. In the line of Vatican II, he develops his theological anthropology according to which the human person is the only creature on earth that "God has wanted for his own sake."[94] The *soul* of every human person is immediately created by God,[95] a spiritual soul that bears in its substantial union with the body the image of the Creator. The Creator intervenes in the creation of every human soul, hence its uniqueness, and irrevocable union with its own body from the moment of its natural conception: "At the origin of each human person there is a creative act of God: no man comes into existence by chance; he is always the result of the creative love of God."[96]

John Paul II considers the relationship between the body and the soul of the human person in light of the Creator's original intention: even though both body and soul make up the constitutive elements of the human person, there is never a question of the superiority of soul over the body. Without any pessimistic Platonism, John Paul includes the body in the created reality of matter that is subjected to corruption. Yet this body maintains its importance in God's plan of salvation because Christ came to save the human person in his totality, as a composite of body and soul. In *Redemptor Hominis*, John Paul II says:

> In Jesus Christ, who was crucified and laid in the tomb and then rose again, 'our hope of resurrection dawned...the bright promise of immortality,' on the way to which man, through the death of the body, shares with the whole of visible creation the necessity to which matter is subject. We intend and are trying to fathom ever more deeply the language of the truth that man's Redeemer enshrined in the phrase 'It is the spirit that gives life, the flesh is of no avail.' In spite of appearances, these words express the highest affirmation of man—the affirmation of the body given life by the Spirit.[97]

---

[93]Pope John Paul II, *Dominum et Vivificantem*, 55; Brian V. Johnstone, "Life in a Culture of Death," *Priests & People* 9 (November 1995): 411; Damian P. Fedoryka, "The Gift of Veritatis Splendor," in *Social Justice Review* 85 (1994): 140; German Grisez, "Veritatis Splendor: Revealed Truth versus Dissent," in *Homiletic and Pastoral Review* 94 (March 1994): 10.

[94]See *Gaudium et Spes*, 24.

[95]See Pope Pius XII, *Humani generis*: *AAS* 42 (1950), 575; Pope Paul VI, *Professio fidei*: *AAS* 60 (1968), 436; Pope John XXIII, *Mater et Magistra*, III: *AAS* 53 (1961), 447.

[96]Pope John Paul II, *Discourse to priests participating in a seminar on "Responsible Procreation*," September 17, 1983, *Insegnamenti di Giovanni Paolo II*, VI, 2 (1983), 562.

[97]Pope John Paul II, *Redemptor Hominis*, 18.

John Paul II does not mix the notions of *person* and *nature*. The body and the soul are the constitutive elements of the nature of the human person. The human nature, a common principle in all human persons, is individualized and exists only in a defined human person. Pope John Paul II refuses the platonic idea of a human nature that exists without being individualized. He remains solidly grounded in the philosophical realism of Aristotle and St. Thomas Aquinas,[98] according to which the generic human nature can exist only in a specific human person. His Encyclical *Dominum et Vivificantem* sheds light on the meaning of the image and likeness of God in the human person, when the Pope says: "This (the image and likeness) means not only rationality and freedom as constitutive properties of human nature, but also, from the very beginning, the capacity of having a personal relationship with God, as 'I' and 'you'..."[99]

Since every human person is a composite of body and soul, all human persons have, in a certain sense, the same nature.[100] Each person individualizes the common human nature according to his specific personhood. Hence, what constitutes the personhood of each person is the possession of his being in himself and not in others. However, they have their being in themselves in relation to others who possess the same nature but different concretization of that nature. As far as the relationality is concerned, the definition of person for John Paul comes very close to that of Richard of St. Victor and St. Thomas Aquinas. What is common to persons is their sharing in the same ontological constitutive elements of body and soul, an idea that was stressed by St. Augustine.[101] What makes them different is the concretization of that nature in each one of them in relationship to himself or to others.

Pope John Paul II, in his *Letter to Families* (1994), without mentioning the name of Descartes, criticizes his principle "*Cogito, ergo sum* (I think, therefore I am)."[102] *Modern rationalism* found in that principle a source of nourishment, because "it is typical of rationalism to make a radical contrast in man between spirit and body, between body and spirit." This platonic distinction which offers to the modern concept of man its distinctive dualistic character, threatens the unity of the human person. The body cannot be reduced to a mere matter

---

[98]See *The Encyclicals of John Paul II*, Ed. J. Michael Miller, Indiana: Our Sunday Visitor Publishing Division, Our Sunday Visitor Inc., 1996, 28.

[99]Pope John Paul II, *Dominum et Vivificantem*, 34.

[100]The Pope is influenced here by St. Gregory of Nyssa.

[101]St. Augustine, *De Gen.* III, 22, 34; *De Trin.* XII, 7, 9; Johann G. Roten, "Mary and Woman in Augustine," in *The University of Dayton Review* 22, no. 3 (Summer 1994): 38.

[102]See also Brian V. Johnstone, "Life in a Culture of Death," *Priests & People* 9 (November 1995): 411.

because the spirit is closely united to the body. As Vatican II states, quoted by John Paul, in the human person there is a unity between body and soul, *"corpore et anima unus."*[103] With no assumption of a direct influence on John Paul, Balthasar also sees in modern rationalism an implicit Gnosticism that "openly animates all those modern world–views which see 'body' and 'spirit,' *bios* and *ethos*, nature and God, in antagonism or opposition."[104] This approach to the human person does not imply that for the Pope there exist no tendencies of tension and struggle between the 'spirit' and the 'body' of which St. Paul spoke. This struggle between the two constitutive elements of the human person, however, "belongs to the heritage of sin, is a consequence of sin and at the same time confirmation of it."[105] If the struggle between body and spirit shows in human experience, this does not mean that philosophical, theological, or even cultural currents should be allowed to promote that dualism. Radical opposition between body and spirit revives the negative Platonism, whose effects are still responsible for many tendencies in today's thought.

Modern rationalism offers to man an increasing experience of separation between body and spirit to the point that man's body is considered like any other bodies present in the world of nature. But if the human body is looked at as a raw material for production of goods for consumption, man's body not only becomes like the bodies of animals used for many experiments, but loses its connection with the spirit. The direct consequence of that radical separation is the arrival at a dreadful ethical defeat. From that very radical opposition between body and spirit proposed by modern rationalism, there emerges *Neo–Manichaeism* which treats man like an object. When the spirit is not considered as giving life to the body and the body as not receiving life from the spirit, "man ceases to live as a person and a subject." The consequences are noticeable on all the levels of human life where people are in contact with each other. Manipulation and exploitation become the rule of the relationships between human beings.[106] *Veritatis Splendor* emphasizes the necessity of

---

[103]See Pope John Paul II, *Letter to Families from Pope John Paul II*, 19; *Veritatis Splendor*, 50; *Celebrate 2000! Reflections on Jesus, the Holy Spirit, and the Father*, Ann Arbor, Michigan: Servant Publications, 1996, 77; *Gaudium et Spes*, 14; Stratford Caldecott, "Cosmology, Eschatology, Ecology: Some Reflections on *Sollicitudo Rei Socialis*," in *Communio* 15 (1988): 307.

[104]See Hans Urs von Balthasar, *The Scandal of the Incarnation*. Irenaeus against the Heresies, San Francisco, 1990, 5; Johann G. Roten, "Im Zeichen der Ellipse. Hans Urs von Balthasars theologische Anthropologie." Doctoral diss., International Marian Research Institute, *MLS* 24 (1992–95), University of Dayton, Dayton, 1995, 146–148; Pope John Paul II, *Evangelium Vitae*, 23.

[105]Pope John Paul II, *Celebrate 2000! Reflections on Jesus, the Holy Spirit, and the Father*, Ann Arbor, Michigan: Servant Publications, 1996, 77. See also Galatians 5:16–17 and 19–21.

[106]See Pope John Paul II, *Letter to Families from Pope John Paul II*, 19. In this letter, the whole analysis of modern rationalism takes place within the framework of the Pope's hermeneutic of the

looking at the totality of the human person in order to avoid this manipulation. In the context of the natural inclinations of the human body, John Paul attributes value to these inclinations only as long as they refer to the entire human person as a "unified totality." Since the body cannot be radically opposed to the soul, all of its natural inclinations involve the human soul and therefore assume a moral relevance through their reference to man as "a soul which expresses itself in a body and a body informed by an immortal spirit."[107] Thus the connection between the entirety of the human person and the natural law as expressed by Pope Paul VI's *Humanae Vitae* and the Congregation for the Doctrine of Faith's *Donum Vitae*:

> The natural moral law expresses and lays down the purposes, rights and duties which are based upon the bodily and spiritual nature of the human person. Therefore this law cannot be thought of as simply a set of norms on the biological level; rather it must be defined as the rational order whereby man is called by the Creator to direct and regulate his life and actions and in particular to make use of his own body.[108]

One notices how Pope John Paul skillfully develops this definition of moral law. The universal nature of man or the very metaphysics of his being are the foundation of the moral actions of the human person as a subject. The natural law finds in the metaphysics of being the necessary ground for the concrete consciousness of the human subject in his actions. Since man is a unified totality of body and soul, his actions flow from the very heart of the reality of his being and they express his subjective consciousness through an act of the *intellectus*. The natural law thus understood does not allow for any division between body and soul, freedom and nature. Such a false dichotomy can be overcome only through the cognitive approach to the moral act in which the actions of the person, as a composite of body and soul, proceed from the truth inscribed in the rational nature of that person, so as to perfect him in his specific order as a unified totality. Here one sees not only the results of John

---

"great mystery" of Ephesians 5:32 [see also Pope John Paul II, *Evangelium Vitae*, 22–23; Anselm K. Min, "John Paul II's Anthropology of Concrete Totality," in *Proceedings of the American Catholic Philosophical Association* 58 (1984): 121; Pope John Paul II, *Orientale Lumen*, 11; Peter Hebblethwaite, *Pope John Paul II and the Church*, Kansas City: Sheed and Ward, 1995, 29; Jack Healy, "*Veritatis Splendor* and the Human Person," in *The Linacre Quarterly* 61 (November 1994): 18].

[107]Pope John Paul II, *Veritatis Splendor*, 50; *Familiaris Consortio*, 11; *Evangelium Vitae*, 23. See also Anselm K. Min, "John Paul II's Anthropology of Concrete Totality," in *Proceedings of the American Catholic Philosophical Association* 58 (1984): 121.

[108]See Pope Paul VI, *Humanae Vitae*, 10; Congregation for the Doctrine of the Faith, *Donum Vitae*, Introduction, 3; Pope John Paul II, *Veritatis Splendor*, 50; *Evangelium Vitae*, 23; Darió Castrillón, "The family in the Magisterium of John Paul II," in *John Paul II. A Panorama of his Teachings*, New York: New City Press, 1989, 116.

Paul's expansion of the traditional Thomism, but also the influence of St. Augustine.[109]

Modern rationalism in its various forms and directions cannot tolerate *mystery*. "It may well acknowledge, in the context of a vague deism, the possibility and even the need for a supreme or divine Being, but it firmly rejects the idea of a God who became man in order to save."[110] The marriage between God and humanity, as a mystery of union and salvation, does not find a fertile ground in modern rationalism. For modern rationalism, it is unthinkable that God should be the Redeemer or the One who initiates that relationship of love inviting man to respond to the initiative of salvation. In an implicit way, it reduces man to a temporal dimension of life by introducing a radical opposition against the mystery of salvation. It rejects any connection between Christology and anthropology: it considers a scandal any theology that tries to understand the whole reality of man under the light of Christ. The words of *Gaudium et Spes*, "Christ reveals man to himself," were in Pope John Paul's deep perception of Vatican II's theology, the Councils' "reply, so long awaited, which the Church has given to modern rationalism."[111]

Analyses and Perspectives of Thomism and Schelerian Phenomenology in the Pontificate of Pope John Paul II

I do not think that Pope John Paul II, as Harvanek asserts,[112] should be interpreted from the point of view of Munich phenomenology and Scheler rather than from the perspective of Thomism and Aristotelism. From the earliest times of his religious formation and his discovery of metaphysics,[113] Wojtyla, as McCool presents it, "realized that the intellectual framework which he needed to unify his personal experience of the world and God had to be an

---

[109]See Pope John Paul II, *Veritatis Splendor*, 50–51; St. Thomas Aquinas, *Summa Theologiae*, I–II, q. 94, a. 2.; St. Augustine, *De Trinitate*, XIV, 15, 21: CCL 50/A, 451; Paul L. Peeters, "*Dominum et Vivificantem*: The Conscience and the Heart," in *Communio* 15 (1988): 150.

[110]See Pope John Paul II, *Letter to Families from Pope John Paul II*, 19.

[111]See Pope John Paul II, *Letter to Families from Pope John Paul II*, 19; *Evangelium Vitae*, 15, 22, 36 and 40; Raymond T. Gawronski, "Redemptor Hominis," in *The Thought of Pope John Paul II*, Rome: Gregorian University, 1993, 222; J. Honoré, "Christ the Redeemer, Core of John Paul's Teaching," in *John Paul II. A Panorama of his Teachings*, New York: New City Press, 1989, 13 and 24; Darió Castrillón, "The family in the Magisterium of John Paul II," in *John Paul II. A Panorama of his Teachings*, New York: New City Press, 1989, 113.

[112]See Robert Harvanek, *Ibid.*, 19.

[113]See Tad Szulc, *Pope John Paul II. The Biography*, New York: Scribner, 1995, 151.

inclusive and coherent philosophy of being."[114] In fact, as John Conley indicates in his answer to Harvanek's study, the "Pope's philosophy of action owes more to scholasticism than Father Harvanek's analysis suggests." I share with Buttiglione his opinion that "even if Wojtyla begins from St. Thomas' ethics, he nonetheless continually refers to his metaphysics. It is, after all, impossible to understand and to participate in Aquinas' ethics if one does not grasp and accept his fundamental ontology."[115] Pope John Paul himself asserted that "my previous Aristotelian–Thomistic formation was enriched by the phenomenological method, and this made it possible for me to undertake a number of creative studies. I am thinking above all of my book *The Acting Person*."[116] I am not asserting that Pope John Paul II should be exclusively interpreted from a Thomistic point of view. Neither do I confirm that the philosophy of John Paul II is exclusively Thomistic. Buttiglione affirms that Pope John Paul always returned to St. Thomas after meeting with each of the modern philosophies, St. John of the Cross, Scheler and Kant: This return, upon which he meditated critically, was the means by which Wojtyla created an original philosophical construction.[117]

The opinion concerning his dependence on Thomistic metaphysics of being does not contradict the belief that the "Pope's phenomenological background clearly shapes the distinctive methodology of his major papal writings."[118] I find Gerald A. McCool's remark in this regard very interesting: "Scheler's phenomenology of consciousness and its world of ideal values and Aquinas' realistic metaphysics of being had been incorporated, in different ways, into his personalist metaphysics of the moral agent."[119] On the other hand, Harvanek

---

[114]See Gerald A. McCool, "The Theology of John Paul II," in *The Thought of Pope John Paul II*, John M. McDermott (ed.), Rome: Gregorian University Press, 1993, 32. See also Pope John Paul II, *Be Not Afraid! Interviews with A. Frossard*, Garden City, N.Y: Doubleday–Image, 1985, 17.

[115]Rocco Buttiglione, *Karol Wojtyla. The Thought of the Man who became Pope John Paul II*, trans. Paolo Guietti and Francesca Murphy, Grand Rapids/Cambridge: William B. Eerdmans Publishing Company, 1997, 72.

[116]Pope John Paul II, *Gift and Mystery. On the Fiftieth Anniversary of my Priestly Ordination*, New York: Doubleday, 1996, 93–94.

[117]Rocco Buttiglione, *Karol Wojtyla. The Thought of the Man who became Pope John Paul II*, trans. Paolo Guietti and Francesca Murphy, Grand Rapids/Cambridge: William B. Eerdmans Publishing Company, 1997, 44; Damian P. Fedoryka, "The Gift of Veritatis Splendor," in *Social Justice Review* 85 (1994): 140.

[118]John J. Conley, "The philosophical foundations of the Thought of John Paul II. A Response," in *The Thought of Pope John Paul II*, John M. McDermott (ed.), Rome: Gregorian University Press, 1993, 23.

[119]Gerald A. McCool, "The Theology of John Paul II," in *The Thought of Pope John Paul II*, John M. McDermott (ed.), Rome: Gregorian University Press, 1993, 29.

himself has confirmed that Lublin Thomism is excessively individualist and subjectivist and "this possibly explains John Paul II's great personal strength and approach to his role as chief bishop of Rome and the Church."[120] If the Lublin Thomism is excessively individualist and subjectivist, a fact that explains the personality and the role of the Pope, why should Pope John Paul II "not be interpreted from the perspective of neo–thomism or neo–scholasticism"?[121]

If the Lublin Thomism is excessively individualistic and subjectivistic, this does not mean that Pope John Paul II follows exactly the same steps. Many factors, including the Second Vatican Council and the mysticism of St. John of the Cross, are at work influencing one and the same person, Karol Wojtyla–Pope John Paul II.[122] "For, after all," said McCool, "the experience of Wojtyla, the metaphysician, whose Thomism would become a personalism under the influence of Scheler, of Wojtyla, the theologian profoundly influenced by his work at the Council, and of Wojtyla, the reflective pastor presenting the Council's teachings to a modern world closed to the values of freedom, spirit, and transcendence, was the integrated experience of the same acting person."[123] Wojtyla's later Thomism, that is when he became the Archbishop of Cracow and then Pope John Paul II, is different from his theologizing as a Thomist when he wrote his first dissertation. Whereas earlier he used the metaphysics of universal nature whose source was the universal structure of man as such formulated in the universal concept, his later Thomism was a philosophy of conscious subjectivity and the concrete person. John McDermott says, "while natures known objectively through concepts in traditional Thomism do not suffice to plumb the mystery of personal subjectivity, persons cannot exist without natures. Person and nature mutually condition each other."[124] What is original in Wojtyla's approach is his

---

[120]Robert Harvanek, *Ibid.*, 19.

[121]Robert Harvanek, *Ibid.*, 19.

[122]See Rocco Buttiglione, *Karol Wojtyla. The Thought of the Man who became Pope John Paul II*, trans. Paolo Guietti and Francesca Murphy, Grand Rapids/Cambridge: William B. Eerdmans Publishing Company, 1997, 45–82 and 177–231.

[123]Gerald A. McCool, "The Theology of John Paul II," in *The Thought of Pope John Paul II*, John M. McDermott (ed.), Rome: Gregorian University Press, 1993, 33. See Pope John Paul II, *Christifideles Laici*, 5; *Veritatis Splendor*, 29; Anselm K. Min, "John Paul II's Anthropology of Concrete Totality," in *Proceedings of the American Catholic Philosophical Association* 58 (1984): 121–124.

[124]John M. McDermott, "The Theology of John Paul II. A Response," in *The Thought of Pope John Paul II*, John M. McDermott (ed.), Rome: Gregorian University Press, 1993, 59. See also K. Wojtyla, "The Task of Christian Philosophy Today," in *Proceedings of the American Catholic Philosophical Association* 53 (1979): 3–4; Anselm K. Min, "John Paul II's Anthropology of

interpretation of St. Thomas which, although based on St. Thomas' ethics, still furnishes a complete vision of his philosophy. The overall philosophy of being of St. Thomas is qualified by Wojtyla as philosophy of the good. But this approach does not place Wojtyla in the category of those philosophers who bring a radical innovation to St. Thomas' metaphysics of being. In fact, as Buttiglione states, "from a Thomistic point of view this operation is wholly legitimate: for *ens et bonum convertuntur* (being and good are convertible)."[125]

John Paul's *Letter to Families* (1994) brings to light his *later Thomism* and explains his understanding of the antithesis between *individualism* and *personalism*. Vatican II's theology of the human person's realization through a sincere gift of self, rooted in St. Thomas' *bonum diffusivum sui*, is the key answer to understanding the difference between individualism and personalism.[126] Individualism "presupposes a use of freedom in which the subject does what he wants, in which he himself is the one to 'establish the truth' of whatever he finds pleasing and useful." In such a case, the criteria of truth are not subject to any objective truth coming from God. Actually, the subject does not tolerate any demands required by an objective truth and refuses to 'give' another anything in the name of that truth. Individualism thus remains egocentric and selfish. On the contrary, personalism exalts the gift of self as the most appropriate way of self–realization; personalism does it in the name of an objective truth revealed by God. The antithesis between individualism and personalism emerges not only on the level of theory, but even more on the level of an 'ethos' which moves the person to become a gift in the very concrete situation of his human existence. Opposite to egoism, personalism is altruistic in the sense that the person, in offering himself as a gift to others, discovers his identity and the joy of being a human person.[127]

As a unique free subject, man is the starting point for metaphysics to underpin contemporary theology. The metaphysics of John Paul II remains a metaphysics of being: "the final question about man drives back to the meta–empirical area, demanding, and hence justifying, metaphysical

---

Concrete Totality," in *Proceedings of the American Catholic Philosophical Association* 58 (1984): 121–124. It is necessary to note that the different direction assumed by Pope John Paul II in respect to metaphysics of universal nature did not eliminate that aspect from his writings. The Pope is still using that approach in many of his writings (see *Mulieris Dignitatem*, 7).

[125]Rocco Buttiglione, *Karol Wojtyla. The Thought of the Man who became Pope John Paul II*, trans. Paolo Guietti and Francesca Murphy, Grand Rapids/Cambridge: William B. Eerdmans Publishing Company, 1997, 73.

[126]Pope John Paul II, *Letter to Families from Pope John Paul II*, 11.

[127]Pope John Paul II, *Letter to Families from Pope John Paul II*, 14; Daniel Callam, "The Gospel of Life," in *The Canadian Catholic Review* 13 (June 1995): 2–3.

considerations, and thus opening human thought to the transcendent."[128] He refers, for example, in *Mulieris Dignitatem*, 6, to Boethius's and Aquinas' traditional definitions of person when explaining the philosophical and theological meaning of person as created in the image and likeness of God. In the context of metaphysics of universal nature, 'image and likeness' indicate man as a rational being, whereas in metaphysics of concrete subjectivity this same man is manifested as a rational being who "can exist only...in relation to another human person...Being a person in the image and likeness of God thus also involves existing in a relationship, in relation to the other 'I.' "[129] Metaphysics of concrete subjectivity should add to the Boethian–Thomistic notion of person, as an 'individual substance endowed with a rational nature,' the proper qualifications, that is, the whole specificity of subjectivity essential to man as a person. This structure of man's subjectivity reaches beyond the individuality of the substantial being of man as possessor of a rational or spiritual nature.[130]

In his moral actions, man experiences himself as a responsible agent who determines himself and continually orients himself to self–fulfillment. Gerald McCool writes, "for the experience on which his reflection is based is man's awareness of himself as an existing being, a subsisting agent whose own reality as a person manifests itself through the self–determining activity in which man must engage in order to possess and fulfil himself."[131] This self–fulfillment requires a self–giving love that will enable the person to participate in and

---

[128]See Karol Wojtyla, "The Task of Christian Philosophy Today," in *Proceedings of the American Catholic Philosophical Association* 53 (1979): 3; Pope John Paul II, *Insegnamenti*, II/2, 542–543; Joseph Cardinal Cordeiro, "The religious sense of man," in *John Paul II. A Panorama of his Teachings*, New York: New City Press, 1989, 77; André Frossard, *Portrait of John Paul II*, San Francisco: Ignatius Press, 1990, 76–77; J. Honoré, "Christ the Redeemer, Core of John Paul's Teaching," in *John Paul II. A Panorama of his Teachings*, New York: New City Press, 1989, 22; Damian P. Fedoryka, "The Gift of Veritatis Splendor," in *Social Justice Review* 85 (1994): 141.

[129]See Pope John Paul II, *Mulieris Dignitatem*, 7; Anselm K. Min, "John Paul II's Anthropology of Concrete Totality," in *Proceedings of the American Catholic Philosophical Association* 58 (1984): 122; Paul L. Peeters, "*Dominum et Vivificantem*: The Conscience and the Heart," in *Communio* 15 (1988): 150.

[130]See Karol Wojtyla, "Subjectivity and the Irreducible in Man," in *Analecta Husserliana* 7 (1979), 109; Anselm K. Min, "John Paul II's Anthropology of Concrete Totality," in *Proceedings of the American Catholic Philosophical Association* 58 (1984): 122; Damian P. Fedoryka, "The Gift of Veritatis Splendor," in *Social Justice Review* 85 (1994): 141.

[131]Gerald A. McCool, *Ibid.*, 37. See also Damian P. Fedoryka, "The Gift of *Veritatis Splendor*," in *Social Justice Review* 85 (1994): 141; Roger Duncan, "On Reading *Laborem Exercens*," *Homiletic and Pastoral Review* 86 (July 1986): 14. See also John M. McDermott, "The Theology of John Paul II. A Response," in *Ibid.*, 59.

interact with the lives of other free persons.[132] Without the self–giving love, the human subject would be unable to fulfill his vocation. The self–giving love establishes the bond of true and authentic *communio* with other human and free subjects within the same community. This, as McCool expresses it, explains the failure of classical liberal capitalism and Marxist communism which did not recognize the dignity of the human subject as a responsible personal agent and therefore "dehumanized man by making him either the servant or the product of impersonal economic forces lower on the scale of being than man himself."[133] Already *Gaudium et Spes*, 24, according to which "man cannot fully find himself except through a sincere gift of self," provided the basis for John Paul's understanding of the paradoxical character of human existence: it is in the calling to give oneself that the human person finds himself. Man's existence fulfills its vocation if it serves the truth in love, a love that causes man to give and to receive something which can be neither bought nor sold, but only given freely and mutually.[134]

If Wojtyla's later Thomism deals with a philosophy of conscious subjectivity remaining however a metaphysics of being, his personalism did not allow any intrusion of *idealism of pure consciousness* or any *sensism* or *logicism of contemporary empiricism*.[135] As Wojtyla relates in his article "The Task of Christian Philosophy Today," "It is necessary to find the correct limits,

[132]See Anna–Teresa Tymieniecka, "The Origins of the Philosophy of John Paul II," in *Proceedings of the American Catholic Philosophical Association* 53 (1979): 18–21; Anselm Min, "John Paul II's Anthropology of Concrete Totality," in *Proceedings of the American Catholic Philosophical Association* 58 (1984): 120–129.

[133]See Gerald A. McCool, *Ibid.*, 37. See also Miroslav Volf, "On Human Work: An Evaluation of the Key Ideas of the Encyclical *Laborem Exercens*," in *Scottish Journal of Theology* 37 (1984): 68–71; Robert A. Destro, "*Laborem Exercens*," in *A Century of Catholic Social Thought*, Edited by George Weigel and Robert Royal, Lanham: University Press of America, 1991, 147–148; Paul Bowe, "*Sollicitudo Rei Socialis*: A Commentary on the Encyclical," in *Doctrine and Life* 38 (1988): 230–231; Roland James Faley, "Pope as Prophet: The New Social Encyclical," *America* 158 (1988): 448; André Frossard, *Portrait of John Paul II*, San Francisco: Ignatius Press, 1990, 101–103; Giacomo Cardinal Biffi, "The Action of the Holy Spirit in the Church and in the World," in *John Paul II. A Panorama of his Teachings*, New York: New City Press, 1989, 43; Joseph Cardinal Cordeiro, "The religious sense of man," in *John Paul II. A Panorama of his Teachings*, New York: New City Press, 1989, 69; Carl Bernstein and Marco Politi, *His Holiness John Paul II and the Hidden History of our Time*, New York: Doubleday, 1996, 7.

[134]See Pope John Paul II, *Letter to Families from Pope John Paul II*, 11.

[135]See Karol Wojtyla, "The Task of Christian Philosophy Today," in *Proceedings of the American Catholic Philosophical Association* 53 (1979): 3; Pope John Paul II, *Christifideles Laici*, 28; *Veritatis Splendor*, 32; Paul L. Peeters, "*Dominum et Vivificantem*: The Conscience and the Heart," in *Communio* 15 (1988): 148–150; J. Honoré, "Christ the Redeemer, Core of John Paul's Teaching," in *John Paul II. A Panorama of his Teachings*, New York: New City Press, 1989, 22; Giacomo Cardinal Biffi, "The Action of the Holy Spirit in the Church and in the World," in *John Paul II. A Panorama of his Teachings*, New York: New City Press, 1989, 42.

according to which the phenomenological analyses, developed from the principles of the philosophy of consciousness, will begin to work to enrich the realistic image of the person."[136] The reason behind this refusal of the philosophy of pure consciousness lies in that objectivity that pertains to the essence of man's experience who, as subject, is given in experience in an objective manner. The emphasis on a partial element of human experience such as pure consciousness, does not work in the philosophical system of Wojtyla. Both idealism and empiricism reduce the concrete intelligibility of man to an abstract intelligibility of something less than man.[137] Far from being a pure consciousness of idealistic phenomenology, "subjectivity for Wojtyla meant man's awareness of his own subsistent being revealed in its activity through what St. Thomas would call an immediate act of *intellectus*. Through that act of intellectual self–awareness, the concrete intelligibility of man revealed itself."[138] Through this intellectual act, man, as a concrete agent, determines his own being and brings his perfection from potency to act by acting upon himself and others.[139] Man's will and the power of self–determination in his ethical action makes Scheler's phenomenology of values fail to be the foundation of Wojtyla's own Christian ethics. Wojtyla's neo–Thomism could then be classified as an expanded form of Thomism that was "an experientially grounded metaphysics of act and potency, immanent and transient action, nature, finality, person, matter, spirit, and the analogous grades of being."[140]

The complicated question of *the relationship between person and*

---

[136]See Karol Wojtyla, "The Task of Christian Philosophy Today," in *Proceedings of the American Catholic Philosophical Association* 53 (1979): 3.

[137]See Karol Wojtyla, "The Task of Christian Philosophy Today," in *Proceedings of the American Catholic Philosophical Association* 53 (1979): 3; Gerald A. McCool, *Ibid.*, 38.

[138]Gerald A. McCool, Ibid., 38. See also K. Wojtyla, "The Subject: Person and Community," in *Review of Metaphysics* 33 (1979): 280–284; *Gaudium et Spes*, 24; Pope John Paul II, *Veritatis Splendor*, 32; *Pastores Dabo Vobis*, 44.

[139]See K. Wojtyla, "The Subject: Person and Community," in *Review of Metaphysics* 33 (1979): 280–284; Pope John Paul II, *Christifideles Laici*, 28; *Veritatis Splendor*, 43; Roger Duncan, "On Reading *Laborem Exercens*," *Homiletic and Pastoral Review* 86 (July 1986): 14; Avery Dulles, "John Paul II and the Truth about Freedom," in *First Things* 55 (1995): 37. In his *Letter to Families* (1994), John Paul brings up the Thomistic notion of the act's orientation to its end: "The person can never be considered a means to an end; above all never a means of 'pleasure.' The person is and must be nothing other than the end of every act. Only then does the action correspond to the true dignity of the person." (Pope John Paul II, *Letter to Families from Pope John Paul II*, 12)

[140]Gerald A. McCool, Ibid., 38. See also Pope John Paul II, *Veritatis Splendor*, 43; Andrew N. Woznicki, *Karol Wojtyla's Existentialist Personalism*, New Britain, Ct.: Mariel Publications, 1980; Rocco Buttiglione, *Karol Wojtyla. The Thought of the Man who became Pope John Paul II*, trans. Paolo Guietti and Francesca Murphy, Grand Rapids/Cambridge: William B. Eerdmans Publishing Company, 1997, 74–75; Avery Dulles, "John Paul II and the Truth about Freedom," in *First Things* 55 (1995): 37–38.

community in the philosophy and the theology of Pope John Paul II cannot be answered by a simple presentation of community as the correlative of person and as the reality that precedes the person. At the very beginning of his Pontificate, John Paul entitled his first Encyclical *Redeemer of Man*, not *Redeemer of Men*. According to J. Honoré, the choice of that title manifests John Paul's primary concern about human persons, seen in the singularity of their beings. He does not talk about human beings in abstract or purely conceptual terms, neither does he allow a melting of the human person's individuality into a pot of a general humanity. Universality can be met only through concrete individuality, because the singular human person is the paradigm of the human nature seen in its totality. The main target is the human being "grasped at the heart of what makes him or herself, in his or her conscious and differentiated personality." This approach to the individuality of the human person in his or her relationship with the universality of nature places Pope John Paul II, according to Honoré, in the line of thought of the Greek Fathers especially in that of the Cappadocian Fathers who always gave priority to the concept of person over that of nature.[141] One can deduce there is no doubt that the individual human subject plays a major and important role in the writings of the Pope. He maintains, "no one can replace us in the responsible freedom that we have as individual persons."[142] The subjectivity of the human person is in many theological and philosophical approaches the point of departure for John Paul II, although he knows how to avoid falling into *Cartesian egoism* or *British individualism*.[143] As *Christifideles Laici*, 40, reads, "the human person has an inherent social dimension which calls a person from the innermost depths of self to communion with others and to the giving of self to others."[144] Another example is found in *Redemptionis Donum*, 10, in the context of a meditation on the evangelical counsels:

---

[141]J. Honoré, "Christ the Redeemer, Core of John Paul's Teaching," in *John Paul II. A Panorama of his Teachings*, New York: New City Press, 1989, 22. See also Raymond T. Gawronski, "Redemptor Hominis," in *The Thought of Pope John Paul II*, Rome: Gregorian University, 1993, 223.

[142]Pope John Paul II, *Evangelium Vitae*, 69; *Pastores Dabo Vobis*, 69; *Christifideles Laici*, 28; Paul L. Peeters, "*Dominum et Vivificantem*: The Conscience and the Heart," in *Communio* 15 (1988): 150; James H. Kroeger, "Rekindling Mission Enthusiasm," in *The Priest* 48 (January, 1992): 35.

[143]See Pope John Paul II, *Familiaris Consortio*, 32; *Redemptionis Donum*, 10; *Salvifici Doloris*, 12; *Christifideles Laici*, 29; *Letter to Families from Pope John Paul II*, 11; Raymond T. Gawronski, "Redemptor Hominis," in *The Thought of Pope John Paul II*, Rome: Gregorian University, 1993, 223; Avery Dulles, "John Paul II and the Truth about Freedom," in *First Things* 55 (1995): 37; Joseph Cardinal Cordeiro, "The religious sense of man," in *John Paul II. A Panorama of his Teachings*, New York: New City Press, 1989, 67.

[144]See also Pope John Paul II, *Pastores Dabo Vobis*, 7.

The entire economy of Redemption is realized precisely through this sensitivity to the mysterious action of the Holy Spirit, the direct Author of all holiness. Along this path the profession of the evangelical counsels opens out in each one of you, dear brothers and sisters, a wide space for the 'new creation' that emerges in your human 'I' precisely from the economy of the Redemption and, through this human 'I,' also into the interpersonal and social dimensions.[145]

One more significant example of the relationship between person and community is brought into the marital context by John Paul II's *Letter to the Families* (1994). Here the "divine 'We' is the eternal pattern of the human 'we,' especially of that 'we' formed by the man and the woman created in the divine image and likeness." The divine "We" is revealed from the very beginning of Genesis when God sought for the pattern of creation in his own being. "Let us make man in our image, after our likeness (Genesis 1:26)" has enabled man, from the very beginning, to understand his own human reality and existence in the divine Being of God. However, every single man and woman, not merely a massive conglomerate of anonymous people, is created in the image and likeness of God. Every person enjoys the singularity that results from God's withdrawal into his divine Being to form the pattern of that specific person, beyond the fact that all people as community reflect the *communio personarum* that exists between the Three Divine Persons. This explains John Paul's opinion concerning the truth about man who, as an individual, is in the image and likeness of God, although that same man is called from the very beginning to live the dimension of *communio personarum* that reflects God's community of Persons.[146] Based on this theory, "communion" and "community" are two closely related yet not identical concepts. Whereas "communion" is concerned with the *communio personarum*, that is with the relationship between "I" and the "thou," "community" transcends this framework and moves towards a "society," a "we." The "communion" between Persons—between man and woman in the context of marriage—gives rise to the "community." Every "community" is "completely pervaded by the very essence of 'communion.'" Since there is no "community" without "communion," John Paul's opinion about this matter is clear; i.e. the person precedes the community, but not without a paradoxical character. Being in the image and likeness of God, man, as an individual, reflects in himself that image of the Trinity. Since the Trinity is a unity of Three Divine Persons, the image of the Triune God in man reveals God's original call for him to be in communion with others. This communion is not

---

[145]Pope John Paul II, *Redemptionis Donum*, 10.

[146]See Pope John Paul II, *Letter to Families from Pope John Paul II*, 6–7. See also Ibid., *Evangelium Vitae*, 19.

just something *ad extra* added to the reality of man because, as reported in *Gaudium et Spes*, 24, quoted in John Paul's *Letter to the Families* (1994), the creation of man in the divine image "refers not only to the divine image and likeness which every human being as such already possesses, but also and primarily to 'a certain similarity between the union of the divine persons and the union of God's children in truth and love.' "[147] Communion rather constitutes one of the essential dimensions of his human existence. Out of that *communio personarum*, in fact, rises the aspect of community that transcends the dimension of a relationship "I"–"thou" and moves towards a "we," a "society" of people. Keeping in mind that John Paul considers the person as the basis of communion and communion as the basis of community, one can understand the Pope's notion of man as the common good. He is a common good of the nation to which he belongs, of the state of which he is a citizen and of his own family. However, "he is such not only as an individual who is part of the multitude of humanity, but rather as 'this individual.' God the Creator calls him into existence 'for himself'..."[148]

Differently from Harvanek, I think that the balance between person and community is produced by the fact that the Pope does work in ontology and metaphysics, and should be interpreted from the perspective of neo–scholasticism.[149] As John Conley states: "Father Harvanek rightly underlines the importance of Scheler and Blondel in Karol Wojtyla's philosophy of action. However, I think it is crucial to underline the Pope's debt to neoscholastic theory in his analysis of the moral act, especially his emphasis upon the intrinsic evil of certain acts."[150] The Pope's insistence that specific acts are *intrinsically* and *universally wrong*,[151] shows his divergence from many personalist and phenomenological ethicians "who easily speak of

---

[147]See Pope John Paul II, *Letter to Families from Pope John Paul II*, 7–8.

[148]Pope John Paul II, *Letter to Families from Pope John Paul II*, 11; Raymond T. Gawronski, "Redemptor Hominis," in *The Thought of Pope John Paul II*, Rome: Gregorian University, 1993, 223; Avery Dulles, "John Paul II and the Truth about Freedom," in *First Things* 55 (1995): 37–38.

[149]See Robert Harvanek, *Ibid.*, 18; Pope John Paul II, *Familiaris Consortio*, 32; *Mulieris Dignitatem*, 7; *Ut Unum Sint*, 28.

[150]John J. Conley, *Ibid.*, 27. See Pope John Paul II, *Familiaris Consortio*, 32.

[151]See Pope John Paul II, *Familiaris Consortio*, 34; *Reconciliatio et Paenitentia*, 18; *Veritatis Splendor*, 51; *Evangelium Vitae*, 19; Aloysius J. Fonseca, "Reflections on the Encyclical Letter *Sollicitudo Rei Socialis*," *Gregorianum* 70 (1989): 20; German Grisez, "Veritatis Splendor: Revealed Truth versus Dissent," in *Homiletic and Pastoral Review* 94 (March 1994): 9; Peter Hebblethwaite, *Pope John Paul II and the Church*, Kansas City: Sheed and Ward, 1995, 29; Giacomo Cardinal Biffi, "The Action of the Holy Spirit in the Church and in the World," in *John Paul II. A Panorama of his Teachings*, New York: New City Press, 1989, 42; Russell Hittinger, "The Pope and the Theorists: The Oneness of Truth," in *Crisis* 11 (December 1993): 34; Jack Healy, "*Veritatis Splendor* and the Human Person," in *The Linacre Quarterly* 61 (November 1994): 22.

'conflicts of value' and who refuse to condemn a particular act as wrong, apart from the act's context of motive and circumstance."[152] A historical relativism such as this could end up leading into an ethical system which, as expressed in *Reconciliatio et Paenitentia*, 18, "relativizes the moral norm, denying its absolute and unconditional value, and, as a consequence, denying that there can be intrinsically illicit acts independent of the circumstances in which they are performed by the subject."[153] The same concept appears again in *Veritatis Splendor*, 37 in which John Paul openly criticizes those moral theologians who establish a sharp distinction between "an ethical order, which would be human in origin and of value for this world alone, and an order of salvation, for which only certain intentions and interior attitudes regarding God and neighbor would be significant." That distinction denies the existence in Divine Revelation of a moral content that is universally valid and permanent. At the same time, since in that specific context Sacred Scripture and Church's teachings become just an exhortation or a generic paraenesis, the human reason assumes the responsibility of establishing its own 'objective' moral norms in order to apply them to concrete historical situations. Human reason acts as if it draws its own truth and authority not from the eternal law that constantly calls the reason to participation[154] in its divine norms, but from a law that man, in an autonomous manner, lays down for himself. Consequently, in their relation to the so–called 'human good' which is the concrete historical situation, moral norms would not belong to the proper content of revelation and would not even be necessary

---

[152]John J. Conley, *Ibid.*, 28; Pope John Paul II, *Evangelium Vitae*, 20. The presentation of the Philosophical background of Pope John Paul's concept of person does not allow me to agree with Olivier Clément who, in his article "Some Orthodox Reflections on Recent Papal Encyclicals," in *One in Christ* 31 (1995): 273–280, proposed the 'economy,' a principle according to which a lesser evil is allowed in some situations of extreme distress, as an answer to abortion.

[153]See also Pope John Paul II, Address to the Bishops of the Eastern Region of France (April 1, 1982), 2: *Insegnamenti* V, 1 (1982), 1081; *Evangelium Vitae*, 20 and 68; German Grisez, "Veritatis Splendor: Revealed Truth versus Dissent," in *Homiletic and Pastoral Review* 94 (March 1994): 8; Peter Hebblethwaite, *Pope John Paul II and the Church*, Kansas City: Sheed and Ward, 1995, 29; Jack Healy, "*Veritatis Splendor* and the Human Person," in *The Linacre Quarterly* 61 (November 1994): 20

[154]Participation is used in the Thomistic sense here: it means, especially in this specific context, a share in the Eternal Reason where, by its natural inclination to its proper act and end, the human reason is already providing for itself and others according to God's plan as revealed in the eternal law: "This participation of the eternal law in the rational creature is called natural law." [St. Thomas Aquinas, *Summa Theologiae*, I–II, q. 91, a. 2; Pope John Paul II, *Veritatis Splendor*, 43; *Evangelium Vitae*, 70; *Pastores Dabo Vobis*, 45 and 51; *Gaudium et Spes*, 15; Daniel Callam, "The Gospel of Life," in *The Canadian Catholic Review* 13 (June 1995): 3; Russell Hittinger, "The Pope and the Theorists: The Oneness of Truth," in *Crisis* 11 (December 1993): 32; Jack Healy, "*Veritatis Splendor* and the Human Person," in *The Linacre Quarterly* 61 (November 1994): 16–17]

or relevant to salvation.[155]

Veritatis Splendor, 51, presents the same problem from the point of view of natural law. Here the relationship between truth, freedom and nature comes into question. The cognitive dimension of John Paul's argument is very clear: the truth about God and the human person determines the true sense of his nature with all the actions resulting from it and the true sense of his freedom as well. That truth involves universality and immutability since it is, and John Paul II refers here to St. Augustine, a reflection of the eternal truth. The freedom of the person should emerge from the truth about his nature. A separation between the freedom of the person and the nature which all have in common "obscures the perception of the universality of the moral law on the part of reason." The natural law should reveal the dignity of the human person because it expresses in actions the reality of his rational nature. Without being in opposition to the individuality of the human person or his or her absolute uniqueness, the universality of the natural law orients the free act of individual and bears witness to the universality of the true good. That universality fosters the *communio personarum* because, when each does what he or she is supposed to do, the true good emerges and the bond of perfect charity resulting from these actions is established.[156] Under the light of these considerations, one understands such an insistence on the Pope's part to refuse to compromise all forms of historical relativism or modern rationalism. That insistence which in itself faithfully reflects the teaching of St. Augustine, of Aquinas, and of Vatican II definitely places him in the tradition of the neoscholastic

---

[155]See Pope John Paul II, *Veritatis Splendor*, 36–37; *Evangelium Vitae*, 74; Address to a Group of Bishops from the United States on Their *ad Limina* Visit (October 15, 1988), 6: *Insegnamenti* XI/3 (1988), 1228; St. Thomas Aquinas, *Summa Theologiae*, I–II, q. 71, a.6; Daniel Callam, "The Gospel of Life," in *The Canadian Catholic Review* 13 (June 1995): 3; Brian V. Johnstone, "Life in a Culture of Death," *Priests & People* 9 (November 1995): 410–411; Giacomo Cardinal Biffi, "The Action of the Holy Spirit in the Church and in the World," in *John Paul II. A Panorama of his Teachings*, New York: New City Press, 1989, 42–43; Russell Hittinger, "The Pope and the Theorists: The Oneness of Truth," in *Crisis* 11 (December 1993): 31–32; Jack Healy, "*Veritatis Splendor* and the Human Person," in *The Linacre Quarterly* 61 (November 1994): 16–17.

[156]See Pope John Paul II, *Veritatis Splendor*, 51; Avery Dulles, "John Paul II and the Truth about Freedom," in *First Things* 55 (1995): 37–38; Alasdair MacIntyre, "How Can We Learn What *Veritatis Splendor* Has To Teach?" in *The Thomist* 58 (1994): 173; Joseph Cardinal Cordeiro, "The religious sense of man," in *John Paul II. A Panorama of his Teachings*, New York: New City Press, 1989, 67; Aloysius J. Fonseca, "Reflections on the Encyclical Letter *Sollicitudo Rei Socialis*," *Gregorianum* 70 (1989): 20; Peter Hebblethwaite, *Pope John Paul II and the Church*, Kansas City: Sheed and Ward, 1995, 28–30; Russell Hittinger, "The Pope and the Theorists: The Oneness of Truth," in *Crisis* 11 (December 1993): 31–32; Jack Healy, "*Veritatis Splendor* and the Human Person," in *The Linacre Quarterly* 61 (November 1994): 16–17; Daniel Callam, "The Gospel of Life," in *The Canadian Catholic Review* 13 (June 1995): 3.

manualists.[157]

Conclusion: Theological Implications of John Paul II's Philosophical Anthropology

I think the originality of Pope John Paul II's approach lies in the fact that he applied a phenomenological method on the philosophy of action, a philosophy that owed more to scholasticism than to Schelerian phenomenology. Tymieniecka affirms that Scheler's phenomenology of values increases, in John Paul's metaphysics of the acting person, the importance of the person's self–awareness.[158] I fully agree with McCool that, despite the continual influence of Schelerian phenomenology sensed here and there in the writings of John Paul, the implementation of the Second Vatican Council in the theology and life of the Church was still shaped by a consistent Thomism: "Despite its (of Schelerian phenomenology) development, however, the metaphysics which he (John Paul) would use to integrate the teaching of Vatican II into his own experience of prayer and culture would remain, in its essentials, the metaphysics of St. Thomas."[159]

The phenomenological method, as John Conley describes it,

...differs from the scholastic or rationalist methods of argumentation inasmuch as it does not seek truth by establishing a proposition, proving the proposition through schematic evidence and refuting counter propositions. The phenomenological method tends to examine a problem by moving from less to more adequate insights as it describes the various dimensions of a particular question.[160]

The Pope moves progressively from the most superficial to the most profound descriptions of the question, and from the narrowest to the broadest

---

[157]See St. Augustine, *Contra Faustum*, Book 22, chapter 27: PL 42, 418; Vatican II, Declaration on Religious Freedom *Dignitatis Humanae*, 3; St. Thomas Aquinas, *Summa Theologiae*, I–II, q. 93, a. 1; Pope John Paul II, *Veritatis Splendor*, 43; *Evangelium Vitae*, 19–20; *Familiaris Consortio*, 32–33; *Reconciliatio et Paenitentia*, 17; Alasdair MacIntyre, "How Can We Learn What *Veritatis Splendor* Has To Teach?" in *The Thomist* 58 (1994): 173; German Grisez, "Veritatis Splendor: Revealed Truth versus Dissent," in *Homiletic and Pastoral Review* 94 (March 1994): 8–10; Giacomo Cardinal Biffi, "The Action of the Holy Spirit in the Church and in the World," in *John Paul II. A Panorama of his Teachings*, New York: New City Press, 1989, 42–43; Russell Hittinger, "The Pope and the Theorists: The Oneness of Truth," in *Crisis* 11 (December 1993): 31.

[158]Anna–Teresa Tymieniecka, "The Origins of the philosophy of John Paul II," in *Proceedings of the American Catholic Philosophical Association* 53 (1979): 16–27.

[159]Gerald A. McCool, "The Theology of John Paul II," in *The Thought of Pope John Paul II*, John M. McDermott (ed.), Rome: Gregorian University Press, 1993, 31.

[160]John J. Conley, "The philosophical foundations of the thought of John Paul II. A Response," in *The Thought of Pope John Paul II*, John M. McDermott (ed.), Rome: Gregorian University Press, 1993, 23.

dimensions of the issue. He invites the reader's thinking to work through successive developments, to go back and forth through the same necessary axis of reference which remains the focus of reflection. This method allows him to place "great values on the attentive description of the various appearances of a question at each step of insight."[161]

Consequently, instead of the Aristotelian epistemology and methodology, the Pope recurs to the Schelerian method of analysis, still with Thomistic content.[162] The Thomistic approach to the person guarantees not only the strong individualistic dimension of the human person as he is acting, but also his or her relationality with others. St. Thomas recurs to Boethius' definition of person: *rationalis naturae individua substantia*. The one who has access to an immaterial knowledge, since he should be defined by a relation to the truth and not as an object within the order of material nature, should have a personal character: "The rational nature does not have a genuine autonomous existence as nature; it subsists as a person. The person, therefore, is an autonomous subject of existence and of action, which otherwise could not be attributed to the rational nature. Not well: this is why God must be a personal being."[163] In fact, for St. Thomas, each Divine Person is *subsistent relation*. Although the relation is subsistent, because each Person possesses the whole Divine nature, each Person is what it is because of the relation with the other Two Persons. St. Thomas' philosophical and metaphysical innovation based on Aristotle is seen most clearly through the affirmation that God's existence as Creator is directly connected with that of the personality of God.[164] I make mine Buttiglione's remark in this regard. "In sum, St. Thomas provides an objective personalism, a set of objective features which are necessary to work out an authentic philosophy of the person."[165] But the Pope then carried his philosophy beyond

---

[161]John J. Conley, *Ibid.*, 24. See also J. Honoré, "Christ the Redeemer, Core of John Paul's Teaching," in *John Paul II. A Panorama of his Teachings*, New York: New City Press, 1989, 14.

[162]See Rocco Buttiglione, Karol Wojtyla. *The Thought of the Man who became Pope John Paul II*, trans. Paolo Guietti and Francesca Murphy, Grand Rapids/Cambridge: William B. Eerdmans Publishing Company, 1997, 78–79.

[163]See Karol Wojtyla, "Il Personalismo Tomista," in *I fondamenti dell'ordine etico*, 141 ff; Rocco Buttiglione, Karol Wojtyla. *The Thought of the Man who became Pope John Paul II*, trans. Paolo Guietti and Francesca Murphy, Grand Rapids/Cambridge: William B. Eerdmans Publishing Company, 1997, 80.

[164]See Rocco Buttiglione, Karol Wojtyla. *The Thought of the Man who became Pope John Paul II*, trans. Paolo Guietti and Francesca Murphy, Grand Rapids/Cambridge: William B. Eerdmans Publishing Company, 1997, 80.

[165]Rocco Buttiglione, Karol Wojtyla. *The Thought of the Man who became Pope John Paul II*, trans. Paolo Guietti and Francesca Murphy, Grand Rapids/Cambridge: William B. Eerdmans Publishing Company, 1997, 82; Karol Wojtyla, "Il Personalismo Tomista," *Ibid.*, 146–147.

the classic Thomist metaphysics of universal nature in its account of man as a conscious acting person. In *Sources of Renewal*, while still Archbishop of Cracow, he had already formed his philosophical/theological vision of the human person in terms of the image and likeness of God.[166] The meaning of this likeness cannot be limited to the capacity of knowing God and the world. Neither can it be reduced to the power of performing good actions through the use of the person's will guided by his intellect. It is mainly his capacity of establishing a relationship of *communio* among himself, God and others. By entering into this *communio*, the human person achieves his perfection through his free self–offering to the others. Isn't this what he said, as Pope John Paul II, when, in *Dominum et Vivificantem*, he explains how the human person is in the image and likeness of God: "This (the image and likeness) means not only rationality and freedom as constitutive properties of human nature, but also, from the very beginning, the capacity of having a personal relationship with God, as 'I' and 'you,' and therefore the capacity of having a covenant, which will take place in God's salvific communication with man."[167] John Paul also refers to *Gaudium et Spes*, 24 in *Salvifici Doloris*, 28 where the Good Samaritan "...gives himself, his very 'I,' opening this 'I' to the other person. Here we touch upon one of the keypoints of all Christian anthropology. Man cannot 'fully find himself except through a sincere gift of himself.' "

The expanded Thomism of the human person explains Pope John Paul II's success in achieving a well–rounded development of the theology of union during his Pontificate. This approach complements and does not deny the strong individualistic tendency that he showed in *The Acting Person*. Nor does this new trend manifest any inconsistency in his philosophical and theological thought; it rather confirms the maturing of thought of a Pope who, being the Pastor of the Universal Church, has been, especially because of his Supreme Office, more in contact with many other resources than the Schelerian phenomenology. Thus, despite the theology of union that he has displayed throughout his Pontificate, John Paul II's approach to the philosophy of the person does not minimize the importance of the individual *in* and *per se*.[168] *Christifideles Laici*, 37, emphasizing the uniqueness and irrepeatability of every human person in his relationship with others, confirms that "the individual can never be reduced by all that seeks to crush and to annihilate the

---

[166]See Karol Wojtyla, *Sources of Renewal: The Implementation of the Second Vatican Council*, San Francisco: Harper and Row, 1980, 61–62 and 133–138.

[167]Pope John Paul II, *Dominum et Vivificantem*, 34. See also Ibid., *Familiaris Consortio*, 51; *Redemptionis Donum*, 4 and 10.

[168]See Pope John Paul II, *Salvifici Doloris*, 28; *Familiaris Consortio*, 22 and 32; *Christifideles Laici*, 37. See also *Gaudium et Spes*, 24.

person into the anonymity that comes from collectivity, institutions, structures and systems."

The christology, anthropology, and metaphysics of *communio* that were developed especially in *Redemptor Hominis* and in many other papal documents find their roots in Karol Wojtyla's pre–papal documents *Sources of Renewal*[169] and *Sign of Contradiction*.[170] The strong individualistic approach cannot be equated with a human self–sufficiency and a resolute attitude of self–seeking. Only through the offering of self does the human person achieves his perfection within the frame work of that *communio*. In the order of creation, this takes place through the establishing of family, society, and the human world; in the order of grace, the perfection of man that flows from his union with God happens through free entering into *communio* with the Church. That *communio* with the Church enables the human person to form "his conscious attitudes toward God, the world, and his fellow men by participating in the Church's own faith–given consciousness."[171] It is love that establishes the *communio* between responsible persons. Whether in the context of marital union or not, responsible love "must be conformed to the truth made known by the mind's conformity to reality. No moral agent could possess himself through an act of responsible self–determination unless that act respected the essential structure of his own human person."[172] The patterns of Wojtyla's reasoning lead us to realize that in his personalist theology, the metaphysics of nature as found in Aquinas will be constantly expanded into a metaphysics of the responsible acting person.[173]

Phenomenology focuses on the correlation between the human person and the object: "not on either the subject (the human person) alone, as in much modern philosophy, or on the object alone, as is common in some kinds of

---

[169]See Karol Wojtyla, *Sources of Renewal: The Implementation of the Second Vatican Council*, San Francisco: Harper and Row, 1980, 61–62 and 133–138.

[170]See Karol Wojtyla, *Sign of Contradiction*, New York: The Seabury Press, 1979, 28–32, 81–90, 130–141, and 150–151.

[171]Gerald A. McCool, "The Theology of John Paul II," in *The Thought of Pope John Paul II*, John M. McDermott (ed.), Rome: Gregorian University Press, 1993, 46. See Karol Wojtyla, *Sources of Renewal: The Implementation of the Second Vatican Council*, San Francisco: Harper and Row, 1980, 61–62 and 133–138; "The Subject: Person and Community," in *Review of Metaphysics* 33 (1979): 292–299.

[172]Gerald A. McCool, "The Theology of John Paul II," in *The Thought of Pope John Paul II*, John M. McDermott (ed.), Rome: Gregorian University Press, 1993, 48–49; Karol Wojtyla, *Fruitful and Responsible Love*, New York: Crossroads, 1979, 16–26.

[173]See Rocco Buttiglione, Karol Wojtyla. *The Thought of the Man who became Pope John Paul II*, trans. Paolo Guietti and Francesca Murphy, Grand Rapids/Cambridge: William B. Eerdmans Publishing Company, 1997, 78–79; Russell Hittinger, "The Pope and the Theorists: The Oneness of Truth," in *Crisis* 11 (December 1993): 34–36.

Scholasticism."[174] This balanced emphasis on both the human person and whatever lies outside of him, whether world or God, enables John Paul to give the human person his due place in the overall picture of the creative order. The transcendence of the subjective reality and the concreteness of the objective reality are both respected. In this sense Avery Dulles asserts that the Pope develops an "original anthropology which owes something to classical Thomism and something to modern personalist phenomenology, especially as represented by Max Scheler..."[175]

With that in mind, the Schelerian phenomenology guarantees the balanced approach of how the act establishes a relationship between the person and the reality. I make John Conley's conclusion my own:

> I believe that the distinctive union between phenomenological method and neoscholastic analysis of the moral act explains part of the difficulty many of us experience when reading the Pope's documents. I often have the impression of banging into scholastic steel as I wander through the phenomenological fog" [176]

The concept of person, whether *human* or *divine* as it appears in the writings of John Paul II reveals the Pope's deep awareness of the Tradition of the Church. It is by being very faithful to the theological content of this Tradition that he reflects on it in a very original way. Throughout all of his Encyclicals and writings, he is primarily interested in establishing a "correct view of the human person and of his unique value."[177] This correct view happens only within the framework of faith because "man's true identity is only fully revealed to him through faith,"[178] and the human person, consequently, receives the meaning of his existence from Divine Revelation:[179] John Paul's well–known personalism is based directly on the uniqueness of the God–man Jesus Christ.[180] Jesus Christ, the *first evangelizer*,[181] and his Apostles

---

[174]*The Encyclicals of John Paul II*, Ibid., 28.

[175]Avery Dulles, "The Prophetic Humanism of John Paul II," *America*, 169 (1993):7.

[176]John J. Conley, *Ibid.*, 28.

[177]*Centesimus Annus*, 11.

[178]*Centesimus Annus*, 54.

[179]See *The Encyclicals of John Paul II*, Edited with Introductions by J. Michael Miller, Indiana: Our Sunday Visitor Publishing Division, Our Sunday Visitor, Inc., 1996, 579.

[180]See James Schall, "*Redemptor Hominis*: The Amazement of God," *Homiletic and Pastoral Review* 80 (October 1979): 14.

[181]See Pope Paul VI, Apostolic Exhortation *Evangelii Nuntiandi*, December 8, 1975, 6; Pope John Paul II, *Redemptor Hominis*, 12.

...preserved, while acting with their full force of spirit, a deep esteem for man, for his intellect, his will his conscience and his freedom. Thus the human person's dignity itself becomes part of the content of that proclamation, being included not necessarily in words but by an attitude toward it.[182]

---

[182]*Redemptor Hominis*, 12.

CHAPTER THREE

THEOLOGY OF CREATION AND THE PRESENCE OF EVIL IN THE THOUGHT OF POPE JOHN PAUL II

The Act of Creation

Pope John Paul II constantly refers to the creative activity of God. He hardly treats any question without introducing something of the theology of creation, the principles of the world's existence and the ethos of the beginning. I think one could say that this basis for his thinking shapes the whole body of papal documents for the entire twenty years of his Pontificate. His interest in these themes becomes evident if one simply notices that his quotes from the Old Testament are mostly from the first chapters of Genesis. At the same time, his vision of the unity between creation and Incarnation has led him to often recur to the theme of creation applying its theological implications to ecclesiological, moral, anthropological, social, and political issues.

The thought of John Paul II in respect to creation becomes clearer when parallels from the different papal writings are viewed together, although such an approach might give the reader the impression of an anachronistic study. It is impossible, however, to draw the main lines of his thinking about creation without considering many of his writings simultaneously. One is impelled to follow this methodology because what he starts to analyze in one document, he often finishes only after tackling the subject from many different points of view and using other documents as well.

The thought of Pope John Paul II concerning creation takes place within the framework of the mystery of it. He never trespasses the boundaries of the human mind; rather his respect for both the *analogy of being* and the *analogy of faith* provide a very sound and valid approach to the mystery of God's creative activity. In *Mulieris Dignitatem*, 8, Pope John Paul II indicates the foundations of anthropomorphism in the biblical language when the image and likeness of God in man is under discussion. If man is created in God's image and likeness, a fact implying that man is 'like' God, it is also true that God too is in some measure 'like man.' This specific likeness enables God to be humanly known, within the limitations of human knowledge that result from the analogy of being. Referring to the Fourth Lateran Council (DS 806), John

Paul analyzes how that analogy imposes limits on the 'likeness' between God and man. John Paul notes, "while man's 'likeness' to God is true, the 'non–likeness' which separates the whole of creation from the Creator is still more essentially true. Although man is created in God's likeness, God does not cease to be the ... 'Different One,' by essence the 'totally Other.' " The Letter of St. Paul to the Romans (Rom 1:20) is evidently his main Scriptural source to reflect on the theology of Vatican I concerning the Revelation of God and man's capacity to know Him through visible creation. His Holiness says, "Although God 'dwells in unapproachable light,' he speaks to man by means of the whole of the universe."[1] In *Redemptoris Missio*, 28–29 as well as in *Dominum et Vivificantem*, 53, John Paul invites all Catholics to ponder the activity of the Spirit throughout the whole of creation. The Holy Spirit enables God's knowledge to be communicated to man through the whole of visible creation.

If by analogy of faith God reveals and communicates Himself in and through Jesus Christ, so also does the analogy of being. God is and will always be a mystery, a mystery that is all the more respected when the process of knowing God uses the valid contemplation of creatures traced out by the Fathers of the First Vatican Council. *Dives in Misericordia* states that "this indirect and imperfect knowledge, achieved by the intellect seeking God by means of creatures through the visible world, falls short of 'vision of the Father.' "[2] Analogy of being and analogy of faith then should be two dimensions that condition any study of the Pope's thought on creation. Having set the analogy as a norm and principle of analyses, one proceeds securely to his deeper considerations regarding the mystery of creation.

Pope John Paul II has constantly searched for the roots of the world's creation and existence in the intra–trinitarian life. The expression of the fatherhood of the Father is the eternal generation of the Son, and their mutual love constitutes the Person of the Holy Spirit.[3] The creation of the world for John Paul II derives from the mutual love between the Father and the Son and is, therefore, the expression of the fatherhood of the Father: "the universe, immense and diverse as it is, the world of all living beings, is inscribed in God's fatherhood, which is its source (cf. Eph 3:14–16)."[4] However, since the

[1]Pope John Paul II, *Dives in Misericordia*, 1. See also Ibid., *Catechesi Tradendae*, 60; Avery Dulles, "John Paul II and the Truth about Freedom," in *First Things* 55 (1995): 38.

[2]Pope John Paul II, *Dives in Misericordia*, 2.

[3]See Pope John Paul II, *Redemptionis Donum*, 3.

[4]Pope John Paul II, *Letter to Families from Pope John Paul II*, 6. See also Raymond T. Gawronski, "Redemptor Hominis," in *The Thought of Pope John Paul II*, Rome: Gregorian University, 1993, 221; Michaël Devaux, "The Truth of Love, the Lie of Death," in *Communio* 23

Holy Spirit is this mutual love in Person, He becomes "the source and the beginning of every giving of gifts to creatures."[5] So, the fatherhood of the Father is communicated *ad extra* because the eternal love that God possesses on His transcendental level as God,[6] manifests itself as *bonum diffusivum sui*, as good diffusive of itself, that is as creative love.[7] This diffusion of good is based on the principle according to which the more common the good, the more properly one's own it will also be: mine–yours–ours. This is the logic behind the creation of the world through the initiative of a good and perfect Father, a goodness that by its very nature is diffusive.

On the level of intratrinitarian life, the expression of the Father's fatherhood is the Word, the Father's image; on the level of creation His fatherhood's expression is man created by the Father in the image and likeness of the Word. The Incarnate Word of God then is the connection between the expression of the Father's fatherhood in divine as well in human existence. In *Redemptor Hominis*, John Paul II says:

> He (Jesus Christ) it was, and he alone, who satisfied the Father's eternal love, that fatherhood that from the beginning found expression in creating the world, giving man all the riches of creation, and making him "little less than God," in that he was created "in the image and after the likeness of God." He and he alone also satisfied that fatherhood of God and that love which man in a way rejected by breaking the first covenant and the later covenants that God "again and again offered to man."[8]

The absolute dependency of man on God results from the Father's "eternal love which, as an irrevocable gift, enters into human history."[9] The relationship between God and the world is, for Pope John Paul II, based on Mercy and

---

(1996): 118; Paul L. Peeters, "Dominum et Vivificantem: The Conscience and the Heart," in *Communio* 15 (1988): 150.

[5]Pope John Paul II, *Dominum et Vivificantem*, 34.

[6]See Pope John Paul II, *Dives in Misericordia*, 15; *General Audience*, December 13, 1978; Joseph Cardinal Cordeiro, "The religious sense of man," in *John Paul II. A Panorama of his Teachings*, New York: New City Press, 1989, 66; Raymond T. Gawronski, "Redemptor Hominis," in *The Thought of Pope John Paul II*, Rome: Gregorian University, 1993, 222.

[7]See Pope John Paul II, *Dominum et Vivificantem*, 37; *Redemptionis Donum*, 3; *Salvifici Doloris*, 10; *Letter to Families from Pope John Paul II*, 10; *Vita Consecrata*, 18; St. Thomas Aquinas, *Summa Theologiae*, I, q. 5, a. 4, ad 2; Raymond T. Gawronski, "Redemptor Hominis," in *The Thought of Pope John Paul II*, Rome: Gregorian University, 1993, 222; Michaël Devaux, "The Truth of Love, the Lie of Death," in *Communio* 23 (1996): 118; Rocco Buttiglione, *Karol Wojtyla. The Thought of the Man who became Pope John Paul II*, trans. Paolo Guietti and Francesca Murphy, Grand Rapids/Cambridge: William B. Eerdmans Publishing Company, 1997, 73.

[8]Pope John Paul II, *Redemptor Hominis*, 9.

[9]Pope John Paul II, *Redemptoris Mater*, 36.

Justice. Through them the Father has established a bond of love that will never end. This bond as described in *Dives in Misericordia*, 4, is a direct consequence of the very act of creation:

> Mercy differs from justice, but is not in opposition to it, if we admit in the history of man—as the Old Testament precisely does—the presence of God, who already as Creator has linked himself to his creature with a particular love. Love, by its very nature, excludes hatred and ill–will toward the one to whom he once gave the gift of himself: *Nihil odisti eorum quae fecisti*, 'you hold nothing of what you have made in abhorrence.'[10]

One notices that here and elsewhere the Pope prefers to place the ontological aspect of God's creational activity before its consequences. Because God is the Creator, His Justice which indicates his transcendent perfection and His Mercy are the basis for His love. This love is the norm of relationality between the Creator and the Creatures. Continuing his comment in *Dives in Misericordia*, the Pope says:

> These words (*Nihil odisti eorum quae fecisti*) indicate the profound basis of the relationship between justice and mercy in God, in his relations with man and the world. They tell us that we must seek the life–giving roots and intimate reasons for this relationship by going back to 'the beginning,' in the very mystery of creation.[11]

In *Redemptoris Mater*, 8, John Paul comments on the opening of St. Paul's Letter to the Ephesians: "Blessed be the God and Father of our Lord Jesus Christ, who has blessed us in Christ with every spiritual blessing in the heavenly places (Eph. 1:3)." The Pope explains the grace that human beings receive in terms of the very act of creation, a grace that originates in the life of God and is revealed and communicated in the Incarnation. The election of man by the Father consists not only in the act that brings man to existence, but in the supernatural grace of Redemption that flows from Christ's act of Incarnation. Christ's supernatural grace is bestowed on humankind throughout history, although that same grace has always been hidden in the mystery of Christ eternally planned by the Father. As the revelation of this mystery tells us, both creation and Redemption are directed to one single goal which is the adoption of men and women as sons and daughters of God:

> In the language of the Bible 'grace' means a special gift, which according to the New Testament has its source precisely in the Trinitarian life of God himself, God who is love (cf. Jn 4:8). The fruit of this love is 'the election' of which the Letter to the Ephesians speaks. On the part of God, this election is the eternal desire to save man

---

[10]Pope John Paul II, *Dives in Misericordia*, 4.

[11]Pope John Paul II, *Dives in Misericordia*, 4.

through a sharing in his own life (cf. 2 Pet 1:4) in Christ: it is salvation through a sharing in supernatural life. The effect of this eternal gift, of this grace of man's election by God, is like a seed of holiness, or a spring which rises in the soul as a gift from God himself, who through grace gives life and holiness to those who are chosen. In this way there is fulfilled, that is to say there comes about, that 'blessing' of man 'with every spiritual blessing,' that 'being his adopted sons and daughters...in Christ,' in him who is eternally the 'beloved Son' of the Father.[12]

When it comes to the theology of creation, John Paul II brings the Augustinian and the Thomistic traditions together, especially regarding the idea of participation. The existence of every being is the participation of *"ens"* in being which occurs *secundum speciem, modum, et ordinem*: "Given that the good is really identified with being, this relation is accompanied by another relation, which is accidental being—which possesses being by participation (*'ens per participationem'*)—and the determinate being—which is an autonomous entity (*'ens subsistens'*)."[13] Not everything that exists participates in being in the same way because there is a hierarchy which articulates itself in the diverse species of being. This metaphysical order which results from the articulation of that hierarchy in order that regulates the relation between the "entities" of the diverse species is also an ethical order. John Paul considers it an ethical order because participation in being is inseparable from participation in value. Projecting this philosophy on man, one realizes that man, as person, comes to maturity through the use of his own freedom and not simply because he fits in a given order. This explains John Paul's notion of creation. God is the Highest Good, and He has the fullness of existence in the sense that He is the superior and transcendent measure of beings. Being the Supreme perfect being, all other beings that find their perfection only in a more perfect being, find in God their end. God recapitulates in Himself the perfection of all beings and, while still infinitely transcending them, He communicates being and goodness to everything which exists:

From this follows the resemblance to God of all creatures in being; this resemblance has its own gradation. Both the resemblance as such and its gradations are gathered together and known in the mind of God as exemplars: the Creator sees in Himself the highest exemplar out of which beings are created and knows them in His image, that is to say, inasmuch as they imitate His essence, which is the first object of

---

[12]Pope John Paul II, *Redemptoris Mater*, 8. See also Ibid., *Dives in Misericordia*, 4. Edna McDonagh, "*Redemptor Hominis* and Ireland" in *The Furrow* 30 (1979): 628.

[13]Karol Wojtyla, "Il fondamento metafisico e fenomenologico della norma morale sulla base delle concezioni di Tommaso d'Aquino e di Max Scheler," 111–112; Rocco Buttiglione, Karol Wojtyla. *The Thought of the Man who became Pope John Paul II*, trans. Paolo Guietti and Francesca Murphy, Grand Rapids/Cambridge: William B. Eerdmans Publishing Company, 1997, 75–76.

knowledge. It is here that we find the nucleus of the normative order.[14]

The fact that the expression of this eternal love of the Father is the life that was given to every creature explains the fundamental truth of humankind's creation *ex Nihilo*: "To create means to call into existence from nothing: therefore, to create means to give existence."[15] Or, as expressed in *Salvifici Doloris*, 10: "For the God of Revelation is first of all the Creator, from whom comes, together with existence, the essential good of creation." To be created out of nothing and to exist means to be able to hold one's existence only in reference to another principle: this other principle, who is God, is essentially existent being. It also means that there is a fundamental unity between man as an intelligent creature and God, a unity which belongs to the internal 'logic' of the very mystery of creation. This total dependency that is the direct consequence of a creation *ex Nihilo*, places the Pope in the line of traditional Thomism's theology of participation and relationality.[16] In *Christifideles Laici*, he says: "The individual's relation to God is a constitutive element of the very 'being' and 'existence' of an individual: it is in God that we 'live, move and have our being' (Acts 17:28)."[17]

The act of creation is an irrevocable gift of a God who, being perfect in Himself and having no need for creatures, decided to bring into existence creatures who, starting to exist at one point in history, are destined to share His eternity:

> This activity (creative activity) by God in the world always continues, as the words of Christ attest: 'My Father is working still...': he works with creative power by sustaining in existence the world that he called into being from nothing, and he works with salvific power in the hearts of those whom from the beginning he has destined

---

[14]Karol Wojtyla, "Il fondamento metafisico e fenomenologico della norma morale sulla base delle concezioni di Tommaso d'Aquino e di Max Scheler," 111–112; Rocco Buttiglione, Karol Wojtyla. *The Thought of the Man who became Pope John Paul II*, trans. Paolo Guietti and Francesca Murphy, Grand Rapids/Cambridge: William B. Eerdmans Publishing Company, 1997, 75–76.

[15]Pope John Paul II, *Dominum et Vivificantem*, 34; Joseph Cardinal Cordeiro, "The religious sense of man," in *John Paul II. A Panorama of his Teachings*, New York: New City Press, 1989, 66.

[16]See Paul L. Peeters, "*Dominum et Vivificantem*: The Conscience and the Heart," in *Communio* 15 (1988): 150; André Frossard, *Portrait of John Paul II*, San Francisco: Ignatius Press, 1990, 77.

[17]Pope John Paul II, *Christifideles Laici*, 39. See also Ibid., *Mulieris Dignitatem*, 9; *Veritatis Splendor*, 43; *Vita Consecrata*, 17.

for 'rest' in union with himself in his 'Father's house.'[18]

In the context of the creation *ex Nihilo*, two notions occupy John Paul's theology: the *origin* of man and his *affinity* to the Creator. Man comes to have a certain affinity with other creatures: he is called to use them, and to be involved with them, although he is still superior to them because God placed them under his dominion.[19] This affinity with other creatures has also a vertical dimension, which is the measure of man's dominion over creation: "But at the same time man must remain subject to the will of God, who imposes limits upon his use and dominion over things (cf. Gen 2: 16–17), just as he promises immortality (cf. Gen 2:9; Wis 2:23). Thus man, being the image of God, has a true affinity with him too."[20] As a human being in the image of God, man is made to represent the Creator in creation: John Paul manifests his awareness of St. Thomas' definition "the name person indicates what is most perfect in nature."[21] The image of God in man is and will always be the fundamental mark of relationship between God and man: "the foundation of the whole human ethos," as also *Mulieris Dignitatem*, 7, reads, "is rooted in the image and likeness of God which the human being bears within himself from the beginning."[22] Two elements are at work here: the image and likeness of God are the causes of man's dominion, but a limited dominion. This implies that a qualified dominion, as a fact of life and not as a mere speciesism, is required of man in his relationship to the world. It is exactly in this sense that *Gaudium et Spes* speaks of man as "the only being God wanted for its own sake."[23]

The image and likeness of God in man as the fundamental criteria for

---

[18]Pope John Paul II, *Laborem Exercens*, 25; *Gift and Mystery. On the Fiftieth Anniversary of my Priestly Ordination*, New York: Doubleday, 1996, 75. See also Joseph Cardinal Cordeiro, "The religious sense of man," in *John Paul II. A Panorama of his Teachings*, New York: New City Press, 1989, 66.

[19]See Pope John Paul II, *Sollicitudo Rei Socialis*, 29; Avery Dulles, "John Paul II and the Truth about Freedom," in *First Things* 55 (1995): 38; Lothar Roos, "On a Theology and Ethics of Work," in *Communio* 11 (1984): 107; Stratford Caldecott, "Cosmology, Eschatology, Ecology: Some Reflections on *Sollicitudo Rei Socialis*," in *Communio* 15 (1988): 307.

[20]Pope John Paul II, *Sollicitudo Rei Socialis*, 29. See also Ibid., *Redemptionis Donum*, 4; *Mulieris Dignitatem*, 7.

[21]See Stratford Caldecott, "Cosmology, Eschatology, Ecology: Some Reflections on *Sollicitudo Rei Socialis*," in *Communio* 15 (1988): 307.

[22]See also Pope John Paul II, *Gift and Mystery. On the Fiftieth Anniversary of my Priestly Ordination*, New York: Doubleday, 1996, 75; André Frossard, *Portrait of John Paul II*, San Francisco: Ignatius Press, 1990, 77.

[23]See Avery Dulles, "John Paul II and the Truth about Freedom," in *First Things* 55 (1995): 37–38; Stratford Caldecott, "Cosmology, Eschatology, Ecology: Some Reflections on *Sollicitudo Rei Socialis*," in *Communio* 15 (1988): 308.

dominion should have *a priori* the very act of existence as its basis. The act of existence precedes and establishes the act of likeness with God along with all its theological implications concerning the nature of the relationship between God and man: to be human means to be called to interpersonal communion through the act of creation out of nothing. From an anthropological point of view, origin and affinity are the constitutive elements of the human person in the act of creation: "The fact is that man was not created, so to speak, immobile and static. The first portrayal of him, as given in the Bible, certainly presents him as a creature and image, defined in his deepest reality by the origin and affinity that constitute him."[24]

The affinity of man to the Creator flows from the nature of the human person who is a unified totality: body and soul are the constitutive elements of the person making him visible and invisible at the same time. The human body is the nexus of the person in his contact with cosmic realities and is, therefore, the 'environment' of the soul. The entire material world enters into contact with the spiritual nature of the person through the body. Thus the human person becomes a little cosmos that represents the spiritual reality of God to all other creatures and, at the same time, is invited to have dominion over those creatures using them with respect to the hierarchy of goods in order to reach his ultimate end. Creation, understood in this way, becomes for John Paul II an approach that respects creation *ex Nihilo* as well as the permanent character of human existence. Both man's visible dimension, that is the body, and the breath of life given to him by God on the day of creation, guarantee a non–preexistent entity to the existence of man as a composite of body and soul. At, the same time, endowed with a spiritual soul, man is created as a reflection of the spiritual reality of God: if the original is eternal, the copy is eternal too. Otherwise, we will be dealing with a spiritual reality that vanishes with the temporal death of man, a fact that contradicts the very notion of creation as it has been revealed in Scripture and developed by the Tradition of the Church.[25]

The intimate interconnectedness between the Father's eternal love and the creation of humankind establishes an unbreakable bond between God and man, the only creature that God created for himself.[26] In the context of the birth of

[24]Pope John Paul II, *Solicitudo Rei Socialis*, 30; Joseph Cardinal Cordeiro, "The religious sense of man," in *John Paul II. A Panorama of his Teachings*, New York: New City Press, 1989, 67–68.

[25]See Pope John Paul II, *Sollicitudo Rei Socialis*, 29; Stratford Caldecott, "Cosmology, Eschatology, Ecology: Some Reflections on *Sollicitudo Rei Socialis*," in *Communio* 15 (1988): 308; Matthew Habiger, "Situating *Sollicitudo Rei Socialis* in Catholic Social Teaching," in *Social Justice Review* 79 (1988): 139.

[26]See *Gaudium et Spes*, 24; Pope John Paul II, *Centesimus Annus*, 11; *Laborem Exercens*, 1; *Redemptionis Donum*, 4; *Mulieris Dignitatem*, 7; Joseph Cardinal Cordeiro, "The religious sense of man," in *John Paul II. A Panorama of his Teachings*, New York: New City Press, 1989, 68.

a child, the words of St. Irenaeus, *"Gloria Dei vivens homo* (the glory of God is for man to be alive)," become one of the focal points of John Paul's *Letter to Families* (1994).[27] The existence and the presence of man on the earth gives meaning to all that exists. Man has the common good of the whole society dwelling in him, because man is first of all the "glory of God." St. Irenaeus' definition, therefore, leads one to "encounter the loftiest definition of man: the glory of God is the common good of all that exists, the common good of the human race." Only with the resurrection of Christ, however, does man's life reach the 'fullness of life' which is in God himself: "I came that they may have life, and have it abundantly (Jn 10:10)." This text of John 10:10 is used by Pope John Paul to illustrate a conviction that has been accompanying him throughout his Pontificate: anthropology is a chapter of christology. Man and all aspects of his life, even his life itself, receives understanding only in light of the Word made flesh. John 10:10 reveals the deepest meaning of *"Gloria Dei vivens homo."*[28]

The first covenant between God and man or the "original covenant with creation in man"[29] is, therefore, a genuine result flowing from the very logic of the act of creation. Before creating man, God, as revealed in the Book of Genesis (1:26), said: "Let us make man in our image, after our likeness." These words suggest an essential difference between the creation of man and the creation of other creatures. With the expression 'let us' one feels that the Creator "withdraws as it were into himself, in order to seek the pattern and inspiration in the mystery of his Being, which is already here disclosed as the divine 'We.' "[30] Hence the mystery of creation in John Paul's opinion should be sought in the very intimate mystery of the Triune God: the divine 'We' is the eternal pattern of the human 'we.' The community of the human family has its ultimate source and model in the community of the Three Divine Persons. It is in that sense that every man and every woman are in *the image and likeness of God*, since "God has imprinted his own image and likeness on man (cf. Gen 1:26), conferring upon him an incomparable dignity."[31] In *Familiaris Consortio*, the love of God expresses in the most significant way the meaning

---

[27]Giacomo Cardinal Biffi, "The action of the Holy Spirit in the Church and in the world," in *John Paul II. A Panorama of his Teachings*, New York: New City Press, 1989, 46.

[28]Pope John Paul II, *Letter to Families from Pope John Paul II*, 11; St. Irenaeus, *Adversus Haereses* IV, 20, 7: PG 7, 1057; SCh 100/2, 648–659.

[29]Pope John Paul II, *Laborem Exercens*, 4. See also Ibid., *Dives in Misericordia*, 7.

[30]Pope John Paul II, *Letter to Families from Pope John Paul II*, 6.

[31]Pope John Paul II, *Centesimus Annus*, 11. See Ibid., 22; *Letter of Pope John Paul II to Women*, 7; Joseph Cardinal Cordeiro, "The religious sense of man," in *John Paul II. A Panorama of his Teachings*, New York: New City Press, 1989, 68.

of the image and likeness of God in man. Here the Pope shows the consequences of God's act of creation: calling man into existence through love, He called him at the same time for love. Love is therefore "the fundamental and innate vocation of every human being."[32] St. Irenaeus, St. Gregory of Nyssa, and St. Augustine are referred to in *Mulieris Dignitatem*, 6, in order to emphasize that the *image and likeness* constitutes

> ...the immutable basis of all Christian anthropology...: man is the high point of the whole order of creation in the visible world; the human race which takes its origin from the calling into existence of man and woman, crowns the whole work of creation; both man and woman are human beings to an equal degree, both created in God's image.[33]

Therefore, as *Mulieris Dignitatem*, 6, again confirms, "the biblical account (of creation) puts forth the truth about the personal character of the human being." This means that, from the very beginning, God's ethos of creating man and woman shines forth in Genesis where "God created man in his own image, in the image of God he created him." John Paul refers to the traditional definition of person within the universal nature as found in Boethius and developed by St. Thomas Aquinas. Man, as a rational being (*animal rationale*), is different from all the other living creatures including those endowed with senses (*animalia*). Besides what was presented in this volume regarding the notion of person and his self–consciousness, this property of rational being, if contemplated in the context of universal nature and categories, enables man to be in the image and likeness of God. In other words, being in the image and likeness of God means for man to be a rational being if he is contemplated in the sense of the Boethian or Thomistic universal nature, and for man to be able to establish a relationship between I and You (including God), if contemplated in the context of his subjective self–consciousness.[34]

Nature of Evil

The terminology concerning evil or sin in its original reality is abundant in the writings of Pope John Paul II. He speaks of it in terms of *mystery of*

---

[32]Pope John Paul II, *Familiaris Consortio*, 11.

[33]Joseph Cardinal Cordeiro, "The religious sense of man," in *John Paul II. A Panorama of his Teachings*, New York: New City Press, 1989, 67–68.

[34]See Pope John Paul II, *Mulieris Dignitatem*, 6; *General Audience*, November 14, 1979; "Persona est naturae rationalis individua substantia:" Manlius Severinus Boethius, *Liber de persona et duabus naturis*, III, PL 64: 1343; St. Thomas Aquinas, *Summa Theologiae*, Ia, q. 29, art. 1; Joseph Cardinal Cordeiro, "The religious sense of man," in *John Paul II. A Panorama of his Teachings*, New York: New City Press, 1989, 67–68.

lawlessness,[35] *inheritance of sin,*[36] *original sin,*[37] *original fall,*[38] *original wound,*[39] *first sin,*[40] *sin of the first parents,*[41] *sin in the descendants of the first Adam,*[42] *mysterium iniquitatis* (using 2 Thess 2:7),[43] *fault,*[44] *breaking of the first covenant,*[45] *breaking,*[46] *disobedience,*[47] *original disobedience,*[48] *disobedience of the first man,*[49] *disobedience of Adam,*[50] *mystery of sin,*[51] *deposit of evil,*[52] *origin of evil,*[53] *root of evil,*[54] *infected sources of evil,*[55] *mystery of evil,*[56] *origin*

---

[35]Pope John Paul II, *Catechesi Tradendae*, 30.

[36]Pope John Paul II, *Redemptionis Donum*, 9 and 10; *Dives in Misericordia*, 8; *Dominum et Vivificantem*, 55; *Sollicitudo Rei Socialis*, 47.

[37]Pope John Paul II, *Redemptor Hominis*, 1 and 8; *Dives in Misericordia*, 8; *Redemptionis Donum*, 9; *Dominum et Vivificantem*, 24; *Mulieris Dignitatem*, 9; *Veritatis Splendor*, 1; *Vita Consecrata*, 87.

[38]Pope John Paul II, *Dominum et Vivificantem*, 13.

[39]Pope John Paul II, *Reconciliatio et Paenitentia*, 3 and 4; *Vita Consecrata*, 87.

[40]Pope John Paul II, *Redemptor Hominis*, 8; *Reconciliatio et Paenitentia*, 14; *Mulieris Dignitatem*, 9.

[41]Pope John Paul II, *Mulieris Dignitatem*, 9.

[42]Pope John Paul II, *Dominum et Vivificantem*, 40.

[43]Pope John Paul II, *To the Youth of the World*, 4; *Reconciliatio et Paenitentia*, 19; *Dominum et Vivificantem*, 31.

[44]Pope John Paul II, *Redemptor Hominis*, 1; *Dominum et Vivificantem*, 31.

[45]Pope John Paul II, *Redemptor Hominis*, 9; *Laborem Exercens*, 4.

[46]Pope John Paul II, *Reconciliatio et Paenitentia*, 4; *Laborem Exercens*, 4.

[47]Pope John Paul II, *Dominum et Vivificantem*, 33, 36, 37; *Sollicitudo rei Socialis*, 30.

[48]Pope John Paul II, *Dominum et Vivificantem*, 33.

[49]Pope John Paul II, *For the 1600th Anniversary of the First Council of Constantinople and the 1550th Anniversary of the Council of Ephesus*, 3; *Dominum et Vivificantem*, 33.

[50]Pope John Paul II, *Dives in Misericordia*, 8.

[51]Pope John Paul II, *To the Youth of the World*, 4 and 12; *Reconciliatio et Paenitentia*, 14; *Redemptionis Donum*, 13; *Dominum et Vivificantem*, 39; *Mulieris Dignitatem*, 9.

[52]Pope John Paul II, *To the Youth of the World*, 6.

[53]Pope John Paul II, *To the Youth of the World*, 15.

[54]Pope John Paul II, *Dives in Misericordia*, 8.

[55]Pope John Paul II, *Reconciliatio et Paenitentia*, 4.

[56]Pope John Paul II, *Mulieris Dignitatem*, 9.

of sin,[57] *the evil implanted from the beginning,*[58] *contamination of sin.*[59]

As far as his reflection on evil is concerned, Pope John Paul II skillfully joins together the Scriptural[60] and the dogmatic theology that relate to this matter.[61] He shows a noticeable influence mainly from the theology of St. Augustine and from the Second Vatican Council. This Council reflects on evil as a reality present in human nature from "the very start of history."[62] And St. Augustine entered into a controversy with the Breton Monk Pelagius who attributed to human nature a state of original justice.[63] The Pope has borrowed many elements from both Augustine and Vatican II when theologizing on the problem of evil, although his thought nevertheless enjoys originality.

For John Paul II, God is the Supreme Being and the Supreme Good.[64] His essence is to exist and His existence in itself is essentially good. Beyond the dimensions of time, on His transcendental level as God the Father, through His Eternal Wisdom and in the Holy Spirit, He decided to create *ex Nihilo* the universe and man in his own image and likeness.[65] The creation of *limited, free, intelligent, good,* and *human* persons is a divine initiative whose purpose is to make these creatures, both as a community and as individuals, share the eternity of the Triune God.[66] This transcendental decision, which is not bound by the laws of time although it took place in time, reveals the eternal love and wisdom of God.

John Paul II follows the steps of St. Thomas Aquinas regarding the relative nature of all created realities and consequently their participation in the

---

[57]Pope John Paul II, *To the Youth of the World*, 15; *Redemptionis Donum*, 9.

[58]Pope John Paul II, *To the Youth of the World*, 15.

[59]Pope John Paul II, *Redemptions Donum*, 4.

[60]The first three chapters of Genesis are essential in the Pope's explanation of the nature of evil. As he himself expressed in *Sign of Contradiction*, the pondering of these chapters is indispensable to understand the nature of evil and its presence in the contemporary world [see Karol Wojtyla, *Sign of Contradiction*, New York: The Seabury Press, 1979, 24; Russell Barta, "Work: In Search of New Meanings," *Chicago Studies* 23 (August 1984): 161].

[61]See A. B. Calkins, *Totus Tuus. John Paul II's Program of Marian Consecration and Entrustment*. U.S.A.: Academy of the Immaculate, 1992, 271–273.

[62]*Gaudium et Spes*, 13.

[63]See O. J. B. Du Roy, "Augustine, St.," in *New Catholic Encyclopedia*, Vol. I, 1055.

[64]See Pope John Paul II, *Vita Consecrata*, 87; Rocco Buttiglione, Karol Wojtyla. *The Thought of the Man who became Pope John Paul II*, trans. Paolo Guietti and Francesca Murphy, Grand Rapids/Cambridge: William B. Eerdmans Publishing Company, 1997, 75–76.

[65]See Pope John Paul II, *Laborem Exercens*, preface.

[66]See Pope John Paul II, *Centesimus Annus*, 53.

Existence of God.[67] Being in the image and likeness of God, the human person shares in the being of God who remains "the origin and the supreme end of man."[68] Although a personal subject endowed with transcendental dignity, he does not exist, however, in the same way God exists because "in his existence and essence he depends on the Creator." He exists only because he shares in God's existence and he will always exist as a limited creature who shares the One, True existence of God.[69] The essence of the human person is not existence itself and, therefore, he does not possess the fulness of Being like God. Failing to possess the fullness of being, man is "in complete ontological and ethical dependence upon the Creator."[70]

Because of his high calling and his being superior to other creatures,[71] man has dominion over the earth, a dominion that has God's image and likeness as its "clear foundation."[72] However, since "man must remain subject to the will of God, who imposes limits upon his use and dominion over things (cf. Gen 2:16–17),"[73] man should naturally and constantly tend with his full freedom toward the Supreme Good.[74] It is the act of the will that determines the

---

[67]See St. Thomas Aquinas, *Summa Theologiae*, I–II, q. 72, a. 5; Pope John Paul II, *Reconciliatio et Paenitentia*, 17; *Christifideles Laici*, 39; *Vita Consecrata*, 99; Rocco Buttiglione, Karol Wojtyla. *The Thought of the Man who became Pope John Paul II*, trans. Paolo Guietti and Francesca Murphy, Grand Rapids/Cambridge: William B. Eerdmans Publishing Company, 1997, 75–76.

[68]Pope John Paul II, *Reconciliatio et Paenitentia*, 18; Avery Dulles, "John Paul II and the Truth about Freedom," in *First Things* 55 (1995): 38.

[69]See Pope John Paul II, *Dominum et Vivificantem*, 36; Rocco Buttiglione, Karol Wojtyla. *The Thought of the Man who became Pope John Paul II*, trans. Paolo Guietti and Francesca Murphy, Grand Rapids/Cambridge: William B. Eerdmans Publishing Company, 1997, 75–76.

[70]Pope John Paul II, *Dominum et Vivificantem*, 44; Lothar Roos, "On a Theology and Ethics of Work," in *Communio* 11 (1984): 107.

[71]See Karol Wojtyla, *Sources of Renewal: The Implementation of the Second Vatican Council*, San Francisco: Harper and Row, 1980, 62; Pope John Paul II, *Redemptor Hominis*, 14; *Dives in Misericordia*, 6; *Sollicitudo Rei Socialis*, 29.

[72]Pope John Paul II, *Sollicitudo Rei Socialis*, 30; *Christifideles Laici*, 43. See also Miroslav Volf, "On Human Work: An Evaluation of the Key Ideas of the Encyclical *Laborem Exercens*," in *Scottish Journal of Theology* 37 (1984): 67; Robert A. Destro, "*Laborem Exercens*," in *A Century of Catholic Social Thought*, Edited by George Weigel and Robert Royal, Lanham: University Press of America, 1991, 146; Aloysius J. Fonseca, "Reflections on the Encyclical Letter *Sollicitudo Rei Socialis*," *Gregorianum* 70 (1989): 15.

[73]Pope John Paul II, *Sollicitudo Rei Socialis*, 29. See Ibid., *Redemptoris Missio*, 58; Avery Dulles, "John Paul II and the Truth about Freedom," in *First Things* 55 (1995): 38; Miroslav Volf, "On Human Work: An Evaluation of the Key Ideas of the Encyclical *Laborem Exercens*," in *Scottish Journal of Theology* 37 (1984): 67 and 74; Jan Schotte, "The Social Teaching of the Church: Laborem Exercens, A New Challenge," in *Review of Social Economy* 40 (1982): 344.

[74]See Pope John Paul II, *Sollicitudo Rei Socialis*, 33; *Veritatis Splendor*, 11; *The Freedom of Conscience and of Religion*, 3; *Redemptionis Donum*, 6; Robert Morneau, "*Redemptor Hominis*:

direction of the being of the human persons. In the context of Christ's Incarnation, Pope John Paul II calls this natural tendency to Christ a *mature humanity*: "Mature humanity means full use of the gift of freedom received from the Creator when he called into existence the man truly made 'in his image, after his likeness.' This gift finds its full realization in the unreserved giving of the whole of one's human person, in a spirit of the love of a spouse, to Christ."[75]

To tend to the Supreme Good does not mean for man to be alienated from the order of creation, because "it was the Creator's will that man should communicate with nature as an intelligent and noble 'master' and 'guardian'..."[76] It rather means that, despite the existence of the 'hierarchy of goods,'[77] man, in his awareness of the principle of the universal destination of goods, should always go beyond them to reach their source, the Supreme Good, "the One who ensures the authentic autonomy of earthly realities."[78] While affirming the essential goodness of creation, man is constantly invited to relativize the created goods by pointing to God as the absolute good. Man should envision the value of his action not only under the light of the creation, but of the Incarnation: in his relationship with nature, the secular and the sacred are united because the act of the person is linked to both creation and

Themes and Theses," in *Review for Religious* 39 (1980): 257; Quentin de la Bedoyere, "Man and His Work," *The Tablet* 235 (1981): 1192; Aloysius J. Fonseca, "Reflections on the Encyclical Letter *Sollicitudo Rei Socialis*," *Gregorianum* 70 (1989): 15.

[75]Pope John Paul II, *Redemptor Hominis*, 21; *Veritatis Splendor*, 17. See also Gregory Baum, "The First Encyclical," in *The Ecumenist* 17 (1979): 56; Russell Barta, "Work: In Search of New Meanings," *Chicago Studies* 23 (August 1984): 157.

[76]Pope John Paul II, *Redemptor Hominis*, 15. See also Ibid., *Laborem Exercens*, 12 and 25; *Redemptoris Missio*, 58; *Lumen Gentium*, 36; Alfred Hennelly, "Pope John Paul's Spirituality of Work," *America* 146 (1982): 31; Miroslav Volf, "On Human Work: An Evaluation of the Key Ideas of the Encyclical *Laborem Exercens*," in *Scottish Journal of Theology* 37 (1984): 67–68; Robert A. Destro, "*Laborem Exercens*," in *A Century of Catholic Social Thought*, Edited by George Weigel and Robert Royal, Lanham: University Press of America, 1991, 146; Stratford Caldecott, "Cosmology, Eschatology, Ecology: Some Reflections on *Sollicitudo Rei Socialis*," *Communio* 15 (1988): 307.

[77]Pope John Paul II, *Laborem Exercens*, 13; *Sollicitudo Rei Socialis*, 34; *Pastores Dabo Vobis*, 30; *Celebrate 2000! Reflections on Jesus, the Holy Spirit, and the Father*, Ann Arbor, Michigan: Servant Publications, 1996, 63; Robert A. Destro, "*Laborem Exercens*," in *A Century of Catholic Social Thought*, Edited by George Weigel and Robert Royal, Lanham: University Press of America, 1991, 146; Stratford Caldecott, "Cosmology, Eschatology, Ecology: Some Reflections on *Sollicitudo Rei Socialis*," *Communio* 15 (1988): 305; Aloysius J. Fonseca, "Reflections on the Encyclical Letter *Sollicitudo Rei Socialis*," *Gregorianum* 70 (1989): 15.

[78]Pope John Paul II, *Tertio Millennio Adveniente*, 20; *Christifideles Laici*, 42; *Veritatis Splendor*, 38. See also Russell Barta, "Work: In Search of New Meanings," *Chicago Studies* 23 (August 1984): 157; Matthew Habiger, "Situating *Sollicitudo Rei Socialis* in Catholic Social Teaching," in *Social Justice Review* 79 (1988): 139.

Redemption.[79] Abstaining from using "with impunity the different categories of beings,"[80] the usage of good should always "contribute to the realization of the human vocation as such," enabling man to share in the creative and the redemptive order.[81]

Concerning the concept of work, the relationship between man and nature should not be viewed as a regrettable by–product of original sin; it should rather be considered a specific vocation addressed to every person to subdue the earth and dominate it.[82] Therefore, in the broad context of man's relationship with the world and with God, "the evil does not consist in 'having' as such, but in 'possessing' without regard to the quality or the ordered hierarchy of the goods one has. Quality and hierarchy arise from the subordination of goods and their availability to man's 'being' and his true vocation."[83] The activity of man, as understood by John Paul II, should be constantly directed to bring order within the whole of creation and therefore be understood as a redeeming activity. Pope John XXIII's *Mater et Magistra*, Vatican II's *Gaudium et Spes*, and Pope John Paul II's *Laborem Exercens*

---

[79]See Pope John Paul II, *Redemptoris Custos*, 22; *Vita Consecrata*, 87; Alfred Hennelly, "Pope John Paul's Spirituality of Work," *America* 146 (1982): 31–32; Russell Barta, "Work: In Search of New Meanings," *Chicago Studies* 23 (August 1984): 157 and 159; Jan Schotte, "The Social Teaching of the Church: Laborem Exercens, A New Challenge," in *Review of Social Economy* 40 (1982): 342; Al Gini, "Meaningful Work and the Rights of the Worker: A Commentary on *Rerum Novarum* and *Laborem Exercens*," in *Thought* 67 (1992): 230.

[80]Pope John Paul II, *Sollicitudo rei Socialis*, 34. See also Helen Ginsburg, "Teaching of John Paul II on Work and the Rights of Workers," in *Social Thought* 13 (Spring–Summer 1987): 48.

[81]Pope John Paul II, *Sollicitudo Rei Socialis*, 28; *Celebrate 2000! Reflections on Jesus, the Holy Spirit, and the Father*, Ann Arbor, Michigan: Servant Publications, 1996, 58. See also Miroslav Volf, "On Human Work: An Evaluation of the Key Ideas of the Encyclical *Laborem Exercens*," in *Scottish Journal of Theology* 37 (1984): 74; Roger Duncan, "On Reading *Laborem Exercens*," *Homiletic and Pastoral Review* 86 (July 1986): 14; Quentin de la Bedoyere, "Man and His Work," *The Tablet* 235 (1981): 1192; Aloysius J. Fonseca, "Reflections on the Encyclical Letter *Sollicitudo Rei Socialis*," *Gregorianum* 70 (1989): 15; Peter Hebblethwaite, *Pope John Paul II and the Church*, Kansas City: Sheed and Ward, 1995, 68–73.

[82]See Pope John Paul II, *Celebrate 2000! Reflections on Jesus, the Holy Spirit, and the Father*, Ann Arbor, Michigan: Servant Publications, 1996, 58–59; Joseph Cardinal Cordeiro, "The religious sense of man," in *John Paul II. A Panorama of his Teachings*, New York: New City Press, 1989, 79; John R. Traffas, "The Spirit of Community and the Spirituality of Work: A Note on *Laborem Exercens*," in *Communio* 10 (1983): 407; Al Gini, "Meaningful Work and the Rights of the Worker: A Commentary on *Rerum Novarum* and *Laborem Exercens*," in *Thought* 67 (1992): 227.

[83]Pope John Paul II, *Sollicitudo Rei Socialis*, 28 and 31; *Celebrate 2000! Reflections on Jesus, the Holy Spirit, and the Father*, Ann Arbor, Michigan: Servant Publications, 1996, 58–59. See also Ronald H. Preston, "Pope John Paul II on Work," in *Theology* 86 (January 1983): 20; Lothar Roos, "On a Theology and Ethics of Work," *Communio* 11 (1984): 103; Gregory Baum, "*Laborem Exercens*," in *The New Dictionary of Catholic Social Thought*, Judith A. Dwyer (ed.), Collegeville: Liturgical Press, 1994, 528.

share the same basic idea: in his relationship with nature, man, through work, becomes more human. He perfects his own being and fulfills his vocation since he is the author, center, and goal of the creative order. As expressed in the *Angelus* of September 20, 1981, "according to God's plans, we must, through our work, not only rule over the earth but also attain salvation. Hence, labor involves not only a temporal dimension, but an eternal one."[84]

Referring to this kind of relationship between man and the world's finality, Paul L. Peeters argues that "finality is not an impulse of nature towards God." Peeters bases his argument on the theology of creation in which the world is created "not only out of love, but for love: a statement of deceptive simplicity which implies that the world does not primarily exist as a cosmos, a finished whole ruled by immanent laws, hierarchies of light and perfection, means and ends, for man's self–realization." He thinks that "finality expresses the theological continuity of creation and grace. It refers to salvific love as a divine process, to the inner action of the divine, sensitive Lover who inspires and attracts us from within, to the presence of the Three Persons..."[85] Somewhat contrary to Peeters, however, I think that the whole Thomistic thinking of Pope John Paul II is Incarnational in that continual desire of man for his ultimate end which is realized through his directing of the whole cosmos to its ultimate finality. This procedure of finality does not contradict positive Revelation because the natural law is a reflection of the eternal law as it was extensively demonstrated in the first part of the present book. For Aquinas as well as for John Paul II, finality is the impulse of nature towards God, an impulse that has its roots in the *datum optimum* of creation and is perfected in the *donum perfectum* of Incarnation and Pentecost.[86]

Being created by the Triune God, every human person is good because he retains the indelible image and likeness of God fulfilling "himself by using his

---

[84]See Pope John XXIII, *Mater et Magistra*, 82; *Gaudium et Spes*, 63; Pope John Paul II, *Laborem Exercens*, 9; *Celebrate 2000! Reflections on Jesus, the Holy Spirit, and the Father*, Ann Arbor, Michigan: Servant Publications, 1996, 58–59; Quentin de la Bedoyere, "Man and His Work," *The Tablet* 235 (1981): 1192; Helen Ginsburg, "Teaching of John Paul II on Work and the Rights of Workers," in *Social Thought* 13 (Spring–Summer 1987): 54; Al Gini, "Meaningful Work and the Rights of the Worker: A Commentary on *Rerum Novarum* and *Laborem Exercens*," in *Thought* 67 (1992): 232; Bartolomeo Sorger, "*Laborem Exercens*: Toward a New Solidarity," in *Official Catholic Social Teaching: Readings in Moral Theology*, Charles Curran and Richard McCormick (eds.), Vol. 5, New York: Paulist Press, 1986, 242; Richard Haas, "The Market Place," *Living Prayer* 27 (July/August 1994): 11; Matthew Habiger, "Situating *Sollicitudo Rei Socialis* in Catholic Social Teaching," in *Social Justice Review* 79 (1988): 139; Joseph Cardinal Cordeiro, "The religious sense of man," in *John Paul II. A Panorama of his Teachings*, New York: New City Press, 1989, 79.

[85]See Paul L. Peeters, "*Dominum et Vivificantem*: The Conscience and the Heart," in *Communio* 15 (1988): 149.

[86]See Avery Dulles, "John Paul II and the Truth about Freedom," in *First Things* 55 (1995): 38.

intelligence and freedom."[87] In her daily life and relating herself to man, the Church "seeks to express the eternal designs and transcendent destiny which the living God, the Creator and Redeemer, has linked with him."[88] So, if human persons are good in themselves just because they are human and if they have a transcendent destiny, where did the idea of evil come from? Following the steps of Vatican II,[89] John Paul II thinks that the question *where does the evil come from?* is a wrong question because evil is not a substantial entity. In the words of Vatican II, man "abused his freedom at the very start of history. He lifted himself up against God, and sought to attain his goal apart from him."[90] Parallel to these words is Pope John Paul II's statement in *Centesimus Annus*: "man is alienated if he *refuses* to *transcend himself* and to live the experience of self–giving and of the formation of an authentic human community *oriented toward his final destiny, which is God.*"[91]

For Vatican II[92] as well for Pope John Paul II, evil starts to exist in the will of the human person only when this person freely disorients himself and his desires from tending to the Supreme Good.[93] From the very beginning of human history, as recalled by *Reconciliatio et Paenitentia*, 14, there is "an exclusion of God through direct opposition to one of his commandments through an act of rivalry, through the mistaken pretension of being 'like him.' " *Reconciliatio et Paenitentia*, 14, describes it boldly again: "Clearly sin is a product of man's freedom." Also *Dominum et Vivificantem* speaks of that matter: "according to the witness concerning the beginning, sin in its original reality takes place in man's will—and conscience—first of all as 'disobedience,' that is, as opposition of the will of man to the will of God."[94]

---

[87]Pope John Paul II, *Centesimus Annus*, 43. See also Aloysius J. Fonseca, "Reflections on the Encyclical Letter *Sollicitudo Rei Socialis*," *Gregorianum* 70 (1989): 15.

[88]Pope John Paul II, *Laborem Exercens*, 4.

[89]See *Gaudium et Spes*, 13 and 14.

[90]*Gaudium et Spes*, 13. See also Pope John Paul II, *Dominum et Vivificantem*, 33; *Mulieris Dignitatem*, 9.

[91]Pope John Paul II, *Centesimus Annus*, 41. See also Ibid., *Dominum et Vivificantem*, 38; St. Augustine, *De Civitate Dei*, XIV, 28; Aloysius J. Fonseca, "Reflections on the Encyclical Letter *Sollicitudo Rei Socialis*," *Gregorianum* 70 (1989): 15; Avery Dulles, "John Paul II and the Truth about Freedom," in *First Things* 55 (1995): 38.

[92]See *Gaudium et Spes* 10, 37 and 39.

[93]See Pope John Paul II, *Veritatis Splendor*, 99; Avery Dulles, "John Paul II and the Truth about Freedom," in *First Things* 55 (1995): 37; Joseph Cardinal Cordeiro, "The religious sense of man," in *John Paul II. A Panorama of his Teachings*, New York: New City Press, 1989, 67.

[94]Pope John Paul II, *Dominum et Vivificantem*, 33. See also *Ibid.*, 39; *Behold Your Mother*, 7; *Mulieris Dignitatem*, 9. The same idea had already been present in *Reconciliatio et Paenitentia*, 14:

In *Redemptoris Mater*, the Pope calls it "the sin of disbelief and of 'little faith' in God,[95] whereas from the very beginning, as *Mulieris Dignitatem*, 10, reports, both man and woman "bear within themselves the constant 'inclination to sin.'"

In *Salvifici Doloris*, 7, John Paul II affirms that "Christianity proclaims the essential good of existence and the good of that which exists, acknowledges the goodness of the Creator and proclaims the good of creatures." This affirmation of the long traditional teaching of the Church eliminates the possibility of evil as an existent substantial entity deriving from a defect in God's creative activity. Like St. Augustine, John Paul sought the answer in the absence of good which exists in a good, limited, intelligent and human will. In other words, the very fact that the intelligent will of the human person does not cling to God, its natural Supreme Good, produces Evil in that will.[96] It is enough for a human will not to be oriented to the Supreme Good to have Evil in it as a deficiency in that good will. Evil, therefore, possesses a paradoxical character because it exists only in a good will. *Salvifici Doloris* describes Evil as "a certain lack, limitation or distortion of good."[97] This disorientation of the human will is sin, called in *Redemptoris Missio*, 23, "the root of all evil." Any tendency to think of "the created and finite reality (*conversio ad creaturam*)"[98] as the Supreme Good, makes room for the existence of evil in the human will. In all cases, consequently, it is the human being who from the very beginning is "the author of the evil of sin."[99]

The tragedy of evil lies in the fact that it *appears to be good* and appeals to the human will as an object of appetite of supreme value. Man does not seek evil because it is evil, but because he is tempted to see it as a good. Unfortunately, the human limitations that exist in the will yield to the "tempting glamor of merely apparent goods, like those held out in every temptation."[100] It is not only a matter of psychological deceit based on the relationship between the "I" of the subject and itself; we are dealing rather with "temptations which sometimes, by diabolical deceit, present themselves under

---

"In the case of Eden there appears in all its seriousness and tragic reality that which constitutes the ultimate essence and darkness of sin: disobedience to God, to his law...

[95]Pope John Paul II, *Redemptoris Mater*, 37.

[96]See Pope John Paul II, *Redemptor Hominis*, 15; *Dives in Misericordia*, 8; St. Augustine, *De Civitate Dei*, XIV, 28.

[97]Pope John Paul II, *Salvifici Doloris*, 7.

[98]Pope John Paul II, *Reconciliatio et Paenitentia*, 17. See also Ibid., *Salvifici Doloris*, 18.

[99]Pope John Paul II, *Mulieris Dignitatem*, 9.

[100]Pope John Paul II, *Letter to Families from Pope John Paul II*, 5.

the appearance of good."[101]

Since Evil is not a substantial entity, but a deficiency that exclusively exists in a good and intelligent human will, it is called by Pope John Paul II the "evil of sin":[102] sin "constitutes the very root of evil in the history of man."[103] Therefore, Evil possesses a paradoxical existence because, on the one hand, it does not exist as a substantial entity like the rest of creatures; yet it exists because it is there as a deficiency in a good and intelligent human will.[104] Evil is a paradoxical non–existent entity in existence because the only reason for its existence is the absence of good. Yes, evil always, "in some way, refers to a good."[105]

Christologically, the transcendental character of the Redemption, although it cannot lose its objective validity because it is God's operation, still could be hindered by man's free will. Therein lies the deepest root of evil and man's self–contradiction. In the context of the Paschal Mystery, the contact between God's total self–offering and man's free choice is described by John Paul II in these words:

> Infinite are the readiness and power of forgiveness which flow continually from the marvelous value of the sacrifice of the Son. No human sin can prevail over this power or even limit it. On the part of man only a lack of good will can limit it, a lack of readiness to be converted and to repent, in other words persistence in obstinacy, opposing grace and truth, especially in the face of the witness of the Cross and Resurrection.[106]

If God always knew, on His transcendental level as God, that a deficiency in a good human will would produce Evil, how is it possible to reconcile this knowledge with His love as expressed in creation? Just as Vatican II confirmed the Tradition of the Church that man was created "in a state of rectitude,"[107] Pope John Paul II likewise confirms that Evil was never intended to be part of

---

[101]Pope John Paul II, *Vita Consecrata*, 38.

[102]See Pope John Paul II, *Redemptoris Mater*, 24; *Reconciliatio et Paenitentia*, 2. The expression *evil of sin* also occurs in the writings of St. Louis Marie de Montfort (See *Secret of the Rosary*, in *God Alone, The Collected Writings of St. Louis Marie de Montfort*, New York: Montfort Publications, 1995, 173).

[103]Pope John Paul II, *Dives in Misericordia*, 8; *Reconciliatio et Paenitentia*, 2; André Frossard, *Portrait of John Paul II*, San Francisco: Ignatius Press, 1990, 78.

[104]Pope John Paul II, *Mulieris Dignitatem*, 9.

[105]Pope John Paul II, *Salvifici Doloris*, 7 and 18. See also Ibid., *Dominum et Vivificantem*, 37.

[106]Pope John Paul II, *Dives in Misericordia*, 13. See also Ralph Martin, "Rich in Mercy" in *New Covenant* 11 (July 1981): 21.

[107]See *Gaudium et Spes*, 13. See also *Gaudium et Spes*, 12.

God's creation[108] simply because God did not create it: "The original source of all that is good is the very act of God, who created both the earth and man, and who gave the earth to man, so that he might have dominion over it by his work and enjoy its fruits (Gen 1:28)."[109] This statement is identical to that of *Gaudium et Spes*, 38 according to which man must "love the things of God's creation: it is from God that he has received them, and it is as flowing from God's hand that he looks upon them and reveres them."

In *Dominum et Vivificantem*, John Paul confirms the essential goodness that creation enjoys because it flows from God, although he condemns as evil that "turning away from the truth contained in the Word of God, who creates the world." Since Christ is the Word of God without Whom nothing came into existence, the sin of the beginning can be compared with the words of Christ in the Upper Room uttered against those who do not believe in him. The Pope says:

> He is the Word who is also the eternal law, the source of every law which regulates the world and especially human acts. When therefore on the eve of his Passion Jesus Christ speaks of the sin of those who 'do not believe in him,' in these words of his, full of sorrow, there is as it were a distant echo of that sin which in its original form is obscurely inscribed in the mystery of creation.[110]

In this text the original reality of sin in human history is linked to the sin of those who did not believe in Christ, as testified by His own words. This is the sin that pervades not only human history as such but stands as a sign of opposition to the whole economy of salvation. The whole truth about creation contained in the Word of God is inscribed in the heart and will of man. In the very act of creation, man's inmost being reflects the truth contained in the Word of the Father, a truth that reveals the original intention of the Creator concerning the destiny of man. In His Word, through Whom creation and salvation happened, the Father already prefigures the remedy of the evil created by man.

Consequently, God did not create Evil; He rather came in redemption of a situation that was created by human beings themselves:

> Moreover, man, who was created for freedom, bears within himself the wound of original sin, which constantly draws him toward evil and puts him in need of redemption. Not only is this doctrine an integral part of Christian revelation, it also

---

[108]See Pope John Paul II, *Dominum et Vivificantem*, 34.

[109]Pope John Paul II, *Centesimus Annus*, 31. See also Encyclical Letter *Redemptor Hominis*, 16.

[110]Pope John Paul II, *Dominum et Vivificantem*, 33.

has great hermeneutical value insofar as it helps one to understand human reality.[111]

It is true that precisely because human persons are limited and free creatures, Evil exists as a deficiency in every good will disoriented from the Supreme Good. Should God have stopped creation just because a deficiency can exist in the good will of a limited human person? Since Jesus Christ is "man's true good"[112] and "the full truth about human freedom is indelibly inscribed on the mystery of the Redemption,"[113] the answer is no. The act of creation, although a mystery in itself,[114] has always been ontologically and transcendentally prefigured by the mystery of Incarnation and Redemption.[115] The only thing that is expected from human persons is to take every opportunity using their "human freedom to cooperate with the merciful plan of God who acts within history."[116] Therefore, the existence of evil can never deny the pure divine love "to which the 'God and Father of our Lord Jesus Christ' is faithful to the uttermost consequences in the history of his covenant with man."[117] That love stands behind the free divine initiative of creating free human beings, although it really is tragic that they use their freedom against the very One who gave it to them. Human freedom, because it is a gift from God, will never lose its authenticity no matter in what conditions it is exercised. In *Centesimus Annus*, Pope John Paul II says:

> Nevertheless, it cannot be forgotten that the manner in which the individual exercises his freedom is conditioned in innumerable ways. While these certainly have an influence on freedom, they do not determine it; they make the exercise of freedom more difficult or less difficult, but they cannot destroy it. Not only is it wrong from the ethical point of view to disregard human nature, which is made for freedom, but in practice it is impossible to do so.[118]

Since Evil exists only in the human will, the moral act of the human person necessarily depends on his freedom, a freedom that constitutes "the condition

---

[111]Pope John Paul II, *Centesimus Annus*, 25.

[112]Pope John Paul II, *Centesimus Annus*, 29. See also Encyclical Letter *Redemptoris Missio*, 7; James Schall, "*Redemptoris Mater*: The Amazement of God," *Homiletic and Pastoral Review* 80 (October 1979): 19.

[113]Pope John Paul II, *Redemptor Hominis*, 21. See also Ibid., *Salvifici Doloris*, 18.

[114]See Pope John Paul II, *Laborem Exercens*, 12.

[115]See Pope John Paul II, *Redemptor Hominis*, 13.

[116]Pope John Paul II, *Centesimus Annus*, 26. See also Ibid., *Sollicitudo Rei Socialis*, 30.

[117]Pope John Paul II, *Dives in Misericordia*, 13.

[118]*Centesimus Annus*, 25.

and the basis for the human person's true dignity."[119]

The abuse of freedom is not, for Pope John Paul II, the only cause of the original reality of sin. For both St. Augustine and John Paul II, the sin of the first parents has its human dimension, an interior measure situated in man's free will; at the same time, however, it also has a certain diabolic characteristic as clearly shown in Genesis 3:15.[120] From the very beginning of creation there has been an external agent at work: the deceiving serpent. Man's original rebellion against the Creator, which has been constantly repeated by him since the beginning of human history, has its origin also in the powers of darkness spoken of by St. Paul in Rm 7:7–25 and in Eph 2:2 and 6:12. *Reconciliatio et Paenitentia* confirms the interconnectedness between human sin and the Evil One:

> Clearly sin is a product of man's freedom. But deep within its human reality there are factors at work which place it beyond the merely human, in the border area where man's conscience, will and sensitivity are in contact with the dark forces which, according to St. Paul, are active in the world almost to the point of ruling it.[121]

In *Dives in Misericordia*, referring to the Epistle of St. John (1 Jn 2:16), Pope John Paul II refers to man as having been always "exposed to the oppressive forces of the threefold concupiscence active within him."[122]

The original reality of sin, as reported in *Dominum et Vivificantem*, is witnessed by Scripture from the very beginning of man's existence. In this sin, the *mysterium iniquitatis* has its beginning because it constitutes the principle and root of all other sins.[123] In *Dominum et Vivificantem*, more than in any other document, the Pope went on to accuse the *father of lies* (Jn 8:44) of being the direct cause of evil in man and the first author of sin in human history: all sin implies a certain consent to and cooperation with the motivation contained in the first temptation of Satan. The original reality of sin is "caused in the will

---

[119]Pope John Paul II, *Redemptor Hominis*, 12; *Familiaris Consortio*, 9; *Reconciliatio et Paenitentia*, 2.

[120]Pope John Paul II, *Mulieris Dignitatem*, 9. See also Michaël Devaux, "The Truth of Love, the Lie of Death," in *Communio* 23 (1996): 118–119; Paul L. Peeters, "*Dominum et Vivificantem*: The Conscience and the Heart," in *Communio* 15 (1988): 152; André Frossard, *Portrait of John Paul II*, San Francisco: Ignatius, 1990, 78–79.

[121]Pope John Paul II, *Reconciliatio et Paenitentia*, 14. See also *Ibid.*, 10; *Salvifici Doloris*, 15.

[122]Pope John Paul II, *Dives in Misericordia*, 14.

[123]Pope John Paul II, *Dominum et Vivificantem*, 33. See also Giacomo Cardinal Biffi, "The Action of the Holy Spirit in the Church and in the World," in *John Paul II. A Panorama of his Teachings*, New York: New City Press, 1989, 41.

of man by the father of lies."[124] He, the father of lies, "is capable of showing God as an enemy of his own creature, and in the first place as an enemy of man, as a source of danger and threat to man."[125] The action of the father of lies is the greatest lie because it twists the entire truth concerning the whole reality of man and God: since man is entirely dependent on his Creator because he was created out of nothing by a pure divine initiative of love, "Satan deceived man, persuading him that he too was a god, that he, like God, was capable of knowing good and evil, ruling the world according to his own will without having to take into account the divine will (cf. Gen 3:5)."[126] Therefore, when the father of lies convinces man to go against his natural tendency toward the Creator, this lie happens in the most anti–truthful and non–logical context.[127] This is why, in the Pope's opinion, Christ chose *father of lies* as the most appropriate name for Satan.

If man was created with the intention of saving him, the whole created order should be oriented towards the redemption of man. Satan, the prince of this world, twists the natural functioning of creation and becomes the one who "from the beginning has been exploiting the work of creation against salvation, against the covenant and the union of man with God."[128] The father of lies is able to do this twisting because he falsifies the whole truth about God and man, in the sense of placing the Creator in a state of suspicion and accusation in the mind of His creature. He falsifies Good itself by making it look bad and, at the same time, hiding the evil of the false good by making it look like the Good. Satan has always challenged man to become the adversary of God by managing to show God as a source of danger and threat to him.[129]

Results of Sin and Condition of Humanity

Personal Sin

Man is alienated from the Supreme Good as soon as he freely determines

---

[124]Pope John Paul II, *Dominum et Vivificantem*, 35. See also Ibid., *Mulieris Dignitatem*, 11; *Veritatis Splendor*, 1; *Tertio Millennio Adveniente*, 7; André Frossard, *Portrait of John Paul II*, San Francisco: Ignatius, 1990, 78–79; Giacomo Cardinal Biffi, "The Action of the Holy Spirit in the Church and in the World," in *John Paul II. A Panorama of his Teachings*, New York: New City Press, 1989, 42.

[125]Pope John Paul II, *Dominum et Vivificantem*, 38.

[126]Pope John Paul II, *Tertio Millennio Adveniente*, 7.

[127]See Pope John Paul II, *Dominum et Vivificantem*, 33 and 37; *Letter to Families from Pope John Paul II*, 23.

[128]Pope John Paul II, *Dominum et Vivificantem*, 27. See also Paul L. Peeters, "*Dominum et Vivificantem*: The Conscience and the Heart," in *Communio* 15 (1988): 151–152.

[129]See Pope John Paul II, *Dominum et Vivificantem*, 37–38.

his own ability to establish the criteria of good and evil. Commenting on Mt 19:16 in *Veritatis Splendor*, 8, where the young man asks Jesus about what moral good should he do in order to earn eternal life, Pope John Paul II says : "People today need to turn to Christ once again in order to receive from him the answer to their questions about what is good and what is evil."[130] The absolute fullness of the goodness of the Creator is the sole reason behind the exclusivity of God in issuing criteria of good and evil. In the Pope's words, "only God can answer the question about what is good, because he is the Good."[131] But God has already answered the question about the good through the very act of creation, an act that orders man to its final end through the natural law.

Pope John Paul II refers to St. Thomas Aquinas' definition of *natural law* which "is nothing other than the light of understanding infused in us by God, whereby we understand what must be done and what must be avoided. God gave this light and this law to man at creation."[132] It is called natural law not because it refers to the nature of irrational beings, but because the reason which promulgates it is proper to human nature. The very act of creation itself reserves for God the exclusive right to give to man the criteria of what is good for him. John Paul does not, however, consider the 'light of understanding' as deriving exclusively from the Divine Revelation of faith. Already natural reason is endowed with the necessary light to enable man to discern good from evil; this light, however, is and will always be a gift from God at creation.

Since God has answered man about good through the natural law, the traditional natural law theory becomes the basis for explaining why certain particular acts are morally unacceptable. I agree with John J. Conley that "this insistence upon the innate moral quality of specific acts squarely places John Paul II in the tradition of the neoscholastic manualists."[133] I disagree with Conley, however, when he says that "the pope's explanation of why these particular acts are morally unacceptable does not follow the theological arguments of traditional natural–law theory."[134]

Both St. Paul's Letter to the Romans and Vatican II's *Gaudium et Spes* are

---

[130]Pope John Paul II, *Veritatis Splendor*, 8. See also Ibid., *Dominum et Vivificantem*, 36.

[131]Pope John Paul II, *Veritatis Splendor*, 9.

[132]Saint Thomas Aquinas, *In Duo Praecepta Caritatis et in Decem Legis Praecepta, Prologus: Opuscula Theologica*, 11, No. 1129, Turin, 1954, 245. See also Ibid., *Summa Theologiae*, I–II, q. 91, a. 2; *Catechism of the Catholic Church*, 1955; Pope John Paul II, *Veritatis Splendor*, 12 and 42.

[133]John J. Conley, "The philosophical foundations of the Thought of John Paul II. A Response," in *The Thought of Pope John Paul II*, John M. McDermott (ed.), Rome: Gregorian University Press, 1993, 28.

[134]John J. Conley, *Ibid.*, 27.

often quoted by Pope John Paul II whenever he meditates on the sinful condition of humankind.[135] In the first chapter of the Letter to the Romans, he sees another kind of flood, a flood where the human conscience can die by drowning in sin. For John Paul, as expressed in *Reconciliatio et Paenitentia*, 13, sin is "an integral part of the truth about man." The Pope shows a realistic grasp of the pervasiveness and depth of the evil affecting man since the beginning of human history,[136] "insinuating itself even into his heart and capable of causing him to perish in Gehenna."[137]

Adam broke the link between God's created good and its source of Wisdom and Love.[138] Since then, creation "has been groaning in travail together until now" and "waits with eager longing for the revelation of the sons of God."[139] Rejecting all forms of Pelagianism, Pope John Paul II does not overlook man's sinful situation in the world: man is in absolute need of Redemption after falling into sin[140] because "Christian life involves a struggle against temptation and the forces of evil...as long as time lasts, the struggle between good and evil continues even in the human heart itself."[141]

In *Redemptor Hominis*, 9, John Paul II says:

> He (the Word) it was, and he alone, who satisfied the Father's eternal love, that fatherhood that from the beginning found expression in creating the world, giving man all the riches of creation, and making him "little less than God (Ps 8:5)," in that he was created "in the image and after the likeness of God (Gen 1:26)." He and he alone also satisfied that fatherhood of God and that love which man in a way rejected

---

[135]See Robert W. Faulhaber, "The Church and Culture–John Paul II's 'On Human Work'," in *Listening* 18 (1983): 103; André Frossard, *Portrait of John Paul II*, San Francisco: Ignatius Press, 1990, 83–84. The contribution of Pope John Paul II to the Pastoral Constitution *Gaudium et Spes* has played a significant role in the theology during his post–election to the papacy. For details concerning that contribution see C.–J. Pinto de Oliveira, "Die theologische Originalität von Johannes Paul II," in *Johannes Paul II und die Menschenrechte*, O. Höffe (ed.), Freiburg, 1981.

[136]See Pope John Paul II, *Redemptor Hominis*, 8; *Dives in Misericordia*, 4; *Dominum et Vivificantem*, 33; *Laborem Exercens*, 27; *Redemptionis Donum*, 9; *Reconciliatio et Paenitentia*, 10; *Mulieris Dignitatem*, 9; Edna Mcdonagh, "*Redemptor Hominis* and Ireland," in *The Furrow* 30 (1979): 626; André Frossard, *Portrait of John Paul II*, San Francisco: Ignatius Press, 1990, 83; Peter Hebblethwaite, *Pope John Paul II and the Church*, Kansas City: Sheed and Ward, 1995, 55–57; Giacomo Cardinal Biffi, "The Action of the Holy Spirit in the Church and in the World," in *John Paul II. A Panorama of his Teachings*, New York: New City Press, 1989, 42.

[137]Pope John Paul II, *Dives in Misericordia*, 7.

[138]See Pope John Paul II, *Redemptor Hominis*, 8; *Dominum et Vivificantem*, 33.

[139]See Rom 8:19–22; Pope John Paul II, *Redemptor Hominis*, 8; *Salvifici Doloris*, 2.

[140]See Pope John Paul II, *Redemptor Hominis*, 13–14; *Redemptionis Donum*, 9; *Reconciliatio et Paenitentia*, 20.

[141]*Centesimus Annus*, 25.

by breaking the first Covenant and the later covenants that God "again and again offered to man (Eucharistic Prayer IV)."[142]

Man's sin is a betrayal of God, but also a betrayal of man himself because he is God's image who has received existence from Him and who is being sustained in life by Him. If image and likeness are the foundation of man's essential goodness, sin is the foundation of that 'non–likeness' to God. Being in the image and likeness of God, man, by sinning, freely "loses his own true identity" as a creature possessing humanity simply because that human identity was given to him by God.[143] Therefore, sin creates an existential crisis because it casts a veil over the meaning of human life, "a meaning that was lost to a considerable extent because of sin."[144] This existential crisis results in the rebellion of nature against man and the refusal to recognize him as its master: although his "claim to ownership and use of created things remains valid, but after sin its exercise becomes difficult and full of suffering."[145] This explains perfectly the statement of *Gaudium et Spes*, 10, concerning the "deeper dichotomy that is in man himself." After sin, man is still made in the image of God and endowed with the dominion over all creatures, yet the exercise of that dominion is most difficult.

The relationality between creatures and the Creator is not only a result of a free decision on the part of God or on the part of man; it belongs to the very logic of creation *ex Nihilo* of free creatures.[146] Analogically, the father's attitude towards the prodigal son emphasizes that that relationality "springs from the very essence of fatherhood, (and) in a way obliges the father to be concerned about his son's dignity."[147]

Pope John Paul II indulges in no Manichean rejection of the world. He is very careful not to reach an extreme pessimism describing the situation of man after sin as almost unredeemable. Sin truly disfigures the likeness of God in

---

[142]Pope John Paul II, *Redemptor Hominis*, 9.

[143]See Pope John Paul II, *Redemptor Hominis*, 13 and 15; *Laborem Exercens*, Preface; *Familiaris Consortio*, 58; *Redemptionis Donum*, 4; *Mulieris Dignitatem*, 9. In *Reconciliatio et Paenitentia*, 15, John Paul calls that rejection of the very principle of life 'suicidal act' (see also *Ibid.*, 31).

[144]Pope John Paul II, *Redemptor Hominis*, 10. See also Ibid., *Reconciliatio et Paenitentia*, 16; Paul L. Peeters, "*Dominum et Vivificantem*: The Conscience and the Heart," in *Communio* 15 (1988): 152; André Frossard, *Portrait of John Paul II*, San Francisco: Ignatius Press, 1990, 78–79.

[145]Pope John Paul II, *Sollicitudo Rei Socialis*, 30 and 34. See also Ibid., *Redemptionis Donum*, 9; Stratford Caldecott, "Cosmology, Eschatology, Ecology: Some Reflections on *Sollicitudo Rei Socialis*," in *Communio* 15 (1988): 309.

[146]See Joseph Cardinal Cordeiro, "The religious sense of man," in *John Paul II. A Panorama of his Teachings*, New York: New City Press, 1989, 66–67.

[147]Pope John Paul II, *Dives in Misericordia*, 6.

man, but man conserves in himself the Creator's 'indestructible image' because of the grace that comes from the very act of creation: "God's fundamental and original intention with regard to man, whom he created in his image and after his likeness, was not withdrawn or cancelled out even when man, having broken the original covenant with God, heard the words: 'in the sweat of your face you shall eat bread.' "[148] Therefore, the reality of sin cannot destroy God's image in man because of man's "unique unrepeatable human reality, which keeps intact the image and likeness of God himself."[149]

In *Redemptor Hominis*, 14, the Pope uses *Gaudium et Spes* to present the concrete situation of man in the world:

> In man himself many elements wrestle with one another. Thus, on the one hand, as a creature he experiences his limitations in a multitude of ways. On the other, he feels himself to be boundless in his desires and summoned to a higher life. Pulled by manifold attractions, he is constantly forced to choose among them and to renounce some. Indeed, as a weak and sinful being, he often does what he would not, and fails to do what he would. Hence he suffers from internal divisions, and from these flow so many and such great discords in society.[150]

John Paul II sees that "the deeper dichotomy that is in man himself "[151] makes him a subject of internal division and intimate suffering: sin "constitutes man's misery."[152] He analyzes this 'deeper dichotomy' in its relationship to the original reality of sin in human history. It is especially in *Dominum et Vivificantem* that this analysis reaches its peak: in the contrast between life according to the Spirit and life according to the flesh. The comment of John Paul on Gal 5:16–21 and Rom 8:5–13, describes the deeper dichotomy that is in man from a spiritual point of view. The words of St. Paul, enable us to know vividly the tension going on in man between openness and resistance to the action of the Holy Spirit. According to the Pope, "in the text of Saint Paul there is a superimposing—and a mutual conpenetration—of the ontological dimension (the flesh and the spirit), the ethical (moral good and evil), and the

---

[148]Pope John Paul II, *Laborem Exercens*, 9. See also Ibid., *Sollicitudo Rei Socialis*, 47; *Mulieris Dignitatem*, 9; *Veritatis Splendor*, 1; *Redemptionis Donum*, 9; André Frossard, *Portrait of John Paul II*, San Francisco: Ignatius, 1990, 78–79.

[149]See Pope John Paul II, *Redemptor Hominis*, 13; *Sollicitudo Rei Socialis*, 47.

[150]*Gaudium et Spes*, 10. See also *Gaudium et Spes*, 37 and 39; Pope John Paul II, *Redemptionis Donum*, 9; Edna McDonagh, "*Redemptor Hominis* and Ireland," in *The Furrow* 30 (1979): 627.

[151]*Gaudium et Spes*, 10.

[152]Pope John Paul II, *Dives in Misericordia*, 4. See also Lothar Roos, "On a Theology and Ethics of Work," in *Communio* 11 (1984): 116.

pneumatological (the action of the Holy Spirit in the order of grace)."[153] The poles of contrast and tension are, on the part of man, his limitations and sinfulness; and on God's part, His unceasing self–giving of divine life in the Holy Spirit. In man's history there has been a continual tension between a perpetual self–offering of God through the gift of Himself and man's reaction to it.

Structures of Sin

The analysis of personal sin leads Pope John Paul II to consider another similar reality: the *structures of sin.*[154] Structures of sin are "rooted in personal sin, and thus always linked to the concrete acts of individuals who introduce these structures, consolidate them and make them difficult to remove."[155] Structures are sinful only in a secondary sense. The primary sin lies in the human heart. *Reconciliatio et Paenitentia,* 16 shows how Pope John Paul II explains the meaning of structures of sin and the way it takes place:

> Whenever the Church speaks of situations of sin, or when she condemns as social sins certain situations or the collective behavior of certain social groups, big or small, or even of whole nations and blocs of nations, she knows and she proclaims that such cases of social sin are the result of the accumulation and concentration of many personal sins. It is a case of the very personal sins of those who cause or support evil or who exploit it; of those who are in a position to avoid eliminate or at least limit certain social evils but who fail to do so out of laziness, fear or the conspiracy of silence, through secret complicity or indifference; of those who take refuge in the supposed impossibility of changing the world, and also of those who sidestep the effort and sacrifice required, producing specious reasons of a higher order. The real responsibility, then, lies with individuals. A situation—or likewise an institution, a structure, society itself—is not in itself the subject of moral acts. Hence a situation cannot in itself be good or bad.[156]

---

[153]Pope John Paul II, *Dominum et Vivificantem,* 55.

[154]See Pope John Paul II, *Reconciliatio et Paenitentia,* 16; *Dominum et Vivificantem,* 47 and 56; *Sollicitudo Rei Socialis,* 36; Robert W. Faulhaber, "The Church and Culture–John Paul II's 'On Human Work'," in *Listening* 18 (1983): 105; Matthew Kiliroor, "Social Doctrine in *Sollicitudo Rei Socialis.*" In *The Month* 21 (1988): 711; Roland James Faley, "Pope as Prophet: The New Social Encyclical," in *America* 158 (1988): 450.

[155]Pope John Paul II, *Sollicitudo Rei Socialis,* 36. See also Matthew Kiliroor, "Social Doctrine in *Sollicitudo Rei Socialis.*" In *The Month* 21 (1988): 713; Paul Bowe, "*Sollicitudo Rei Socialis*: A Commentary on the Encyclical," in *Doctrine and Life* 38 (1988): 232; Roger M. Mahony, "Perspectives for Viewing the Social Concerns Encyclical," *Origins* 18 (1988): 71; Matthew Habiger, "Situating *Sollicitudo Rei Socialis* in Catholic Social Teaching," in *Social Justice Review* 79 (1988): 139.

[156]See also Matthew Kiliroor, "Social Doctrine in *Sollicitudo Rei Socialis.*" In *The Month* 21 (1988): 712; J. Bryan Heir, "Taking on the Super–Rivals: Reactions to the Pope's Latest Encyclical," in *Commonweal* 115 (1988): 170.

The accumulation and the concentration of many personal sins is not only a quantitative, but also a qualitative addition where the personal evil coming from many different persons could negatively influence the society. That influence is produced through a variety of behaviors and actions the responsibility of which lies with individuals. A situation, a structure, an institution, or society itself does not act. The agent of the moral act is exclusively the human person on whom falls the responsibility of sin. Any attempt to escape that responsibility by throwing it on situations does not justify the presence of evil in the structure of the human society. This idea of sin as present in society under this collective form is developed throughout *Reconciliatio et Paenitentia*, although John Paul confirms from the very beginning that "however disturbing these divisions may seem at first sight, it is only by a careful examination that one can detect their root: It is to be found in a wound in man's inmost self."[157]

Like any other approach in his theology, in this specific aspect of structural sin Pope John Paul II follows the same patterns as far as the relationship between the person and the community is concerned. He uses Vatican II's *Gaudium et Spes*, 10, in order to confirm the teaching of the Council regarding structural sin: although rooted in personal responsibility, sin is also present in its social dimension. That social dimension is constantly dependent on and is a sign of the action of the individual, wherein the accumulation of personal sins lead into a very complex reality that affects the whole society.[158]

According to the principle of a mysterious and intangible human solidarity, there is a communion of saints and communion of sin. In the law of ascent, to use the words of Elizabeth Leseur as quoted in *Reconciliatio et Paenitentia*, 16, "every soul that rises above itself, raises up the world." To that law of ascent there unfortunately corresponds the law of descent: a soul that "lowers itself through sin drags down with itself the Church and, in some way, the whole world."[159] This means that there is no sin, even the most secret and strictly individual one, that does not possess, somehow, a social dimension: it effects the ecclesial body and the human family.

---

[157]Pope John Paul II, *Reconciliatio et Paenitentia*, 2. See also Roland James Faley, "Pope as Prophet: The New Social Encyclical," in *America* 158 (1988): 450; William J. Byron, "Solidarity: Path to Development and Peace," in *America* 158 (1988): 445.

[158]See Pope John Paul II, *Reconciliatio et Paenitentia*, 3–4; William J. Byron, "Solidarity: Path to Development and Peace," in *America* 158 (1988): 446; Aloysius J. Fonseca, "Reflections on the Encyclical Letter *Sollicitudo Rei Socialis*," *Gregorianum* 70 (1989): 19.

[159]Pope John Paul II, *Reconciliatio et Paenitentia*, 16.

State of Original Justice

Another theological area to be investigated in the writings of Pope John Paul II is man's state of original justice. Does Pope John Paul II consider man's original justice a concrete historical reality or only a state of being that was originally intended by God, but has never actually taken place in man's history? In other words, were Adam and Eve, historically speaking, without sin before the original fall? The hermeneutical approach of Pope John Paul II to the account of Genesis is in favor of a historical dimension of man's original justice. In *Dives in Misericordia*, 5, the Pope compares the prodigal son to every man, but especially to the one "who was the first to lose the inheritance of grace and original justice."[160]

The logic of Pope John Paul II in confirming the historicity of the state of original justice lies in the fact that if sin is intrinsically linked to human history, so is its antithesis, justice. In *Laborem Exercens* and in the context of human work as a fundamental truth revealed in the Book of Genesis, Pope John Paul II says: "These truths are decisive for man from the very beginning, and at the same time they trace out the main lines of his earthly existence, both in the state of original justice and also after the breaking, caused by sin, of the Creator's original covenant with creation in man."[161] It is evident, at least in this text, that original justice belongs to man's earthly existence. Man's original justice is a historical reality, not only an ontological plan that God, always on his transcendental level, wanted man to have, but was never applied to him because of the plan of Redemption. Pope John Paul is not of the opinion that man's original justice is a reality that just remained in God's original intention without being applied historically to man, with the excuse that Redemption was eternally preestablished for the salvation of man and, therefore, it does not matter whether original justice is historical or not. The reason behind John Paul's refusal lies in the fact that sin, as a historical reality, cannot be the breaking away from a mere ontological dimension in man's existence. All three, original justice, sin, and Redemption are real and historical.

In *Mulieris Dignitatem*, the state of original justice enjoys a personal and philosophical characteristic. Here the Pope goes down deep to the very roots of the existence of the human person as person, and analyzes what it means for his proper subject to be a product of the justice of that beginning. Instead of

---

[160]Pope John Paul II, *Dives in Misericordia*, 5; André Frossard, *Portrait of John Paul II*, San Francisco: Ignatius, 1990, 78–79.

[161]Pope John Paul II, *Laborem Exercens*, 4. See also Ibid., *Sollicitudo Rei Socialis*, 30; Stratford Caldecott, "Cosmology, Eschatology, Ecology: Some Reflections on *Sollicitudo Rei Socialis*," in *Communio* 15 (1988): 309.

remaining in the categories of universal nature, now the state of original justice consists in a relationship with God, in a "union with God as the source of the unity within his (man's) own 'I,' in the mutual relationship between man and woman ('*communio personarum*') as well as in regard to the external world, to nature."[162]

In the General Audience of October 6, 1982, John Paul II says: "The holiness originally bestowed on the human person by the Creator is part of the reality of the 'sacrament of creation.' " Sacrament of creation indicates that what originates from God is naturally ordered to be a visible sign of God thus pointing to Him and making human beings aware of His existence and His action. Such an understanding of creation as a primordial sacrament, allows John Paul II to see in the visibility and the corporality of creation a guarantee and a visible sign of the transcendent and divine reality itself. Consequently, creation must be understood as a making visible the invisible: this sacramentality is in John Paul's opinion an evident basis for the state of original grace and justice that man and woman enjoyed at the beginning of creation.[163]

---

[162]Pope John Paul II, *Mulieris Dignitatem*, 9.

[163]See also Pope John Paul II, *General Audiences* of July 28, 1982, September 29, 1982, October 20, 1982; *Congress for Catholic Education*, November 1, 1983; Hans Cardinal Groër, "The Church Sacrament of Salvation," in *John Paul II. A Panorama of his Teachings*, New York: New City Press, 1989, 32.

CHAPTER FOUR

THEOLOGY OF REDEMPTION

The Divine Dimension of Redemption

It seems that Redemption, or at least this particular expression, has somewhat faded from the forefront of Catholic and Christian thinking and writing. Expressions such as *salvation history* or *liberation* occupied the center of post–Vatican II christology, especially in the sixties and the seventies.[1] There is no doubt that Pope John Paul II, although he uses the newer language, does so without any unilateral emphasis but as a part of the whole christology,[2] and thus has restored the importance of the theme of Redemption.[3] J. Honoré sees in John Paul II's approach to Christology an attempt to meditate on the Christian mystery more in its economical dimension of Redemption than in its *ab aeterno* essence as a revealed truth *per se*. His approach, according to Honoré, comes mostly from the theological orientations of St. Irenaeus and the Cappadocian Fathers. The Pope puts the dogmas of the Catholic Church in relational perspective instead of spending his whole energy in explaining them. He prefers to show the internal logic of Divine Revelation and connect the different disciplines to each other displaying their significance with respect to salvation.[4] I add to Honoré's remark that Pope John Paul does not fail to

---

[1] See Edna McDonagh, "*Redemptor Hominis* and Ireland," in *The Furrow* 30 (1979): 625; Raymond T. Gawronski, "Redemptor Hominis," in *The Thought of Pope John Paul II*, Rome: Gregorian University, 1993, 221.

[2] See Pope John Paul II, *Reconciliatio et Paenitentia*, 7; *Salvifici Doloris*, 14.

[3] See Pope John Paul II, *Redemptor Hominis, Redemptoris Mater, Redemptoris Missio, Redemptionis Donum, Redemptoris Custos; Letter of the Pope to Children in the Year of the Family,* Pauline Books and Media, 1994, 12–13; *Letter to Families from Pope John Paul II*, 16; *Orientale Lumen*, 1; *Gift and Mystery. On the Fiftieth Anniversary of my Priestly Ordination*, New York: Doubleday, 1996, 82; Raymond T. Gawronski, "Redemptor Hominis," in *The Thought of Pope John Paul II*, Rome: Gregorian University, 1993, 221–222; Angelo Scola, " 'Claim' of Christ, 'Claim' of the world: On the trinitarian Encyclicals of John Paul II," in *Communio* 18 (1991): 323–324; J. Honoré, "Christ the Redeemer, Core of John Paul's Teaching," in *John Paul II. A Panorama of his Teachings*, New York: New City Press, 1989, 12–13.

[4] See J. Honoré, "Christ the Redeemer, Core of John Paul's Teaching," in *John Paul II. A Panorama of his Teachings*, New York: New City Press, 1989, 12–13. See also Raymond T.

consider the revealed truths of faith in themselves: speculations and abstract thinking are spread all through his Christology. This fact is understandable because he is very well acquainted with the philosophy and the theology that are behind contemporary christological currents, as chapter five will show.

The Redemption as developed in the writings of Pope John Paul II has a divine and a human dimension.[5] The *divine dimension of Redemption* consists in that the Redeemer enables humankind to meet and partake of the absolute in God's mystery. Without Christ, marriage between the human and the divine would be impossible and man, for his part, would never be able to come in contact with the divine. The divine economy of salvation is the completion of the salvific acts. John Paul's *analogia fidei* which is present in *Redemptor Hominis*, in *Dives in Misericordia* and in *Dominum et Vivificantem*, remains very faithful to the theology of St. John the Evangelist: "No one has ever seen God. It is God the only Son, ever at the Father's side, who revealed Him."[6]

In the context of the divine dimension of Redemption, the mystery is identified with love that is manifested through the Son's Revelation. In the thought of Pope John Paul, as explained in the section on *The Act of Creation*, the creative love of God becomes a "redeeming love."[7] The Pope develops throughout his writings the commitment of the Triune God to the mystery of creation. Since the mystery of God was expressed through love that is creative, that same mystery of love is expressed once again through the Redemption: the creative love becomes a redeeming love: "It is precisely this love that constitutes the true price of the Redemption of man and the world."[8]

In his deep and extensive considerations of the reality and the existence of sin, John Paul II presents sin as a debt that human beings owe to God: every sin is a debt which we contract with God, and He, in His justice, requires

---

Gawronski, "Redemptor Hominis," in *The Thought of Pope John Paul II*, Rome: Gregorian University, 1993, 222.

[5]See Pope John Paul II, *Celebrate 2000! Reflections on Jesus, the Holy Spirit, and the Father*, Ann Arbor, Michigan: Servant Publications, 1996, 70; Raymond T. Gawronski, "Redemptor Hominis," in *The Thought of Pope John Paul II*, Rome: Gregorian University, 1993, 222.

[6]See John 1:18; Pope John Paul II, *Dives in Misericordia*, 2; *Dominum et Vivificantem*, 23; J. Honoré, "Christ the Redeemer, Core of John Paul II's Teaching," in *John Paul II. A Panorama of his Teachings*, New York: New City Press, 1989, 16–17; Raymond T. Gawronski, "Redemptor Hominis," in *The Thought of Pope John Paul II*, Rome: Gregorian University, 1993, 222.

[7]Pope John Paul II, *Redemptionis Donum*, 3. See also Raymond T. Gawronski, "Redemptor Hominis," in *The Thought of Pope John Paul II*, Rome: Gregorian University, 1993, 222.

[8]Pope John Paul II, *Redemptionis Donum*, 3. See also Terence P. Curley, "*Evangelium Vitae* and Our Culture," in *The Priest* 51 (October 1995): 19; Aloysius J. Fonseca, "Reflections on the Encyclical Letter *Sollicitudo Rei Socialis*," *Gregorianum* 70 (1989): 15–16; Raymond T. Gawronski, "Redemptor Hominis," in *The Thought of Pope John Paul II*, Rome: Gregorian University, 1993, 222.

payment down to the last farthing: "God," as he says in *Reconciliatio et Paenitentia*, 31, "is always the one who is principally offended by sin—'*Tibi soli peccavi*!'—and God alone can forgive."[9] The roots of this idea can be found in the theology of St. Augustine, St. Anselm and St. Louis Marie Grignon de Montfort.[10]

In order to reach the original state of justice and share again in the communion which exists between the Father and the Son, the debt of sin has to be paid by the shedding of the blood of the Son of God.[11] Describing in *Redemptor Hominis* the perpetual character of the Sacrifice at Calvary through the celebration of the Eucharist, Pope John Paul II says:

> By celebrating and also partaking of the Eucharist we unite ourselves with Christ on earth and in heaven who intercedes for us with the Father but we always do so through the redeeming act of his sacrifice, through which he has redeemed us, so that we have been 'bought with a price.' The 'price' of our Redemption is likewise a further proof of the value that God himself sets on man and of our dignity in Christ.[12]

In *Dives in Misericordia*, 7, the Pope penetrates to the very heart of the mystery of the Redemption, understood as a payment on the part of Christ to the Father.[13] The positive attitude of the Father in accepting payment for humanity's debt of sin, is the ultimate expression of mercy. This mercy which manifests the relationship between God's justice and His love reveals the essence of God's holiness: *the debt of sin was paid by the sacrifice of Him who never committed it in the first place.*[14] Sin offends God; God is committed to His love for humankind, although an absolute justice has to be expressed. The

---

[9]See also Pope John Paul II, *Salvifici Doloris*, 10; Joseph Cardinal Cordeiro, "The religious sense of man," in *John Paul II. A Panorama of his Teachings*, New York: New City Press, 1989, 80.

[10]See St. Louis Marie de Montfort, *Secret of the Rosary*, in *God Alone, The Collected Writings of St. Louis Marie de Montfort*, New York: Montfort Publications, 1995, 173.

[11]See also Pope John Paul II, *Redemptionis Donum*, 3; Raymond T. Gawronski, "Redemptor Hominis," in *The Thought of Pope John Paul II*, Rome: Gregorian University, 1993, 222.

[12]Pope John Paul II, *Redemptor Hominis*, 20. See also Ibid., *Redemptoris Missio*, 23; Raymond T. Gawronski, "Redemptor Hominis," in *The Thought of Pope John Paul II*, Rome: Gregorian University, 1993, 222.

[13]See also Pope John Paul II, *Redemptionis Donum*, 3; Terence P. Curley, "*Evangelium Vitae* and Our Culture," in *The Priest* 51 (October 1995): 18; Angelo Scola, " 'Claim' of Christ, 'Claim' of the World: On the Trinitarian Encyclicals of John Paul II," in *Communio* 18 (1991): 324.

[14]See K. Lehmann, *Der bedrohte Mensch und die Kraft des Erbarmens. Die Enzyklika über das Erbarmen Gottes Papst Johannes Paul II*, Freiburg, 1981, 112; Terrence Prendergast, " 'A Vision of Wholeness': A Reflection on the Use of Scripture in a Cross–section of Papal Writings," in *The Thought of Pope John Paul II*, Rome: Gregorian University, 1993, 86–87; Joseph Cardinal Cordeiro, "The religious sense of man," in *John Paul II. A Panorama of his Teachings*, New York: New City Press, 1989, 80.

relationship between His love and His absolute justice is His mercy. His Mercy does not abolish His justice, neither does His Justice obscure His love. But an absolute justice can be obtained only if it is done according to the measure of God. Therefore, it is the God–man Jesus Christ Who, as a human and a divine agent at the same time, is able to obtain that absolute justice. Yet, only love can explain why Christ, being One with the Father and the One who did not know any sin, has paid the debt of sin in order to satisfy God. Thus justice to 'God's measure' could be brought about only by the action of Christ, God and man, who fulfilled the criteria of God for the possibility of Redemption:

> Indeed this Redemption is the ultimate and definitive revelation of the holiness of God, who is the absolute fullness of perfection: fullness of justice and of love, since justice is based on love, flows from it and tends toward it. In the passion and death of Christ—in the fact that the Father did not spare his own Son, but 'for our sake made him sin'—absolute justice is expressed, for Christ undergoes the Passion and Cross because of the sins of humanity. This constitutes even a 'superabundance' of justice, for the sins of man are 'compensated for' by the sacrifice of the Man–God. Nevertheless, this justice, which is properly justice 'to God's measure,' springs completely from love: from the love of the Father and of the Son, and completely bears fruit in love.[15]

The parable of the prodigal son, from the perspective of his relationship with his father, confirms the reaction of God in regard to the decisions of human beings. His reaction is a liberating *mercy*. Mercy cannot be defined merely as an attitude of a just God whose love is greater than His justice. Mercy is a commitment on the part of God to constantly *bring back the order of creation to its original value*. It is an action that God performs in order to prove His creative power of love "which does not allow itself to be 'conquered by evil,' but overcomes 'evil with good.' "[16] As the Pope says in *Dives in Misericordia*, 9, this is the mystery of the "overwhelming encounter of divine transcendent justice with love: that 'kiss' given by mercy to justice":

[15]Pope John Paul II, *Dives in Misericordia*, 7; Terrence Prendergast, " 'A Vision of Wholeness': A Reflection on the Use of Scripture in a Cross–section of Papal Writings," in *The Thought of Pope John Paul II*, Rome: Gregorian University, 1993, 86–87; Raymond T. Gawronski, "Redemptor Hominis," in *The Thought of Pope John Paul II*, Rome: Gregorian University, 1993, 222.

[16]Pope John Paul II, *Dives in Misericordia*, 6. See also *Sollicitudo Rei Socialis*, 31; Pinchas Lapide, "*Dives in Misericordia*: An Encyclical for Christians and Jews," in *Journal of Ecumenical Studies* 18 (1981): 141; Terrence Prendergast, " 'A Vision of Wholeness': A Reflection on the Use of Scripture in a Cross–section of Papal Writings," in *The Thought of Pope John Paul II*, Rome: Gregorian University, 1993, 86–87. In *Sollicitudo Rei Socialis*, 31, Pope John Paul refers *Praeconium Paschale, Missale Romanum*, editio typica altera, 1975, 272: "O certe necessarium Adae peccatum, quod Christi morte deletum est! O felix culpa, quae talem ac tantum meruit habere Redemptorem!".

The true and proper meaning of mercy does not consist only in looking, however penetratingly and compassionately, at moral, physical or material evil: mercy is manifested in its true and proper aspect when it restores to value, promotes and draws good from all the forms of evil existing in the world and in man.[17]

Sin introduced a foreign element into human nature, an element that God did not intend to exist when He created it.[18] Thus, this nature needs to be remolded and again created in the image and the likeness of God. The Father's eternal love needs to be satisfied[19] not because of an anger that should be calmed; rather in the sense of restoring the Father's original dimension of love by re–creating the ontological status of human creatures.[20] In *Redemptor Hominis*, 9, John Paul says:

> The Redemption of the world—this tremendous mystery of love in which creation is renewed (*Gaudium et Spes*, 37; *Lumen Gentium*, 48)—is, at its deepest root, the fullness of justice in a human heart—the heart of the firstborn Son—in order that it may become justice in the hearts of many human beings, predestined from eternity in the First–born Son to be children of God (Rom 8:29–30) and called to grace, called to love.

This does not mean that we are subjecting God to the temporal categories of creation. It rather indicates that God, always on His transcendental level, reacts in the face of human acts. However, if man's concrete and historical situation does not match God's original plan of salvation, God does not change this plan because He has also eternally planned the event of the Incarnation. This theology is beautifully expressed at the conclusion of *Redemptoris Mater*:

> If he (God) has eternally willed to call man to share in the divine nature (cf. 2 Pet 1:4), it can be said that he has matched the 'divinization' of man to humanity's historical conditions, so that even after sin he is ready to restore at a great price the eternal plan of his love through the 'humanization' of his Son, who is of the same being as himself.[21]

---

[17]Pope John Paul II, *Dives in Misericordia*, 6; Terrence Prendergast, " 'A Vision of Wholeness': A Reflection on the Use of Scripture in a Cross–section of Papal Writings," in *The Thought of Pope John Paul II*, Rome: Gregorian University, 1993, 86–87.

[18]See also Pope John Paul II, *Dominum et Vivificantem*, 35.

[19]See Pope John Paul II, *Redemptor Hominis*, 9.

[20]See Pope John Paul II, *Dives in Misericordia*, 7; German Grisez, "Veritatis Splendor: Revealed Truth versus Dissent," in Homiletic and Pastoral Review 94 (March 1994): 8; Joseph Cardinal Cordeiro, "The religious sense of man," in *John Paul II. A Panorama of his Teachings*, New York: New City Press, 1989, 81.

[21]Pope John Paul II, *Redemptoris Mater*, 51. See also Ibid., *Dives in Misericordia*, 7.

Dominum et Vivificantem examines the divine dimension of Redemption from an anthropological perspective. This approach allows Pope John Paul II to display not only the mission of Christ as extended throughout history, but that of the Holy Spirit.[22] It has always been asserted that the Holy Spirit extends the salvific work of Christ in space and time, but how does He accomplish this mission? The analysis of John 16: 7–11 serves for the purpose of answering the question: "The Holy Spirit will convince the world concerning sin and righteousness and judgment." "The Holy Spirit convinces the world of sin" is, in its primary meaning, directed against those who rejected Jesus Christ by hanging him on the cross. However, because of the universality of the Redemption, the historical activity of the Spirit is inseparably linked to the witness borne to the Paschal Mystery throughout the whole history of the Church: "The revelation of the mystery of the Redemption opens the way to an understanding in which every sin wherever and whenever committed has a reference to the cross of Christ..."[23] Thus the mission of the Holy Spirit in convincing the world concerning sin as described by the words of the Redeemer in the Upper Room, becomes part of every age; the statement 'convince the world concerning sin' takes on the widest possible meaning and therefore should be including all the sin in the history of humanity. Consequently, since convincing the world concerning sin is related to the historicity of the Church, Pope John Paul II naturally relates the words of the Upper Room with the event of Pentecost. By the power of Pentecost, through the lips of Peter and later on throughout the whole life of the Church, the Spirit convinces the world concerning the sin of rejecting Jesus Christ.[24]

The Holy Spirit convinces the world concerning sin in two senses. In the first sense, since Christ came to save the world not to condemn it, the Holy Spirit, by revealing to the world the gravity of rejecting Christ, invites people to conversion. Conversion includes "the interior judgment of conscience, and this, being a proof of the action of the Spirit of truth in man's inmost being, becomes at the same time a new beginning of the bestowal of grace and

---

[22]See Michael O'Carroll, "Dominum et Vivificantem," in *Veni Creator Spiritus: A Theological Encyclopedia of the Holy Spirit*, Collegeville: Liturgical Press, 1990, 71; Giacomo Cardinal Biffi, "The Action of the Holy Spirit in the Church and in the World," in *John Paul II. A Panorama of his Teachings*, New York: New City Press, 1989, 41–42.

[23]See Pope John Paul II, *Dominum et Vivificantem*, 29. See also Ibid., 31; Giacomo Cardinal Biffi, "The Action of the Holy Spirit in the Church and in the World," in *John Paul II. A Panorama of his Teachings*, New York: New City Press, 1989, 442–43.

[24]See Pope John Paul II, *Dominum et Vivificantem*, 30; *Celebrate 2000! Reflections on Jesus, the Holy Spirit, and the Father*, Ann Arbor, Michigan: Servant Publications, 1996, 75; Giacomo Cardinal Biffi, "The Action of the Holy Spirit in the Church and in the World," in *John Paul II. A Panorama of his Teachings*, New York: New City Press, 1989, 43.

love."[25] This dimension, which is anthropological, focuses on the action of the Spirit vis–à–vis the heart of man as understood in the biblical sense of his spiritual entirety. This entity includes not only the conscience, but also all the inner faculties that make up the inmost being of the person. The convincing of sin through this anthropological dimension is in direct reference to 'righteousness', because definitive salvation is its ultimate goal.[26]

In the second sense, which has a christological dimension, the Holy Spirit convinces the world concerning sin in reference to Christ. By the very act of convincing the world concerning sin, the Holy Spirit convinces it concerning the remission of sin, a remission that became possible through the same One who was rejected: "The Holy Spirit, who takes from the Son the work of the Redemption of the world, by this very fact takes the task of the salvific 'convincing of sin.' "[27] *Dominum et Vivificantem* takes the aspect of the payment of the debt of sin one step further. Here, says the Pope, the Holy Spirit is the divine agent who convinces the world of sin, but always in relationship to the cross of Christ. This convincing does not concern humanity's collective guilt. It concerns every individual personal sin of whatever place or time. Evil in all its dimensions is revealed as evil through the cross of Christ. In every circumstance where a human person commits evil, the Holy Spirit turns the whole human person toward the cross of Christ and convinces that individual human being of the gravity of the evil performed by him or her. The Spirit unveils to the human conscience the full evil of sin by pointing out its roots and redirecting it from its evil actions.[28]

If the two dimensions are combined together, one realizes that the mission of the Holy Spirit has two implications: it condemns sin itself by inviting the person to interior conversion, and, by the same move, reveals the salvation brought by Christ. The Pope expresses this when he says that "in this

---

[25]Pope John Paul II, *Dominum et Vivificantem*, 31; *Celebrate 2000! Reflections on Jesus, the Holy Spirit, and the Father*, Ann Arbor, Michigan: Servant Publications, 1996, 75; Giacomo Cardinal Biffi, "The Action of the Holy Spirit in the Church and in the World," in *John Paul II. A Panorama of his Teachings*, New York: New City Press, 1989, 43.

[26]See Pope John Paul II, *Dominum et Vivificantem*, 28; Michael O'Carroll, "Dominum et Vivificantem," in *Veni Creator Spiritus: A Theological Encyclopedia of the Holy Spirit*, Collegeville: Liturgical Press, 1990, 71; Giacomo Cardinal Biffi, "The Action of the Holy Spirit in the Church and in the World," in *John Paul II. A Panorama of his Teachings*, New York: New City Press, 1989, 43.

[27]Pope John Paul II, *Dominum et Vivificantem*, 28. See also Ibid., *Reconciliatio et Penitentia*, 19–22.

[28]See Pope John Paul II, *Dominum et Vivificantem*, 29, 32, 43 and 44; *Celebrate 2000! Reflections on Jesus, the Holy Spirit, and the Father*, Ann Arbor, Michigan: Servant Publications, 1996, 75; J. Honoré, "Christ the Redeemer, Core of John Paul's Teaching," in *John Paul II. A Panorama of his Teachings*, New York: New City Press, 1989, 19.

'convincing concerning sin' we discover a double gift: the gift of the truth of conscience and the gift of the certainty of Redemption."[29] And with reference to convincing the world concerning judgment, he notes, "vast horizons open up for understanding 'sin' and also 'righteousness.' "[30] The Pope explains: "The Holy Spirit, by showing sin against the background of Christ's Cross in the economy of salvation (one could say 'sin saved'), enables us to understand how his mission is also 'to convince' of the sin that has already been definitively judged ('sin condemned')."[31] This text introduces us to the details and the manner of Redemption that is being accomplished by the Holy Spirit. In the same act where the Holy Spirit reveals the nature of evil, He draws out good, because He confirms the Redemption of Christ. The Spirit of truth cannot but reveal the reality of sin that abides in the world; but as soon as this reality comes to light, the christological content of Redemption emerges, intervening on behalf of man and relieving him, in a certain sense, from judgment.[32] It is in this sense that Christ says "the Holy Spirit will take from what is mine and declare it to you."

No one but the Spirit of truth, the Holy Spirit, is able to "convince the world." The reason, in John Paul's opinion, rests in the trinitarian mystery of God: to the Father—in the Son—through the Holy Spirit. Since the Third Divine Person, the Holy Spirit, "searches the depths of God," we, faced with the mystery of sin, should also search not only the human conscience, but also the depths of God in order to find an answer. Thus in his search, the human person inevitably encounters the Holy Spirit and is convinced by Him concerning sin because the Spirit, from the depths of God, "draws God's response to man's sin."[33]

For Pope John Paul, apart from the cross of Christ, sin cannot be revealed to man in its entire mystery: this theology of sin is developed to understand all sin, including sin in its original reality, or original sin.[34] The paschal mystery reveals all the dimensions of evil proper to the sin of man. But the mission of the Holy Spirit constantly stands in relationship with the Paschal Mystery. Therefore, apart from the action of the Holy Spirit, man is absolutely ignorant

---

[29]Pope John Paul II, *Dominum et Vivificantem*, 31.

[30]Pope John Paul II, *Dominum et Vivificantem*, 28.

[31]Pope John Paul II, *Dominum et Vivificantem*, 28.

[32]See Pope John Paul II, *Dominum et Vivificantem*, 28; Michael O'Carroll, "Dominum et Vivificantem," in *Veni Creator Spiritus: A Theological Encyclopedia of the Holy Spirit*, Collegeville: Liturgical Press, 1990, 71.

[33]Pope John Paul II, *Dominum et Vivificantem*, 32.

[34]See Michael O'Carroll, "Dominum et Vivificantem," in *Veni Creator Spiritus: A Theological Encyclopedia of the Holy Spirit*, Collegeville: Liturgical Press, 1990, 71.

of the reality of the *mysterium iniquitatis* and only the Spirit convinces the world concerning sin. So, man is at first ignorant of the reality of sin, but the Cross of Christ reveals it and, then, relative to the Cross of Christ, the Holy Spirit convinces the world concerning it. In the context of this relationship Christianity, as the Pope attests, rejects any 'fatalism' regarding sin:

> Sin, shown in this relationship (with the cross of Christ), is recognized in the entire dimension of evil proper to it, through the 'mysterium iniquitatis' which is hidden within it. Man does not know this dimension—he is absolutely ignorant of it apart from the cross of Christ. So he cannot be 'convinced' of it except by the Holy Spirit...[35]

In its relationship with the cross of Christ, sin is identified not only in the entire dimension of evil proper to it, but also in the full dimension of the *mysterium pietatis*. Man is also "absolutely ignorant of this dimension of sin apart from the cross of Christ. And he cannot be 'convinced' of this dimension either, except by the Holy Spirit: the one who searches the depths of God."[36] Since the Holy Spirit is the mutual Love between the Father and the Son and therefore the uncreated source of every gift to creatures, when He reveals the *mysterium pietatis*, "in him we can picture as personified and actualized in a transcendent way that mercy which the patristic and theological tradition, following the line of the Old and New Testament, attributes to God."[37]

A further step is needed to explain *how* the Spirit's 'convincing concerning sin' takes place in man. The Pope points to the conscience, "the most secret core and sanctuary of a man, where he is alone with God, whose voice echoes in his depths."[38] In order to avoid a subjectivistic approach, John Paul immediately affirms that the conscience "is not an independent and exclusive capacity to decide what is good and what is evil." It is bound by a principle of obedience to the objective norms that come from the natural law and the Divine Revelation.

The Holy Spirit accomplishes his mission of 'convincing concerning sin' "in no other way except through the conscience."[39] An upright conscience identifies good and evil as good and evil and, under the action of the Holy Spirit, leads man to discover the roots of sin in him. Through the joint efforts

---

[35]Pope John Paul II, *Dominum et Vivificantem*, 32. See also *Ibid.*, 44.

[36]Pope John Paul II, *Dominum et Vivificantem*, 32.

[37]Pope John Paul II, *Dominum et Vivificantem*, 39; Michael O'Carroll, "Dominum et Vivificantem," in *Veni Creator Spiritus: A Theological Encyclopedia of the Holy Spirit*, Collegeville: Liturgical Press, 1990, 72.

[38]*Gaudium et Spes*, 16; Pope John Paul II, *Dominum et Vivificantem*, 43.

[39]Pope John Paul II, *Dominum et Vivificantem*, 43.

of both the Holy Spirit and the human conscience, the 'convincing the world concerning sin' is accomplished. The conscience commands, forbids, judges in the light of interior dictates and prohibitions, and determines the paths of human conversion; the Holy Spirit enables this conscience to share in the suffering of God who repented 'at having created man.' Isn't the suffering of the conscience "an echo of that 'reprobation' which is interiorized in the 'heart' of the Trinity and by virtue of the eternal love is translated into the suffering of the Cross, into Christ's obedience unto death?"[40]

The Cross and the Mystery of Redemption

John Paul II emphasizes the universality of the Christ event: the mystery of Redemption reaches all human beings whether they are believers in Christ or not.[41] In *Centesimus Annus*, he says: "We are not dealing here with man in the 'abstract,' but with the real, 'concrete,' 'historical' man. We are dealing with *each individual*, since each one is included in the mystery of Redemption, and through this mystery Christ has united himself with each one forever."[42]

The reason for this outreach to all humankind is the authentic humanity Christ assumed for the sake of Redemption. The human nature of the Incarnate Word became, in a certain sense, a 'universal nature' through its identification with the nature of every human person. However, the Son of God assumed the human nature in its most sublime condition, as it was prefigured by the Creator since the beginning of creation: He was "by his very nature absolutely innocent and free from sin, and His coming into the world was untainted by the disobedience of Adam and the inheritance of original sin."[43] In *Redemptor Hominis*, John Paul II says:

> The life of Christ speaks, also, to many who are not capable of repeating with Peter: "you are the Christ, the Son of the living God (Mt 16:16)." He, the Son of the living God, speaks to people also as Man: it is his life that speaks, his humanity, his fidelity to the truth, his all–embracing love.[44]

If the Incarnation is the point of departure, albeit the second step after creation of God's self–offering to humanity, the Paschal Mystery constitutes for John Paul II the culminating point of the Son's redeeming activity, an activity that manifests His daily self–giving to humanity in its most concrete circumstances.

---

[40]Pope John Paul II, *Dominum et Vivificantem*, 45.

[41]See Pope John Paul II, *Redemptor Hominis*, 13.

[42]Pope John Paul II, *Centesimus Annus*, 53. See also Ibid., *Dives in Misericordia*, 7.

[43]Pope John Paul II, *Dives in Misericordia*, 8.

[44]Pope John Paul II, *Redemptor Hominis*, 7.

Therefore, the irrevocable commitment of the Son in His union with human nature through the Incarnation, found its utmost expression in the shedding of His blood on the cross. Incarnation and Redemption constitute an organic and indissoluble unity, in which, as the second Vatican Council relates, "the plan of revelation is realized by words and deeds which are intrinsically bound up with each other."[45] This is how John Paul describes the importance of the mystery of Redemption for the Church:

> The Church never ceases to relive his death on the Cross and his Resurrection, which constitute the *content of the Church's daily life*...The Church lives his (Christ's) mystery, draws unwearyingly from it and continually seeks ways of bringing this mystery of her Master and Lord to humanity—to the peoples, the nations, the succeeding generations, and every individual human being—as if she were ever repeating, as the Apostle did: "For I decided to know nothing among you except Jesus Christ and him crucified (1 Cor 2:2)." The Church stays within the sphere of the mystery of the Redemption, which has become the fundamental principle of her life and mission.[46]

The debt of sin can be paid by the Son because the cross becomes the ultimate expression of the Father's love to humanity. As *Redemptor Hominis*, 9, expresses it:

> The cross on Calvary, through which Jesus Christ—a Man, the Son of the Virgin Mary, thought to be the son of Joseph of Nazareth—"leaves" this world, is also a fresh manifestation of the eternal fatherhood of God, who in him draws near again to humanity, to each human being, giving him the thrice holy "Spirit of Truth (Jn 16:13)."[47]

Both sin and cross are brought to be in relationship with the fatherhood of the Father in the same context of *Redemptor Hominis*, 9. Sin breaks the bond between the Father's fatherhood which was expressed in creation. The cross reveals the fatherhood of the Father, a fatherhood which was previously expressed through the gift of creation.[48] The damage done to the Father's eternal fatherhood through sin, is restored through the cross. Since the cross manifests in a fresh way the fatherhood of the Father, a fatherhood that was expressed through the act of creation, the cross accomplishes the re–creation of humanity in the image and likeness of God. This is the *divine dimension* of

---

[45]*Dei Verbum*, 2; Pope John Paul II, *Redemptoris Custos*, 6; J. Honoré, "Christ the Redeemer, Core of John Paul's Teaching," in *John Paul II. A Panorama of his Teachings*, New York: New City Press, 1989, 16–17.

[46]Pope John Paul II, *Redemptor Hominis*, 7.

[47]See Pope John Paul II, *Redemptor Hominis*, 9.

[48]See Pope John Paul II, *Redemptor Hominis*, 9; *Dives in Misericordia*, 7.

the Redemption that

> ...enables us, I would say, in the most empirical and 'historical' way, to uncover the depth of that love which does not recoil before the extraordinary sacrifice of the Son, in order to satisfy the fidelity of the Creator and Father toward human beings, created in his image and chosen from 'the beginning,' in this Son, for grace and glory.[49]

The cross stands as a *sign of contradiction* against sin, the sin that does nothing but destroy human life: "Here we touch indirectly on the mystery of the divine 'economy' which linked salvation and grace with the Cross."[50] In *Redemptor Hominis*, 9, John Paul II says:

> If he (the Father) 'made to be sin' him (the incarnate Son) who was without any sin whatever, it was to reveal the love that is always greater than the whole of creation, the love that is he himself, since 'God is love (1 Jn 4:8, 16)'. Above all, love is greater than sin, than weakness, than the 'futility of creation (cf. Rom 8:20)'; it is stronger than death; it is a love always ready to raise up and forgive, always ready to go to meet the prodigal son...This revelation of love is also described as mercy (St. Thomas Aquinas, Summa Theologiae, III, q. 46, a. 1, ad 3), and in man's history this revelation of love and mercy has taken a form and a name: that of Jesus Christ.[51]

This text explains how the debt of sin is paid. For John Paul II, the cross is a contradiction because through it the Incarnate Son pays a debt that humanity owes God, not a debt that He owes humanity. Because God is love, love is greater than the accidental changing of human condition that led human persons to sin. God is committed to creation first through the very act of creation and then through the cross. Since God decided to act *ad extra* and create human persons, God is committed to deal with all the consequences of His free act. However, there is a tragic relationship between Him and humans because the very act that comes from Him out of love, is switched by them to bring about the paradoxical reality of evil.

The balance between Christology from above and Christology from below makes it clear *how* the debt of sin is paid. This balance idea is what makes John Paul II original in his understanding of how the redemption took place. By 'high Christology,' in this specific context, is meant the absolute difference between the human nature of the Word and that of human persons. Difference not in the constitutive elements, but in the absence of any sin or disorder in His nature. By 'Christology from below' is meant the absolute identification

---

[49]Pope John Paul II, *Dives in Misericordia*, 7.

[50]Pope John Paul II, *Redemptor Hominis*, 11. See also Ibid., *Dominum et Vivificantem*, 28.

[51]See Pope John Paul II, *Redemptor Hominis*, 9.

between the human nature of the Word and ours in its constitutive elements. Quoting *Gaudium et Spes,* 22, John Paul says in *Redemptor Hominis*:

> Human nature, by the very fact that it was assumed, not absorbed, in him, has been raised in us also to a dignity beyond compare. For, by his Incarnation, He, the Son of God, in a certain way united himself with each man (22). He worked with human hands, he thought with human mind. He acted with human will, and with human heart he loved. Born of the Virgin Mary, he has truly been made one of us, like to us in all things except sin, he, the Redeemer of man.[52]

The cross in the theology of Pope John Paul II is also an *eschatological sign.* Even if the cross "is like a touch of eternal love upon the most painful wounds of man's earthly existence,"[53] its fruits will be earned only in the *eschaton.* In fact, the ultimate victory of Christ's cross upon evil could happen only when man is not capable of sinning anymore. However, the Pope shows an extraordinary awareness that the theology of the kingdom always obeys the tension of *already* and *not yet.* Yes, the sacrifice of the Cross has already conquered sin and death, yet its final fulfillment will only be in the *eschaton*:

> In the Paschal Mystery the limits of the many sided evil in which man becomes a sharer during his earthly existence are surpassed: the Cross of Christ, in fact, makes us understand the deepest roots of evil, which are fixed in sin and death; thus the Cross becomes an eschatological sign. Only in the eschatological fulfillment and definitive renewal of the world will love conquer, in all the elect, the deepest sources of evil, bringing as its fully mature fruit the kingdom of life and holiness and glorious immortality. The foundation of this eschatological fulfillment is already contained in the Cross of Christ and in his death.[54]

The power of the cross will be fulfilled in the *eschaton,* but "while in the temporal phase, in human history, which is at the same time the history of sin and death, love must be revealed above all as mercy and must also be actualized as mercy."[55] In this context, Pope John Paul II brings out a truly original idea: the cross is the ultimate revelation of God's mercy, in the sense of an *admirabile commercium.* Mercy is not a unilateral action that emanates from God through Christ towards humanity, and it should never be confused

---

[52]See Pope John Paul II, *Redemptor Hominis,* 8.

[53]Pope John Paul II, *Dives in Misericordia,* 8. See also Ibid., *Dominum et Vivificantem,* 39; Ralph Martin, "Rich in Mercy," in *New Covenant* 11 (July 1981): 20.

[54]Pope John Paul II, *Dives in Misericordia,* 8.

[55]Pope John Paul II, *Dives in Misericordia,* 8.

with pity which demeans. The mercy of God never degrades but transforms.[56] Nor does mercy presuppose or maintain a certain distance between the one practicing it and the one benefitting from it. It is also a mercy on the Son of God Who "stand(s) at the door and knock(s)... In a special way, God also reveals his mercy when he invites man to have 'mercy' on his only Son, the Crucified One."[57] That invitation that is based on God's eternal love for man, possesses in itself a tragic dimension because it encounters the limited, human yet authentic freedom. That encounter of divine and human freedom that reaches its highest point in the cross of Christ, expresses the ultimate love of the One Who gave existence to the human freedom and, respecting that responsible freedom, keeps somewhat begging for mercy the humans He eternally loved. Christ, as the Crucified One, will never fail to knock at the heart of every man in order, "without restricting his freedom, but instead seeking to draw from this very freedom love, which is not only an act of solidarity with the suffering Son of man, but also a kind of 'mercy' shown by each of us to the Son of the eternal Father."[58] Nothing is more paradoxical about man than the consequence of this theology: "in obtaining mercy, he is in a sense the one who at the same time 'shows mercy.' "[59] Therefore, as the Pope concludes in *Dives in Misericordia*, 14, "true mercy is, so to speak, the most profound source of justice."

This *admirabile commercium* reveals the deepest details of God's logic and how He applied it in His plan of Redemption. This plan is one of dual responsibilities between God who offers salvation through Christ and man who, by accepting that Redemption, saves himself and effects God's plan: "This exchange is a law of the very plan of salvation, a law which is simple, strong and at the same time 'easy.' "[60] The exchange shows how God relates to the world, and how this relation is the expression of "the deep mystery of God: that inscrutable unity of Father, Son and Holy Spirit..."[61] The whole idea about *admirabile commercium* is possible because of the Paschal Mystery. This mystery is, therefore, Christ at the center of the revelation of the inscrutable

---

[56]See Joseph O'Hare, "Mercy Appears," in *America* 143 (1980): 402; Joseph Cardinal Cordeiro, "The religious sense of man," in *John Paul II. A Panorama of his Teachings*, New York: New City Press, 1989, 80–81.

[57]Pope John Paul II, *Dives in Misericordia*, 8.

[58]Pope John Paul II, *Dives in Misericordia*, 8. See also Joseph O'Hare, "Mercy Appears," in *America* 143 (1980): 402.

[59]Pope John Paul II, *Dives in Misericordia*, 8.

[60]Pope John Paul II, *Dives in Misericordia*, 8.

[61]Pope John Paul II, *Dives in Misericordia*, 8. See also Joseph O'Hare, "Mercy Appears," in *America* 143 (1980): 402.

mystery of God.[62]

The Mystery of Redemptive Suffering

When it comes to the question of suffering as expounded in *Salvifici Doloris*, Pope John Paul II reinforces his arguments with Scripture as well as philosophy. The mystery of suffering, as a specific aspect of the whole mystery of man, is revealed to man only *in the light of the Word made flesh*. John Paul recurs to the theology of Vatican II: since the mystery of man could be understood only in and through the mystery of the Incarnation, also suffering, as part of that mystery, should be approached from exactly the same perspective. The Pope uses a cognitive approach to understanding suffering: the truth of Divine Revelation demonstrates the mystery of suffering and inserts it in God's plan of salvation. The process of discerning the good in human suffering assumes different stages, taking however the truth of divine Revelation as its point of departure.

Pope John Paul II's *Salvifici Doloris* considers the *reality of suffering* as a starting point to treat the question: whatever form it takes, suffering is almost inseparable from man's existence.[63] By the word 'suffering' is expressed something essential to the nature of man. Since suffering belongs to the very reality of man, it goes with his condition as a limited and yet transcendent being. Suffering is a concomitant characteristic of man's existence. It is ever inside of him. He has to get beyond it. The paradoxical character of suffering is evident from the very beginning of *Salvifici Doloris*: "It (suffering) is as deep as man himself, precisely because it manifests in its own way that depth which is proper to man, and in its own way surpasses it. Suffering seems to belong to man's transcendence: it is one of those points in which man is in a certain sense 'destined' to go beyond himself, and he is called to this in a mysterious way."[64] The world of suffering exists in every single individual not only as a small part of that 'world,' but also as a finite and unrepeatable entity. With all its dimensions, the whole world of suffering is present in the human subject, although as a finite entity.[65]

The Pope does not approach the question of suffering as if it is a problem

---

[62]Pope John Paul II, *Dives in Misericordia*, 8. See also Ralph Martin, "Rich in Mercy," in *New Covenant* 11 (July 1981): 20.

[63]See Pope John Paul II, *Salvifici Doloris*, 2–3; Joseph Cardinal Cordeiro, "The religious sense of man," in *John Paul II. A Panorama of his Teachings*, New York: New City Press, 1989, 79–80.

[64]Pope John Paul II, *Salvifici Doloris*, 2; Joseph Cardinal Cordeiro, "The religious sense of man," in *John Paul II. A Panorama of his Teachings*, New York: New City Press, 1989, 79–80.

[65]See Pope John Paul II, *Salvifici Doloris*, 8.

that needs an answer; nor as a reality that needs description. Rather, instead of being a problem, suffering is a *mystery* hidden within the broader picture of the relationship between man and God as Creator and Redeemer. In it "is contained the greatness of a specific mystery."[66] It is a mystery because of the need of the human heart to command the person to overcome fear, and because of the imperative of faith that "provides the content, in the name of which and by virtue of which we dare to touch what appears in every man so intangible: for man, in his suffering, remains an intangible mystery."[67] In its objective reality, suffering assumes an inexpressible and non–transferable character, although its existence is totally evident from a subjective point of view.

The double character of the human person indicates that both his spiritual and bodily elements are immediate or direct subjects of suffering. Thus, there is a *physical suffering* when the body is hurting, and a *moral suffering* when the soul is in pain. This latter possesses a spiritual as well as a psychological nature that usually accompanies both physical and moral suffering. Especially developed in the Old Testament are those moral sufferings that, although less identifiable because of their spiritual nature, still enjoy a physical or somatic element and their presence is often reflected in the condition of the entire organism.[68]

In the theology and terminology of the Old Testament, suffering and evil are identified with each other: man suffers whenever he experiences any kind of evil. Thanks to the New Testament and the Greek verb 'pasko,' suffering is no longer identified with objective evil; rather it "expresses a situation in which man experiences evil and in doing so becomes the subject of suffering."[69] This subjective dimension of suffering does not eliminate its passive character. Suffering remains something passive in its metaphysical essence, although the subject himself is the agent that experiences it and often brings it on himself. No matter how passive it is, suffering is constantly marked by a specific 'activity' of pain always caused by a certain experience of evil.

The very *essence of evil*, then, is the question to be dealt with when the reality of suffering is in question. Since the problem of evil has already been extensively treated in this volume, a short note on the relationship between suffering and evil should be sufficient. The influence of St. Augustine on the mind of John Paul in this area is very noticeable. Christians, by virtue of

---

[66]Pope John Paul II, *Salvifici Doloris*, 4; Joseph Cardinal Cordeiro, "The religious sense of man," in *John Paul II. A Panorama of his Teachings*, New York: New City Press, 1989, 80.

[67]Pope John Paul II, *Salvifici Doloris*, 4.

[68]See Pope John Paul II, *Salvifici Doloris*, 6.

[69]Pope John Paul II, *Salvifici Doloris*, 7; Joseph Cardinal Cordeiro, "The religious sense of man," in *John Paul II. A Panorama of his Teachings*, New York: New City Press, 1989, 80.

Divine Revelation, believe and proclaim the essential goodness of existence and the goodness of that which exists. The reason of that goodness is to be sought in the ultimate source of existence: God who is Good by nature. In this context of natural goodness of all that exists

> ...man suffers on account of evil, which is a certain lack, limitation or distortion of good. We could say that man suffers because of a good in which he does not share, from which in a certain sense he is cut off, or of which he has deprived himself. He particularly suffers when he 'ought —in the normal order of things—to have a share in this good, and does not have it. Thus, in the Christian view, the reality of suffering is explained through evil, which always, in some way, refers to a good.[70]

This confirms the aspects we spoke of in the section on the *Nature of Evil*. Here the suffering is put in direct relation to the essence of evil: when we address the problem of *the existence of evil*, "we are always, at least to a certain extent, asking a question about suffering too."[71]

Pope John Paul II lays it down very clearly that suffering is not always a result of sin. In the case that it is a punishment for the evil done by the person, that decision on the part of God is justified by the necessity of guaranteeing the moral order. To the evil of sin that transgresses the moral order established in a transcendent way by the will of the Creator, corresponds a punishment of a God who is a just Judge. This aspect of God is a fundamental truth of faith that was confirmed by Divine Revelation, a truth that rejects the idea of a God who is exclusively a God of love and mercy. A God of love and mercy does not compromise His faithfulness to the objective moral order established through creation. Nothing in the Old or in the New Testament violates the transcendent moral order based upon justice. From this point of view, suffering appears as a 'justified evil.'[72] Here again one finds the cognitive dimension of the mystery of suffering: John Paul proceeds from the truth of Revelation in order to draw out of it what is good for human beings. Thus punishment should not be approached merely or exclusively from a negative point of view, that is as a repayment for the evil done. Punishment, therefore, possesses a positive dimension which allows a rebuilding of goodness in the subject who suffers.

The Pope gives the example of Job in order to approach the question of suffering from a different angle: suffering is not always the result of evil and should not therefore be always linked to the moral order. The suffering of the innocent, like the case of Job, "must be accepted as a mystery, which the

---

[70]Pope John Paul II, *Salvifici Doloris*, 7.

[71]Pope John Paul II, *Salvifici Doloris*, 9.

[72]Pope John Paul II, *Salvifici Doloris*, 10.

individual is unable to penetrate completely by his own intelligence."[73] If the transcendent moral order based upon justice should never be violated, at the same time the principles of that order cannot be applied in an exclusive and superficial way. Suffering has the nature of a punishment when it connected with the evil of sin, but "it is not true that all suffering is a consequence of a fault and has the nature of a punishment."[74] Especially in the case of Job that reality becomes very evident: the Lord consents to test Job in order to demonstrate his righteousness.

For John Paul, suffering, although it should not be always considered as a punishment of concrete sins, is still connected somehow to the beginning of sin. There exists a sinful backdrop to the collective activity of persons, called by St. John the 'sin of the world.' *Sin* stands in a very complicated relationship to *suffering* which has in some way infected the whole of creation.[75] In its original reality, sin causes an *ipso facto* suffering because sin rejects the relationality between the human person and God, a relationality that permits the very possibility of human existence.[76] Therefore, sin in its temporal and historical dimension remains a mystery because it cannot be identified as a direct cause of suffering but, on the other hand, this principle is not exclusive because of the mysterious relationship between suffering and the sin of the beginnings: "Though it is not licit to apply here the narrow criterion of direct dependence (as Job's three friends did), it is equally true that one cannot reject the criterion that, at the basis of human suffering, there is a complex involvement with sin."[77]

When it comes to the question of *death* in the relationship to sin and suffering, death is not a form of suffering in the temporal sense. However, death still primarily "involves the dissolution of the entire psychophysical personality of man," as a "definitive summing up of the destructive work both in the bodily organism and in the psyche." The soul survives after death and the body undergoes gradual decomposition according to the words of the Lord uttered after Adam's sin at the beginning of history: "you are dust and to dust you shall return." Sin causes death and suffering. Sin could be the direct cause of suffering, but it is not the exclusive cause. Hence, the mysterious relationship between suffering and the original reality of sin. Death is caused

---

[73]Pope John Paul II, *Salvifici Doloris*, 11.

[74]Pope John Paul II, *Salvifici Doloris*, 11.

[75]Pope John Paul II, *Salvifici Doloris*, 15. See also Ibid., *Dominum et Vivificantem*, 39.

[76]See Pope John Paul II, *Salvifici Doloris*, 15. See also Ibid., *Familiaris Consortio*, 58; Robert Morneau, "*Redemptor Hominis*: Themes and Theses," in *Review for Religious* 39 (1980): 249.

[77]Pope John Paul II, *Salvifici Doloris*, 15.

by sin, but goes beyond any form of temporal and historical suffering. However, it is not possible to ignore the fact that death is still experienced by human beings as a suffering which possesses a total and definitive character. This total character is the definitive summing–up of human suffering, and it goes beyond all forms of temporal and historical suffering.[78]

Sin, suffering, and death, like any reality that belongs to the human condition and to man's existence, should be included in the mechanism of Redemption as accomplished by the passion of Christ.[79] Herein the theme of suffering assumes a totally new dimension, the dimension of Redemption. With this dimension, suffering receives its fundamental and definitive meaning, a meaning that surpasses its historical and temporal dimension. John Paul II applies the text of John 3:16: "For God so loved the world that he gave his only Son, that whoever believes in him should not perish but have eternal life." Final damnation is what constitutes the ultimate danger for the human person. That damnation involves a definitive, eschatological suffering: man can escape it only through the intervention of the loving Only–begotten Son. Since the mystery of suffering should not be limited to its temporal and historical dimension, the Son of God "must strike evil right at its transcendental roots from which it develops in human history. These transcendental roots of evil are grounded in sin and death: for they are at the basis of the loss of eternal life."[80]

The Redeemer had to deal with all three realities of sin, death and suffering. Regarding sin, Jesus Christ has bestowed upon humanity sanctifying grace through His Incarnation. As God in Person Who assumes a human nature like ours except sin, "He blots out from human history the dominion of sin, which took root under the influence of the evil spirit beginning with original sin." By His resurrection from the dead he opened the road for future resurrection of the bodies and has thus destroyed the dominion of death. By triumphing over sin and death, Christ has recuperated the two essential conditions of 'eternal life,' the life spoken of by St. John the Evangelist in the text of Jn 3:16 quoted above. These two essential conditions re–establish man's union with God, a reality that, in the eschatological perspective, eliminates suffering. Ultimately, suffering will be destroyed and man's definitive happiness in his union with God will shape his eschatological existence.[81] The fact that man's destiny is an

---

[78]Pope John Paul II, *Salvifici Doloris*, 15.

[79]See Pope John Paul II, *Salvifici Doloris*, 3; *Celebrate 2000! Reflections on Jesus, the Holy Spirit, and the Father*, Ann Arbor, Michigan: Servant Publications, 1996, 63. See also André Frossard, *Portrait of John Paul II*, San Francisco: Ignatius Press, 1990, 67–68.

[80]Pope John Paul II, *Salvifici Doloris*, 14. See also Ibid., *Christifideles Laici*, 54; Arthur Macdonal Allchin, "*Redemptoris Mater*: An Anglican Response," in *One in Christ* 23 (1988): 324.

[81]See Pope John Paul II, *Salvifici Doloris*, 15; Joseph Cardinal Cordeiro, "The religious sense of man," in *John Paul II. A Panorama of his Teachings*, New York: New City Press, 1989,

eternal union with God opens a new door for viewing the realities of sin, suffering and death: on his transcendental plan, positive though incomprehensible in every detail, God reveals Himself as committed to the work of salvation and Redemption. In spite of sin in all its forms, the love between the Father and the Son on the intratrinitarian level that stands at the very root of creation is expressed in time through the Incarnation which enables the Son to draw close in a salvific way to the whole world of suffering in which man shares and to strike at the very roots of human evil.[82]

Pope John Paul II refers to the words of Is 53:2–6 in order to describe the redemptive way through which Christ draws close to the world of suffering. "The Lord has laid on him the iniquity of us all" should be understood as a 'substitutive' and 'redemptive' suffering. If the whole reality of suffering 'is measured' by the evil suffered, then that whole extent of evil and suffering is what was thrown on Christ's shoulders. In other words, "all human sin in its breadth and depth becomes the true cause of the Redeemer's suffering."[83] That substitutive suffering can take place only because of the identity of the Only–begotten and His relationship of love with the Father. He can annihilate sin because of the love He has for the Father that overcomes the evil of every sin: In Gethsemane, Christ proved the truth of love through the truth of suffering. Suffering shines forth as a new reality directly connected with the truth of love.[84]

After the event of Gethsemane, the words of Christ "my God, my God, why have you abandoned me?" on Golgotha, bear witness to the depth of evil of the suffering experienced. These words receive a paradoxical dimension because they are spoken by a Person who is God and man at the same time. Being God, He enjoys an inseparable unity with the Father, although that same inseparable unity is the condition of possibility, as it were, of complete separation between the Father and the sin of the world as it is thrown on the shoulders of Christ. Evil in all its dimensions and in its entirety, as was spoken by St. Paul's 2 Cor 5:21 "for our sake he made him to be sin who knew no sin", was cast upon Jesus Who, being human like us except for sin, assumes the responsibility of bearing the sin of humanity and experiencing the ultimate estrangement between God and the evil brought about by the sin of man. The text of *Salvifici Doloris*, 18 in this regard reads as follows:

80.

[82]See Pope John Paul II, *Salvifici Doloris*, 15.

[83]Pope John Paul II, *Salvifici Doloris*, 17.

[84]See Pope John Paul II, *Salvifici Doloris*, 17–18.

One can say that these words on abandonment are born at the level of that inseparable union of the Son with the Father, and are born because the Father 'laid on him the iniquity of us all'...Together with this horrible weight, encompassing the 'entire' evil of the turning away from God which is contained in sin, Christ, through the divine depth of His filial union with the Father, perceives in a humanly inexpressible way this suffering which is the separation, the rejection by the Father, the estrangement from God. But precisely through this suffering He accomplishes the Redemption...[85]

Only in that context of the Son's suffering does suffering in general become salvific. In other words, from the perspective of the suffering of Christ, the suffering of every person enters into a completely new dimension and a new order. The good that the human person draws out of suffering parallels the supreme good of Redemption. Since this Redemption happened through suffering, it gave it a new meaning and dimension, precisely a salvific one. Again the God of Creation is revealed as the God of salvation, as the God who will do everything to bring the man he created to the happiness of Redemption. A mystery such as suffering assumes a salvific dimension for every human being because the love between the Father and the Son that created the world is being outpoured again through the Incarnation that finds its culminating point in transforming the reality of suffering into Redemption. In this sense the suffering of Christ becomes the price of Redemption. Therefore, the key answer to understand that transformation for John Paul II is love. Suffering is linked to love, to that love which "creates good, drawing it out by means of suffering, just as the supreme good of the Redemption of the world was drawn from the cross of Christ."[86]

His identity as God and man has enabled Christ to act as the personal subject of redemptive suffering, a subject that is endowed with a duality of nature. This Son Whom the Father 'gave' is consubstantial with the Father as to the divinity, yet has suffered as a man. Although the suffering of Christ has a human dimension because he suffered as a man, that human suffering still possesses an incomparable intensity because the subject of suffering is the Only–begotten Son of the Father. Therefore, He alone can cover that spiritual space of the relationship between God and man, a space that was filled with evil since the beginning of the history of man on earth. In that specific space pervaded by evil, only Christ replaces evil by good because He only is capable of assessing the measure of evil contained in the sin of man.[87] By filling this

---

[85]Pope John Paul II, *Salvifici Doloris*, 18.

[86]Pope John Paul II, *Salvifici Doloris*, 18. See also Ibid., *Vita Consecrata*, 28; *Celebrate 2000! Reflections on Jesus, the Holy Spirit, and the Father*, Ann Arbor, Michigan: Servant Publications, 1996, 63–65.

[87]See Pope John Paul II, *Salvifici Doloris*, 17.

space with good, Christ does not leave any space for complaint from man who would otherwise be able to accuse God of not knowing the limitations of the human condition, a condition that constantly experiences the pain of suffering. Life, even the one full of suffering, becomes meaningful especially in view of a God who creates and is committed to all the dimensions of the life of His Creatures.

St. Paul says in Col 1:24: "In my flesh I complete what is lacking in Christ's afflictions for the sake of his body, that is, the Church." The good of Redemption accomplished by Christ cannot be augmented by any man. It is by itself inexhaustible and infinite. Col. 1:24 is for John Paul a key text for understanding why the suffering of Christ, although it pays the full price of Redemption, does not exclude the participation of the human person in it. Each person has his own share in the Redemption because each person is called to share in the suffering of Christ. Precisely because Christ's suffering redeemed all human suffering, the sharing in that suffering of Christ is also a sharing in the Redemption. As if through their suffering people "repay the infinite price of the passion and death of Christ, which became the price of our Redemption."[88] Especially in His mystical Body, the Church, Christ opens His own redemptive suffering to all human suffering: "Insofar as man becomes a sharer in Christ's suffering...to that extent he in his own way completes the suffering through which Christ accomplished the Redemption of the world." This does not mean that the Redemption achieved by Christ is incomplete. It means the Redemption that is accomplished once and for all is still being constantly accomplished and extended in human history through the suffering of human beings. If Christ has perfectly achieved the whole reality of Redemption through suffering, this does not imply that He has brought it to a close. In its very essence, that suffering must be continually completed. That completeness of Christ's Redemption never excludes the fact that it "remains always open to all love expressed in human suffering."[89] Only within the framework of a Church that extends in history and time the redemptive work of Christ, it is possible to understand the completeness of Christ's suffering which should be unceasingly completed.

To conclude, the whole mystery of suffering cannot be looked upon from a merely human point of view, because it necessarily enjoys the supernatural

---

[88]See Pope John Paul II, *Salvifici Doloris*, 19–21 and 24; Hans Cardinal Groër, "The Church Sacrament of Salvation," in *John Paul II. A Panorama of his Teachings*, New York: New City Press, 1989, 34–35.

[89]Pope John Paul II, *Salvifici Doloris*, 24; *Celebrate 2000! Reflections on Jesus, the Holy Spirit, and the Father*, Ann Arbor, Michigan: Servant Publications, 1996, 66; Hans Cardinal Groër, "The Church Sacrament of Salvation," in *John Paul II. A Panorama of his Teachings*, New York: New City Press, 1989, 33–34.

dimension. That dimension is rooted in the divine mystery of the Redemption of the world. At the same time, suffering "is deeply human because in it the person discovers himself, his own humanity, his own dignity, his own mission." Christ does not answer in the abstract the human questions about the meaning of suffering. As much as man probes the mystery of suffering in both its human and divine dimensions, only by becoming a sharer in the suffering of Christ, does he receive a direct answer concerning his own suffering. Only at the level of Christ's suffering does man discover the meaning of his own suffering and realize that he should necessarily orient it to an eschatological fulfillment where the whole mystery will then make full sense.[90]

The Human Dimension of the Mystery of Redemption

The *human dimension* of Redemption, as it is called by John Paul II in *Redemptor Hominis*, 10, lies in the mystery of Christ who "fully reveals man to himself (*Gaudium et Spes*, 22)" and sheds light on the human condition as such. These words of *Gaudium et Spes* constitute the fundamental basis for the Pope's theological anthropology: the human dimension of the mystery of Redemption is what Redemption, as an exclusive act of God, inflicts on man with all the anthropological implications drawn from it. *Redemptor Hominis*, with its striking philosophy of existence, turns to the very core of the human person's identity, nature, and destiny, forecasting the line of thought of John Paul for the coming years of his Pontificate: the mystery of Christ reveals the truth of the human person's being, his vocation and the very meaning of his existence. The principle of the Pope's anthropological reflection in *Redemptor Hominis* is contained in the axiom of "...the mystery of the Redemption, in which the question of man is inscribed with a special vigor of truth and love."[91]

In this section it is necessary to present how Pope John Paul II distinguishes between the order of creation and the order of salvation when seeking to establish the relations among sin, death, and Redemption. The reality of death is that tragedy "which from the beginning of man's history had been allied to sin."[92] In the order of creation, death entered the world because of the sin of Adam and Eve, a fact that is scripturally evident in the Letter of St. Paul to the Romans. As far as the order of salvation is concerned, the Church Fathers' theory of *procedure of inversion* seems to be the method adopted by Pope John

---

[90]See Pope John Paul II, *Salvifici Doloris*, 26 and 31.

[91]Pope John Paul II, *Redemptor Hominis*, 10, 11, 13, 18; Raymond T. Gawronski, "Redemptor Hominis," in *The Thought of Pope John Paul II*, Rome: Gregorian University, 1993, 222; J. Honoré, "Christ the Redeemer, Core of John Paul's Teaching," in *John Paul II. A Panorama of his Teachings*, New York: New City Press, 1989, 21.

[92]Pope John Paul II, *Dives in Misericordia*, 8.

Paul II. He argues that since the sin of Adam has caused death, only the death of the sinless Christ can cause justification: "Death has justice done to it at the price of the death of the one who was without sin and who alone was able—by means of his own death—to inflict death upon death."[93]

The relationship between Christ and Adam as reported in *Gaudium et Spes*, 22 is the main text that inspires the theology of Pope John Paul II concerning the connection between creation and Incarnation. The text of *Gaudium et Spes*, 22 reads:

> The truth is that only in the mystery of the Incarnate Word does the mystery of man take on light. For Adam, the first man, was a type of him who was to come (Rm 5:14), Christ the Lord. Christ, the new Adam, in the very revelation of the mystery of the Father and of his love, fully reveals man to himself and brings to light his most high calling...He who is the image of the invisible God (Col 1:15), is himself the perfect man who has restored in the children of Adam that likeness to God which had been disfigured ever since the first sin.

John Paul II quotes this text of *Gaudium et Spes* in *Redemptor Hominis*, 8 and sees in it the most important point reached by the Council: man in his deepest human consciousness. In John Paul's opinion, the Council has already made "contact with the inward mystery of man, which in biblical and non–biblical language is expressed by the word '*heart*.' Christ, the Redeemer of the world, is the one who penetrated in a unique, unrepeatable way into the mystery of man and entered his 'heart.' "[94] Explicit references to the term *heart* appear more than fifty times in *Dominum et Vivificantem*, and they are frequently linked to the theme of conscience. Rather than a faculty or an inherent potentiality of the human being in relation to love, the heart denotes a temple, a field, a spatiality that serves to emphasize innate dependence and passivity: "the heart is the locality where truth as revelation and love as gift take place."[95]

Adam was only a type of Him who was to come, because the Incarnation is not only the culmination of creation, but also, ontologically speaking, *a priori* includes the reality of creation and therefore stands at the center of God's

---

[93]Pope John Paul II, *Dives in Misericordia*, 8; Romanus Cessario, "Moral Absolutes in the Civilization of Love," in *Crisis* 13 (May 1995): 21.

[94]Pope John Paul II, *Redemptor Hominis*, 8. See also Pope John Paul II, *Centesimus Annus*, 47; *Laborem Exercens*, 1; Mary Craig, *Man from a Far Country. A Portrait of Pope John Paul II*, London: Hodder And Stoughton, 1982, 150; Raymond T. Gawronski, "Redemptor Hominis," in *The Thought of Pope John Paul II*, Rome: Gregorian University, 1993, 222.

[95]See Paul L. Peeters, "*Dominum et Vivificantem*: The Conscience and the Heart," in *Communio* 15 (1988): 148.

economy of salvation.[96] Christ Himself, as God–man, is the perfect and substantial image of the Father and, being a perfect man, perfectly reflects in Himself the image of God in man. The image and likeness that God intended man to have from the beginning but was disfigured by the first sin is now reproduced in an ever perfect way in Christ, God and man. As far as this concept is concerned, there is a parallel to this text of *Redemptor Hominis*, 8 in *Redemptionis Donum* 4: "For this Redemption gives back to God the work of creation which had been contaminated by sin, showing the perfection which the whole of creation, and in particular man, possesses in the thought and intention of God Himself."[97]

So the link between the good creation and God as its source, broken by Adam, was restored through the intervention of Christ who fully reveals the Father and ontologically renews the interiority, the 'heart' of man.[98] The renewal of man is not only social, emotional and psychological, it reaches the very ontological being of the human person:

> In the mystery of the Redemption man becomes newly 'expressed' and, in a way, is newly created...The man who wishes to understand himself thoroughly—and not just in accordance with immediate, partial, often superficial, and even illusory standards and measures of his being—he must with unrest, uncertainty and even his weakness and sinfulness, with his life and death, draw near to Christ. He must, so to speak, enter into him with all his own self, he must 'appropriate' and assimilate the whole of the reality of the Incarnation and Redemption in order to find himself. If this profound process takes place within him, he then bears fruit not only of adoration of God but also of deep wonder at himself.[99]

The mystery of the Incarnate Word penetrates into the deepest dimension of human consciousness and reaches the very inner mystery of man: "To man, created to the image of God, the Holy Spirit gives the gift of conscience, so that in this conscience the image may faithfully reflect its model, which is both Wisdom and eternal Law, the source of the moral order in man and in the

---

[96]See also Pope John Paul II, *Centesimus Annus*, 62; *Redemptionis Donum*, 4; Raymond T. Gawronski, "Redemptor Hominis," in *The Thought of Pope John Paul II*, Rome: Gregorian University, 1993, 222–223.

[97]Pope John Paul II, *Redemptionis Donum*, 4. See also Ibid., *Mulieris Dignitatem*, 11; Raymond T. Gawronski, "Redemptor Hominis," in *The Thought of Pope John Paul II*, Rome: Gregorian University, 1993, 222.

[98]See Pope John Paul II, *Redemptor Hominis*, 11; Raymond T. Gawronski, "Redemptor Hominis," in *The Thought of Pope John Paul II*, Rome: Gregorian University, 1993, 222–223.

[99]Pope John Paul II, *Redemptor Hominis*, 10. See also Pope John II, *Redemptoris Mater*, 52; *Centesimus Annus*, 62; Raymond T. Gawronski, "Redemptor Hominis," in *The Thought of Pope John Paul II*, Rome: Gregorian University, 1993, 223.

world."[100] The whole reality of man is revealed and understood only in the light of Christ, because the theocentric revelation of God necessarily contains an anthropological dimension and "Christian anthropology therefore is really a chapter of theology."[101] *Veritatis Splendor* speaks of the anthropological implications resulting from Divine Revelation: "What man is and what he must do becomes clear as soon as God reveals himself."[102] Pope Paul VI affirmed that "in order to know man, authentic man, man in his fullness, one must know God."[103] Paul VI went on to quote Saint Catherine of Siena, who expressed the same idea: "In your nature, O eternal Godhead, I shall know my own nature."[104] Pope John Paul II quoted both Pope Paul VI and Saint Catherine in *Centesimus Annus*.[105] The relationship between man and the Incarnation does not take place *ad extra*, on the outside dimension of man. It is a relationship of new creation, parallel to the relationship of dependency that starts with creation *ex nihilo* of the human person.[106] Creation and Redemption are parallel mysteries: both are intended to create man in the image and likeness of the Creator. Creation creates man *ex nihilo* to be a living being in the world; Redemption ontologically recreates this same human being into a new creature united to Christ. In *Redemptor Hominis*, Pope John Paul II affirms that the re–creation of man through the mystery of Redemption happens at the ontological level:

> This union of Christ with man is in itself a mystery. From the mystery is born 'the new man,' called to become a partaker of God's life, and newly created in Christ for the fullness of grace and truth. Christ's union with man is power and the source of power, as Saint John stated so incisively in the prologue of his Gospel: '(The Word) gave power to become children of God.' Man is transformed inwardly by this power as the source of a new life that does not disappear and pass away but lasts to eternal life. This life which the Father has promised and offered to each man in Jesus Christ, his eternal and only Son, who, 'when the time had fully come,' became incarnate and was born of the Virgin Mary, is the final fulfillment of man's vocation. It is in a way

---

[100]Pope John Paul II, *Dominum et Vivificantem*, 36.

[101]Pope John Paul II, *Centesimus Annus*, 55. See also Pope John Paul II, *Laborem Exercens*, 1; *Veritatis Splendor*, 10; Romanus Cessario, "Moral Absolutes in the Civilization of Love," in *Crisis* 13 (May 1995): 20; Joseph Cardinal Cordeiro, "The religious sense of man," in *John Paul II. A Panorama of his Teachings*, New York: New City Press, 1989, 65–66.

[102]Pope John Paul II, *Veritatis Splendor*, 10.

[103]Pope Paul VI, Homily at the Final Public Session of the Second Vatican Ecumenical Council (December 7, 1965): *AAS* 58 (1966), 58.

[104]*Ibid.*

[105]Pope John Paul II, *Centesimus Annus*, 55.

[106]See Pope John Paul II, *Redemptor Hominis*, 13; *Redemptionis Donum*, 4.

the fulfillment of the 'destiny' that God has prepared for him from eternity.[107]

The Incarnation of the Son is not only a restoration of creation to its original status before the fall. Christ's redeeming activity does not only reveal the original beauty of God's creation, but also elevates the nature of every human person to a new ontological level:[108]

> God, as Christ has revealed him, does not merely remain closely linked with the world as the Creator and the ultimate source of existence. He is also Father: he is linked to man, whom he called to existence in the visible world, by a bond still more intimate than that of creation. It is love which not only creates the good but also grants participation in the very life of God: Father, Son and Holy Spirit. For he who loves desires to give himself.[109]

The text of *Redemptor Hominis*, 20, that we need to analyze is outlined in a deep reflection of the theology of the Eucharist:

> The 'price' of our Redemption is likewise a further proof of the value that God himself sets on man and of our dignity in Christ. For by becoming 'children of God,' adopted sons, we also become in his likeness 'a kingdom and priests' and obtain 'a royal priesthood,' that is to say we share in that unique and irreversible restoration of man and the world to the Father that was carried out once for all by him, who is both the eternal Son and also true Man. The Eucharist is the sacrament in which our new being is most completely expressed and in which Christ himself unceasingly and in an ever new manner 'bears witness' in the Holy Spirit to our spirit that each of us, as a sharer in the mystery of the Redemption, has access to the fruits of the filial reconciliation with God that he himself actuated and continually actuates among us by means of the Church's ministry.[110]

By *new* it is not meant what John Paul means when he speaks of *new evangelization*. New evangelization is not new in its content, because the Gospel is always the same. New evangelization means a new way of expressing and communicating it, albeit accurately and faithfully, to all people.[111] In this case, the new way of revealing the fundamental truth of

---

[107]Pope John Paul II, *Redemptor Hominis*, 18. See also *Redemptor Hominis*, 20.

[108]See Karol Wojtyla, *Sources of Renewal: The Implementation of the Second Vatican Council*, San Francisco: Harper and Row, 1980, 133–138; Pope John Paul II, *Redemptor Hominis*, 10; *Redemptionis Donum*, 4.

[109]Pope John Paul II, *Dives in Misericordia*, 7.

[110]Pope John Paul II, *Redemptor Hominis*, 20.

[111]Pope John Paul II, *Centesimus Annus*, 5; *Pastores Dabo Vobis*, 70; Joseph A. Loya, "John Paul II's Encyclical *Slavorum Apostoli*: An Ecumenical Assessment." In *Ecumenical Trends* 14 (1985): 168; Josef Kalvoda, "The Cyrilo–Methodian Idea." In *The Priest* 42 (February 1986): 18.

creation means a new approach to the reality of creation itself. The ontological reality of creation acquires a new dimension because God the Son assumed a new dimension:[112] human nature. In the same way that creation *ex nihilo* brings a being out of nothing, "in the mystery of the Redemption man becomes newly 'expressed' and, in a way, is newly created!"[113] Redemption as a new creation, happens *ex nihilo* because it brings a being *ex nihilo* to a new creation. Both creations are ontological and both happen on the level of the innermost being of the human person. Again in *Redemptor Hominis*, John Paul II says:

> This revelation of the Father and outpouring of the Holy Spirit, which stamp an indelible seal on the mystery of the Redemption, explain the meaning of the Cross and death of Christ. The God of creation is revealed as the God of Redemption, as the God who is "faithful to himself (1 Thess 5:24)," and faithful to his love for man and the world, which he revealed on the day of creation.[114]

The entrance of the Son of God in history has sanctified all the elements of creation. Both creation and Redemption are oriented to make man a sharer in the eternity of God. But man lives in space and time; therefore, Redemption has to have a *cosmic dimension*.[115] Commenting on the words of St. Paul in Galatians 4:4, Pope John Paul II says in *Redemptoris Mater*: "This 'fullness' marks the moment when, with the entrance of the eternal into time, time itself is redeemed, and being filled with the mystery of Christ becomes definitively 'salvation time.' "[116] The pope explains that the expression 'fullness' cannot be considered only as "the conclusion of a chronological process but also and especially the coming to maturity or completion of a particularly important period, one directed toward the fulfillment of an expectation, a coming to completion which thus takes on an eschatological dimension."[117] So not only is man being 'newly created' but also time is being newly transformed into a history of salvation. Again in *Redemptoris Mater*, John Paul says: "In the

---

[112]See also Pope John Paul II, *Catechesi Tradendae*, 29; *Pastores Dabo Vobis*, 55.

[113]Pope John Paul II, *Redemptor Hominis*, 9. See also Ibid., *Catechesi Tradendae*, 20; *Redemptionis Donum*, 7.

[114]Pope John Paul II, *Redemptor Hominis*, 9.

[115]See also Pope John Paul II, *Dominum et Vivificantem*, 50; *Reconciliatio et Paenitentia*, 7; Michael O'Carroll, "Dominum et Vivificantem," in *Veni Creator Spiritus: A Theological Encyclopedia of the Holy Spirit*, Collegeville: Liturgical Press, 1990, 72.

[116]Pope John Paul II, *Redemptoris Mater*, 1. See also Ibid., *Redemptoris Mater*, 49; *Dominum et Vivificantem*, 49; *Mulieris Dignitatem*, 3.

[117]*The Encyclicals of John Paul II*, Edited with Introductions by Michael Miller, Indiana: Our Sunday Visitor Publishing Division, Our Sunday Visitor, Inc., 1996, 354: Pope John Paul II, *Redemptoris Mater*, 1, note 2.

following reflections we wish to concentrate first of all on the present, which in itself is not yet history, but which nevertheless is constantly forming it, also in the sense of the history of salvation."[118] Since, in the Incarnation, time has been transformed into salvation time because it is filled with the mystery of Christ, the regular normal history of souls has become history of salvation. In *Dominum et Vivificantem*, 49, the Pope again describes the fullness of time in which "human history has been wholly permeated by the 'measurement' of God himself: a transcendent presence of the eternal 'now.' "

In *Redemptoris Mater*, John Paul analyzes Ephesians 1:3 and draws a parallel to Gal 4:4. He uses Ephesians to designate the Father's eternal plan of creation and Galatians to designate His eternal plan of Redemption. In the text, a perfect parallel between the time of creation and the time of Redemption is drawn:

> These words of the Letter to the Ephesians reveal the eternal design of God the Father, his plan of man's salvation in Christ. It is a universal plan, which concerns all men and women created in the image and likeness of God (cf. Gen 1:26). Just as all are included in the creative work of God 'in the beginning,' so all are eternally included in the divine plan of salvation, which is to be completely revealed, in the 'fullness of time,' with the final coming of Christ.[119]

Later on in *Tertio Millennio Adveniente*, Pope John Paul II picked up the same theological idea of the cosmic implications resulting from the theology of Redemption. It is evident that the Pope does not attribute the existence of a spiritual soul to any other creature but man. The cosmic dimension of Christ's redeeming activity recuperates the original order of creation in its relation to man. Therefore, there exists a certain parallel between time as inserted in the order of creation and time as inserted in the order of Redemption. The 'fullness of time' as conceived by God eternally reveals itself to be the 'redemption' of time, in the same way the order of Redemption has eternally been prefigured by God as concomitant with the order of creation:

> The fact that in the fullness of time the Eternal Word took on the condition of a creature gives a unique cosmic value to the event which took place in Bethlehem two thousand years ago. Thanks to the Word, the world of creatures appears as a 'cosmos,' an ordered universe. And it is the same Word who, by taking flesh, renews the cosmic order of creation.[120]

John Paul follows the traditional thought of St. Thomas Aquinas, according

---

[118]Pope John Paul II, *Redemptoris Mater*, 6; *Mulieris Dignitatem*, 3.

[119]Pope John Paul II, *Redemptoris Mater*, 7.

[120]Pope John Paul II, *Tertio Millennio Adveniente*, 3. See also *Ibid.*, 9–10.

to which the grace of creation was perfected by the supernatural grace of Redemption. By 'fullness of grace' the Pope confirms that the grace of God that was given to man in the very act of creation reaches its fullness in the mystery of Redemption. It is not meant that the grace of creation is deficient or is not sufficient to maintain man in life. However, because of the historical reality of sin, the act of creation had to be renewed through the act of recreation and, therefore, the supernatural grace of the Incarnation was necessary to grant to man the fullness of grace he was called to possess from the beginning of creation.[121]

So, against any implicit Pelagianism, the efforts of man to find himself can be successful only if the reality of Incarnation and Redemption is assimilated. At the same time, the grace of Redemption cannot work in human persons unless they take the initiative to assume all the dimensions of the Incarnation. The incarnate Word presents the possibility of Redemption and man, by his own free will, has to put into act this possibility: Redemption in act happens when man cooperates with God, although God is exclusively the Redeemer.[122] *Veritatis Splendor* reports the inseparable connection between the Lord's grace and human freedom: the famous prayer of St. Augustine, "Da quod iubes et iube quod vis (grant what you command and command what you will)," serves to demonstrate that intimate link.[123] By few words of *Centesimus Annus*, Pope John Paul II summarizes the theory of cooperation between God and man in Redemption: "Grace, in cooperation with human freedom, constitutes that mysterious presence of God in history which is providence."[124]

The re–creation of the human person in the image and likeness of God, requires two conditions: the acting person has to be Divine and the human nature assumed by Him has to be assumed of the lump of Adam without the foreign element of sin.[125] Against any tendency of reducing Christ to a mere human being in solidarity with human beings, Pope John Paul II emphasizes the uniqueness of the Incarnation. The Incarnation of the Son, although it takes

---

[121]See German Grisez, "Veritatis Splendor: Revealed Truth versus Dissent," in Homiletic and Pastoral Review 94 (March 1994): 9.

[122]See Pope John Paul II, *Catechesi Tradendae*, 72, where he quotes St. Augustine: "Both (our believing and our doing good) are ours because of the choice of our will, and yet both are gifts from the Spirit of faith and charity." (*Retractationum Liber I*, 23, 2: PL 32, 621) See also Romanus Cessario, "Moral Absolutes in the Civilization of Love," in *Crisis* 13 (May 1995): 21.

[123]See St. Augustine, *Confessiones*, X, 29, 40: CCL 27, 176; Pope John Paul II, *Veritatis Splendor*, 24; German Grisez, "Veritatis Splendor: Revealed Truth versus Dissent," in Homiletic and Pastoral Review 94 (March 1994): 8.

[124]Pope John Paul II, *Centesimus Annus*, 59; German Grisez, "Veritatis Splendor: Revealed Truth versus Dissent," in Homiletic and Pastoral Review 94 (March 1994): 9.

[125]See Pope John Paul II, *Tertio Millennio Adveniente*, 4.

place in space and time, is still a transcendental event: "God entered the history of humanity and, as man, became an *actor* in that history, one of the thousands of millions of human beings but at the same time *unique!*"[126]

The picture of the Son in the Incarnation is very close to Hans Urs von Balthasar's perception, according to which God himself is the one who steps "forth onto the world stage as a particular and special character vis–à–vis other particular and special characters."[127] There is no doubt, however, that the designation of the Son as an actor has its roots in the Pope's Christian personalism and in his experience as an actor who performed many theatrical shows. The choice of the expression *actor* is of extreme importance in *Redemptor Hominis*: it brings the Son, as a man, down to the level of human being. The situation of the Son is identified with the most concrete situation of every man in this world: He is one among His brethren. The image of the actor is a different way of expressing the Johannine verse: "the Word became flesh and dwelt among us."[128] The Pope quotes this verse just before referring to the image of the actor. *Dwelt among us* is in Greek *eskenosen* which means, in its literary sense, He settled his tent among us. The expression *actor*, at the same time, stands in paradoxical contradiction to the *uniqueness* of the Incarnate Word. He is among us as one of us, yet He is still unique.

One of the anthropological implications of Redemption is the freedom given to man by Christ. How does John Paul connect freedom to truth in the overall picture of salvation? In *Veritatis Splendor*, Pope John Paul II, describing the *Auseinandersetzung* between moral theologians and the Magisterium of the Church in respect to many moral issues, points out the roots of dissent by saying:

> It is no longer a matter of limited and occasional dissent, but of an overall and systematic calling into question of traditional moral doctrine, on the basis of certain anthropological and ethical presuppositions. At the root of these presuppositions is the more or less obvious influence of currents of thought which end by detaching human freedom from its essential and constitutive relationship to truth.[129]

The reason for such a false contradiction between truth and freedom resides in the several currents of thought in ethics that have given rise to an alleged conflict between freedom and law. Although far–reaching by its very nature, freedom cannot be unlimited because it is called to accept the divine law of

---

[126]Pope John Paul II, *Redemptor Hominis*, 1.

[127]H.U.v. Balthasar, *Theodrama II. Dramatis Personae: Man in God*, San Francisco, 1990, 189.

[128]Jn 1:14.

[129]Pope John Paul II, *Veritatis Splendor*, 4.

God and halt before the tree of knowledge of good and evil. By obeying that law, human freedom finds its authentic and complete fulfillment. By establishing a false dichotomy between human freedom and divine law, such currents of thought allow individuals and groups to determine what is good and what is evil, as if human freedom were able to create values and enjoy a primacy over truth. In that case, truth would become a creation of freedom and, consequently, "freedom would thus lay claim to a moral autonomy which would actually amount to an absolute sovereignty."[130]

In the opinion of Pope John Paul II, freedom and truth are intimately connected:[131] human freedom cannot be detached from "obedience to the truth."[132] The words of St. John the Evangelist: "You will know the truth, and the truth will make you free (Jn 8:32)," contain both

> ...a fundamental requirement and a warning: the requirement of an honest relationship with regard to truth as a condition for authentic freedom, and the warning to avoid every kind of illusory freedom, every superficial unilateral freedom, every freedom that fails to enter into the whole truth about man and the world.[133]

As an exclusive gift from God, "freedom attains its full development only by accepting the truth."[134] Since the truth about God and the human person is revealed to humanity through the twofold mystery of creation and Redemption, freedom is bound to the truth which God makes available.[135]

Consequently, when freedom is detached from objective truth, it degenerates into license:

---

[130]Pope John Paul II, *Veritatis Splendor*, 35; Giacomo Cardinal Biffi, "The Action of the Holy Spirit in the Church and in the World," in *John Paul II. A Panorama of his Teachings*, New York: New City Press, 1989, 43; Manuel Ureña, "The Missionary Impulse in the Church according to Redemptoris Missio," in *Communio* 19 (1992): 95.

[131]See Karol Wojtyla, *The Acting Person*, 155, 162, 165, 172, 235 and 288; *Amore e Responsabilità*, 103, 105; Pope John Paul II, *Centesimus Annus*, 12; *Dives in Misericordia*, 11; *Spiritus Domini*, 3; *Veritatis Splendor*, 31; *Evangelium Vitae*, 19 and 96; *Letter to Families from Pope John Paul II*, 13; *Vita Consecrata*, 91; John M. McDermott, "The Theology of John Paul II. A Response," in *The Thought of Pope John Paul II*, John M. McDermott (ed.), Rome: Gregorian University, 1993, 59; James Schall, "*Redemptor Hominis*: The Amazement of God," *Homiletic and Pastoral Review* 80 (October 1979): 16.

[132]*Centesimus Annus*, 17.

[133]*Redemptor Hominis*, 12.

[134]Pope John Paul II, *Centesimus Annus*, 46. See also Robert Morneau, "*Redemptor Hominis*: Themes and Thesis," in *Review for Religious* 39 (1980): 257.

[135]See Manuel Ureña, "The Missionary Impulse in the Church according to Redemptoris Missio," in *Communio* 19 (1992): 95; *Encyclicals of John Paul II*, Edited with Introductions by Michael Miller, Indiana: Our Sunday Visitor Publishing Division, Our Sunday Visitor, Ins., 1996, 579.

The Mystery of the Trinity

A person who is concerned solely or primarily with possessing and enjoying, who is no longer able to control his instincts and passions, or to subordinate them by obedience to the truth, cannot be free: obedience to the truth about God and man is the first condition of freedom, making it possible for a person to order his needs and desires and to choose the means of satisfying them according to a correct scale of values.[136]

In the same *Centesimus Annus*, Pope John Paul II attests to the importance of Pope Leo XIII's Encyclical *Libertas Praestantissimum*[137] regarding the relationship between freedom and truth. Pope Leo's Encyclical "called attention to the essential bond between human freedom and truth, so that freedom which refused to be bound to the truth would fall into arbitrariness and end up submitting itself to the vilest of passions, to the point of self–destruction."[138]

Predestination

The anthropological implications of the divine dimension of Redemption do not lead Pope John Paul II to fall into the trap of *predestination*. Predestination is a theological doctrine "proclaiming 'God's unchangeable decision for eternity of all that is to be' and 'God's destination of men to everlasting happiness or misery.' "[139] Yes, man's destiny is eternally willed by God to be a sharing in His immeasurable life: from eternity God has thought of us and loved us as unique individuals. In the unfolding of history, God reveals His plan to every man in a gradual process that happens day by day.[140] But man with his free will is able to oppose and change God's plan for his life. Therefore, it is not proper to say that man's destiny will take place according to God's eternal plan, since man is in reality able to change this plan. In *Familiaris Consortio*, John Paul recurs to St. Augustine to elucidate the question: "This shows that history is not simply a fixed progression towards what is better, but rather an event of freedom, and even a struggle between freedoms that are in mutual conflict, that is, according to the well–known expression of St. Augustine, a conflict between two loves: the love of God to the point of disregarding self, and the love of self to the point of disregarding

---

[136]*Centesimus Annus*, 41.

[137]Pope Leo XIII, *Encyclical Libertas Praestantissimum*, June 20, 1888.

[138]Pope John Paul II, *Centesimus Annus*, 591–592.

[139]Tad Szulc, *Pope John Paul II. The Biography*, New York: Scribner, 1995, 53.

[140]Pope John Paul II, *Christifideles Laici*, 58; Angelo Scola, " 'Claim' of Christ, 'Claim' of the World: On the Trinitarian Encyclicals of John Paul II," in *Communio* 18 (1991): 324; André Frossard, *Portrait of John Paul II*, San Francisco: Ignatius Press, 1990, 168–169.

God."[141]   To prove the same point in *Veritatis Splendor*, 43, Aquinas now becomes the Pope's theologian of reference: God provides for man not 'from without,' i.e. through the laws of physical nature, but 'from within,' through reason that is able, by the natural knowledge of God's eternal law, to show man the right direction to take in his free actions. Man's own physical and spiritual constitutions provide him with all the necessary power to unfold God's eternal plan in history, especially that God has revealed Himself in and through Jesus Christ. "In this way God calls man to participate in his own providence, since he desires to guide the world—not only the world of nature but also the world of human persons—through man himself, through man's reasonable and responsible care."[142]   Again, in *Pastores Dabo Vobis* and in the context of priestly vocation, John Paul proclaims the destiny of man as the result of the encounter between God's grace and human freedom. Predestination does not reflect the face of God as revealed in and through Jesus Christ. Predestination is widespread because more and more people have a confused idea of God which compromises the interaction between the free divine initiative of grace and the human response. As a consequence, their religiosity becomes a religiosity without God since, implicitly, "God's will is seen as an immutable and unavoidable fate to which one has to bend and resign oneself in a totally passive manner."[143]

In his *Letter to the Families* (1994), John Paul approaches the problem of predestination from a different perspective, referring to the theology of St. Augustine. The question that arises is this: how is it possible that God wills man "for his own sake" whereas he is created to share in the divine life of God? Can man truly exist "for his own sake" if he is destined for an eschatological destiny that is totally immersed in the Being of God? What is the relationship between the life of the person and its eschatological fulfillment in sharing in the life of the Trinity? There is no doubt that "it might appear that in destining man for divine life God definitively takes away man's existing 'for his own sake.'" St. Augustine's famous words, "our heart is restless until it rests in thee," sheds a new light on John Paul's understanding of the question: between the two finalities of man's existence, that is, between earthly existence and his destiny as willed by God, there is no contradiction. Actually, there is a perfect complementarity and unity between man who, by his very genealogy as a creature in God's image, exists "for his own sake" and the fulfillment of

[141]St. Augustine, *De Civitate Dei*, XIV, 28: CSEL 40, II, 56–57; Pope John Paul II, *Familiaris Consortio*, 6; André Frossard, *Portrait of John Paul II*, San Francisco: Ignatius Press, 1990, 78.

[142]See St. Thomas Aquinas, *Summa Theologiae*, I–II, q. 90, a. 4, ad 1; Pope John Paul II, *Veritatis Splendor*, 43.

[143]Pope John Paul II, *Pastores Dabo Vobis*, 37.

his earthly existence by sharing in God's life. The very act of creating man in God's image presupposes an eschatological fulfillment because the content of man's self–fulfillment on earth is "the fullness of life in God, proclaimed by Christ (cf. Jn 6:37–40), who redeemed us precisely so that we might come to share it (cf. Mk 10:45)." At the moment of conception itself, man is already destined to eternity in God, although "our human will is always and inevitably subject to the law of time and change. The divine will, on the other hand, is eternal."[144] A perfect harmony and complementarity between the destiny of man as willed by God and his earthly existence cannot compromise his free will and its subjection to the laws of human change: man is still able to change God's eternal plan for his life. *Vita Consecrata* refers to the example of the saints, the great champions of apostolic activity who "have always taught...that we need to trust in God as if everything depended on him and, at the same time, to work generously as if everything depended on us."[145]

What does man's original destiny as prethought by God (creation–glory) mean for man's history couched freedom? How can an immutable God, who from the beginning wanted man to be glorified in Christ, relate to historical man endowed with authentic freedom? A christocentric vision of man, still far from falling into blind Fideism, is the only answer. Only a superficial study that ignored the dynamism of human freedom could turn the christocentric approach to anthropology into fideism. It is in the works of Grillmeier and von Balthasar that John Paul finds his answer:[146] "objective christocentrism," an expression that is not used by John Paul, is the train of thought followed by the Pope in seeking an answer to the problem of predestination. The dynamic nature of the human freedom, just mentioned, does not allow a christ–centered explanation become Fideism or predestination. In the salvific logic of God, Christ "becomes the original whole within which the research of human reason unfolds itself, respected in its autonomy, as long as it does not attempt to close the circle by itself." Human reason is constantly invited to be open to the fulfillment of God's grace: this fulfillment is a necessity that offers itself simply as a hypothesis to be posited by reason without a direct capacity on the part of reason to describe its detail. This kind of objective christocentrism creates a constant cooperation between reason and faith, nature and the supernatural, without any confusion of these elements with each other in the

---

[144]See Pope John Paul II, *Letter to Families from Pope John Paul II*, 9; St. Augustine, *Confessiones* I, 1: CCL 27, 1.

[145]Pope John Paul II, *Vita Consecrata*, 73.

[146]See Angelo Scola, " 'Claim' of Christ, 'Claim' of the World: On the Trinitarian Encyclicals of John Paul II," in *Communio* 18 (1991): 326–327; Hans Urs von Balthasar, "Résumé of My Thought," *Communio* 15, 4 (Winter, 1988): 468–473.

united reality which is the christic whole.[147] Christocentrism therefore gives an answer to the enigma of man not in the sense of preemptively deciding his fate, but in radicalizing it. To man is left the decision of selecting the mechanism of Redemption in which Christ's response to the relationship between man's historicity and God's predestination for him in Christ, determines the ultimate outcome. The fundamental anthropological *datum* which finds in Christ its radicalization and not its preemptive decision, sheds light on the question of the true meaning of predestination: no other answer can be given to man and yet his freedom can fail to ratify that answer. Based on that, history becomes the unfolding of God's infinite freedom and answer in Christ as encountered by man's limited and finite freedom. To the degree that finite freedom withdraws itself from this encounter, the initiative of the father of lies inserts itself on the stage. Thus, man's life experiences a continual dialectic between an objective christocentrism that offers Redemption and man's freedom to encounter or not encounter God's free Redemption. As a result of that indispensable christocentric dimension of approach to anthropology, the anthropology does not die because man's mystery is understood thanks to the context of the christic whole. It is in that sense that John Paul II understands *Gaudium et Spes'* "Christ reveals man to himself."

---

[147]Angelo Scola, " 'Claim' of Christ, 'Claim' of the World: On the Trinitarian Encyclicals of John Paul II," in *Communio* 18 (1991): 326.

CHAPTER FIVE

THE CHRISTOLOGY OF POPE JOHN PAUL II
AND CONTEMPORARY CHRISTOLOGICAL TRENDS

Introduction

Within six months of assuming the Petrine ministry, Pope John Paul II started to set forth his trinitarian theology by signing his first Encyclical Letter *Redemptor Hominis* in which he, as he himself confesses in *Redemptoris Missio*, 4, sets forth the program of his pontificate. It is a deep and reflective presentation on the Incarnation of the Second Person of the Trinity and His redeeming activity: It places the Incarnation at the center of God's plan of salvation.[1] The Encyclical outlines the Pope's anthropological and Christological vision. In announcing its publication at an Angelus he said:

> The Encyclical contains those thoughts which then, at the beginning of this new life, were pressing with particular forcefulness in my mind and which, certainly, had already been maturing in me previously, during the years of my service as a priest, and then as a bishop. I am of the opinion that, if Christ called me in this way with such thoughts..., it was because he wanted these calls of the intellect and of the heart...to ring out in my new and universal ministry, right from its beginning. Therefore as I see and feel the relationship between the Mystery of the Redemption in Christ Jesus and the dignity of man, so I would like so much to unite the mission of the Church with service of man in his impenetrable mystery. I see in that the central task of my new ecclesial service.[2]

---

[1] See Pope John Paul II, *Tertio Millennio Adveniente*, 15; *Catechesi Tradendae*, 5–6; *Reconciliatio et Paenitentia*, 10; *Redemptoris Custos*, 1; *Letter of the Pope to Children in the Year of the Family*, Pauline Books and Media, 1994, 8–10; J. Honoré, "Christ the Redeemer, Core of John Paul's Teaching," in *John Paul II. A Panorama of his Teachings*, New York: New City Press, 1989, 12–13; Raymond T. Gawronski, "Redemptor Hominis," in *The Thought of Pope John Paul II*, Rome: Gregorian University, 1993, 222; Angelo Scola, "'Claim' of Christ, 'Claim' of the World: On the Trinitarian Encyclicals of John Paul II," in *Communio* 18 (1991): 322; Ibid., "Con Cristo al cuore dell'uomo," *Synesis* 6 (1989): 1–2 and 47–61; John Saward, *Christ is the Answer. The Christ–Centered Teaching of Pope John Paul II*, New York: Alba House, 1995, 3–10.

[2] Angelus, March 11, 1979, *L'Osservatore Romano* 12 (March 19, 1979): 2. See also *The Encyclicals of John Paul II*, Edited with Introductions by J. Michael Miller, Indiana: Our Sunday

Many years later, in his *Crossing the Threshold of Hope* Pope John Paul II commented again on the publication of *Redemptor Hominis* affirming that "I was actually carrying its content within me. I had only to 'copy' from memory and experience what I had already been living on the threshold of the papacy."[3] The fundamental truths of Incarnation and Redemption are linked to John Paul II's Petrine ministry from its first moment:[4] *Redemptor Hominis* (1979), his first Encyclical, inaugurates the present Pontificate[5] and is concerned with the identity and the work of the Incarnate Son. The christocentricity of John Paul presents itself as a *nexus mysteriorum*, that is the connection of each revealed truth with the person of Jesus Christ and his redemptive actions. In a society where "contemporary theological journals are full of efforts to 'de–incarnationalize,' as it were, Christ," and where "certain political options require for intellectual integrity a non–divine, non–unique Christ,"[6] the first words of the new Supreme Pontiff were spoken out very loudly:"The Redeemer of man, Jesus Christ, is the center of the universe and of history."[7] And "Jesus Christ is the chief way for the Church. He himself is our way to the Father's house (Jn 14:1 ff.) and is the way to each man."[8] While Vatican II's *Lumen Gentium* and *Dei Verbum* have given a strong emphasis to christocentrism, *Redemptor Hominis* picks up the themes of Vatican II and deepens them further.[9]

The impassioned cry that was heard at the beginning of his Petrine ministry, "do not be afraid! Open, indeed, open wide the doors to Christ!,"[10] will re–echo throughout his whole Pontificate. He calls the Incarnation *key truth of faith*,[11]

Visitor Publishing Division, Our Sunday Visitor, Inc., 1996, 31.

[3]Pope John Paul II, *Crossing the Threshold of Hope*, New York: Random House, 1994, 48.

[4]See Pope John Paul II, *Redemptor Hominis*, 2.

[5]See Pope John Paul II, *Redemptor Hominis*, 3.

[6]James Schall, "*Redemptor Hominis*: The Amazement of God," *Homiletic and Pastoral Review* 80 (October 1979): 11–19. See also Mary Craig, *Man from a Far Country. A Portrait of Pope John Paul II*, London: Hodder And Stoughton, 1982, 143.

[7]Pope John Paul II, *Redemptor Hominis*, 1. See also Gregory Baum, "The first Encyclical," in *The Ecumenist* 17 (1979): 56.

[8]Pope John Paul II, *Redemptor Hominis*, 13.

[9]See Gerard Philips, *La Chiesa e il suo mistero*, vol. 1, Milano, 1969, 69–70; J. Honoré, "Christ the Redeemer, Core of John Paul's Teaching," in *John Paul II. A Panorama of his Teachings*, New York: New City Press, 1989, 12–13.

[10]See Pope John Paul II, *Christifideles Laici*, 34; Peter Hebblethwaite, *Pope John Paul II and the Church*, Kansas City: Sheed and Ward, 1995, 62.

[11]Pope John Paul II, *Redemptor Hominis*, 1; *Dominum et Vivificantem*, 49.

the first fundamental truth,[12] and *the fundamental event in the economy of salvation,*[13] because, as expressed in *Redemptoris Missio*, "the whole economy of salvation has its center in Christ."[14] With the influence of Ephesians 1:10 and St. Irenaeus, *Reconciliatio et Paenitentia* places the Incarnation at the center of God's economy of salvation:"For, according to our faith, the Word of God became flesh and came to dwell in the world; he entered into the history of the world, summing it up and recapitulating it in himself."[15] Christ, in *Pastores Dabo Vobis*, 10, is "the Lord and Master, the key, the center and the purpose of the whole of human history."

The christocentrism of John Paul II is the key to the trinitarian triptych, *Redemptor Hominis*, *Dives in Misericordia*, and *Dominum et Vivificantem*. *Redemptoris Hominis* was followed by the Encyclical *Dives in Misericordia* (1980) on the Person of the Father, an Encyclical that is more theological and more immediately God–centered. It appeared in a very critical period filled with social catastrophes.[16] On the First Sunday of Advent in 1980, the Pope announced the reason for his second Encyclical Letter *Dives in Misericordia*, On The Mercy of God:"Its main purpose is to recall the Father's love, revealed in the whole messianic mission of Christ, beginning with his coming into the world up to the Paschal Mystery of his Cross and Resurrection."[17]

On May 18, 1986, Pope John Paul II published *Dominum et Vivificantem*, the last encyclical of his trinitarian trilogy and the longest treatment of the Holy Spirit in the papal Magisterium of any age.[18] It is a document that deals specifically with the Person of the Holy Spirit, His identity and role in the life of the Church and the world. Three parts make up this Encyclical: The Spirit of the Father and the Son given to the Church; The Spirit who convinces the world concerning sin; The Spirit who gives life. It has only a few patristic references, but the rich use of Holy Scripture in it is striking.

One reason for this Encyclical is to present the faith in the Holy Spirit that

[12]Pope John Paul II, *Redemptor Hominis*, 2.

[13]Pope John Paul II, *Redemptoris Mater*, 39. See also Ibid., *Mulieris Dignitatem*, 3.

[14]Pope John Paul II, *Redemptoris Missio*, 44.

[15]Pope John Paul II, *Reconciliatio et Paenitentia*, 10.

[16]See Joseph O'Hare, "Mercy Appears," *America* 143 (1980): 402.

[17]Angelus, November 30, 1980, *L'Osservatore Romano* 49 (1980): 2. See also Ralph Martin, "Rich in Mercy," in *New Covenant* 11 (July 1981): 20.

[18]See Cardinal Hamer's statement presenting the Encyclical to the Press, 30 May in English tr. Vatican Polyglot Press, Catholic Truth Society, London: *L'Osservatore Romano*, English ed. 9 June 1986, 16–17; Michael O'Carroll, "Dominum et Vivificantem," in *Veni Creator Spiritus: A Theological Encyclopedia of the Holy Spirit*. Collegeville: Liturgical Press, 1990, 70; André Frossard, *Portrait of John Paul II*, San Francisco: Ignatius Press, 1990, 101.

has been uninterruptedly professed by the Church, especially in recent years by Leo XIII's *Divinum Illud Munus* (1897), as well as Pius XII's *Mystici Corporis* (1943), and by the Second Vatican Council as reported by Pope Paul VI.[19] The second reason for this Encyclical is commemoration of the sixteenth centenary of the First Council of Constantinople, celebrated in 1981 simultaneously in Constantinople and Rome. This commemoration which constitutes "one of the most important ecclesial events of recent years," inspired the Pope to theologize on the Holy Spirit as the "supreme source of unity" between East and West.

With *Dominum et Vivificantem*, the full exposition of St. Paul's 2 Cor 13:13, "the grace of our Lord Jesus Christ (*Redemptor Hominis*) and the love of God (*Dives in Misericordia*) and the fellowship of the Holy Spirit (*Dominum et Vivificantem*) be with you all," comes to a completion.[20] At the dawn of the Second Millennium, the Holy Spirit, like the Father and the Son, stands "at the center of the Christian faith and is the source and dynamic power of the Church's renewal."[21]

All three Encyclicals, *Redemptor Hominis*, *Dives in Misericordia*, and *Dominum et Vivificantem*, although they form a well–planned trinitarian trilogy, still do not exhaust the thinking of the Pope about the Triune God. So, further investigation of the documents of John Paul II is necessary in order to create the fitting framework of his trinitarian theology. This theology will be presented in chapters six and seven of the present volume. For now, it is necessary to focus on the christology of John Paul II in its relationship with contemporary christology.

Pope John Paul II and Christology in Scripture

As a man of his time, Pope John Paul II reveals an extraordinary awareness of the christological trends that have been taking place in the Church, especially since the beginning of the 1980s.[22] He deals with these christological approaches in a comprehensive way, presenting skillfully and convincingly the consistent teaching of the Church. *Redemptor Hominis* and other writings of

---

[19]See Pope Paul VI, Address at General Audience (June 6, 1973): *Insegnamenti* XI (1973), 477.

[20]See Terrence Prendergast, "'A Vision of Wholeness': A Reflection on the Use of Scripture in a Cross–section of Papal Writings," in *The Thought of Pope John Paul II*, Rome: Gregorian University, 1993, 87–88; *The Encyclicals of John Paul II*, Edited with Introductions by Michael Miller, Indiana: Our Sunday Visitor Publishing Division, Our Sunday Visitor, Inc., 1996, 254; Pope John Paul II, *Pastores Dabo Vobis*, 12.

[21]Pope John Paul II, *Dominum et Vivificantem*, 2. See also Michael O'Carroll, "Dominum et Vivificantem," in *Veni Creator Spiritus: A Theological Encyclopedia of the Holy Spirit*. Collegeville: Liturgical Press, 1990, 70.

[22]See Pope John Paul II, *Tertio Millennio Adveniente*, 42.

Pope John Paul II deal with the attitude and the teaching of the Church toward these contemporary Christologies.[23] The Pope does not fly beyond the concrete situation of theology: he faces it explaining to the reader and convincing him or her about the reason behind the faith of the Church.[24] The contemporary christological currents are presented in this section with the clear yet concise views of Pope John Paul II.

Recently, there has been an obvious tendency shared by many theologians to re–evaluate *Christology in Scripture*.[25] The main line of thought in this type of Christology lies in focusing on the redemption of humankind as a historical event that happened through the concrete earthly Jesus of Nazareth. The story of Jesus is the fundamental basis for understanding the pre–existent Christ, the paschal Christ and the post–paschal Christ. Pope John Paul II does not explicitly enter into theological argument with Bultmann or any other theological school that separates the historical Jesus from the Christ of the Kerygma, but Bultmann's method was once criticized by the Pope in an interview with André Frossard. The Pope does not use the historical critical method in his hermeneutical approach to the Sacred Scriptures.[26] But he definitely establishes a continuity between the preexistent Word, the historical Jesus, and the Christ of faith. In *Redemptoris Missio* he says:

> Jesus is the Incarnate Word — a single and indivisible person. One cannot separate Jesus from the Christ or speak of a 'Jesus of history' who would differ from the 'Christ of faith.' The Church acknowledges and confesses Jesus as 'the Christ, the Son of the living God' (Mt 16:16): Christ is none other than Jesus of Nazareth; he is the Word of God made man for the salvation of all.[27]

---

[23]See Pope John Paul II, *Duodecimum Saeculum*, 8–9.

[24]See Pope John Paul II, *Catechesi Tradendae*, 5–9.

[25]See Commission Biblique Pontificale, *Bible et Christologie*, Paris: Cerf, 1984; Aldo Moda, *La Cristologia contemporanea nell'area Tedesca, Olandese, Francese e Italiana*, in Giovanni Iammarrone (a cura) *La Cristologia Contemporanea*, Padova: Edizioni Messagero Padova, 1992, 36–74; Angelo Amato, *Prospettive Cristologiche*, in *Ibid.*, 388–390.

[26]See Pope John Paul II, *Dominum et Vivificantem*, 21; André Frossard, *Portrait of John Paul II*, San Francisco: Ignatius Press, 1990, 106–108; Terrence Prendergast, "'A Vision of Wholeness': A Reflection on the Use of Scripture in a Cross–section of Papal Writings," in *The Thought of Pope John Paul II*, Rome: Gregorian University, 1993, 73–83 and 86; James Swetnam, "'A Vision of Wholeness': Response," in *The Thought of Pope John Paul II*, Rome: Gregorian University, 1993, 94; Manuel Ureña, "The Missionary Impulse in the Church according to *Redemptoris Missio*," in *Communio* 19 (1992): 97.

[27]Pope John Paul II, *Redemptoris Missio*, 6. See also Ibid., *Pastores Dabo Vobis*, 13; Terrence Prendergast, "'A Vision of Wholeness': A Reflection on the Use of Scripture in a Cross–section of Papal Writings," in *The Thought of Pope John Paul II*, Rome: Gregorian University, 1993, 86; James Swetnam, "'A Vision of Wholeness': Response," in *The Thought of Pope John Paul II*, Rome: Gregorian University, 1993, 94–95; Manuel Ureña, "The Missionary Impulse in the Church

The act of existence of the Person of Christ is the only guarantee for the continuity of his pre–existent personality, his historical identity and His post–resurrectional reality. The person, hypostasis, is the only reality that was present in the Word before assuming human nature, remained during the earthly existence of Jesus Christ, and is risen from the dead in a glorified human nature.[28]

Another method used by Pope John Paul II to display the continuity between the historical Jesus and the Christ of faith is the biblical data of the virginal conception of Mary. Like many other contemporary theologians,[29] for John Paul the *virginal conception* of Mary links the two moments of the pre– and the post–paschal period. Mary, as Virgin and Mother, experienced the historicity of God in the pre– and post paschal period thus linking the Annunciation with the paschal mystery and Pentecost. Her virginal conception therefore, assures the continuity in the identity of Christ, who, being of a divine origin, became man in the womb of a virgin and, after experiencing human life with all its dimensions except sin, died and was risen from the dead.

In my second volume on the Mariology of the Pope, *Mary in the Theology of Pope John Paul II: Immaculate Conception, Virgin, and Mother,* I will extensively treat the question of Mary. Here, however, it is sufficient to realize how implicit and hidden contemporary Gnosticism can influence the understanding of the Incarnation by attacking two areas: the virginity of Mary and the maleness of Jesus. Both areas are directly related to the bodily aspects of Divine Revelation. Note that Mary and Jesus are the two protagonists of the Incarnation: one is human and the other is human and divine. Humanity is the common element in both of them. Since Gnosticism tends to emphasize the spiritual and divine dimension of the Redemption at the expense of any human element that God has included in the economy of salvation, Mary's virginity and the maleness of Jesus become *per se* irrelevant theological realities. How does Pope John Paul II avoid Gnosticism when relating the Incarnation to the virginity of Mary, in whom "the hypostatic union of the Son of God with human nature, is accomplished and fulfilled"?[30] There is a theological tendency nowadays that considers the virginity of the Lord's Mother not an essential element in Divine Revelation. The argument runs as follows: as long

according to *Redemptoris Missio,*" in *Communio* 19 (1992): 97.

[28]See Terrence Prendergast, "'A Vision of Wholeness': A Reflection on the Use of Scripture in a Cross–section of Papal Writings," in *The Thought of Pope John Paul II,* Rome: Gregorian University, 1993, 86; James Swetnam, "'A Vision of Wholeness': Response," in *The Thought of Pope John Paul II,* Rome: Gregorian University, 1993, 95.

[29]See Johann G. Roten, *The Word of God made man by the Holy Spirit,* 13–14.

[30]Pope John Paul II, *Redemptoris Mater,* 9.

as Mary gives birth to God the Son, her virginity is not a constitutive dimension in God's plan of Redemption. In itself, the virginity of Mary is used by Gnostics to foster their theory concerning the spiritual flesh of Christ: they permit Mary's virginity as long as it serves their christological purpose. As a theological reality that belongs to the overall picture of God's plan of Redemption or as an element of Divine Revelation, Mary's virginity is generally disdained by Gnostics.

In Pope John Paul's theology, the virginity of Mary is a factor that determines the nature of the relationship between the Mother and the Son in the context of the Incarnation. The hypostatic union of the two natures in the Person of the incarnate Word *a priori* presupposes Mary's virginity. Since the motherhood of Mary is "a result of her total self–giving to God in virginity,"[31] the virginity of Mary is a theological reality that is intrinsically important in God's plan of salvation expressing the bodily aspect of Divine Revelation and eliminating Gnostic tendencies.

The other element that ensures a continuity between the historical Jesus and the Christ of the Kerygma is the *Paschal Mystery*. This Mystery reveals the mercy of the Father from a historical as well as from an eschatological point of view. The historical dimension of mercy is the direct result of the death and Resurrection of Christ who, sending down the Holy Spirit on the Apostles, gave them the power to forgive sins and revealed that here on earth and throughout human history, mercy is "more powerful than sin."[32] The eschatological dimension of mercy is manifested through the mutual love between the Son and the Father, a love that constitutes the basis of the Resurrection of Christ and is "more powerful than death."[33] Therefore, "the paschal Christ is the definitive incarnation of mercy, its living sign in salvation history and in eschatology."[34] Referring to the words of Mary in Lk 1:50: "His mercy is...from generation to generation," the Pope concludes:"At the very moment of the Incarnation, these words open up a new perspective of salvation history. After the Resurrection of Christ, this perspective is new on both the historical and the eschatological level."[35]

The final stage of Revelation of the Father in and through the Paschal Mystery of Jesus Christ is the evident guarantee of the continuity between the

---

[31]Pope John Paul II, *Redemptoris Mater*, 39. See also Ibid., *Mulieris Dignitatem*, 3.

[32]Pope John Paul II, *Dives in Misericordia*, 8. See also Ralph Martin, "Rich in Mercy," in *New Covenant* 11 (July 1981): 20.

[33]Pope John Paul II, *Dives in Misericordia*, 8. See also Ralph Martin, "Rich in Mercy," in *New Covenant* 11 (July 1981): 20.

[34]Pope John Paul II, *Dives in Misericordia*, 8.

[35]Pope John Paul II, *Dives in Misericordia*, 9.

historicity of the Revelation and its eschatological dimension. Jesus Christ, after his Resurrection, reveals the exact same face of the loving Father whose mercy, applied to the historical life of the Church, is more powerful than sin and, applied on the eschatological existence of human persons, is more powerful than death. The actuality of mercy is especially emphasized by the fact that mercy, as the summary of the messianic message of the Gospel, encapsules the core of the Old Testament's message about a merciful Father. With this actual mercy, *Dives in Misericordia* demonstrates the Pope's definitive refutation of any theological approach that would assert a contradiction between the Old Testament God of vengeance and the New Testament God of love.[36]

John Saward describes some of the feminist views concerning the maleness of Jesus saying:"The refusal of the feminists to ascribe any positive significance to the maleness of Jesus has led some of them to dust down the old Gnostic myth of an androgynous risen Christ."[37] Saward reacts against Elizabeth A. Johnson's argument that Jesus' maleness is "intrinsically important for his own historical identity and the historical challenge of his ministry, but not theologically determinative of his identity as the Christ."[38] For Johnson, Christ is a pneumatological reality, a creation [*sic*] of the Spirit who is not limited by whether one is Jew or Greek, slave or free, male or female.[39] Johnson's conclusion is then drawn: "Christ, in contrast to Jesus, is not male, or more exactly not exclusively male."[40] In Saward's opinion, Johnson

> ...takes up the heresy of the Gnostic Cerinthus by claiming that 'Jesus' and the 'Christ' are not strictly the same person...The Resurrection, on Johnson's view, would appear to destroy Jesus in His bodily and male humanity and replace Him with the androgynous figure of 'the whole Christ'.[41]

Saward thinks that contemporary feminism is fascinated with Gnosticism.[42]

---

[36]See Pinchas Lapide, "*Dives in Misericordia*: An Encyclical for Christians and Jews," in *Journal of Ecumenical Studies* 18 (1981): 140.

[37]John Saward, *Christ is the Answer. The Christ–Centered Teaching of Pope John Paul II*, xiv–xv, note 15.

[38]Elizabeth A. Johnson, *She Who is. The Mystery of God in Feminist Theological Discourse*, New York, 1992, 156.

[39]See *Ibid.*, 162.

[40]*Ibid.*

[41]John Saward, *Christ is the Answer. The Christ–Centered teaching of Pope John Paul II*, xiv–xv, note 15.

[42]See *Ibid.*

Saward's attitude is one of many theologians who are watching an implicit Gnosticism infiltrating not only into the theology, but also into the worship of the Church. This summary explains what is happening in the world of scriptural christology here at the end of the Second Millennium and Pope John Paul II shows a comprehensive awareness of all of these theological arguments, as will be evident below.

I do not think however that Elizabeth A. Johnson was claiming that the historical Jesus and the risen Christ are not strictly the same person, in the sense that Cerinthus did. Her intention was to emphasize that the Christ–event, although rooted in history, still enjoys a transcendental dimension that surpasses the limitations of the culture and the history of Jesus' life on earth. Johnson was trying to analyze the famous text of St. Paul's letter to the Galatians 3:27–28:"All baptized in Christ, you have all clothed yourselves in Christ, and there are no more distinctions between Jew and Greek, slave and free, male and female, but all of you are one in Christ Jesus."

Johnson's position in respect to the theological importance of Jesus' maleness jeopardizes another long tradition in the Church that started with St. Paul and was taken up by many Fathers of the Church: Christ is the new Adam who recapitulates in Himself the whole history of salvation. The sin introduced by Adam is canceled by the new Adam. The theory of recapitulation imposes as a necessity that the maleness of Jesus Christ should be theologically determinative of His identity as the Christ, because Christ is part of the history of salvation. Christ does not fall from heaven, He is the fulfillment of a long history of salvation that started with the creation of Adam and Eve and went through many stages in the Old Testament. A Christ that falls from heaven is a Gnostic Christ. In that specific culture, in that specific time, in those specific limitations, Christ, as Jesus, a male human being, fulfills the history of salvation.

It is not a question of discrimination or inequality between male and female. The proof lies in Galatians 3:28–29: everybody is looked at in the category of person, not male or female. I disagree nevertheless with Elizabeth Johnson that the maleness of Jesus is not theologically determinative of his identity as the Christ. First of all, in Galatians 3:27–28 St. Paul is looking at all human beings from a resurrectional point of view. This is not to erase the differences between Jews and Gentiles, male and female. The key is to look at all people in their personal reality: St. Paul considers them from the point of view of person. This approach maintains the functional difference between male and female but erases all cultural discrimination because they all are human persons. In *Mulieris Dignitatem*, 11, the hermeneutic of Galatians 3:28–29 is looked at by John Paul in terms of correction of a condition that was caused by that original division between man and woman. In the New Covenant, precisely, "in Christ the mutual opposition between man and woman — which is the inheritance of original sin — is essentially overcome."[43]

In regard to the maleness of Jesus and its theological importance, John Paul in *Mulieris Dignitatem*, 25, recurs to St. Paul's Letter to the Ephesians (5:25–32) where Christ and the Church are analogously described as the bridegroom and the bride. It is in this context of 'Great mystery' that the Pope analyzes the connection among God's love for His people in the Old Testament, Christ's love for His Church in the New Covenant, and the love between man and woman. Since the divine initiative of creation is based on the love of God that was manifested to His People from the beginning of creation, the same mechanism happens in the culmination of God's revelation in and through Jesus Christ. Christ's love for His Church is the definitive answer and Revelation of God's love for humanity. However, the concept of Church itself includes both man and woman. Therefore, "'being the bride,' and thus the 'feminine' element, becomes a symbol of all that is 'human'..." All human beings, men and women, are called to be the bride of Christ who "has entered this history and remains in it as the Bridegroom who 'has given himself...(as) a sincere gift in the most complete and radical way." It is not a matter of discrimination; it is rather dealt with here as an expression of the divine love of the Father humanly manifested in the person of Jesus of Nazareth. Since Christ incarnates in Himself the divine initiative of the Father's love, he and only He, as a man and at the same time as a Divine Person equal to the Father, can offer to the Church the whole measure of love that God had for humanity since the beginning of human history. Therefore, the establishment of a relationship between time and eternity in the context of salvation history should be very carefully defined. One cannot emphasize the transcendental and ahistorical identity of Christ at the expense of the historical Jesus or *vice versa*. The text of *Mulieris Dignitatem*, 25, elucidates the whole issue:

> Christ is the Bridegroom. This expresses the truth about the love of God who 'first loved us' (cf. 1 Jn 4:19) and who, with the gift generated by this spousal love for man, has exceeded all human expectations...The Bridegroom — the Son consubstantial with the Father as God — became son of Mary; he became the 'son of man,' true man, a male. The symbol of the Bridegroom is masculine. This masculine symbol represents the human aspect of the divine love which God has for Israel, for the Church, and for all people...Precisely because Christ's divine love is the love of a Bridegroom, it is the model and pattern of all human love, men's love in particular.[44]

Since God is absolutely beyond every creaturely category, the whole question

---

[43]See also Pope John Paul II, *Evangelium Vitae*, 99; *Vita Consecrata*, 58.

[44]See also Pope John Paul II, *Letter to Families from Pope John Paul II*, 18; *Vita Consecrata*, 34.

whether God is male or female is in itself an invalid question, although God is spoken of in Scriptures as a father and mother in anthropomorphic language.[45] The question concerning the femininity of God, however, assumes a different shape if it is treated from the point of view of the Incarnation. Remaining at the level of the Immanent and transcendent Triune God, this question does not really have a theological value, because God in His very life does not fall under the categories of gender: Scripture speaks of him with both maternal and paternal characteristics.[46] It is, therefore, in the context of Incarnation that the question concerning the masculinity of the incarnate God must be treated.

To that question of Jesus' maleness is connected the question of femininity, not only of Mary but also of women in general. In my second volume on the Mariology of the Pope, *Presence and Mediation of Mary in the Theology of Pope John Paul II*, the question of woman and her relationship with Mary's identity and role in God's plan of salvation, will be extensively treated. Here, it is enough to mention the problem in its relationship to Jesus' maleness.

The identity and role of women in the order of creation and in the order of salvation has become an important concern in contemporary theology as well as in official documents of the Catholic Church. It is enough to mention the presence of this theme in a number of Pope Pius XII's Discourses[47] and in the Encyclical *Pacem in Terris* of Pope John XXIII.[48] In Vatican II the topic of the vocation and dignity of women was brought up by the Pastoral Constitution *Gaudium et Spes*,[49] the Decree on the Apostolate of the Laity *Apostolicam Actuositatem*,[50] and the Closing Message of the Second Vatican Council addressed to women.[51] After the Second Vatican Council, Pope Paul VI underscored the contributions of woman by bestowing the title "Doctor of the Church" on both St. Teresa of Jesus and St. Catherine of Siena.[52] At the request

---

[45]See Pope John Paul II, *Orientale Lumen*, 9.

[46]See Pope John Paul II, *Dives in Misericordia*, 15; *Behold Your Mother*, 4–5; *Mulieris Dignitatem*, 8; *Orientale Lumen*, 9.

[47]See Pius XII, Address to Italian Women (October 21, 1945), *AAS* 37 (1945): 284–295; Address to the World Union of Catholic Women's Organizations (April 24, 1952), *AAS* 44 (1952): 420–424; Address to the participants in the XIV International Meeting of the World Union of Catholic Women's Organizations (September 29, 1957), *AAS* 49 (1957): 906–922.

[48]See Pope John XXIII, Encyclical Letter *Pacem in Terris* (April 11, 1963), AAS 55 (1963): 267–268; Pope John Paul II, *Christifideles Laici*, 49.

[49]See *Gaudium et Spes*, 8, 9, and 60.

[50]See *Apostolicam Actuositatem*, 9.

[51]See The Council's Message to Women (December 8, 1965); *AAS* 58 (1966): 13–14.

[52]See proclamation of St. Teresa of Jesus as a "Doctor of the Universal Church" (September 27, 1970), *AAS* 62 (1970): 590–596; Proclamation of St. Catherine of Siena as a "Doctor of the

of the 1971 Assembly of the Synod of Bishops, the same Paul VI set up a special commission to study the contemporary problems concerning the "effective promotion of the dignity and the responsibility of women."[53]

The Encyclical Letter *Redemptoris Mater* (1987), *Mulieris Dignitatem* (1988), and *Letter to Women* (1995) are the three main documents that afford Pope John Paul II the opportunity to "address the contemporary challenge posed by the various women's liberation movements."[54] For a Pope who was deeply influenced by the inner personality of his own mother Emilia, the question of liberation is grounded in an ontological and theological dignity to be preserved against many false ideologies that deride the role of woman.[55] The first and fundamental aspect that John Paul extensively treats in *Christifideles Laici* and *Mulieris Dignitatem* resides in God's original plan Who willed from the very 'beginning' to create the human being as a 'unity of the two.' This unity which forms the prime community of persons, and is the source of every other community, is at the same time 'sign' of "that interpersonal communion of love which constitutes the mystical, intimate life of God, One in Three."[56] How is it possible to even think of a discrimination if the original personal intercommunion between man and woman is a reflection of the trinitarian communion?

The dignity of woman, as expressed in *Mulieris Dignitatem*, 4, consists "in the supernatural elevation to union with God in Jesus Christ, which determines the ultimate finality of the existence of every person both on earth and in eternity."[57] John Paul prescinds from imprisoning the dignity of woman in

---

Universal Church" (October 4, 1970), *AAS* 62 (1970): 673–678; Pope John Paul II, *Letter of Pope John Paul II to Women*, 11.

[53]See *AAS* 65 (1973): 284f.; Pope John Paul II, *Mulieris Dignitatem*, 1.

[54]See *The Encyclicals of John Paul II*, Edited with Introductions by J. Michael Miller, Indiana: Our Sunday Visitor Publishing Division, Our Sunday Visitor, Inc., 1996, 341.

[55]See Pope John Paul II, *Familiaris Consortio*, 22; *Mulieris Dignitatem*, 1; *Letter of Pope John Paul II to Women*, 1 and 6; *The Thought of Pope John Paul II*, Edited by John M. McDermott, Rome: Gregorian University press, 1993, XX; Donal Dorr, "The New Social Encyclical," in *The Furrow* 32 (1981): 703–705; Arthur Macdonal Allchin, *"Redemptoris Mater*: An Anglican Response," in *One in Christ* 23 (1988): 324; Carl Bernstein and Marco Politi, *His Holiness John Paul II and the Hidden History of our Time*, New York: Doubleday, 1996, 22.

[56]See Pope John Paul II, *Christifideles Laici*, 52; *Mulieris Dignitatem*, 7; *Redemptoris Custos*, 19. Cardinal Law refers to John Paul II's understanding of the communio personarum between man and woman in the context of marriage as the image of the Blessed Trinity (See Bernard Cardinal Law, *Christian Marriage. A Covenant of Love and Life*, Boston: Daughters of St. Paul, 1998, 16–17 and 35).

[57]See also Pope John Paul II, *Letter of Pope John Paul II to Women*, 1; Hans Cardinal Groër, "The Church Sacrament of Salvation," in *John Paul II. A Panorama of his Teachings*, New York: New City Press, 1989, 33.

merely temporal functions. The union of both man and woman with God, whether in time or in eschatology, is the criterion for understanding the vocation, destiny and meaning of the existence of all persons: the ethos of creation and of salvation determines the framework in which man and woman find respectively their own true identity and role in life and in eternity. This is the reason why in *Christifideles Laici*, 51, John Paul recurs to the theology of *Inter Insigniores* as proposed by the Congregation for the Doctrine of the Faith: there is a difference between a function and a dignity of holiness. The organic nature of the ecclesial structure is totally ordered to the holiness of Christ's members. Although the Church is an organic communion with a hierarchical structure, the union with God is the ultimate goal of that structure and, consequently, the holiness is far more important than a function or a difference that exists between man and woman either in the order of creation or in the order of salvation.[58] The same theology occurs again in *Mulieris Dignitatem*, 5, "the dignity of every human being and the vocation corresponding to that dignity find their definitive measure in union with God."[59] This does not mean that the Pope disregards the historical categories of maleness and femininity and their respective role and vocation in humanity and in the Church. He insists rather on avoiding a discrimination that emphasizes the difference between them at the expense of their original unity as human persons: the image and likeness of God conferred on persons, primarily as persons, constitutes the immutable basis of all Christian anthropology.[60]

At the same time, mankind, fundamentally created in God's image, can exist *only as male and female* because "male and female he created them": from the very beginning, man exists only as a 'unity of the two.' The primary and fundamental act of creation refers to the human person as a person before going into the details of that personality as it reveals its existence in masculinity and femininity. That is why, continues John Paul, "man is person, man and woman equally so, since both were created in the image and likeness of the personal God." Therefore, the human person as the image of God is for John Paul the essential basis for equal dignity between man and woman because both are persons. This essential equality from the point of view of their humanity, however, does not contradict the difference between their maleness

---

[58]See Pope John Paul II, *Christifideles Laici*, 51; *Mulieris Dignitatem*, 27; *Ordinatio Sacerdotalis*, 3; Congregation for the Doctrine of the Faith, Declaration on the Question of Admission of Women to the Ministerial Priesthood *Inter Insigniores* (October 15, 1976), 6: *AAS* 69 (1977), 115.

[59]See Pope John Paul II, *Christifideles Laici*, 50; Peter Hebblethwaite, *Pope John Paul II and the Church*, Kansas City: Sheed and Ward, 1995, 30.

[60]See Pope John Paul II, *Mulieris Dignitatem*, 6; *Christifideles Laici*, 50.

and femaleness. The Pope refers to Origen, Clement of Alexandria and St. Augustine to confirm an equality based on a humanity created in the image and likeness of God: both male and female are two different 'I's who share a common humanity. An equality of man and woman based on the image and likeness definitely places John Paul II in the Augustinian tradition.[61]

In *Redemptor Hominis*, 10, John Paul II uses Galatians 3:28 in the context of new creation:

> In the mystery of the Redemption man becomes newly 'expressed' and, in a way, is newly created. He is newly created! 'There is neither Jew nor Greek, there is neither slave nor free, there is neither male nor female; for you are all one in Christ Jesus'. The man who wishes to understand himself thoroughly — and not just in accordance with immediate, partial, often superficial, and even illusory standards and measures of his being — he must with his unrest, uncertainty and even his weakness and sinfulness, with his life and death, draw near to Christ. He must, so to speak, enter into him with all his own self, he must 'appropriate' and assimilate the whole of the reality of the Incarnation and Redemption in order to find himself. If this profound process takes place within him, he then bears fruit not only of adoration of God but also of deep wonder at himself.[62]

Galatians 3:28 applies to the theory of new creation in the theology of Pope John Paul II. Every human person regardless of race, sex, color, or social status can become newly created in Christ. In the light of Christ every human being is looked at as a *person* in the image and likeness of God. Instead of focusing on the differences between people in Galatians 3:28, Pope John Paul stresses the unity resulting from the act of Redemption.[63] This unity never cancels the differences between people; it rather enriches the relationship between them. The mystery of Christ, instead of erasing the differences between Jews and Greeks, male and female, eventually reveals the identity of each one of them to him–or herself. Instead of erasing the difference, the new creation in Christ brings forth 'new Greek' and 'new Jew,' 'new male' and 'new female.' The new creation implies neither a static and undifferentiated equality, nor an irreconcilable and inexorably conflictual difference. It is a unity without

---

[61]See Pope John Paul II, *Mulieris Dignitatem*, 4 and 6; *Letter to Families from Pope John Paul II*, 6–7; St. Augustine, *De Gen.* III, 22, 34; *De Trin.* XII, 7, 9; Johann G. Roten, "Mary and Woman in Augustine," in *The University of Dayton Review* 22, no. 3 (Summer 1994): 37–38; Hans Cardinal Groër, "The Church Sacrament of Salvation," in *John Paul II. A Panorama of his Teachings*, New York: New City Press, 1989, 33; Joseph Cardinal Cordeiro, "The religious sense of man," in *John Paul II. A Panorama of his Teachings*, New York: New City Press, 1989, 67.

[62]Pope John Paul II, *Redemptor Hominis*, 10.

[63]See also Pope John Paul II, *Familiaris Consortio*, 22; *Mulieris Dignitatem*, 4–5; *Christifideles Laici*, 50; *Letter to Families from Pope John Paul II*, 18.

confusion of functions; it is a difference with reconcilable complemetarity.[64] The mystery of Christ emphasizes the difference between man and woman because it reveals their personal and individual identity.[65] Male and female are different because of the ethos of creation, but are one because of the mystery of Christ. It is a difference within the unity of humankind, a unity that keeps the difference between man and woman. That same theology occurs again in *Mulieris Dignitatem*, 2, where the Pope, using *Gaudium et Spes*, 22, affirms that "this eternal truth about the human being, man and woman...at the same time constitutes the mystery which only in 'the Incarnate Word takes on light...(since) Christ fully reveals man to himself and makes his supreme calling clear." If the whole reality of man can be revealed only under the light of the Word of God made flesh, the difference between man and woman, whether from an ontological, anthropological, or theological point of view, should follow the same principle. This is the basis for discovering the identity, role and vocation of woman, as it was established by the ethos of creation and culminated in the order of salvation. In this context, the truth about woman as revealed by God determines what is her true good; what is good, or seems to be good for woman cannot determine the truth of her identity and vocation. Therefore, the role and identity of woman should not be measured by the criteria of functionality typical in human societies. The sacramental economy established by the free and sovereign choice of Christ as attested by the Gospel and the Church's constant tradition determines what is specific to being male and female.[66] John Paul II somewhat follows the thinking of Saint Augustine "that a woman, for all her physical qualities as a woman, is actually renewed in the spirit of her mind in the knowledge of God according to the image of her Creator, and therein there is no male or female...(some people) do not realize that there could have been no distinction of male and female except in relation to the body."[67]

---

[64]John Paul's *Letter to Women* (1995) asserts that womanhood and manhood are complementary not only from the physical and psychological points of view, but also from the ontological. This means that because of the ethos of creation, man and woman fulfill their vocation through a duality of the "masculine" and the "feminine." In the context of marriage, because of the "unity of the two" expressed in Genesis, they lead their being to perfection when they experience their interpersonal relationship as a gift through a relational "uni–duality" (See Pope John Paul II, *Letter of Pope John Paul II to Women*, 7).

[65]See also Pope John Paul II, *Familiaris Consortio*, 23; *Behold Your Mother*, 4–5; *Mulieris Dignitatem*, 16; *Letter to Families from Pope John Paul II*, 6–7.

[66]See also Pope John Paul II, *Letter of Pope John Paul II to Women*, 11; James Swetnam, "'A Vision of Wholeness': Response," in *The Thought of Pope John Paul II*, Rome: Gregorian University, 1993, 94.

[67]St. Augustine, *De Gen.* III, 22, 34; *De Trin.* XII, 7, 9. For details see also Johann G. Roten, "Mary and Woman in Augustine," in *The University of Dayton* Review vol. 22, no. 3, (Summer

As it can be deduced, in his approach to the realities of faith, Pope John Paul II often bases his argument on cognitive grounds: he proceeds from the truth to the good. "More than anything else," the Pope says in his *Letter to Women* (1995), "the word of God enables us to grasp clearly the ultimate anthropological basis of the dignity of women, making it evident as a part of God's plan for humanity."[68] Since the truth is nothing but the product of the divine law, it can only be intrinsically good. This way of treating the question affords the Pope the opportunity to avoid a purely positivistic approach to Divine Revelation: the good of the human person cannot be merely a production of the natural reason. The ultimate source of natural reason is the eternal divine law of God. Therefore, good can come only from the revealed truth about man and God and, only in this sense, is truly Good.

John Paul II applies this cognitive dimension to the Church's understanding of woman as found in Scripture, Tradition and the Magisterium's teaching. In that way of perceiving the relationship between truth and good, he presents the identity and role of woman in the economy of salvation.[69] In *Familiaris Consortio*, 22, he shows how the Divine Revelation confirms the authenticity of woman's dignity for the natural reason. Putting it in a mariological perspective, through Mary he identifies the function of woman in the Church:"God then manifests the dignity of women in the highest form possible, by assuming human flesh from the Virgin Mary, whom the Church honors as the Mother of God, calling her the New Eve and presenting her as the model of redeemed woman."[70] Also in *Mulieris Dignitatem*, 1, John Paul refers to the cognitive dimension: the ethos of creation is the only principle that opens the doors to a true and authentic perception of the identity and role of woman, first in creation and specifically in the ecclesial structure of the Church. Reinforcing his cognitive approach with *Gaudium et Spes*, 10, John Paul is convinced that a true understanding of the question of woman requires that one go back "to the foundations which are to be found in Christ, to those 'immutable' truths and values of which he himself remains the 'faithful witness' (cf. Rev 1:5) and

---

1994): 37–38.

[68]*Letter of Pope John Paul II to Women*, 6; André Frossard, *Portrait of John Paul II*, San Francisco: Ignatius Press, 1990, 101; Peter Hebblethwaite, *Pope John Paul II and the Church*, Kansas City: Sheed and Ward, 1995, 29–30; Richard J. Taylor, *"Redemptoris Mater*: Pope John Paul II's Encyclical for the Marian Year: Some Reflections," in *Priest & People* 2 (1988): 135.

[69]See Pope John Paul II, *Behold Your Mother*, 5; *Letter to Families from Pope John Paul II*, 6–7; Richard J. Taylor, *"Redemptoris Mater*: Pope John Paul II's Encyclical for the Marian Year: Some Reflections," in *Priest & People* 2 (1988): 135.

[70]See Pope John Paul II, *Familiaris Consortio*, 22. The Pope recurs to the same idea in *Familiaris Consortio*, 25 where he quotes St. Ambrose (see St. Ambrose, *Exameron*, V, 7, 19: CSEL 32, I, 154).

Teacher. A different way of acting would lead to doubtful, if not actually erroneous and deceptive results."[71]   Since the order of salvation is an indispensable and essential perfection of the order of creation, woman cannot be assigned to the two orders in contradictory ways:

> It is a question of understanding the reason for and the consequences of the Creator's decision that the human being should always and only exist as a woman or a man. It is only by beginning from these bases, which make it possible to understand the greatness of the dignity and vocation of women, that one is able to speak of their active presence in the Church and in society.[72]

A Note on Systematic Christology in Pope John Paul II

Pope John Paul II faithfully reflects the tradition of the Church when it comes to *Systematic Christology*, a discipline that entails many ramifications in the contemporary period.[73] His main line of thought consists in presenting in a deep and skillful way the teaching of Chalcedon: the full humanity assumed of the Virgin Mary and the pre–existent divine nature are united in the one and the same Person of the Son. This One and same Person, endowed with a duality of nature, becomes the single personal subject of all His actions.[74] Neither of the two natures should be emphasized at the expense of the other, an idea that was also developed by Cardinal Ratzinger.[75]

In Pope John Paul II's opinion, the sanctification of human nature happened through the *hypostatic union*[76] of the Divine Nature and the human nature in the person of the Word. Referring to St. Thomas Aquinas in *Dominum et Vivificantem*, 50, John Paul II calls the Incarnation '*supreme grace, the grace*

---

[71]See also Pope John Paul II, *Letter of Pope John Paul II to Women*, 11.

[72]Pope John Paul II, *Mulieris Dignitatem*, 1 and 28; *Letter of Pope John Paul II to Women*, 11.

[73]See Raymond T. Gawronski, "Redemptor Hominis," in *The Thought of Pope John Paul II*, Rome: Gregorian University, 1993, 222; Aldo Moda, *La Cristologia Contemporanea nell'area Tedesca, Olandese, Francese e Italiana*, in Giovanni Iammarrone (a cura) *La Cristologia Contemporanea*, Padova: Edizioni Messagero Padova, 1992, 74–93 and 126–247.

[74]See Pope John Paul II, *Salvifici Doloris*, 17; Raymond T. Gawronski, "Redemptor Hominis," in *The Thought of Pope John Paul II*, Rome: Gregorian University, 1993, 222.

[75]See J. Ratzinger, "Jesus Christ today," in *Communio* 17 (1990): 69.

[76]See Pope John Paul II, *Redemptor Hominis*, 20; *Behold Your Mother*, 1; *Dominum et Vivificantem*, 21 and 50; *Redemptoris Mater*, 9; *Duodecimum Saeculum*, 8; *Tertio Millennio Adveniente*, 3; *Salvifici Doloris*, 17; *Mulieris Dignitatem*, 4; *Celebrate 2000! Reflections on Jesus, the Holy Spirit, and the Father*, Ann Arbor, Michigan: Servant Publications, 1996, 32; Michael O'Carroll, "Dominum et Vivificantem," in *Veni Creator Spiritus: A Theological Encyclopedia of the Holy Spirit*, Collegeville: Liturgical Press, 1990, 72; Raymond T. Gawronski, "Redemptor Hominis," in *The Thought of Pope John Paul II*, Rome: Gregorian University, 1993, 222.

of union,' source of every other grace.[77] That same hypostatic union enabled His saving 'acts,' especially His death and resurrection, to be salvific.[78] Incarnation and Redemption are two different processes of the same Christ–event. Chronologically, the Incarnation in the womb of Mary precedes Christ's death and resurrection. Ontologically, both aspects constitutes one complex reality. So, John Paul II does not focus exclusively on the Paschal Mystery in his theology of Redemption. *The Incarnation is already redemption.*[79] In *Redemptor Hominis* he says:

> We also are in a certain way in a season of a new Advent (end of the second millennium), a season of expectation:"In many and various ways God spoke of old to our fathers by the prophets; but in these last days he has spoken to us by a Son...," by the Son, his Word, who became man and was born of the Virgin Mary. *This act of Redemption* marked the high point of the history of man within God's loving plan.[80]

Pope John Paul II's emphasis on the hypostatic union as the first step of Redemption, chronologically speaking, is a method of condemning the implicit Gnosticism that is infiltrating the devotion and the theology of the Church.[81] It also prevents one from falling into the Docetism that "is reproduced in the disdain of some contemporary theologians for the bodily aspects of Divine Revelations: the *Virginity of the Lord's Mother, His Resurrection in the flesh, His real presence in the Eucharist.*"[82] In the context of ecclesiology, it prevents *gnostic feminism,* and an elitist and *spiritualistic view of Christ's Mystical body.*

St. John of the Cross picks up the Tradition of the Fathers, especially that of St. Thomas Aquinas, when he speaks of the hypostatic union as a marriage of divinity and humanity in the Word.[83] Pope Paul VI speaks of marriage of

---

[77]St. Thomas Aquinas, *Summa Theologiae,* III, q. 2, aa. 10–12; q. 6, a. 6; q. 7, a. 13.

[78]See Pope John Paul II, *Mulieris Dignitatem,* 3; *Redemptoris Custos,* 6–7 and 27.

[79]See also Pope John Paul II, *Redemptoris Missio,* 40; *Salvifici Doloris,* 10; *Mulieris Dignitatem,* 3; Lothar Roos, "On a Theology and Ethics of Work," *Communio* 11 (1984): 103.

[80]Pope John Paul II, *Redemptor Hominis,* 1. See also Ibid., *Tertio Millennio Adveniente,* 1 and 3.

[81]See Pope John Paul II, *Mulieris Dignitatem,* 3; *Redemptoris Custos,* 6. For the presence of Gnosticism in today's theology, see Terrence Prendergast, "'A Vision of Wholeness': A Reflection on the Use of Scripture in a Cross–section of Papal Writings," in *The Thought of Pope John Paul II,* Rome: Gregorian University, 1993, 86; John Saward, *Christ is the Answer. The Christ–Centered Teaching of Pope John Paul II,* New York: Alba House, 1995, xiv–xvii.

[82]John Saward, *Christ is the Answer. The Christ–Centered Teaching of Pope John Paul II,* xiv.

[83]See St. John of the Cross, *Romance VII, Poems,* ET by Roy Campbell, Harmondsworth, 1960, 89.

divine and human action in the great economy of the Redemption."[84] This hypostatic union in the theology of John Paul II is an eternal marriage between the Word and the human nature He assumed, a nature that is true and authentic. John Paul refers to the theology of Vatican II, according to which the human nature of the Word became the instrument of salvation of humankind. *Redemptoris Custos* presents the humanity of Jesus in the context of the mystery of Incarnation; His humanity under the light of that mystery constitutes "the efficacious instrument of his divinity for the purpose of sanctifying man."[85] In *Mulieris Dignitatem*, 11, the Pope says:"the essence of the New Covenant consists in the fact that the Son of God, who is of one substance with the eternal Father, becomes man: he takes humanity into the unity of the divine Person of the Word."[86]

Pope John Paul II's View on the Relationship Between Jesus and Anthropology as Expressed in Culture

The relationship between Jesus and *Anthropology* as expressed in culture is currently predominant in all Christology. In this approach, Christ's humanity is the most important element, not from a dogmatic, but from a cultural point of view. This anthropological approach to Christ entails different ramifications that are worth studying.

Absolute Identification

Many contemporary christological trends look at Jesus from a mere humanistic point of view: He is the universal man, the model of an authentic humanity, and the pillar of moral ideals.[87] In this context a psychological approach to Jesus perceives Him as a perfectly balanced human person. He is an efficient instrument of psychological transformation for others.[88] In this scenario, the *absolute identification* of Christ with humanity runs the risk of downgrading His divine nature. The effort to replace a metaphysical Christ

---

[84]Pope Paul VI, Discourse (March 19, 1969): *Insegnamenti* VII (1969): 1269; Pope John Paul II, *Redemptoris Custos*, 21.

[85]Pope John Paul II, *Redemptoris Custos*, 21.

[86]See also Pope John Paul II, *Redemptoris Custos*, 7.

[87]See Johann G. Roten, *The Word of God made man by the Holy Spirit*, 20; K. Jaspers, *I grandi filosofi*, Milano: Longanesi, 1973, 280–307; L. Kolakowski, *Senso e non–senso della tradizione cristiana*, Assisi: Cittadella, 1975, 32–39; M. Machovec, *Gesù per gli atei*, Assisi: Cittadella, 1974, 40 ff.

[88]See H. Wolff, *Gesù la maschilità esemplare*, Brescia: Queriniana, 1979; Ibid., *Gesù psicoterapeuta. L'attegiamento di Gesù nei confronti degli uomini come modello della moderna psicoterapia*, Brescia: Queriniana, 1982.

with a social, merely human Jesus has been widely adopted by many theologians such as Knox, Pittenger, and Robinson.[89] How does Pope John Paul II keep the balance between Christ's identification with every human person and His transcendental identity?

The first and most important argument against the approach of absolute identification is the relationship between creation, Incarnation, and sanctification: that relationship is directly connected to the Word made flesh in the strict sense of the word. By establishing a solid bond between these three aspects of the economy of salvation, the Pope avoids what many contemporary theologians fall into, namely a lack of unity in their outlook on God's activity in history. That lack prompts a sequence of events that are attributed to God without a coherent intrinsic logic about the divine activity: many theologians attribute the act of creation to God in terms of a pre–trinitarian idea of God; others see in Christ the Redeemer without considering that this Redeemer is the Word as such. The result of lack of coherence in theological thinking concerning the continuity between the different aspects of the history of salvation are evident especially at the level of trinitarian theology. The immediate consequence is recognizable in a separation between the Immanent and the Economic Trinity, as it will be discussed at the last two chapters of the present volume.

At the very beginning of his Pontificate, Pope John Paul II confirmed that the power of truth about the creation of man and the world is "contained in the mystery of the Incarnation and the Redemption."[90] Since there is an "intrinsic unity between creation and redemption,"[91] the act of creation constitutes, as it were, the first step of God's plan of salvation. In this eternal, transcendental, and positive plan, the whole truth about the creation of humankind finds its climax in the mystery of the Son's Incarnation. In fact, "God's salvific giving of himself and his life, in some way to all creation but directly to man, reaches

---

[89]See James Schall, *"Redemptor Hominis:* The Amazement of God," *Homiletic and Pastoral Review* 80 (October 1979): 13.

[90]Pope John Paul II, *Redemptor Hominis*, 13. See also Ibid., *Dives in Misericordia*, 7; Herbert McCabe, "Redemptor Hominis," in *New Blackfriars* 60 (1979), 146; Aloysius J. Fonseca, "Reflections on the Encyclical Letter *Sollicitudo Rei Socialis*," *Gregorianum* 70 (1989): 15–16; Terrence Prendergast, "'A Vision of Wholeness': A Reflection on the Use of Scripture in a Cross–section of Papal Writings," in *The Thought of Pope John Paul II*, Rome: Gregorian University, 1993, 86.

[91]See Pope John Paul II, *Dominum et Vivificantem*, 49–50; *Salvifici Doloris*, 10; James Schall, *"Redemptor Hominis:* The Amazement of God," *Homiletic and Pastoral Review* 80 (October 1979): 14; Paul L. Peeters, *"Dominum et Vivificantem:* The Conscience and the Heart," in *Communio* 15 (1988): 149.

one of its high points in the mystery of the Incarnation."[92] And, as expressed in *Dominum et Vivificantem*, 52, "Creation is thus completed by the Incarnation and since that moment is permeated by the powers of the Redemption, powers which fill humanity and all creation." In *Slavorum Apostoli*, Pope John Paul II says:"Your plan of creation, O Father, culminating in the Redemption, touches the living man and embraces his entire life and the history of all peoples."[93]

What kind of relationship does Creation have to Incarnation? Or, how is it possible to establish a relationship between two realities, one of them temporal and still taking place through history (Creation), and the other, although it took place once and for all in history, is still transcendent by nature (Incarnation)? How does the Pope escape the narrow bounds of Molinist christocentrism, and how does he display his thinking about the logic of salvation history in a pattern that is more lucid than a mere linear chronology?[94]

The relationship between the visible and the invisible, the created and the Uncreated, time and eternity, man and the divine, is and will always be a necessary question to consider when developing a sound theology.[95] In *Duodecimum Saeculum* and in the context of the Iconoclast controversy, Pope John Paul II recalls the dilemma posed by the iconoclasts and affirms that this dilemma "called into question the whole Christian vision of the reality of the Incarnation and therefore the relationships of God and the world, grace and nature, in short, the specific character of the 'new covenant' that God made with humanity in Jesus Christ."[96]

St. Augustine felt that dilemma at the very beginning of his theological activity. In his *Confession* he says: "Lord, since eternity is Yours, are You unaware of what I am saying to you? Or do You see in time what takes place in time?"[97] Or, along the same line of St. Augustine's thought: "For it is an

---

[92]Pope John Paul II, *Redemptoris Mater*, 9. See also *Redemptoris Mater*, 37; *Dominum et Vivificantem*, 52; Aloysius J. Fonseca, "Reflections on the Encyclical Letter *Sollicitudo Rei Socialis*," *Gregorianum* 70 (1989): 15–16.

[93]Pope John Paul II, *Slavorum Apostoli*, 30.

[94]See Pope John Paul II, *Redemptor Hominis*, 13; Angelo Scola, "'Claim' of Christ, 'Claim' of the World: On the Trinitarian Encyclicals of John Paul II," in *Communio* 18 (1991): 325.

[95]See Pope John Paul II, *Redemptor Hominis*, 18; *Dominum et Vivificantem*, 50; *Tertio Millennio Adveniente*, 9; *Centesimus Annus*, 51; André Frossard, *Portrait of John Paul II*, San Francisco: Ignatius Press, 1990, 168–169.

[96]Pope John Paul II, *Duodecimum Saeculum*, 9. See also Ibid., *Letter to Families from Pope John Paul II*, 20.

[97]*Confessions of St. Augustine*, Revision of the translation of Rev. J. M. Lelen, New Jersey: Catholic Book Publishing Co., 1997, Bk. 11, Ch. 1, 326.

unusual and sublime concept, O Lord, to behold Your immutable eternity creating changeable things, and these must therefore be before them."[98]

In the context of relationship between time and eternity, St. Augustine brings up the question of priority. For him, one should "...discern the distinction between priority in eternity, in time, in choice, and in origin: priority in eternity, as God precedes all things; in time, as the flower precedes the fruit, in choice, as the fruit precedes the flower; in origin, as the sound precedes the song."[99] It is beyond human imagination and knowledge to understand how God, Who is eternal, can precede temporal creatures. It is also difficult to figure out how the sound can precede the song, since "there is not first a formless sound that afterward is shaped into a song. For as soon as each sound is heard, it passes away, nor can you find anything of it that you may collect and compose into a song. Therefore, the song has its being in its sound, and this sound is its matter."[100]

The reason behind presenting the theory of St. Augustine is to clarify the position of Pope John Paul II when he establishes the relationship between creation and Incarnation. Creation is not prior to Incarnation in eternity, because creation itself is not co–eternal with God. Neither is creation prior to Incarnation by choice because the Son's Incarnation has brought about the supernatural grace of Redemption far beyond what the grace of creation has bestowed on human beings.[101] As the Pope attests, the dignity of the human person "already forged in the creative act of God, is raised immeasurably higher in the mystery of the Incarnation of the Son of God."[102] In fact, against all forms of Pelagianism, the grace of creation is not sufficient to redeem humankind: in the divine economy, a factor that is sufficient unto itself, "the human action which is ours — though capable of nothing (cf. Jn 15:5), is never dispensed from a humble but conditional and ennobling collaboration."[103]

The relation of creation to Incarnation is like the relation of the song to the sound. Creation has its being in Incarnation, because creation does not have any meaning without the Incarnation. This means that in the very logic of creation itself, God has already prefigured and preestablished the reality of the

---

[98]*Ibid.*, Bk. 12, Ch. 29, 397.

[99]*Ibid.*

[100]*Ibid.*

[101]See Pope John Paul II, *Redemptoris Mater*, 36; *Dives in Misericordia*, 7; *Dominum et Vivificantem*, 9 and 50.

[102]Pope John Paul II, *Celebrate 2000! Reflections on Jesus, the Holy Spirit, and the Father*, Ann Arbor, Michigan: Servant Publications, 1996, 29.

[103]See Pope John Paul II, *Redemptoris Custos*, 30.

Incarnation.[104] Therefore, Incarnation is a "new revelation of God" and a "new 'self–giving' of God."[105] In deep but simple terms Pope John Paul II reflects on the Tradition of the Church: the creation, ontologically not chronologically, happened in vision of the Incarnation:

> The divine plan of salvation — which was fully revealed to us with the coming of Christ — is eternal. And according to the teaching contained in the Letter just quoted (Ephesians 1:4–6) and in other Pauline Letters (cf. Col 1:12–14; Rom 3:24; Gal 3:13; 2 Cor 5: 18–29), it is also eternally linked to Christ.[106]

When it comes to eternity, things cannot precede each other because otherwise eternity would not be eternity. Since God's plan of salvation in Christ is eternal, creation can precede Incarnation only in the sense that the beginning of creation took place before the coming of Christ in the flesh. On the transcendental level of God and in His eternal presence, creation and salvation are simultaneous.[107] It is amazing how Pope John Paul expresses this in *Redemptoris Mater*:

> If he has eternally willed to call man to share in the divine nature (cf. 2 Pet 1:4), it can be said that he has matched the 'divinization' of man to humanity's historical conditions, so that even after sin he is ready to restore at a great price the eternal plan of his love through the 'humanization' of his Son, who is of the same being as himself.[108]

So in time, creation took place before the Incarnation, but according to the divine plan "which begins from eternity in Christ, the perfect 'image of the Father, and which culminates in him, 'the firstborn from the dead' (Col 1:18),"[109] Incarnation is concomitant to creation: God eternally intended for

---

[104]See Pope John Paul II, *Redemptor Hominis*, 16; *Sollicitudo Rei Socialis*, 31; *Celebrate 2000! Reflections on Jesus, the Holy Spirit, and the Father*, Ann Arbor, Michigan: Servant Publications, 1996, 48; J. Honoré, "Christ the Redeemer, Core of John Paul's Teaching," in *John Paul II. A Panorama of his Teachings*, New York: New City Press, 1989, 13; Lothar Roos, "On a Theology and Ethics of Work," *Communio* 11 (1984): 103; Aloysius J. Fonseca, "Reflections on the Encyclical Letter *Sollicitudo Rei Socialis*," *Gregorianum* 70 (1989): 15–16.

[105]Pope John Paul II, *Redemptoris Mater*, 36. See also Ibid., *Dominum et Vivificantem*, 21 and 49–50.

[106]Pope John Paul II, *Redemptoris Mater*, 7.

[107]See J. Honoré, "Christ the Redeemer, Core of John Paul's Teaching," in *John Paul II. A Panorama of his Teachings*, New York: New City Press, 1989, 13.

[108]Pope John Paul II, *Redemptoris Mater*, 51. See also André Frossard, *Portrait of John Paul II*, San Francisco: Ignatius Press, 1990, 168–169.

[109]Pope John Paul II, *Sollicitudo Rei Socialis*, 31.

human persons to share His divine life, and this sharing becomes possible only through the supernatural grace of Incarnation.[110] At the beginning of his first Encyclical, *Redemptor Hominis*, Pope John Paul II says:

> Through the Incarnation God gave human life the dimension that he intended man to have from his first beginning; he has granted that dimension definitively — in the way that is peculiar to him alone, in keeping with his eternal love and mercy, with the full freedom of God — and he has granted it also with the bounty that enables us, in considering the original sin and the whole history of the sins of humanity, and in considering the errors of the human intellect, will and heart, to repeat with amazement the words of the sacred liturgy:"O happy fault...which gained us so great a Redeemer!"[111]

The same theology occurs at the closing of the Encyclical Letter *Centesimus Annus* where Pope John Paul II declares:

> But the Christian knows that the newness which we await in its fullness at the Lord's second coming has been present since the creation of the world, and in a special way since the time when God became man in Jesus Christ and brought about a 'new creation' with him and through him (2 Cor 5:17; Gal 6:15).[112]

In *Redemptoris Mater*,1, Pope John Paul II comments on the words of St. Paul in his Letter to the Galatians (4:4). The expression "'fullness' indicates the moment fixed from all eternity when the Father sent his Son 'that whoever believes in him should not perish but have eternal life' (Jn 3:16)."[113] This shows that the plan of God, although it happens in space and time, is still a transcendental design that was planned from all eternity: considering the various aspects of the mystery of Christ, one should never lose sight of its unity.[114] The fullness indicates, at the same time, that God's entrance into

---

[110]See also Pope John Paul II, *Dominum et Vivificantem*, 9; *Mulieris Dignitatem*, 9.

[111]Pope John Paul II, *Redemptor Hominis*, 1. See also Ibid., *Dives in Miseriordia*, 7; Terrence Prendergast, "'A Vision of Wholeness': A Reflection on the Use of Scripture in a Cross–section of Papal Writings," in *The Thought of Pope John Paul II*, Rome: Gregorian University, 1993, 86; J. Honoré, "Christ the Redeemer, Core of John Paul's Teaching," in *John Paul II. A Panorama of his Teachings*, New York: New City Press, 1989, 13.

[112]Pope John Paul II, *Centesimus Annus*, 62.

[113]Pope John Paul II, *Redemptoris Mater*, 1. See also Ibid., *Tertio Millennio Adveniente*, 1; Thomas H. Stahel, "Redemptoris Mater," in *America* 156 (1987): 353; Felipe Gomez, "A New Encyclical Letter: The Mother of the Redeemer," in *East Asian Pastoral Review* 24 (1987): 108.

[114]See also Pope John Paul II, *Dominum et Vivificantem*, 52; *Redemptoris Missio*, 6; Felipe Gomez, "A New Encyclical Letter: The Mother of the Redeemer," in *East Asian Pastoral Review* 24 (1987): 108; Terrence Prendergast, "'A Vision of Wholeness': A Reflection on the Use of Scripture in a Cross–section of Papal Writings," in *The Thought of Pope John Paul II*, Rome: Gregorian University, 1993, 86.

history does not reduce Him to temporal and historical categories.[115] So, the determination of the categories according to which the divine is related to the human is and will always be the exclusive prerogative of God. We find ourselves again dealing with the dilemma of how could Eternity enter time and how could an uncreated God be present according to the manner of created categories, at the same time maintaining His own transcendence.

Tertio Millennio Adveniente, 66, a text that needs extensive analysis, affords the Pope the opportunity to comment on St Paul's *fullness of time* as found in Gal 4:4:

> Thanks to God's coming on earth, human time, which began at Creation, has reached its fullness. 'The fullness of time' is in fact eternity, indeed, it is the One who is eternal, God himself. Thus to enter into 'the fullness of time' means to reach the end of time and to transcend its limits, in order to find time's fulfillment in the eternity of God. In Christianity time has a fundamental importance. Within the dimension of time the world was created; within it the history of salvation unfolds, finding its culmination in the 'fullness of time' of the Incarnation, and its goal in the glorious return of the Son of God at the end of time. In Jesus Christ, the Word made flesh, time becomes a dimension of God, who is himself eternal. With the coming of Christ there begin 'the last days' (cf. Heb 1:2), the 'last hour'' (cf. 1 Jn 2:18), and the time of the Church, which will last until the Parousia.[116]

This text of *Tertio Millennio Adveniente* reveals that the Pope's philosophy of time is influenced by the views of St. Augustine. For John Paul II, time is a category in the creational order of the world, but it is not like any other categories. Is it possible that time was created before the world? If creation took place in time, then time was created before creation. But if time was not created before creation, it means that time is one of the created categories. Time was created in order for the creation of the whole world to be possible: time is a dimension that allows the other categories to exist. Since creation was created one thing after the other, time must have been created in a concomitant way with the first elements that were created, that is with the formless heaven and earth. It is impossible that time is not concomitant with the whole creation because creation took place as a succession of things created 'one at a time.' This explains why the Pope says: within the dimension of time the world was created.

By offering the creational order the category in which to exist, time

---

[115]See also Pope John Paul II, *Catechesi Tradendae*, 29; J. Honoré, "Christ the Redeemer, Core of John Paul's Teaching," in *John Paul II. A Panorama of his Teachings*, New York: New City Press, 1989, 14.

[116]Pope John Paul II, *Tertio Millennio Adveniente*, 9–10; J. Honoré, "Christ the Redeemer, Core of John Paul's Teaching," in *John Paul II. A Panorama of his Teachings*, New York: New City Press, 1989, 14.

becomes a dimension of man. There is no possibility for any creature on earth to exist outside this dimension. Yet, as the Pope goes on, this dimension becomes the 'dimension of God' because of the Incarnation. However, since God is 'himself eternal,' time assumes an eschatological dimension. Therefore the coming of Christ has directed time towards its eschatological fulfillment and, in this sense, has made time become 'fullness of time.' Time for the world is still linear because it is historical, although that linear dimension is changed to a circular form that, as the image of eternity, experiences the tension between the *already* and the *not yet* of the presence of the Kingdom.

In the presentation of the relationship between Incarnation and creation, the influence of *St. Louis De Montfort* on John Paul is quite noticeable.[117] It concerns the connection between the goodness of creation and its source in divine Wisdom and Love. The text of *Redemptor Hominis* reads:

> The Redeemer of the world! In him has been revealed in a new and more wonderful way the fundamental truth concerning creation to which the Book of Genesis gives witness when it repeats several times:'God saw that it was Good'. The good has its source in Wisdom and Love. In Jesus Christ the visible world which God created for man — the world that, when sin entered, 'was subjected to futility' — recovers again its original link with the divine source of Wisdom and Love.[118]

This text of John Paul II show a noticeable influence from St. Louis De Montfort's theology. For De Montfort, in the general sense of the term, wisdom means a delectable knowledge, a taste for God and his truth. There are several kinds of wisdom. First: true and false wisdom. True wisdom is a taste for truth without falsehood or deception. False wisdom is a taste for falsehood disguised as truth. Natural wisdom is knowledge, in an outstanding degree, of natural things in their principles. Supernatural wisdom is knowledge of supernatural and divine things in their origin. This supernatural wisdom is divided into substantial or uncreated Wisdom and accidental or created wisdom. Accidental or created wisdom is the communication that uncreated Wisdom makes of himself to mankind. Substantial or Uncreated Wisdom is the Son of God, the second person of the most Blessed Trinity. In other words, it is Eternal Wisdom in eternity or Jesus Christ in time.[119]

St. Louis de Montfort was familiar with the writings of St. Augustine, because he refers to him many times in his treatises. It seems that De Montfort

---

[117]See Pope John Paul II, *Gift and Mystery. On the Fiftieth Anniversary of my Priestly Ordination*, New York: Doubleday, 1996, 29–30.

[118]Pope John Paul II, *Redemptor Hominis*, 8. See also Ibid., *Dives in Misericordia*, 4.

[119]See *God Alone, The Collected writings of St. Louis Marie de Montfort*, New York: Montfort Publications, 1995, 53.

has taken from St. Augustine the theological concept of Wisdom, as the creating Word of God. This Wisdom is the source of all beings that were brought out of nothing into existence. St. Augustine says in his *Confession*:

> How and from where could this be but from You, from Whom are all things, insofar as they exist? The further a thing is from You, so much the more is it unlike You, for the distance is not of space. Therefore, You, O Lord...in the Beginning, which is of You, in Your Wisdom, which is born of You, You did make something, and that out of nothing. For You made heaven and earth, not of Your own substance, for then they should have been equal to Your only–begotten Son and consequently to Your own Self.[120]

Also in the same Book, Chapter 19, St. Augustine says:"It is true, O Lord, that You have made Heaven and earth, and it is true that the *Beginning* is Your *Wisdom, in which You did create all things* (Ps 104:24)."[121]

It is the Augustinian and Montfortian concept of uncreated and substantial Wisdom that John Paul II refers to when connecting the goodness of creation to its source of Wisdom and Love. The texts confirm this connectedness because the overall picture of *Redemptor Hominis*, 8 presents the Incarnation as the new creation of humankind. Therefore, Wisdom and Love can fit in this context, only if they refer to the person of Jesus Christ, instead of the generic gift of wisdom. After stating that *the good has its source in Wisdom and Love*, the Pope refers immediately to the person of Jesus Christ. Goodness of creation has its source in Wisdom and Love in the sense that goodness is the consequence of the Eternal Wisdom's action *ad extra*. John Paul affirms this idea again in *Tertio Millennio Adveniente* when, commenting on the Jn 1:1–4 and Col 1:15, he brings together the identity and the works of the Word in a context of creation:"God created the world through the Word. The Word is Eternal Wisdom; the Thought and Substantial Image of God..."[122]

Pope John Paul II and Ideological Tendencies in Contemporary Christology

Christ is used in some contemporary thinking as the expression of socio–critical attitude and is absorbed in a specific intent which has a practical

---

[120]*Confessions of St. Augustine*, Revision of the Translation of Rev. J. M. Lelen, New Jersey: Catholic Book Publishing Co., 1997, Bk. 12, Ch. 7, 367. See also Bk 12, Ch. 15, 375–379.

[121]*Confessions of St. Augustine*, Revision of the Translation of Rev. J. M. Lelen, New Jersey: Catholic Book Publishing, Co., 1997, Bk. 12, Ch. 7, 383.

[122]Pope John Paul II, *Tertio Millennio Adveniente*, 3.

meaning: Christ justifies liberation movements.[123] In terms of Von Balthasar, the figure of Jesus is, in this instance, 'cut up into pieces'[124] because He becomes the hero figure of identification for socialists and is expected to explain everything. This type of Christology is a dangerous *Ideology* in which Christ is used to justify certain political actions and needs.[125]

Cardinal Joseph Ratzinger draws a parallel between the Incarnate Word with respect to His contemporaries and the Church today, the visible body of Christ, with respect to its contemporaries:"The Church is not an idea but a Body, and the scandal of becoming flesh over which so many of Jesus' contemporaries stumbled continues in the scandalous character of the Church."[126] With these few words, the prefect of the *Propaganda fidei* summarizes the presence of many gnostic approaches in today's theology. At the dawn of the Church, St. Ignatius of Antioch fought Gnosticism because it neglected the visible dimension of the Incarnation along with its consequences on the Church, the visible body of Christ.[127] This Christological Docetism, by considering Christ's mystical body compared with His individual body, viewed this mystical body exclusively from an elitist and spiritualistic point of view. John Saward describes this situation by saying:"The Docetists believed that the 'true Church' was an invisible clique of superior 'knowing' people, and so they felt free to ignore the hierarchy, despise the poor, and shun what they saw as the coarse of materialism of the Mass."[128] Something similar is happening in our own time.

In his pre–Papacy studies of the theology of the Second Vatican Council, Karol Wojtyla developed an anti–idealistic idea about the identity of the Church. For Wojtyla every person is called to enrich the supernatural faith which is the source of the Church's consciousness of her own nature and of the

---

[123]See J.M. Bonino (a cura di), *Ni vencido ni monarca celestial*, Buenos Aires: Tierra Nueva, 1977; S. Trnidad, *Cristología–Conquista–Colonización*, in Equipo Seladoc, *Panorama de la teologia latinoamericana. Cristología en America Latina.* VI: Materiales, Salamanca, 1981, 204–220; B. Mack, *The Lost Gospel: The Book of Q and Christian Origins*, Harper, 1993; St. Mitchell, *The Gospel according to Jesus*, Harper/Collins, 1991, 13.

[124]Hans Urs von Balthasar, *A short Primer for Unsettled Laymen*, ET (San Francisco, 1985), 27.

[125]See Johann G. Roten, *The Word of God made man by the Holy Spirit*, 17–18; Pope Paul VI, *Evangelii Nuntiandi*, 58..

[126]Cardinal Joseph Ratzinger, "Die Ekklesiologie des Zweiten Vatikanischen Konzils", in *Kirche, Ökumene und Politik. Neue Versuche zur Ekklesiologie*, Einsiedeln, 1987, 15.

[127]See St. Ignatius of Antioch, *Epistola ad Smyrnaeos*, 6.

[128]John Saward, *Christ is the Answer. The Christ–Centered Teaching of Pope John Paul II*, xv.

relationship with the source of her very existence, the Triune God.[129] The Church, being of divine origin, is the gift of this Triune God to every man through the redeeming death of Jesus Christ.[130]

Pope John Paul II, abstaining from all kinds of *Auseinandersetzungen* with contemporary ideologies, still shows a full awareness of the many problems.[131] He develops a theology of *universal Redemption* as an implicit response to the unilateral paths of ideology. By *universal Redemption* it is meant what *Lumen Gentium*, 1, brought to the consciousness of the Church. The Church is a kind of sacrament of Christ, that is, a sign and instrument of deepest union with God as well as for the unity of all humankind. Hans Cardinal Groër believes that the concept of sacrament in this instance was broadened by John Paul II who sees in it not only in the traditional use of the word, but also as a grand synthesis: the Church is a sacrament in the order of salvation as well as creation. With the necessary cautions, in the analogous way in which the concept *sacrament* must be applied to the Church, John Paul has a universal tone when, on several occasions he emphasizes the universality of the Church's sacramentality: the Church is not only a sacrament of salvation, but also a sacrament of unity for the human race: "since this unity is already based upon and guaranteed by our common human nature, his (John Paul's) idea here seems to refer to a unity for the whole human race brought about by grace, in a way that earlier theology did not so readily perceive."[132]

The Pope believes that the desire of the Redeemer is the unity of all people,[133] a unity that is based on the facts that the God–man is Jesus Christ,

---

[129]See Karol Wojtyla, *Sources of Renewal: The Implementation of the Second Vatican Council*, San Francisco: Harper and Row, 1980, 35–41.

[130]See Karol Wojtyla, *Sources of Renewal: The Implementation of the Second Vatican Council*, San Francisco: Harper and Row, 1980, 35–41, 45–65 and 86–97.

[131]See Pope John Paul II, *Catechesi Tradendae*, 52; *Letter to Families from Pope John Paul II*, 14; Bartolomeo Sorger, "*Laborem Exercens*: Toward a New Solidarity," in *Official Catholic Social Teaching: Readings in Moral Theology*, Charles Curran and Richard McCormick (eds.), Vol. 5, New York: Paulist Press, 1986, 242.

[132]See Pope John Paul II, *Urbi et Orbi*, October 17, 1978; *Homily*, December 31, 1979; *General Audience*, September 8, 1982; *Ut Unum Sint*, 3; Hans Cardinal Groër, "The Church Sacrament of Salvation," in *John Paul II. A Panorama of his Teachings*, New York: New City Press, 1989, 28–29; Jon Nilson, "The Challenges of *Ut Unum Sint*," in *Ecumenical Trends* 25 (1996): 8; Richard John Neuhaus, "'That They May All Be One': The Pope's Twelfth Encyclical," in *Crisis* 13 (September 1995): 26; Josef Cardinal Tomko, "Mission and dialogue in the teaching of John Paul II," in *John Paul II. A Panorama of his Teachings*, New York: New City Press, 1989, 83. Many aspects of the unity in the thought of John Paul II are displayed in the recently published volume of Darcy O'Brien, *The Hidden Pope*, New York: Daybreak Books, 1998.

[133]See Pope John Paul II, *Slavorum Apostoli*, 6, 14 and 25; *Redemptoris Mater*, 30; *Ut Unum Sint*, 1, 9, and 88–95; Richard John Neuhaus, "'That They May All Be One': The Pope's Twelfth Encyclical," in *Crisis* 13 (September 1995): 26; Jon Nilson, "The Challenges of *Ut Unum Sint*," in

One and the same, and that He is One with the Father. The 'visibility' of God resulting from the Incarnation event is the criterion for any relationship between all the faithful and Christ. Therefore, this "full communion in visible unity"[134] of God's people must have the Incarnation as its fundamental constitutive element.[135] The Church, today more than ever before, is orienting her prime concern towards man's vocation in Christ who "united himself with each man."[136]

The meaning of man, of every man, "is inscribed with a special vigor of truth and love"[137] in the mystery of the Redemption.[138] If Christ unites himself to every man through the Incarnation, the Church "lives more profoundly her own nature and mission by penetrating into the depths of this mystery and into its rich universal language. It was not without reason that the Apostle speaks of Christ's body, the Church."[139] The nature and the mission of the Church from the point of view of universality has been declared by the Second Vatican Council.[140] Therefore, reaching out to every man without exception by her very internal nature, the Church, guided by her awareness of herself as a supernatural *communio*, rejects believing in her identity as a community of

Ecumenical Trends 25 (1996): 8; *The Encyclicals of John Paul II*, Edited with Introductions by J. Michael Miller, Indiana: Our Sunday Visitor Publishing Division, Our Sunday Visitor, Inc., 1996, 223–224; R. McFarlane, "An Anglican Response to the Encyclical *Ut Unum Sint*," in *Ecumenical Trends* 25 (1996): 12.

[134]Pope John Paul II, Apostolic Letter *Duodecimum Saeculum*, 1. See also Ibid., *Redemptoris Missio*, 47; Jon Nilson, "The Challenges of *Ut Unum Sint*," in *Ecumenical Trends* 25 (1996): 8.

[135]See Pope John Paul II, *Duodecimum Saeculum*, 9. In this text, the Pope recalls St. John Damascene's beautiful expression concerning the Incarnation that express the One who "deigned to dwell in matter and bring about our salvation through matter." (*Discourse on images*, I, 16; PG 94: 1246 A) See also Edna McDonagh, "*Redemptor Hominis* and Ireland," in *The Furrow* 30 (1979): 625; Richard John Neuhaus, "'That They May All Be One': The Pope's Twelfth Encyclical," in *Crisis* 13 (September 1995): 26.

[136]*Gaudium et Spes*, 22; Pope John Paul II, *Redemptor Hominis*, 18.

[137]Pope John Paul II, *Redemptor Hominis*, 18.

[138]See Gregory Baum, "The First Encyclical," in *The Ecumenist* 17 (1979): 56.

[139]Pope John Paul II, *Redemptor Hominis*, 18 and 22. See also Ibid., *The Freedom of Conscience and Religion*, 1; Ruth Reardon, "'A Source of Joy': *Ut Unum Sint* and Interchurch Families," in *One in Christ* 31 (1995): 281. This idea was already developed in the pre–papal document on the Second Vatican Council (see Karol Wojtyla, *Sources of Renewal: The Implementation of the Second Vatican Council*, San Francisco: Harper and Row, 1980, 19–34 and 114–121).

[140]See *Lumen Gentium*, 13; Pope John Paul II, *Slavorum Apostoli*, 16; Josef Cardinal Tomko, "Mission and dialogue in the teaching of John Paul II," in *John Paul II. A Panorama of his Teachings*, New York: New City Press, 1989, 83.

elitist people:[141]

> In this way, turning to man and his real problems, his hopes and sufferings, his achievements and falls — this too also makes the Church as a body, an organism, a social unit perceive the same divine influences, the light and strength of the Spirit that come from the crucified and risen Christ, and it is for this very reason that she lives her life. The Church has only one life: that which is given her by her Spouse and Lord. Indeed, precisely because Christ united himself with her in his mystery of Redemption, the Church must be strongly united with each man.[142]

A similar concept is also found in *Centesimus Annus* but more in a social context:"Christian truth is not of this kind. Since it is not an ideology, the Christian faith does not presume to imprison changing socio–political realities in a rigid schema, and it recognizes that human life is realized in history in conditions that are diverse and imperfect." The Church's approach is a strictly theological one since her original vocation is to preach the Gospel avoiding any establishment of partisan ideological preconceptions.[143]

In *Redemptoris Mater*, Pope John Paul II uses the *Magnificat* of Mary to aptly describe God's special love for the poor. Since this canticle is "an inspired profession of her faith, in which her response to the revealed word is expressed,"[144] it is a bold proclamation of the "undimmed truth about God".[145] Therefore, in the *Magnificat* the Church constantly sees her teaching confirmed: the truth about God who is the source of every gift, "cannot be separated from the manifestation of his love of preference for the poor and humble."[146]

---

[141]See Pope John Paul II, *Slavorum Apostoli*, 16; *Reconciliatio et Paenitentia*, 10; *Christifideles Laici*, 8; Paul Bowe, "*Sollicitudo Rei Socialis*: A Commentary on the Encyclical," in *Doctrine and life* 38 (1988): 233; Gerald McCool, "The Theology of John Paul II," in *The Thought of Pope John Paul II*, John M. McDermott (ed.), Rome: Gregorian University Press, 1993, 41; Hans Cardinal Groër, "The Church Sacrament of Salvation," in *John Paul II. A Panorama of his Teachings*, New York: New City Press, 1989, 28–29.

[142]Pope John Paul II, *Redemptor Hominis*, 18.

[143]Pope John Paul II, *Centesimus Annus*, 46. See also Ibid., *Redemptoris Mater*, 25; *The Freedom of Conscience and of Religion*, 1; *Reconciliatio et Paenitentia*, 16; Mary Craig, *Man from a far Country. A Portrait of Pope John Paul II*, London: Hodder And Stughton, 1982, 144; Paul Bowe, "*Sollicitudo Rei Socialis*: A Commentary on the Encyclical," in *Doctrine and life* 38 (1988): 233; Roland James Faley, "Pope as Prophet: The New Social Encyclical," in *America* 158 (1988): 449; Aloysius J. Fonseca, "Reflections on the Encyclical Letter *Sollicitudo Rei Socialis*," in *Gregorianum* 70 (1989): 7 and 16.

[144]Pope John Paul II, *Redemptoris Mater*, 36.

[145]Pope John Paul II, *Redemptoris Mater*, 37.

[146]Pope John Paul II, *Redemptoris Mater*, 37. See also Ibid., *Dives in Misericordia*, 3; *Laborem Exercens*, 8; *Sollicitudo Rei Socialis*, 41–43; *Familiaris Consortio*, 47; Address to the Residents of

It is not intended here to present with all its complexity the social teachings of the Church and her relationship with society. It is enough to note that the Church sides with the poor, although in many political situations of the past, the Church used a cautious attitude in order to avoid political controversy with civil authorities. The Church's attitude, however, does not mean at all that the Church has neglected the defense of human rights throughout her history. Didn't the Church undergo heavy persecution wherever human rights were denied her members? During those times and during every period of sinful actions against the rights of any people the Church sided with the poor, but according to her own identity as a divine–human institution and not according to methods of revolution or violence that are often used by a political governments.[147] As the Second Millennium of Christianity draws near, in terms of John Paul II's *Tertio Millennio Adveniente*,

> ...the Church should become more fully conscious of the sinfulness of her children, recalling all those times in history when they departed from the spirit of Christ and his Gospel and, instead of offering to the world the witness of a life inspired by the values of faith, indulged in ways of thinking and acting which were truly forms of counter witness and scandal.[148]

This text is clearly inspired by Vatican II's *Lumen Gentium*, 8, where the Fathers of the Council affirmed the Church's need for continual purification.

In John Paul's *Letter to Families* (1994), there emerges the strong position of a Pope who condemns a civilization that does not protect the right of each and every person. That kind of selfish society is rooted in contemporary positivism that results in agnosticism in theory and utilitarianism in practice and in ethics. John Paul's teaching concerning utilitarianism throughout all his theological and social writings, is presented in this *Letter to Families* in terms of a civilization of production and of use, a civilization of 'things' and not of persons. Evidently, a person's rights, especially the rights of the poor and marginalized, are abused because in such a utilitarian civilization "woman can become an object for man, children a hindrance to parents, the family an institution obstructing the freedom of its members."[149] A utilitarian system that constantly is in quest of momentary and optimum worldly happiness, cuts the

---

'Favela Vidigal,' Rio de Janeiro (July 2, 1980), 4: *AAS* 72 (1980), 854.

[147]See Pope John Paul II, *Reconciliatio et Paenitentia*, 16; William J. Byron, "Solidarity: Path to Development and Peace," in *America* 158 (1988): 446; Roland James Faley, "Pope as Prophet: The New Social Encyclical," in *America* 158 (1988): 450; Mary Craig, *Man from a Far Country. A Portrait of Pope John Paul II*, London: Hodder And Stughton, 1982, 140–143.

[148]Pope John Paul II, *Tertio Millennio Adveniente*, 33.

[149]Pope John Paul II, *Letter to Families from Pope John Paul II*, 13.

total image of Christ to pieces. Such a "utilitarian happiness," recognized simply as an immediate gratification for the exclusive benefit of the individual, deprives the mechanism of Redemption of its possibility of effectiveness. This mechanism follows a divine law that cannot be reduced to just another human measure of healing or to a passing gratification resulting from a momentary remedy for human misery. The objective demands of the true good of man transcends the ideology of 'utilitarian happiness' to reach the ultimate happiness of the human person as established by the divine accomplishment of Redemption.[150] Therefore, I have to disagree with Gregory Baum who, at the conclusion of his article *The First Papal Encyclical*,[151] having accused the Church of neglecting in the past the defense of human rights, wonders why this topic was not brought up in Pope John Paul II's Encyclical Letter *Redemptor Hominis*: his claim that the Church does not live what it preaches on human rights does not seem to be supported by valid theological arguments.[152]

The Encyclical *Redemptoris Missio*, in criticizing a contemporary deficient image of Christ, presents the thought of the Pope from a different angle. The doctrinal underpinnings of this Encyclical deal with some ideological approaches to christology dealing with Christ's relationship with the kingdom of God. The many dimensions of the kingdom of God and its orientation to eschatology have been thoroughly investigated by Pope Paul VI and later by the International Theological Commission.[153] Pope Paul VI insisted that an 'integral development' should be constantly open to the Absolute.[154] John Paul II, along the same line of theological thought, rejects the secular interpretation of the kingdom, one which easily translates it into "one more ideology of purely earthly progress."[155] The activity of the Church, if performed for the

---

[150]Pope John Paul II, *Letter to Families from Pope John Paul II*, 14; William J. Byron, "Solidarity: Path to Development and Peace," in *America* 158 (1988): 446; Roland James Faley, "Pope as Prophet: The New Social Encyclical," in *America* 158 (1988): 450; Aloysius J. Fonseca, "Reflections on the Encyclical Letter *Sollicitudo Rei Socialis*," in *Gregorianum* 70 (1989): 14–15.

[151]See Gregory Baum, "The First Papal Encyclical," *The Ecumenist* 17 (1979): 58–59.

[152]See Pope John Paul II, *Laborem Exercens*, 11; *Sollicitudo Rei Socialis*, 41.

[153]See Pope John Paul II, *Redemptoris Missio*, 20; *Catechesi Tradendae*, 29; Pope Paul VI, *Evangelii Nuntiandi*, 34; International Theological Commission, *Select Themes of Ecclesiology on the Occasion of the Twentieth Anniversary of the Closing of the Second Vatican Council* (October 7, 1985), 10: "The Eschatological Character of the Church: Kingdom and Church."

[154]See Pope Paul VI, *Populorum Progressio*, 19–21 and 41–42. See also Fabio Giardini, "Trinitarian Communion and Christian Mission in *Redemptoris Missio*," in *Euntes* 47 (1994): 153.

[155]Pope John Paul II, *Redemptoris Missio*, 17. See also Ibid., *Catechesi Tradendae*, 35; *Sollicitudo Rei Socialis*, 41; *Documents of the Third General Conference of Latin American Bishops*, Puebla (1979), 3760 (1145); Carl E. Braaten, "A Papal Letter on the Church's Missionary Mandate," in *Dialog* 30 (1991): 181; Timothy O'Donnell, "The Crisis of Faith and the Theology of Mission: A Reflection on *Redemptoris Missio*," in *Faith and Reason* 18:3 (1992): 8–9; Fabio Giardini,

accomplishment of earthly progress, would be promoting human development rather than bringing people to the mystery of Redemption through conversion and baptism. True Christian freedom achieved by Redemption transcends the earthly task of liberating the human person from sin and opening for him life in abundance. As Michael Miller says in his introduction to the Encyclical *Redemptoris Missio*, "the Church's principal contribution to the development of peoples is not technical expertise or works of charity but the formation of consciences."[156] Her mission, John Paul says, "consists essentially in offering people an opportunity not to 'have more' but to 'be more,' by awaking their consciences through the Gospel."[157] It is through conversion of mind and heart and through the recognition of human dignity that the true meaning of liberation comes to light. The reduction of man to a horizontal scale of human values is an ideology that severs him from the essential relationship with the transcendental Christ. In the mind of John Paul, it is not possible to justify the lop–sided tendencies that reduce the multi–dimensional Gospel of Jesus Christ transforming the proclamation and witness of faith into an element of exclusively human and social liberation. That approach is not the answer for man's relationship with God in the world. Therefore, as the Pope again underscores in *Redemptoris Missio*, 20, "it must immediately be added that this temporal dimension of the kingdom remains incomplete unless it is related to the Kingdom of Christ present in the Church and straining toward eschatological fullness."[158] *Orientale Lumen*'s presentation of the tension between the 'already' and the 'not yet' of the kingdom, makes the Church flow back and forth between a continuity with the past (tradition) and eschatological expectation for the future. The Church should not make absolute what it does because it has a sacramental nature that is expressed in her faithful transmission of the Word of God, in her celebration of the sacraments, and in

---

"Trinitarian Communion and Christian Mission in *Redemptoris Missio*," in *Euntes* 47 (1994): 153–154.

[156]*The Encyclicals of John Paul II*, Edited with Introductions by Michael Miller, Indiana: Our Sunday Visitor Publishing Division, Our Sunday Visitor, Inc., 1996, 485. See also Pope John Paul II, *Familiaris Consortio*, 49; Roland James Faley, "Pope as Prophet: The New Social Encyclical," in *America* 158 (1988): 450; Carl E. Braaten, "A Papal Letter on the Church's Missionary Mandate," in *Dialog* 30 (1991): 181; James H. Kroeger, "Rekindling Mission Enthusiasm," in *The Priest* 48 (January, 1992): 33.

[157]Pope John Paul II, *Redemptoris Missio*, 58; Fabio Giardini, "Trinitarian Communion and Christian Mission in *Redemptoris Missio*," in *Euntes* 47 (1994): 154.

[158]See also Pope John Paul II, *Reconciliatio et Paenitentia*, 26; *Pastores Dabo Vobis*, 7; *Vita Consecrata*, 1; Timothy O'Donnell, "The Crisis of Faith and the Theology of Mission: A Reflection on *Redemptoris Missio*," in *Faith and Reason* 18:3 (1992): 8–9; James H. Kroeger, "Rekindling Mission Enthusiasm," in *The Priest* 48 (January, 1992): 33; Fabio Giardini, "Trinitarian Communion and Christian Mission in *Redemptoris Missio*," in *Euntes* 47 (1994): 154.

her participation in the prophetic, priestly and kingly mission of Jesus. The absolutization of the Church's actions denies the difference between her mission in history and the fullness of the kingdom:"whatever takes place in time can never be identified with the fullness of the kingdom, which is always a free gift." The eschatological dimension of the fullness of the kingdom does not compromise the promise of the Lord; yet that promise finds its ultimate dimension in the fullness of the kingdom. A constant tension between the 'already' and the 'not yet' of the kingdom guarantees the supremacy of the Lord in giving the kingdom always as a gift flowing from the divine initiative of God.[159]

Pope John Paul II and Approaches of Reduction in Contemporary Christology

An approach of *reduction* makes Christ the ultimate expression of secularization. Religion then is absorbed by society and its virtues are presented without relationship to any particular institution. This view reduces the image of the *Christus totus* and negates the existence of any specific religion. The Jesus Seminar, for example, mentions among its seven pillars of scholarly wisdom one especially that reflects this reductionist sense of Incarnation. It stipulates that Jesus was not an eschatological figure and that his understanding of mission was limited to a kingdom of strictly temporal dimensions. Incarnation is confused with ordinariness.[160]

Pope John Paul II says in *Redemptoris Missio*:

> The temptation today is to reduce Christianity to merely human wisdom, a pseudo–science of well–being. In our heavily secularized world a 'gradual secularization of salvation' has taken place, so that people strive for the good of man, but man who is truncated, reduced to his merely horizontal dimension. We know, however, that Jesus came to bring integral salvation, one which embraces the whole person and all mankind, and opens up the wondrous prospect of divine filiation.[161]

The mission and identity of the Church as developed is the Encyclical

---

[159]See Pope John Paul II, *Orientale Lumen*, 26. See also Ibid., *Vita Consecrata*, 1 and 16; Hans Cardinal Groër, "The Church Sacrament of Salvation," in *John Paul II. A Panorama of his Teachings*, New York: New City Press, 1989, 36; Timothy O'Donnell, "The Crisis of Faith and the Theology of Mission: A Reflection on *Redemptoris Missio*," in *Faith and Reason* 18:3 (1992): 8–9; James H. Kroeger, "Rekindling Mission Enthusiasm," in *The Priest* 48 (January, 1992): 33.

[160]See *The Five Gospels: The Search for the Authentic Words of Jesus*, Macmillian, 1993; Johann G. Roten, *The Word of God made man by the Holy Spirit*, 17–18; A. N. Wilson, *Jesus*, W. W. Norton, 1992, 17; L. T. Johnson, *The Real Jesus*, Harper, 1996, 46; M. Borg, *Jesus, A New Visions: Spirit, Culture, and the Life of Discipleship*, Harper and Row, 1987, 97–171.

[161]Pope John Paul II, *Redemptoris Missio*, 11. See also Ibid., *Catechesi Tradendae*, 29.

Redemptoris Missio, afford Pope John Paul II the opportunity to respond to this reductionism. He bases his approach on the theology of Vatican II, according to which the Church has been established as the universal sacrament of salvation.[162] In the opinion of the Pope, the Church is closely linked to the unique and necessary mediation of Christ as an indispensable sign and instrument by which God chooses to save humanity. Sound Christology cannot be separated from Church, because the Church, in the mystery of God's plan, is Christ's "co–worker in the salvation of the world."[163] Ecclesiology goes hand in hand with Christology, both being necessary in God's integral saving plan for all humanity. The grace of Redemption of every human person comes from Christ, a grace which, in turn, always has "a mysterious relationship to the Church."[164] Since this grace is the grace of Christ and is communicated through His Church, "the eschatological reality," as the Pope affirms in *Redemptoris Missio*, 13, "is not relegated to a remote 'end of the world,' but is already close and at work in our midst."[165] This type of relationship between Christology and Ecclesiology within the context of God's plan of salvation, serves to avoid confusing the Incarnation with any ordinary reality. Actually, it confirms the transcendent character of the mission of Christ and, by being incarnate in the divine–human institution of the Church, it takes the vitality out of any ecclesiological Gnosticism. The unwavering foundation and the supreme purpose of the Church, proceed from and are rooted in the transcendental and eternal plan of the Three Divine Persons.[166]

The Church is not merely a human or a 'man–made' institution, because it is necessarily based on Christological foundations: Christianity should never represent, as *Vita Consecrata* states, the transcendent dimension of the culture

---

[162]See *Lumen Gentium*, 48; *Gaudium et Spes*, 43; *Ad Gentes*, 7 and 21; Pope John Paul II, *Redemptoris Missio*, 9; *Catechesi Tradendae*, 32; Hans Cardinal Groër, "The Church Sacrament of Salvation," in *John Paul II. A Panorama of his Teachings*, New York: New City Press, 1989, 33–35; Josef Cardinal Tomko, "Mission and dialogue in the teaching of John Paul II," in *John Paul II. A Panorama of his Teachings*, New York: New City Press, 1989, 83; Timothy O'Donnell, "The Crisis of Faith and the Theology of Mission: A Reflection on *Redemptoris Missio*," in *Faith and Reason* 18:3 (1992): 8–9.

[163]Pope John Paul II, *Redemptoris Missio*, 9. See also Ibid., Letter to the Fifth Plenary Assembly of Asian Bishops' Conferences (June 23, 1990), 4: *AAS* 83 (1991), 101–102; *Dominicae Cenae*, 4; Hans Cardinal Groër, "The Church Sacrament of Salvation," in *John Paul II. A Panorama of his Teachings*, New York: New City Press, 1989, 33–35.

[164]Pope John Paul II, *Redemptoris Missio*, 10.

[165]See also Pope John Paul II, *Catechesi Tradendae*, 60; Timothy O'Donnell, "The Crisis of Faith and the Theology of Mission: A Reflection on *Redemptoris Missio*," in *Faith and Reason* 18:3 (1992): 8–9.

[166]See Josef Cardinal Tomko, "Mission and dialogue in the teaching of John Paul II," in *John Paul II. A Panorama of his Teachings*, New York: New City Press, 1989, 83–84.

itself.[167] Pope Paul VI has already dealt with this approach to Ecclesiology in his overall program of spreading the teaching of Vatican II concerning the identity and the role of the Church. Quoted by Pope John Paul II in *Redemptoris Missio*, 19, Pope Paul VI summarizes his understanding of the profound link between Christ and the Church: the Church "is not an end unto herself, but rather is fervently concerned to be completely of Christ, in Christ and for Christ, as well as completely of men, among men and for men."[168]

In *Tertio Millennio Adveniente*, the answer of Pope John Paul II to the reductionist approach to christology, is based on the extraordinary character of Christianity. What this religion brings about is the necessity of institutionalizing the Revelation of God in a Church that is human and divine at the same time. The necessity of a specific religion does not contradict the transcendence of God since Christianity is an incarnational faith that respects the eschatological and transcendent character of Christ's kingdom. In *Tertio Millennio Adveniente*, Pope John Paul II says:

> In Christ this pedagogy (of the Old Covenant) achieves its purpose: Jesus does not in fact merely speak 'in the name of God' like the Prophets, but he is God himself speaking in his Eternal Word made flesh. Here we touch upon the essential point by which Christianity differs from all the other religions, by which man's search for God has been expressed from earliest times. Christianity has its starting–point in the Incarnation of the Word.[169]

For John Paul, if Christ becomes the ultimate expression of secularization, the transcendental aspect of the Incarnation as it is expressed in the mission of the Church is reduced to a mere humanism. In *Christifideles Laici*, John Paul II manifests the danger resulting from such an approach, especially because it disconnects man's relationship with any transcendental divinity with the excuse of a self–sufficiency. Even if Christ is brought into the picture by humanism, it is solely because he is presented an example with an exclusively temporal character: humanism, as the world philosophy, becomes a false humanism if it reduced to the world of physics without going to metaphysics which interprets the real significance of being. The elimination of the metaphysics of being which is the result of a false humanism endangers the religious sense of man and his constant need for the transcendent:"A certain

---

[167]See Pope John Paul II, *Vita Consecrata*, 79; *Dominicae Cenae*, 4; Hans Cardinal Groër, "The Church Sacrament of Salvation," in *John Paul II. A Panorama of his Teachings*, New York: New City Press, 1989, 33–35.

[168]Pope Paul VI, Address at the Opening of the Third Session of the Second Vatican Ecumenical Council (September 14, 1964): *AAS* 56 (1964): 810; Hans Cardinal Groër, "The Church Sacrament of Salvation," in *John Paul II. A Panorama of his Teachings*, New York: New City Press, 1989, 36.

[169]Pope John Paul II, *Tertio Millennio Adveniente*, 6. See also Ibid., *Catechesi Tradendae*, 52.

type of humanism founded on an explicit antimetaphysical premise, which has invaded so many philosophical expressions in modern times, constitutes an intentional effort to dissociate the empirical from the transcendent, the contingent from the absolute; and, in the last analysis, this is an anti–religious undertaking."[170]

Many times, humanism deprive Christ of any extraordinary or supernatural qualities as if these qualities are a threat for the human person. "It has been said," observes the Pope, "that ours is the time of 'humanism': paradoxically, some of its atheistic and secularistic forms arrive at a point where the human person is diminished and annihilated; other forms of humanism, instead, exalt the individual in such a manner that these forms become a veritable and real idolatry."[171]

In *Pastores Dabo Vobis* rationalism is considered as that specific type of humanism that is totally subjective and does not leave any space for contact between man and divinity. Unfortunately, "it is still very widespread and, in the name of a reductive concept of 'science,' it renders human reason insensitive to an encounter with revelation and with divine transcendence."[172] This is a somewhat secularist outlook on life and human destiny, an outlook that is described by Pope Paul VI, quoted by John Paul's *Pastores Dabo Vobis*, 7. In his acute and wise vision, Paul VI detected that the individual is "...all bound up in himself, this man who makes himself not only the center of his every interest, but dares to propose himself as the principle and reason of all reality."[173] By proposing himself as the principle of all reality, man implicitly acquires a sense of false self–sufficiency that, without any explicit opposition to God, will lead him to feel that he is simply able to do without God. Such an outlook on human existence still invades today's mentality despite the fall of the ideologies which made materialism a dogma and denied the need for religion. Thus a practical and existential atheism, in John Paul's opinion, contaminates the widespread secularist outlook on human life and man's destiny: without considering God, man's explanation of the reality of the world

---

[170]See Pope John Paul II, *Insegnamenti*, II/2, 542; Joseph Cardinal Cordeiro, "The religious sense of man," in *John Paul II. A Panorama of his Teachings*, New York: New City Press, 1989, 77; Darió Castrillón, "The family in the Magisterium of John Paul II," in *John Paul II. A Panorama of his Teachings*, New York: New City Press, 1989, 114–115.

[171]Pope John Paul II, *Christifideles Laici*, 5; J. Honoré, "Christ the Redeemer, Core of John Paul's Teaching," in *John Paul II. A Panorama of his Teachings*, New York: New City Press, 1989, 24–25; Joseph Cardinal Cordeiro, "The religious sense of man," in *John Paul II. A Panorama of his Teachings*, New York: New City Press, 1989, 77.

[172]Pope John Paul II, *Pastores Dabo Vobis*, 7.

[173]Pope Paul VI, homily at the ninth session of the Second Vatican Council (Dec. 7, 1965): *AAS* 58 (1966), 55; Pope John Paul II, *Pastores Dabo Vobis*, 7.

becomes a dangerous weapon that implicitly denies God's existence.

John Paul's *Letter to Families* (1994) looks for the roots of christological reduction in the phenomenon of the *Enlightment*. According to this approach, man is 'more' human if he is merely human: everything transcendental that belongs to man and that was given him by the Creator and the Redeemer, is reduced to just what man is in himself. Consequently, the constant tension between man's limitations and his transcendence is reduced to the ordinariness of a being who is boxed into his own reality without any reference to his relationship of creation, Redemption, and sanctification with the Three Divine Persons. Anthropology then loses its intimate connection with christology and becomes an anthropomonism.[174]

Pope John Paul II and Meditative Exploration of Transcendence

The last anthropological approach to Christ focuses on a meditative exploration of transcendence where Christ is used merely as a symbol in order to express it. There is an incomprehensibility and an inaccessibility of God on which we project our ideas, ambitions, needs, wishes and representations. This *projection* stresses the divine and, consequently, neglects the unity between humanity and divinity in the person of Christ.[175]

Already in Wojtyla's first doctoral dissertation, *Faith According to Saint John of the Cross*,[176] the *anthropological* analysis of man's relationship with God presupposes an authentic understanding of the historical data of Divine Revelation. That understanding sheds light on the impossibility for the human mind, even in its mystical experience of God, to go beyond the historicity of Revelation to reach transcendence through meditative exploration. In mystical experience the living faith becomes the supernatural virtue that perfects the intellect of a soul elevated by grace to God.[177] This happens, however, through a process of purification in which the mind is purged of conceptual knowledge of God derived from the abstraction of their content from sense experience.[178]

---

[174]Pope John Paul II, *Letter to Families from Pope John Paul II*, 15.

[175]See R. Arnaldez, *Jésus, fils de Marie, prophète de l'Islam*, Paris: Desclée, 1980; G. De Rosa, *Cristianesimo, religioni e sètte non cristiane a confronto*, Roma: Città Nuova, 1989; J. Dupuis, *Gesù Cristo incontro alle religioni*, Assisi: Cittadella, 1989; J. Vernette, *Jésus dans la nouvelle religiosité*, Paris: Desclée, 1987.

[176]For an analysis of *Faith According to Saint John of the Cross*, see Rocco Buttiglione, *Karol Wojtyla. The Thought of the Man who became Pope John Paul II*, trans. Paolo Guietti and Francesca Murphy, Grand Rapids/Cambridge: William B. Eerdmans Publishing Company, 1997, 45–53.

[177]See *Faith According to Saint John of the Cross*, 237–238; Rocco Buttiglione, *Karol Wojtyla. The Thought of the Man who became Pope John Paul II*, trans. Paolo Guietti and Francesca Murphy, Grand Rapids/Cambridge: William B. Eerdmans Publishing Company, 1997, 46.

[178]See *Faith According to Saint John of the Cross*, 241–243 and 252–253.

This purification is a cooperation between an intellect drawn to God through an act of faith and God's own operation. In that cooperation the human person realizes that his or her mind receives more and more infused supernatural knowledge that is the exclusive gift of God who reveals Himself. McCool's description of Wojtyla's dissertation in that respect reads: "And so, through the active and passive purification of its knowledge, the adherence of the believing intellect to God's revelation came to depend less on its natural operation as a mind and more on the infused light which it owed to its supernatural participation in God's own divine knowledge."[179] Since the supernatural virtue of faith bestows on the mind the infused supernatural knowledge of God, the object of the mind cannot but be the truth coming from Divine Revelation. In other words, in the mystical encounter between the believing mind and God, the very matter of that supernatural knowledge of God is provided by the truth of historical Revelation. Mystical knowledge of God could never, therefore, rise above or surpass in its clarity or content historical Revelation which remains the "highest form of knowledge of God in the power of any human soul united to its body."[180]

Wojtyla explains more: to the living faith is added the infused theological virtue of charity which is the gift of the Holy Spirit who brings the habit of charity from potency to act. This virtue gives to faith the necessary strength to adhere to the truths of Divine Revelation. Both living faith and the infused theological virtue of charity accomplish the ontological union between the believing mind and God. That "ontological union with God however could not overcome the innate imperfection of knowledge through faith on the psychological level."[181]   This imperfection comes from the conceptual knowledge abstracted from the experiences of the senses. Therefore, the faith of the believing mind does not grow when it acquires more clarity in conceptual knowledge; rather, the growth takes place when the mind increases its ability to put aside that conceptual knowledge in order to adhere to the 'substance' of Revelation.[182] Therefore, the ultimate source of contemplative wisdom is inevitably faith, "for no knowledge of God's own inner being available to the human mind could be more direct or immediate than the

---

[179]Gerald A. McCool, "The Theology of John Paul II," in *The Thought of Pope John Paul II*, 33.

[180]*Faith According to Saint John of the Cross*, 245, 257–261, and 264. See also Gerald A. McCool, "The Theology of John Paul II," in *The Thought of Pope John Paul II*, John M. McDermott (ed.), Rome: Gregorian University Press, 1993, 35; Williams, *The Mind of John Paul II*, 106 ff.

[181]Gerald A. McCool, *Ibid.*, 34. See *Faith According to Saint John of the Cross*, 251–261; Rocco Buttiglione, *Karol Wojtyla. The Thought of the Man who became Pope John Paul II*, trans. Paolo Guietti and Francesca Murphy, Grand Rapids/Cambridge: William B. Eerdmans Publishing Company, 1997, 46.

[182]See Gerald McCool, *Ibid.*, 35.

knowledge given by God Himself in revelation and accepted by man through faith."[183]

As short as this summary is on that specific section of *Faith According to Saint John of the Cross*, it shows how the young Wojtyla was firmly founded on the indispensable truth coming from Divine Revelation that took place in and through the historical Jesus of Nazareth. No form of mystical knowledge could ever rise above historical revelation and no form of non–conceptual wisdom could ever take the place of faith that accepts Divine Revelation and adheres to it.

As the Archbishop of Cracow, Wojtyla developed the theme of the origin of the Church in his *Sources of Renewal*. This work is an exposition of Vatican II's theology of the Church and treats the question of the Church's consciousness of her own nature in relation to the Trinity. This link between the theology of the Church and trinitarian theology was already made by *Lumen Gentium* and followed up by many post–conciliar theologians. As it was said in the Introduction to the present volume, the *Sources of Renewal* presents the proper order of the revealed truths: *Creation, Incarnation, Redemption*, and the *sending of the Holy Spirit*.[184] The logic of faith suggests this ordering of the revealed truths in order to understand properly the Church's consciousness of her own origin and nature: "In the logical order of faith, the origin of the Church was subsequent to the Father's mission of His Son, and of His Holy Spirit, through His Son, to perform the work of divine redemption."[185] Note that the redemptive work of the Son stands at the center of the Church's consciousness of her own origin and nature. This is the reason behind the opening words of *Redemptor Hominis*, 1: "The Redeemer of man, Jesus Christ, is the center of the universe and of history," a theology that John Paul II had already been living for a long time before his election to the see of St. Peter. Obviously, Wojtyla's theology of the Church had to be built upon his favored

---

[183]Gerald A. McCool, *Ibid.*, 35. See also John M. McDermott, "The Theology of John Paul II. A Response," in *The Thought of Pope John Paul II*, John M. McDermott (ed.), Rome: Gregorian University Press, 1993, 55; Rocco Buttiglione, *Karol Wojtyla. The Thought of the Man who became Pope John Paul II*, trans. Paolo Guietti and Francesca Murphy, Grand Rapids/Cambridge: William B. Eerdmans Publishing Company, 1997, 46.

[184]See Karol Wojtyla, *Sources of Renewal: The Implementation of the Second Vatican Council*, San Francisco: Harper and Row, 1980, 35–41.

[185]Gerald A. McCool, "The Theology of John Paul II," in *The Thought of Pope John Paul II*, John M. McDermott (ed.), Rome: Gregorian University Press, 1993, 44; Karol Wojtyla, *Sources of Renewal: The Implementation of the Second Vatican Council*, San Francisco: Harper and Row, 1980, 44; J. Honoré, "Christ the Redeemer, Core of John Paul's Teaching," in *John Paul II. A Panorama of his Teachings*, New York: New City Press, 1989, 24–25.

theology of the Trinity and the Incarnation.[186] McCool states with perspicuous insight that, in this area, the theologies of Wojtyla and Rahner come close together, although Rahner does not seem to have had any direct influence on Wojtyla:"Nevertheless, in both theologies, a metaphysics based upon the experience of the free self–conscious person links the Church to the Trinity and the Incarnation and grounds an intrinsic continuity between the orders of creation and redemption."[187]

Consequently, the Church is not in communion with the Triune God through a meditative exploration of His transcendence. Instead, the very origin and nature of the Church are transcendent as such because the Church is constantly aware that she has been commissioned by the Father, through the Incarnation of the Son and the sending of the Holy Spirit: the Church as mystery and communion reflects in time the eternal and ineffable mystery and the intrinsic communion of God, Three in One.[188] This vertical dimension of the Church's consciousness, since it is a prime dimension in the theology of Karol Wojtyla, is emphasized later on in the whole ecclesiological approach of Pope John Paul II.

Later on, in his papal writings, Pope John Paul II picked up again the whole issue of a faith that is incarnational in a Church in order to steer away from an exclusively meditative study of the transcendent God. By incarnational faith it is meant what the Pope says in *Christifideles Laici* when describing the role of the lay faithful in the society: "Thus for the lay faithful, to be present and active in the world is not only an anthropological and sociological reality, but in a specific way, a theological and ecclesiological reality as well."[189] The Pope warns again against a denial of the saving Incarnation of Christ as he meditates in *Vita Consecrata* on the witness that religious and other consecrated persons should give when faced with superficial solutions to the

[186]Gerald A. McCool, "The Theology of John Paul II," in *The Thought of Pope John Paul II*, John M. McDermott (ed.), Rome: Gregorian University Press, 1993, 44; Karol Wojtyla, *Sources of Renewal: The Implementation of the Second Vatican Council*, San Francisco: Harper and Row, 1980, 57–59 and 66–100.

[187]Gerald A. McCool, "The Theology of John Paul II," in *The Thought of Pope John Paul II*, John M. McDermott (ed.), Rome: Gregorian University Press, 1993, 50. See also Manuel Ureña, "The Missionary Impulse in the Church according to *Redemptoris Missio*," in *Communio* 19 (1992): 97–98.

[188]Karol Wojtyla, *Sources of Renewal: The Implementation of the Second Vatican Council*, San Francisco: Harper and Row, 1980, 36–41 and 397–408. See also Pope John Paul II, *Christifideles Laici*, 31; Josef Cardinal Tomko, "Mission and dialogue in the teaching of John Paul II," in *John Paul II. A Panorama of his Teachings*, New York: New City Press, 1989, 83–84.

[189]Pope John Paul II, *Christifideles Laici*, 15; Josef Cardinal Tomko, "Mission and dialogue in the teaching of John Paul II," in *John Paul II. A Panorama of his Teachings*, New York: New City Press, 1989, 84–85.

question of human existence raised by contemporaries. All the dimensions of human reality should be taken into account including the redeeming grace that actually comes from both the creation and the Incarnation. Consecrated persons are invited to be aware of the fine line existing between a search for God and a search for self which is subconsciously based on pure selfishness: "They constitute a warning against confusing that search (for God) with a subtle search for self or a flight into Gnosticism."[190]

He emphasizes the fact that the Incarnation, ontological and transcendental as it is, still happened in human history. Therefore, Incarnation constitutes the one and only source of salvation: the final sanctification of humankind draws its possibility from the Incarnation of the Son. There are two poles that are the constitutive elements of the Redemption. One is the *hypostatic union*[191] of the two natures in the Person of the Word; the other is His *death and resurrection*.[192] This mechanism of Redemption, in a historical and objective way, provides the grace of forgiveness of sins and of salvation because man cannot achieve it on his own. As expressed in *Reconciliatio et Paenitentia*, 20: "The Christian has received the guarantee and the necessary strength not to sin. It is not a question therefore of a sinlessness acquired through one's own virtue or even inherent in man, as the Gnostics thought."[193]

Both the Incarnation and the Paschal Mystery are indispensable and complementary, but the first is the basis and even the condition of the other:"In the salvific design of the Most Holy Trinity, the mystery of the Incarnation constitutes the superabundant fulfillment of the promise made by God to man after original sin, after that first sin whose effects oppress the whole earthly history of man (cf. Gen 3:15)."[194] Pope John Paul II does not combine both aspects in a syncretic way; he rather gives to each its place in God's economy of salvation.

Christ cannot be taken as a mere symbol that points to the transcendence of the divine, because "it is 'God, who is rich in mercy (Eph 2:4)' whom Jesus Christ has revealed to us as Father: it is his very Son who, in himself, has

---

[190]See Pope John Paul II, *Vita Consecrata*, 103.

[191]See Ecumenical Council of Chalcedon, *Definitio fidei: Conciliorum Oecumenicorum Decreta*, Ed. Istituto per le Scienze Religiose, 3rd ed., Bologna, 1973, 86 (DS 301) quoted by Pope John Paul II, *Redemptoris Mater*, 31. See also Pope John Paul II, *Redemptoris Mater*, 9 and 39; *Tertio Millennio Adveniente*, 3; Gregory Baum, "The First Encyclical," in *The Ecumenist* 17 (1979): 56.

[192]See Pope John Paul II, *Redemptor Hominis*, 20; *Dives in Misericordia*, 7; Robert Morneau, "*Redemptor Hominis*: Themes and Thesis," in *Review for Religious* 39 (1980): 250.

[193]See also Hans Cardinal Groër, "The Church Sacrament of Salvation," in *John Paul II. A Panorama of his Teachings*, New York: New City Press, 1989, 33–35.

[194]Pope John Paul II, *Redemptoris Mater*, 11.

manifested him and made him known to us."[195] Commenting on John 1:18 where St. John writes that "the only Son, who is in the bosom of the Father, he has made him known," Pope John Paul II says: "This 'making known' reveals God in the most profound mystery of his being, one and three, surrounded by 'unapproachable light'."[196] This statement confirms that there is no part of the transcendence that is not incarnate in Jesus Christ, because Christ is the definitive self–revelation of God and not just one more spiritual guru in religious history. The idea that "a sort of void which is sometimes suggested as existing between Christ and the Logos," does not fit into the categories of a true Incarnation. By Christ, one has to understand not simply the Word pre–existent to the Incarnation, as the new forms of cosmic theocentrism would present it. Against neo–modernist theology, John Paul confirms Christ's full awareness of his unique and universal mediation.[197]

Consequently, the whole of divinity is fully revealed and manifested in and through Christ Who Himself, as God and man at the same time, died and is risen. Jesus Christ is not just one of the many possible manifestations of the Word in history. There is an absolute identification between Him and the Word. Recalling the binding teaching of Chalcedon against Nestorius, John Paul II asserts in *Redemptoris Missio*: "Jesus is the Incarnate Word — a single and indivisible person. One cannot separate Jesus from the Christ...Christ is none other than Jesus of Nazareth."[198]

The uniqueness of Christ, consequently, has an absolute and universal significance. All grace of Redemption flows from the objective and historical event of the Paschal mystery, in which Christ reveals Himself to be the exclusive Savior of humanity. Even those who do not know Christ and His mediation, are nonetheless saved through him, because they share in that mystery in a way known to God alone. The universality of salvation that is accomplished in and through Christ cannot be narrowed down by any system

---

[195]Pope John Paul II, *Dives in Misericordia*, 1.

[196]Pope John Paul II, *Dives in Misericordia*, 2.

[197]Pope John Paul II, *Redemptoris Missio*, 29. See also *Ibid.*, 5; Manuel Ureña, "The Missionary Impulse in the Church according to *Redemptoris Missio*," in *Communio* 19 (1992): 97; Timothy O'Donnell, "The Crisis of Faith and the Theology of Mission: A Reflection on *Redemptoris Missio*," in *Faith and Reason* 18:3 (1992): 6; James H. Kroeger, "Rekindling Mission Enthusiasm," in *The Priest* 48 (January, 1992): 33; Hans Cardinal Groër, "The Church Sacrament of Salvation," in *John Paul II. A Panorama of his Teachings*, New York: New City Press, 1989, 33–35; Fabio Giardini, "Trinitarian Communion and Christian Mission in *Redemptoris Missio*," in *Euntes* 47 (1994): 152.

[198]Pope John Paul II, *Redemptoris Missio*, 6. See also Ibid., *Dominum et Vivificantem*, 19; Manuel Ureña, "The Missionary Impulse in the Church according to *Redemptoris Missio*," in *Communio* 19 (1992): 97; Timothy O'Donnell, "The Crisis of Faith and the Theology of Mission: A Reflection on *Redemptoris Missio*," in *Faith and Reason* 18:3 (1992): 7; James H. Kroeger, "Rekindling Mission Enthusiasm," in *The Priest* 48 (January, 1992): 33.

of knowledge: all are saved by Him whether they know it or not. All saving grace comes from Christ and is the result of His Sacrifice.[199]

Pope John Paul II follows the steps of the Second Vatican Council in developing a theology of presence and activity of Christ and the Spirit outside the visible boundaries of the Church. Nonetheless, avoiding all forms of 'ecclesiocentrism' which would make the Church a more important element in the economy of salvation than Christ, he contends that the Church has a "specific and necessary role"[200] in God's saving plan: "the Church is the ordinary means of salvation and...she alone possesses the fullness of the means of salvation."[201] The Church is a universal sacrament or sign and the universal instrument of salvation. As the universal sacrament of Redemption, the Church effects what it signifies: the divine grace of Redemption. As a universal instrument of salvation, the Church, moved by the Holy Spirit, is used by Christ to carry out His mission: "The universal activity of the Spirit is not to be separated from his particular activity within the body of Christ."[202] The reason is the fact that all activities of the Holy Spirit are oriented toward their fulfillment in Christ, and Christ is the head of the Church. Here again, it should be made clear that the pneumatological dimension of Redemption enjoys a christological content and is necessarily therefore ecclesiological. In conclusion, the salvation made possible to all human beings by the Redemption, in a real but hidden way necessarily involves "a mysterious

---

[199]See Pope John Paul II, *Redemptoris Missio*, 10; Carl E. Braaten, "A Papal Letter on the Church's Missionary Mandate," in *Dialog* 30 (1991): 181–182; Manuel Ureña, "The Missionary Impulse in the Church according to *Redemptoris Missio*," in *Communio* 19 (1992): 97; Timothy O'Donnell, "The Crisis of Faith and the Theology of Mission: A Reflection on *Redemptoris Missio*," in *Faith and Reason* 18:3 (1992): 7; Hans Cardinal Groër, "The Church Sacrament of Salvation," in *John Paul II. A Panorama of his Teachings*, New York: New City Press, 1989, 33–35; Fabio Giardini, "Trinitarian Communion and Christian Mission in *Redemptoris Missio*," in *Euntes* 47 (1994): 154–155.

[200]Pope John Paul II, *Redemptoris Missio*, 18; Josef Cardinal Tomko, "Mission and dialogue in the teaching of John Paul II," in *John Paul II. A Panorama of his Teachings*, New York: New City Press, 1989, 84–85.

[201]Pope John Paul II, *Redemptoris Missio*, 55. See also Hans Cardinal Groër, "The Church Sacrament of Salvation," in *John Paul II. A Panorama of his Teachings*, New York: New City Press, 1989, 28; Josef Cardinal Tomko, "Mission and dialogue in the teaching of John Paul II," in *John Paul II. A Panorama of his Teachings*, New York: New City Press, 1989, 85.

[202]Pope John Paul II, *Redemptoris Missio*, 29; Josef Cardinal Tomko, "Mission and dialogue in the teaching of John Paul II," in *John Paul II. A Panorama of his Teachings*, New York: New City Press, 1989, 84–86; Manuel Ureña, "The Missionary Impulse in the Church according to *Redemptoris Missio*," in *Communio* 19 (1992): 101; James H. Kroeger, "Rekindling Mission Enthusiasm," in *The Priest* 48 (January, 1992): 36.

relationship to the Church."[203] The Church, as sacrament, not only signifies and brings about union with God in the order of salvation, but also signifies and brings about unity of all humankind in the order of creation. The expansion of the traditional concept of sacrament applied to the Church, demonstrates the extraordinary skill of John Paul II who, having selected the words of *Lumen Gentium*, 1, developed them throughout his writings insisting on the necessary analogy involved in using the word sacrament as applied to the Church or to the seven sacraments: the text of *Lumen Gentium* states that the Church is *like* a sacrament, not *a sacrament*. One must speak of the sacramentality of the Church in an analogous, but identical manner, to the seven sacraments instituted by Christ and administered by the Church. The development of the concept of sacrament as found in *Lumen Gentium* throughout the writings of John Paul II, explains the grounds for his continual reference to ecclesiology as he is theologizing on various disciplines.[204]

Whereas meditative exploration of the transcendence would focus on the subjective efforts of the human person searching the divine mystery, it would overlook the divine dimension of Redemption.[205] This dimension offers the objective grace of salvation, a grace that is imparted to humanity exclusively by God. The whole mechanism of Redemption is incarnational and is therefore trinitarian: "no one, therefore, can enter into communion with God except through Christ, by the working of the Holy Spirit."[206] Pope John Paul II believes that one can speak about Redemption in two senses: the first is the reality of Redemption itself that is the exclusive action of the incarnate Word; the second is the application of that Redemption to individuals who accept and cooperate with it.[207] Here the familiar saying of St. Augustine is very meaningful: the One who created you without your choice, does not save you without your choice.

The concept of the kingdom of God as handed down in the tradition and theology of the Church is another aspect of the theology of Pope John Paul II that opposes a merely meditative exploration of the transcendence. The Pope

---

[203]Pope John Paul II, *Redemptoris Missio*, 10. See also Hans Cardinal Groër, "The Church Sacrament of Salvation," in *John Paul II. A Panorama of his Teachings*, New York: New City Press, 1989, 28.

[204]See Pope John Paul II, *General Audience*, September 8, 1982; Hans Cardinal Groër, "The Church Sacrament of Salvation," in *John Paul II. A Panorama of his Teachings*, New York: New City Press, 1989, 28.

[205]See Pope John Paul II, *Redemptor Hominis*, 9.

[206]Pope John Paul II, *Redemptoris Missio*, 5.

[207]See Pope John Paul II, *Redemptoris Missio*, 10; Lothar Roos, "On a Theology and Ethics of Work," *Communio* 11 (1984): 110.

demonstrates that the kingdom of God cannot be exclusively presented theocentrically; it should always be linked to Christ and the Church because of the trinitarian character of the Divine Revelation.[208] Since Christ incarnating the kingdom with His very Person; since the Church (*Lumen Gentium*, 5) is the kingdom's "seed and beginning"[209] on earth and also is, as *Redemptoris Missio* puts it, the "co–worker (of Christ) in the salvation of the world,"[210] then Christ and the Church cannot be subordinate to the kingdom. Their purpose cannot be reduced to serving the kingdom in the sense that this kingdom is alone supreme in God's plan. Otherwise, Christ and the Church would be reduced merely to two among many symbols that express a meditative exploration of transcendence, whereas both are necessary and complementary truths that must be professed at one and the same time. The Pope therefore concludes that the kingdom is "not a concept, a doctrine, or a program subject to free interpretation, but is before all else a person with the face and name of Jesus of Nazareth."[211]

---

[208]See Pope John Paul II, *Redemptoris Missio*, 17–18; *Redemptionis Donum*, 11; *Chrsitifideles Laici*, 36; *Pastores Dabo Vobis*, 12; *The Encyclicals of John Paul II*, Edited with Introduction by Michael Miller, Indiana: Our Sunday Visitor Publishing Division, Our Sunday Visitor, Inc., 1996, 481.

[209]Pope John Paul II, *Christifideles Laici*, 36; *Pastores Dabo Vobis*, 12; Timothy O'Donnell, "The Crisis of Faith and the Theology of Mission: A Reflection on *Redemptoris Missio*," in *Faith and Reason* 18:3 (1992): 8.

[210]Pope John Paul II, *Redemptoris Missio*, 9; Manuel Ureña, "The Missionary Impulse in the Church according to *Redemptoris Missio*," in *Communio* 19 (1992): 98–99; Timothy O'Donnell, "The Crisis of Faith and the Theology of Mission: A Reflection on *Redemptoris Missio*," in *Faith and Reason* 18:3 (1992): 8.

[211]Pope John Paul II, *Redemptoris Missio*, 18; Manuel Ureña, "The Missionary Impulse in the Church according to *Redemptoris Missio*," in *Communio* 19 (1992): 96–99; Timothy O'Donnell, "The Crisis of Faith and the Theology of Mission: A Reflection on *Redemptoris Missio*," in *Faith and Reason* 18:3 (1992): 8–9; Fabio Giardini, "Trinitarian Communion and Christian Mission in *Redemptoris Missio*," in *Euntes* 47 (1994): 153.

CHAPTER SIX

IMMANENT AND ECONOMIC TRINITY
IN THE THEOLOGICAL THOUGHT OF JOHN PAUL II

An Outlook on the Theology of Revelation in Contemporary Period

The first Vatican Council, when speaking about the Divine Revelation, proposed that God reveals *qualities about Himself* that go beyond the capacity of human intelligence. *Dei Filius* affirms that there would be no means of understanding these qualities if God did not reveal them to us.[1] Since the mysteries concerning God surpass the capacities of the human intellect, the authority of God is the only guarantee of their truthfulness.[2] Therefore there are two orders of knowledge of Divine Revelation: knowledge based on faith and knowledge based on reason. Vatican I, by limiting Divine Revelation to *characteristics about God*, reached only a partial exposition which would later be completed by the Fathers of the Second Vatican Council.

The *Second Vatican Council* moved the emphasis from a revelation *of qualities about God* (Vatican I) to *God's self–communication*.[3] In comparison with Vatican I, Vatican II employs a deeper concept of Divine Revelation that is fully trinitarian and christological.[4] The historical event of Jesus Christ is the actual reality of the Triune God's self–communication. Divine Revelation is not seen anymore in contrast with history, but is understood in the historical perspective of Jesus Christ's redemptive work.[5] The fulness of the Divine

---

[1] See *DS*, 3015.

[2] See First Vatican Ecumenical Council, Dogmatic Constitution on the Church of Christ *Pastor Aeternus*: Conciliorum Oecumenicorum Decreta, Ed. Istituto per le Scienze Religiose, 3rd ed., Bologna, 1973, 811–816; *Lumen Gentium*, 25; Pope John Paul II, *Redemptor Hominis*, 19.

[3] See *Dei Verbum*, 2.

[4] See *Dei Verbum*, 4.

[5] R. Latourelle extensively investigated the historico–salvific dimension of the theology of Revelation: from the Old Testament until the coming of Christ and throughout the history of the Church, all the scriptural data in their historical evolvement become a reading of God's self–manifestation (see *Dei Verbum*, 24; R. Latourelle, *La Révélation chrétienne. Notion biblique, notion théologique*. Excepta ex dissertatione, 1956 cat. P.U.G. 1101; Rino Fisichella, "Il Contributo

Revelation of the Triune God is realized through the death and resurrection of Christ and the descent of the Holy Spirit.[6] Consequently, Vatican II clearly affirms the fact that Christian Revelation is adequately understood only in a trinitarian perspective. This Council recuperates the centrality of the mystery of the Trinity in the faith and the theology of the Church: at the core of the New Testament stands the belief that the God we believe in is a Triune God.

The Second Vatican Council that was, in terms of John Paul II, "in a special way an 'ecclesiological' Council,"[7] was primarily concerned with the theme of Church. Since this Council is also "essentially 'pneumatological',"[8] the Fathers of this Council found in the trinitarian and the christological character of God's Revelation[9] the best soil for a fruitful thinking about the role and identity of the Church. In fact, the Council emphasized that the Church is missionary by nature and dynamically bases her mission on the trinitarian mission of the Three Divine Persons.[10] In the path of Vatican II, both Pope Paul VI and Pope John Paul II brought out the need for a new study of the doctrine on the Holy Spirit. Paul VI asserted: "The Christology and particularly the ecclesiology of the Council must be succeeded by a new study of and devotion to the Holy Spirit, precisely as the indispensable complement to the teaching of the Council."[11] While the Second Vatican Council is especially concerned with ecclesiology, "the teaching of this Council," as Pope John Paul II asserts on the other hand, "is essentially 'pneumatological': it is permeated by the truth about the Holy Spirit, as the soul of the Church."[12] Clearly, in this area, the influence of the ecclesiology of Hans Urs von Balthasar on the Council is relevant. Such an ecclesiological orientation[13] opened the door to Pope Paul VI and John Paul II to connect the mystery of the Trinity to all the aspects of the Church's faith and its theology as well.

---

di R. Latourelle alla Teologia Fondamentale," in Rino Fisichella (ed.), *Gesù Rivelatore*, Piemme, 1988, 14).

[6]See *Dei Verbum*, 4.

[7]Pope John Paul II, *Dominum et Vivificantem*, 26.

[8]Pope John Paul II, *Dominum et Vivificantem*, 26.

[9]See especially *Lumen Gentium*, 2, 3, 4, 8 and 9.

[10]See Pope John Paul II, *Redemptoris Missio*, 1.

[11]Address at General Audience (June 6, 1973): *Insegnamenti* XI (1973), 477.

[12]Pope John Paul II, *Dominum et Vivificantem*, 26.

[13]For details concerning the ecclesiological revival of Vatican II, see the list of theological works in N. Ciola, *Il dibattito ecclesiologico in Italia. Uno studio bibliografico* (1963–1984), Roma, 1986. See also Salvador Pié–Ninot, "La Chiesa come Tema Teologico Fondamentale," in *Gesù Rivelatore*, Editor Rino Fisichella, Eidizioni Piemme, 1988, 148–152; Mary Craig, *Man from a Far Country. A Portrait of Pope John Paul II*, London: Hodder And Stoughton, 1982, 64–65.

The enormous contribution of R. Latourelle to the theology of Revelation is very noticeable in the world of Catholic theology. The valid preoccupation of Vatican II with consideration of the Word of God primarily in its theological framework,[14] did not stop Latourelle from presenting the *preambula fidei* or the *motivum fidei* that promotes a lively presentation of the faith without leading the Christian community into Fideism.

Latourelle thoroughly develops a theology of Revelation that is Christocentric. The mystery of God's Revelation is not merely an abstract idea, but a real concrete Person. Christ as the Revealer and simultaneously the Revelation of the Father, is the unique reality of God's self–expression: Christ is in our midst as the Revelation in Person, in Him everything is given and revealed to us.[15] It is through the Word made flesh, therefore, that this definitive and full Revelation of God is made possible. The Incarnation is the reality that expresses the fullness of the mystery: the God–man becomes perfectly connatural with the human language of salvation as well as God's divine plan.[16]

The thought of Latourelle shows that the theology of Revelation as found proposed in *Dei Verbum* of the Second Vatican Council, did not go unheeded. Latourelle and many others have fully developed and explained the christological and the trinitarian dimensions of the Divine Revelation.

Pope *Paul VI* took up Vatican II's trinitarian and christological approach to Divine Revelation and applied it especially to ecclesiology.[17] It was possible to develop a trinitarian ecclesiology because the Fathers of the Second Vatican Council had already prepared the road for that task.[18] This ecclesiology was thoroughly delineated in *Ecclesiam Suam* at the very beginning of Pope Paul VI's Pontificate. It is, at the same time, a pneumatological ecclesiology that emphasizes the role of the Holy Spirit in strengthening the Church's

---

[14]See R. Latourelle, "Assenza e presenza della Fondamentale al Concilio Vaticano II," in R. Latourelle (ed.), *Vaticano II. Bilancio e prospettive*, Vol. II, Assisi, 1988, 1383–1395; Rino Fisichella, "Il Contributo di R. Latourelle alla Teologia Fondamentale" in Rino Fisichella (ed.), *Gesù Rivelatore*, Piemme, 1988, 11.

[15]See R. Latourelle, *Teologia della Rivelazione*, Assisi, 1967, 242.

[16]See R. Latourelle, *Teologia della Rivelazione*, Assisi, 1967, 411. It is fitting to conclude Latourelle's thought concerning the necessity of the historicity of God's self–revelation in and through Jesus Christ by quoting an excerpt from the same document:"l'Incarnazione è la via scelta da Dio per rivelare e per rivelarsi. Essa ha lo scopo di rendere possibile, a livello dell'uomo, la conoscenza di Dio e del suo piano salvifico. Perciò è esatto dire che l'Incarnazione del Figlio, intesa concretamente, è la Rivelazione del Figlio e, per mezzo suo, del Padre." (*Ibid.*, 419)

[17]See Pope Paul VI, *Ecclesiam Suam; Marialis Cultus*, 25–27.

[18]See *Lumen Gentium*, 2, 3, 4, 8 and 9.

consciousness of both her divine and her human reality.[19] When describing the difficult time that Pope Paul VI went through right after the Second Vatican Council, John Paul II says:

> What the Spirit said to the Church through the Council of our time, what the Spirit says in this Church to all the Churches (Revelation 2:7) cannot lead to anything else — in spite of momentary uneasiness — but still more mature solidity of the whole People of God, aware of their salvific mission.[20]

Therefore "Can we fail to have trust — in spite of all human weakness and all the faults of past centuries — in our Lord's grace as revealed recently through what the Holy Spirit said and we heard during the Council?"[21]

The ecclesiological orientation of the Second Vatican Council and of Pope Paul VI was also accompanied by an anthropological thrust. The consequence was the establishment of Christology at the center of contemporary theology. This did not happen for methodological reasons, rather, it happened because Christ is the center of Christian Revelation.[22] The necessity of a christological revival was sensed especially by Italian theologians in 1967 immediately after the Second Vatican Council. This revival spread simultaneously in many other countries and began to show its fruits in the 1980's.[23] Since then, the concentration of the Church's theological thinking on the mystery of Jesus Christ has become dominant. In his *L'uomo e I suoi problemi alla luce di Cristo*,[24] R. Latourelle describes the contemporary christological approaches of K. Barth, E. Mersch, R. Guardini, K. Rahner, and Hans Urs von Balthasar. These theologians guided the ecclesiological and the anthropological revival of Vatican II to its success: Christ remains the indispensable condition and most secure guarantee for understanding the dynamic situation of man.[25]

---

[19]See also Pope John Paul II, *Redemptor Hominis*, 3, 7.

[20]Pope John Paul II, *Redemptor Hominis*, 3.

[21]Pope John Paul II, *Redemptor Hominis*, 6.

[22]See Johann Roten's unpublished article "The Word of God made man by the Holy Spirit," 2; J. Dupuis, "The Uniqueness of Jesus Christ in the Early Christian Tradition," in *Religious Pluralism, Jeevadhara* 47 (1978): 406—407.

[23]See *La Cristologia Contemporanea*, (a cura di Giovanni Iammarrone), Padova: Edizioni Messagero Padova, 1992, 5.

[24]Assisi: Cittadella, 1982.

[25]See *La Cristologia Contemporanea*, (a cura di Giovanni Iammarrone), Padova: Edizioni Messagero Padova, 1992, 9. The evidence of that christological reinstallation and its relationship with the other disciplines is given through the abundant material that appeared since the 1980s (see *Ibid.*, 22–33; John Macquarrie, *Jesus Christ in Modern Thought*, Philadelphia: Trinity Press, 1990; Johann Roten, *The Word of God made man by the Holy Spirit*, 14–16).

On the level of the Church's Magisterium, Pope John Paul II, having observed the successful Petrine ministry of Pope Paul VI, went further to develop a Christ–centered theology in many fields: trinitarian theology, Christology, Mariology, Ecclesiology and Anthropology. The center of Christian faith is the Person of Jesus Christ. This primacy however is not reduced to only the salvific work of Redemption accomplished by Christ. Rather the christocentricity of John Paul II's thinking refers to Christ's primacy in all theological disciplines because that centrality cannot simply derive from a dependence on Adam's sin. Christ is truly the Alpha and the Omega, the one in whom everything was thought, willed, and created. There isn't a single truth of faith or a single demand of Christian praxis that can be separated from the fact that Jesus Christ is the Son of God who became man in the womb of the Virgin, lived among us, died for us and is risen from the dead. A certain paradoxical character is noticeable in John Paul's christocentricity because the totality of the mystery of Redemption has in its own being the basis of its own credibility. The truth about Jesus Christ becomes the *crede ut intelligas* of John Paul II. The entire economy of salvation depends on understanding the mystery of Jesus Christ.[26]

All these aspects reach far beyond a Christology that limits itself to a mere dependence on a sinful humanity that brought a Redeemer down from heaven.[27] Christ stands at the center when the name of God, Father–Son–Holy Spirit, is pronounced. In creation, the Father created through the Son in the Holy Spirit and here Christ again occupies the middle position. The Incarnation, historically speaking, takes place between the economy of the Father (Old Testament) and the economy of the Holy Spirit (Era of the Church). The sanctification of the people of God redeemed by Christ happens by the Holy Spirit who leads them through Christ to the Father. Throughout the whole economy of salvation, creation–Incarnation–sanctification, Jesus occupies the center: this theory will be noticed throughout the writings of John Paul II. Jesus Christ is the center of Christian faith in the sense that he "is the stable principle and fixed center of the mission that God himself has entrusted to man."[28] For John Paul II the Revelation of God is necessarily Christological.[29] Being one of the main architects of the Second Vatican

---

[26]See J. Honoré, "Christ the Redeemer, Core of John Paul II's Teaching," in *John Paul II. A Panorama of his Teachings*, New York: New City Press, 1989, 15.

[27]See Pope John Paul II, *Catechesi Tradendae*, 2 and 5; *Vita Consecrata*, 15; Angelo Scola, "'Claim' of Christ, 'Claim' of the World: On the Trinitarian Encyclicals of John Paul II," in *Communio* 18 (1991): 323.

[28]Pope John Paul II, *Redemptor Hominis*, 11.

[29]See Pope John Paul II, *Catechesi Tradendae*, 22.

Council's *Lumen Gentium* and *Gaudium et Spes*,[30] was not a fact that deterred Pope John Paul II from his effort to approach all disciplines of theology from a christological point of view. His christocentricity is at once Marian, Ecclesial, Eucharistic, and Trinitarian.[31] Actually, he intended the ecclesiology of the Council to be christocentric in the sense that Cardinal Ratzinger displays it: "*Lumen Gentium sit Christus*. Because Christ is the light of the nations, there exists a mirror of His glory, the Church, that reflects His radiance."[32] During the celebration in the Sistine Chapel right after his election, John Paul immediately indicated that he thought that theology should give major attention to ecclesiology. He views the Church along the line of Pope John XXIII whose words became the basic theme of *Lumen Gentium*: "The Church is the universal sacrament of salvation."[33] Later on, quoting *Lumen Gentium*, 1, in *Redemptor Hominis*, 7, John Paul says: "'By her relationship with Christ, the Church is a kind of sacrament or sign and means of intimate union with God, and of the unity of all mankind (LG, 1),' and the source of this is he, he himself, he the Redeemer."[34] John Paul II, although placing Christ at the center of the Church's faith, still takes Pope Paul VI's ecclesiology as the point of departure of his own Christology. He links Paul VI's ecclesiology to his own Christology with such extraordinary skill: the awareness of the Church as deftly developed by Paul VI needs a specific source, and this fountainhead is Jesus Christ:[35]

> Faced with these tasks that appear along the ways for the Church, those ways that Pope Paul VI clearly indicated in the first Encyclical of his Pontificate, and aware of the absolute necessity of all these ways and also of the difficulties thronging them, we feel all the more our need for a profound link with Christ.[36]

John Paul II, consequently, switched the ecclesiological orientation of Paul

---

[30]See Edward D. O'Connor, "The roots of Pope John Paul II's devotion to Mary," in *Marian Studies* XXXIX (1988): 87.

[31]See Mary Craig, *Man from a Far Country. A Portrait of Pope John Paul II*, London: Hodder and Stoughton, 1982, 70–71; John Saward, *Christ is the Answer. The Christ–Centered Teaching of Pope John Paul II*, New York: Alba House, 1995, 2.

[32]J. Ratzinger, *Kirche, Ökumene und Politik*. Neue Versuche zur Ekklesiologie, Einsiedeln, 1987, 14; John Saward, *Christ is the Answer. The Christ–Centered Teaching of Pope John Paul II*, New York: Alba House, 1995, 1–2.

[33]See Hans Cardinal Groër, "The Church Sacrament of Salvation," in *John Paul II. A Panorama of his Teachings*, New York: New City Press, 1989, 27.

[34]Pope John Paul II, *Redemptor Hominis*, 7; *Christifideles Laici*, 2.

[35]See Pope John Paul II, *Centesimus Annus*, 3.

[36]Pope John Paul II, *Redemptor Hominis*, 22.

VI to a christological one, maintaining however that an ecclesiological dimension is always necessary for a sound christocentrism:

> Our spirit is set in one direction, the only direction for our intellect, will and heart is — toward Christ our Redeemer, toward Christ, the Redeemer of man. We wish to look toward him — because there is salvation in no one else but him, the Son of God — repeating what Peter said:"Lord, to whom shall we go? You have the words of eternal life (Jn 6:68)".[37]

The Christocentrism of Pope John Paul II has always been a balanced approach within the theology of the Church throughout his pontificate. In the mode of Bonaventure, the Pope's Christocentrism has avoided becoming a Christomonism, because none of the Divine Persons could ever monopolize the whole economy of salvation at the expense of the other two.[38] If Christ is at the center of that economy, it should be constantly kept in mind that the other two persons are also at the center, yet each according to His divine properties. One could picture the situation as the Three Divine Persons on one circle representing eternity. On that circle each Person can be considered to be at the center of the economy according to the angle from which one approaches the mystery of salvation. All the characteristics of the Son in the framework of the economy of creation–Incarnation–sanctification are also applied to the Father and the Holy Spirit, always respecting the different properties of each Person. Respecting the different properties in this context means the Father and the Holy Spirit were in some sense 'incarnate' without becoming man like Jesus Christ. Their 'incarnation' respects their divine properties as Father who is 'incarnate' through the Incarnation of the Son and as Holy Spirit who is 'incarnate' to extend in history the historical Incarnation of the Son. The same thing could be applied to the Father in His relationship with the Son and the Holy Spirit, and to the Holy Spirit in his relationship with the Father and the Son. This I think is the true meaning of the christocentrism of John Paul II, a christocentrism that constitutes the foundations of the Pope's trinitarian theology.

Once the idea of christocentrism is understood in that way, one grasps easily that there is no contradiction between John Paul's christocentrism and his vision of the trinitarian mystery as the center of the Church's faith. The daily content of the Church's kerygma and all ecclesial mission is trinitarian by nature, because the mystery of the Trinity is the "typically Christian

---

[37]Pope John Paul II, *Redemptor Hominis*, 7.

[38]See St. Bonaventure, *In Hexaëmeron* 1, 10; *Opera Omnia*, vol. 5, Quaracchi, 1891, 330B; Josef Seifert, "Karol Cardinal Wojtyla (Pope John Paul II) as Philosopher and the Cracow/Lublin School of Philosophy," in *Aletheia* 2 (1981): 130–199; John Saward, *Christ is the Answer. The Christ–Centered Teaching of Pope John Paul II*, New York: Alba House, 1995, 3–4.

mystery,"[39] and "God's self–communication (that happens) in the Holy Spirit,"[40] is the "inscrutable unity of the Trinity."[41] Commenting on the Letter of St. Paul to the Galatians (4:4–7) in *Tertio Millennio Adveniente*, Pope John Paul II shows the reason behind his trinitarian approach: the Christocentric approach must not become a christomonism because "the mystery of the Incarnation contains the revelation of the mystery of the Trinity and the continuation of the Son's mission in the mission of the Holy Spirit."[42] Every day of her life and through the Holy Spirit, the Church, the fruit of the redeeming activity of the Son, witnesses to the Divine Revelation of the Triune God. Therefore, although centered on Christ, the core of the New Testament is the Revelation of God as a Trinity of Persons.[43] In the same line of thought as Vatican II and Pope Paul VI, John Paul II emphasizes the christological and the trinitarian dimension of the Divine Revelation of God introducing it as the fundamental truth for all the aspects of the faith of the Church.

In his Encyclical Letter *Redemptoris Missio*, Pope John Paul II, without developing the theme at length, reaffirms the essential connection of trinitarian doctrine to the theology of Revelation. The tactic sometimes taken by those who wish to emphasize a theocentric approach to the mystery of God, runs the risk of disconnecting that mystery from its trinitarian nature. This approach jeopardizes the very essence of the New Testament Revelation of God as a Trinity of Persons. That tactic presents the kingdom of God theocentrically without stressing its necessary link with Christ Who *is* the kingdom in Person. Such a theocentric approach aims to find common ground in the one divine reality. But, says the Pope, this "is not the kingdom of God as we know it from revelation."[44] Here is John Paul's awareness of the many implicit theological tendencies that, although with good intention, sometimes compromise the essence and core of the Church's faith.

---

[39] *Prayers and Devotions from Pope John Paul II*, Edited and with an Introduction by Bishop Peter Canisius Johannes Van Lierde, Translated by Firman O'Sullivan, New York: Viking, A Giniger Book, 1984, 445. See also Pope John Paul II, *Vita Consecrata*, 14; *The Encyclicals of John Paul II*, Edited with Introductions by Michael Miller, Indiana: Our Sunday Visitor Publishing Division, Our Sunday Visitor, Inc., 1996, 479.

[40] Pope John Paul II, *Dominum et Vivificantem*, 51; *Christifideles Laici*, 2; *Vita Consecrata*, 5.

[41] Pope John Paul II, *Mulieris Dignitatem*, 3.

[42] Pope John Paul II, *Tertio Millennio Adveniente*, 1; Terrence Prendergast, "'A Vision of Wholeness': A Reflection on the Use of Scripture in a Cross–section of Papal Writings," in *The Thought of Pope John Paul II*, Rome: Gregorian University, 1993, 87–88.

[43] See Pope John Paul II, *Dives in Misericordia*, 1; *Slavorum Apostoli*, 18.

[44] See Pope John Paul II, *Redemptoris Missio*, 17–18.

Analogy of Being and Analogy of Faith

"We are in a position to know more about what the One and Triune God is not than about what he is. If we could explain him adequately with our reason, that would mean that we should have captured and reduced him to the measure of our minds," said Pope John Paul II in a reflection on the occasion of Trinity Sunday.[45] It should constantly be kept in mind that the Pope's theology on the Trinity, whether in its economic or immanent aspect, always respects the dimension of mystery. He appropriates in his Pontificate the thought process that belongs to both a doctor of the faith and a theologian: this process was identified by Vatican I as *analogy of being* and *of faith*. This analogy guarantees the transcendent character of the truths of faith in themselves and the correlation of the dogmas between these truths and the way that they are expressed in theology. At the same time, analogy enables faith and theology to understand each other, retaining a hierarchy of value between the truths of faith as communicated by Divine Revelation.[46]

There are many ways to reflect on the Triune God within the Tradition of the Church, but imprisoning God in the box of our thoughts would be wrong. Therefore, in John Paul II's opinion the *via negativa* is still a valid method to theologize on the mystery of the Trinity, especially because it has been a method handed down in the Church by both Greek and Latin Traditions.[47] St. Augustine's famous words *Deus semper maior* and St. Thomas' fascination before the Tri–unity of God which always remains a mystery for human reason, find many expressions in John Paul II's theology of Revelation.[48]

The Revelation of the Father in and through Jesus Christ reveals at once the whole truth about God and about man. What the First Vatican Council avoided, namely to speak of a Revelation and a communication of God Himself, the Second Vatican Council and later Pope John Paul II went far beyond. Of course, the Fathers of Vatican I were respecting the transcendent nature and the inaccessibility of God. But this transcendence in the theology of Vatican II and

---

[45]*Prayers and Devotions from Pope John Paul II*, Edited and with an Introduction by Bishop Peter Canisius Johannes Van Lierde, Translated by Firman O'Sullivan, New York: Viking, A Giniger Book, 1984, 446. See also Pope John Paul II, *Catechesi Tradendae*, 60; *Dives in Misericordia*, 2.

[46]See J. Honoré, "Christ the Redeemer, Core of John Paul II's Teaching," in *John Paul II. A Panorama of his Teachings*, New York: New City Press, 1989, 15–16; Hans Cardinal Groër, "The Church Sacrament of Salvation," in *John Paul II. A Panorama of his Teachings*, New York: New City Press, 1989, 31.

[47]See Yves Congar, *Credo nello Spirito Santo*, Vol. 3, Brescia: Queriniana, 1987, 21.

[48]See St. Augustine, *Enarratio in Psalmum* LXII, 16: CCL 39, 804; St. Thomas Aquinas, *I Sent.* d. 3, q. 1, a. 4; *C. Gentiles* I, 3; IV, 1; *De Pot.*, q.9, a. 5; q. 10, a. 1; *Summa Theologiae* Ia, q. 1, a. 8 ad 2; Pope John Paul II, *Veritatis Splendor*, 41; *Letter to Families from Pope John Paul II*, 7.

of Pope John Paul II was never compromised because the analogy of being and of faith protected it: "If in himself he remains ineffable and unsearchable, still more ineffable and unsearchable is he in the reality of the Incarnation of the Word, who became man through the Virgin of Nazareth."[49] A christological approach to Revelation, therefore, was for Vatican II the only way to provide a true Revelation of the Triune God without any threat to the traditional belief in the awesome incomprehensibility of the Divine Nature: the life, words and actions of the historical Jesus Christ reveals and communicates God Himself.

The Encyclical *Dives in Misericordia* dedicated by Pope John Paul II to a theological reflection on the Person of the Father, opens with the following words: "It is 'God, who is rich in mercy' whom Jesus Christ has revealed to us as Father: it is his very Son who, in himself, has manifested him and made him known to us."[50] Jn 1:18 and Heb 1:1–2 are the Scriptural foundations for the Pope's opening statement. In this text as well as in *Dives in Misericordia*, 2, Pope John Paul II comments on St. John 1:18: "No one has ever seen God, the only Son, who is in the bosom of the Father, he has made him known." The same theology occurs in *Redemptoris Missio*, 5: "In this definitive Word of his revelation, God has made himself known in the fullest possible way. He has revealed to mankind who he is." The 'making Him known' indicates two things. First of all, that the Divine Revelation is total, complete, and perfect in itself; it encompasses the whole truth about the Father: "This making known reveals God in the most profound mystery of his being, one and three, surrounded by 'unapproachable light'."[51] Second, that the categories according to which the divine exists should be respected as a mystery. The mystery in itself lies typically and essentially outside the human person's vision and cognitive knowledge, although God wanted to reveal it and communicate it in a way comprehensible for that person: the sacrament — whether Church as Sacrament or the seven sacraments — is the means to accomplish that communication. Hence, the *analogia fidei*, in John Paul's opinion, is that constant approach to God that paradoxically keeps two dimensions that seem to exclude each other, yet both are necessary for the cognitive dimension of the

[49]Pope John Paul II, *Redemptoris Mater*, 51.

[50]Pope John Paul II, *Dives in Misericordia*, 1.

[51]Pope John Paul II, *Dives in Misericordia*, 2. See also Ibid., *Mulieris Dignitatem*, 3; *Vita Consecrata*, 17–19; Angelo Scola, "'Claim' of Christ, 'Claim' of the World: On the Trinitarian Encyclicals of John Paul II," in *Communio* 18 (1991): 324; J. Honoré, "Christ the Redeemer, Core of John Paul's Teaching," in *John Paul II. A Panorama of his Teaching*, New York: New City Press, 1989, 17; Hans Cardinal Groër, "The Church Sacrament of Salvation," in *John Paul II. A Panorama of his Teachings*, New York: New City Press, 1989, 31.

human knowledge of the mystery of God.[52]

One more element that was added to Vatican I's understanding of Divine Revelation by Vatican II and was displayed in an even deeper way by Pope John Paul II was the *anthropological implication* of this Divine Revelation. Hegel, Marx, Kierkegaard, and Max Scheler have extensively treated the question of man with a new sort of science, call it "philosophical anthropology." Pope John Paul II saw in the demoralization of man that the very meaning of his own being was threatened: there emerges a "systematic renunciation of the healthy ambition of being a man." There is a fragmentation of man in both theory and practice; some of his functions are absolutized and others simply suppressed or reduced to a concept that does not reflect the whole picture of man or the whole structure of his subjective personality. John Paul rejects any system that does not look at "the whole man, in the whole truth of his spiritual and corporeal subjectivity." John Paul's obvious thrust in giving a privileged status to the question of man over all other questions and disciplines of philosophy, has made him a pioneering figure in the field of that "philosophical anthropology."[53]

John Paul's effort to establish a well founded philosophical anthropology spotlights the long standing dichotomy between subjectivism and objectivism. Whereas realists, wanting to safeguard the objectivity of both human being and human knowing, see in subjectivity a constant threat of falling into subjectivism, objectivism and positivism on the contrary tend to arouse fear among idealists. Idealists, especially in the post–Cartesian period, have so emphasized 'pure consciousness,' that in many areas of their thinking man seems to be cut off from reality.[54]

John Paul II who attempted to break down this antinomy, found himself dealing with the question of subjectivism vs. objectivism not only in philosophical but also in theological framework: the core of the reflections of John Paul II, whether theology, Church's politics or social teachings, is

---

[52]Hans Cardinal Groër, "The Church Sacrament of Salvation," in *John Paul II. A Panorama of his Teachings*, New York: New City Press, 1989, 31.

[53]See Karol Wojtyla, "The Task of Christian Philosophy Today," in *Proceedings of the American Catholic Philosophical Association* 53 (1979): 3; *The Acting Person*, Boston: Reidel, 1979, 4 and 21; *Toward a Philosophy of Praxis: An Anthology*, ed. Alfred Bloch and George T. Czuczka, New York: Crossroad, 1980, 12; Pope John Paul II, *Evangelium Vitae*, 15, 36 and 96; Anselm K. Min, "John Paul II's Anthropology of Concrete Totality," in *Proceedings of the American Catholic Philosophical Association* 58 (1984): 120; Pope John Paul II, *The Person, The Nation and The State*, ed. William Murphy, Vatican City: Pontifical Commission on Justice and Peace, 1980, 47 and 51; *Redemptor Hominis*, 13.

[54]See Karol Wojtyla, "Subjectivity and the Irreducible in man," in *Analecta Husserliana* 7 (1979): 108; Anselm K. Min, "John Paul II's Anthropology of Concrete Totality," in *Proceedings of the American Catholic Philosophical Association* 58 (1984): 121.

undoubtedly philosophical. But the expansion to include theology is further justified by the added light which derives from theology, especially because Karol Wojtyla is now Pope John Paul II, prime teacher of the Catholic Church.[55]

Both *Gaudium et Spes* and *Dei Verbum* rely upon a personalistic approach to Divine Revelation. Pope John Paul II confirms Vatican II's *Dei Verbum* and indirectly some modern theologians like Karl Rahner,[56] when considering christological and trinitarian Revelation of God as at the same time anthropological. The Pope clearly testifies that anthropology and theology are increasingly important factors: "The more the Church's mission is centered upon man — the more it is, so to speak, anthropocentric — the more it must be confirmed and actualized theocentrically, that is to say, be directed in Jesus Christ to the Father."[57] In Jesus Christ, God communicates Himself to every human person and, therefore, the event of God's Revelation also necessarily has an anthropological dimension. The event of Christ allows one to counteract the error of "various currents of human thoughts ...(that) tend to separate theocentrism and anthropocentrism."[58] Pope John Paul confirms in *Dives in Misericordia* that theological trends that separate anthropocentrism from theocentrism "violate a fundamental teaching of the Second Vatican Council:"[59]

> While the various currents of human thought both in the past and at the present have tended and still tend to separate theocentrism and anthropocentrism, and even to set

---

[55]See Anna–Teresa Tymieniecka, "The Origins of the Philosophy of John Paul II," in *Proceedings of the American Catholic Philosophical Association* 53 (1979): 16 and 24; Pope John Paul II, *Evangelium Vitae*, 15 and 20.

[56]See Gregory Baum, "The First Papal Encyclical," *The Ecumenist* 17 (1979): 55; Anna–Teresa Tymieniecka, "The Origins of the Philosophy of John Paul II," in *Proceedings of the American Catholic Philosophical Association* 53 (1979): 25,

[57]Pope John Paul II, *Dives in Misericordia*, 1. See also Ibid., *Redemptionis Donum*, 4; Angelo Scola, "'Claim' of Christ, 'Claim' of the World: On the Trinitarian Encyclicals of John Paul II," in *Communio* 18 (1991): 324; Joseph Cardinal Cordeiro, "The religious sense of man," in *John Paul II. A Panorama of his Teachings*, New York: New City Press, 1989, 73; Darió Castrillón, "The family in the Magisterium of John Paul II," in *John Paul II. A Panorama of his Teachings*, New York: New City Press, 1989, 113.

[58]See Pope John Paul II, *Dives in Misericordia*, 1; Australia, November 26, 1986; *Celebrate 2000! Reflections on Jesus, the Holy Spirit, and the Father*, Ann Arbor, Michigan: Servant Publications, 1996, 52–53 Joseph Cardinal Cordeiro, "The religious sense of man," in *John Paul II. A Panorama of his Teachings*, New York: New City Press, 1989, 73; Angelo Scola, "'Claim' of Christ, 'Claim' of the World: On the Trinitarian Encyclicals of John Paul II," in *Communio* 18 (1991): 324.

[59]*The Encyclicals of John Paul II*, Edited with Introductions by Michael Miller, Indiana: Our Sunday Visitor Publishing Division, Our Sunday Visitor, Inc., 1996, 98.

them in opposition to each other, the Church, following Christ, seeks to link them up in human history, in a deep and organic way. And this is also one of the basic principles, perhaps the most important one, of the teaching of the last Council.[60]

Since the Incarnation is the Revelation of God's union with the entire human family: a theocentric approach to Divine Revelation is necessarily *anthropological* by nature. In *Dives in Misericordia*, Pope John Paul II refers to *Gaudium et Spes*, 22: "'Christ the new Adam...fully reveals man to himself and brings to light his lofty calling,' and does it 'in the very revelation of the mystery of the Father and of his love'."[61] This means that man "cannot be manifested in the full dignity of his nature without reference — not only on the level of concepts but also in an integrally existential way — to God. Man and man's lofty calling are revealed in Christ through the revelation of the mystery of the Father and his love."[62] And in *Redemptor Hominis*, by revealing God as a Trinity of Persons, the Son "fully reveals man to himself. If we may use the expression, this is the human dimension of the mystery of the Redemption. In this dimension man finds again the greatness, dignity and value that belong to his humanity."[63]

The Revelation of the mystery of the Father directly includes the Revelation of the mystery of man and both took place through the Incarnation of the Word. In and through Jesus Christ, the increasing assimilation and understanding of the Father's Revelation naturally implies an increase in comprehending the truth about man. Actually, the culminating point of Divine Revelation, not from a theocentric but from an anthropological point of view, resides in manifesting the nature of the relationship between man and the Father. Nobody before Pope John Paul II has put so much emphasis on the anthropological dimension of the Divine Revelation of God through Jesus Christ. This is what he asserts when commenting on Jn 1:18 in *Dives in Misericordia*:

Nevertheless, through this 'making known' by Christ we know God above all in his relationship of love for man: in his 'philanthropy.' It is precisely here that 'his invisible nature' becomes in a special way 'visible,' incomparably more visible than through all the other 'things that have been made': it becomes visible in Christ and through Christ, through his actions and his words, and finally through his death on

---

[60]Pope John Paul II, *Dives in Misericordia*, 1.

[61]Pope John Paul II, *Dives in Misericordia*, 1.

[62]Pope John Paul II, *Dives in Misericordia*, 1. See also *Tertio Millennio Adveniente*, 4.

[63]Pope John Paul II, *Redemptor Hominis*, 10. See also Ibid., *Dominum et Vivificantem*, 59; *Redemptionis Donum*, 4.

the Cross and his resurrection.[64]

Operations of the Triune God

The task now of discerning the role of each of the Divine Persons in the economy of salvation, preparatory to a treatment of the procession of the Holy Spirit, follows the pattern of Pope John Paul II whose pneumatology is inseparable from his reflections on the Triune God. This methodology is shared by many contemporary theologians.[65]

It is a long tradition in the Church to think of the Son and the Holy Spirit as the arms of the Father in the world: the "mystery of the Father and of his love, made manifest and freely given in Jesus through the Spirit."[66] Pope John Paul II develops this tradition in an extensive way, especially in his Encyclical Letters, *Redemptor Hominis*, *Dives in Misericordia*, and *Dominum et Vivificantem*. In his pre–papal document on the theology of the Second Vatican Council, *Sources of Renewal*, Karol Wojtyla had already started to theologize on the proper action of each of the Divine Persons in God's *economy of salvation*. As far as the *Economic Trinity*[67] is concerned, in general terms the Father is the Creator, the Son is the Redeemer, the Holy Spirit is the Sanctifier.[68] Throughout his Pontificate John Paul II would continue to develop such a theology that meditates on the specific economy of each Divine Person.[69] These qualifications of the Three Divine Persons in the writings of the Pope vary from one document to another according to the intention and topic proper to that document.

In *Redemptoris Mater*, 1, Pope John Paul II thinks that St. Paul's words in Galatians 4:4 "celebrate together the love of the Father, the mission of the Son, the gift of the Holy Spirit, the role of the woman from whom the Redeemer was born, and our divine filiation, in the mystery of the 'fullness of time'."[70] At the

---

[64]Pope John Paul II, *Dives in Misericordia*, 2.

[65]See Yves Congar, *Credo nello Spirito Santo*, Vol. III, Brescia: Queriniana, 1987, 7.

[66]Pope John Paul II, *Redemptoris Missio*, 12; Paul L. Peeters, "*Dominum et Vivificantem*: The Conscience and the Heart," in *Communio* 15 (1988): 148.

[67]Pope John Paul II does not use the terminology *Economic Trinity* or *Immanent Trinity*. These expressions are introduced in this volume in order to respectively refer to the Blessed Trinity in its work in history or on the intra–trinitarian life.

[68]See Karol Wojtyla, *Sources of Renewal: The Implementation of the Second Vatican Council*, San Francisco: Harper and Row, 1980, 45–65.

[69]See Pope John Paul II, *Redemptionis Donum*, 10; *Reconciliatio et Paenitentia*, 35; *Pastores Dabo Vobis*, 19; *Veritatis Splendor*, 10; *Letter to Families from Pope John Paul II*, 4; *Vita Consecrata*, 17.

[70]Pope John Paul II, *Redemptoris Mater*, 1. See also Ibid., *Redemptoris Missio*, 12.

beginning of *Redemptoris Mater*, John Paul II is committed to the Pauline trinitarian formula. This is the reason why love, mission, and gift are attributed to the Three Divine Persons.

Slavorum Apostoli, 20, describes the humanity as "created by God the Father, redeemed by the Son our Savior and enlightened by the Holy Spirit."[71] *Enlightened by the Holy Spirit* is explained in what John Paul says towards the end of *Slavorum Apostoli*: "To you, therefore, God the Father Almighty, God the Son who have redeemed the world, God the Spirit who are the sustainer and teacher of all holiness, I desire to entrust the whole Church of yesterday, today and tomorrow..."[72] The expression *enlightened* is close in meaning to the concept of St. Augustine where, in his theology of creation, *enlightening* designates the act of maintaining in existence and causing holiness and sanctification.[73] In his *Confessions*, St. Augustine connects God's creation of light as it appears in Genesis and the descent of the Holy Spirit during Pentecost: "For behold, it is as by the very command of God saying, Let there be lights in the firmament of Heaven (Gen 1:14), and suddenly there came a sound from Heaven, as of a violent wind blowing, and there appeared parted tongues as of fire, which settled upon each of them (Acts 2:2–3)."[74]

In *Slavorum Apostoli*, 30, Pope John Paul II explains more explicitly, the different functions of the Divine Persons. Describing the mission of the two Apostles of the Slavs, Cyrill and Methodius, the Pope says that they bore witness

> ...that you are the Creator of man, that you are our Father and that in you we are all brethren; that through the Son, your eternal Word, you have given existence to all things, and have called human beings to share in your life without end; that you have so loved the world as to grant it the gift of your only–begotten Son, who for us men and for our salvation came down from heaven and by the power of the Holy Spirit became incarnate in the womb of the Virgin Mary and was made man; and that finally you have sent the Spirit of power and consolation so that every human being, redeemed by Christ, may in him receive the dignity of a child and become a co–heir of the unfailing promises which you have made to humanity.[75]

Notice how John Paul II always relates the activity of the Holy Spirit in the economy of salvation to the Redemption of Christ. The Holy Spirit enables

---

[71]Pope John Paul II, *Slavorum Apostoli*, 20.

[72]Pope John Paul II, *Slavaorum Apostoli*, 31. See also Ibid., *Sollicitudo Rei Socialis*, 40.

[73]See Pope John Paul II, *Sollicitudo Rei Socialis*, 47; *Redemptionis Donum*, 10.

[74]*Confessions of St. Augustine*, Bk. 13, Ch. 19, Revision of the Translation of Rev. J. M. Lelen, New Jersey: Catholic Book Publishing Co., 1997, 423.

[75]Pope John Paul II, *Salavorum Apostoli*, 30.

every human being to have the dignity of child in Christ, simply because every human being was redeemed by Christ.[76] The fatherhood of the Father expressed through the act of creation, is fulfilled by the Son in the Holy Spirit. To this act of creation corresponds the mystery of "divine adoption received by man in Christ through the grace of the Holy Spirit."[77] Here Redemption is clearly identified as a process of inversion in respect to creation: in the act of creating God's children, the schema would be 'Father → Son → Holy Spirit;' in the act of recreating God's children, the schema would be 'Holy Spirit → Son → Father.'[78]

It is obvious for Pope John Paul II, however, that the role of each of the Three Divine Persons in the economy of salvation cannot be understood as monopolized by that specific Divine Person.[79] The reason for this lies in the fact that the universal plan for the salvation in the world, as expressed in *Slavorum Apostoli*, 20, is the result of the "eternal design of the Most Holy Trinity."[80] Nearly identical expressions occur in other documents: 'providential plan of the Most Holy Trinity' in *Redemptoris Mater*, 3, 'salvific design of the Most Holy Trinity' in *Redemptoris Mater*, 11. Because the eternal design of the Most Holy Trinity is evidently designed equally by the Father, by the Son, and by the Holy Spirit, all three fulfill that plan. They do not accomplish it individually; they act each according to His properties as Father, as Son, or as Holy Spirit.[81] All activities that emanate from the "great God, (who is) One in Trinity;"[82] they are all done by the same and One God but by Three different Divine Persons. In this sense J. Honoré, commenting on the Pope's thought, said: "the work of salvation, through the joint action of the Father, the Son, and the Spirit, reveals the depth of the divine mystery that sustains their trinitarian

---

[76]See also Pope John Paul II, *Redemptor Hominis*, 18; *Dominum et Vivificantem*, 52; *Redemptoris Mater*, 1; *Chrsitifideles Laici*, 16; *Tertio Millennio Adveniente*, 1.

[77]Pope John Paul II, *Redemptor Hominis*, 18. See also *Redemptoris Mater*, 8 and 43; *The Encyclicals of John Paul II*, Edited with Introductions by J. Michael Miller, Indiana: Our Sunday Visitor Publishing Division, Our Sunday Visitor, Inc., 1996, 344.

[78]This schema was reported by the Pope himself when explaining how the counciliar texts of Vatican II "move us to penetrate ever deeper into the Trinitarian mystery of God himself...: to the Father, through Christ, in the Holy Spirit." (Pope John Paul II, *Dominum et Vivificantem*, 2. See also Ibid., *Dominicae Cenae*, 3; *Familiaris Consortio*, 59; *Behold Your Mother*, 7)

[79]See Pope John Paul II, *Slavorum Apostoli*, 30; *Vita Consecrata*, 66.

[80]Pope John Paul II, *Slavorum Apostoli*, 20. See also Ibid., *Dives in Misericordia*, 9; *Dominum et Vivificantem*, 64; *Dominicae Cenae*, 3.

[81]See Pope John Paul II, *Christifideles Laici*, 16.

[82]Pope John Paul II, *Slavorum Apostoli*, 30. See also Ibid., *Reconciliatio et Paenitentia*, 31.

distinction and the infinity of their being and eternity."[83]

Pope John Paul II comes very close to the trinitarian theology of St. Thomas Aquinas who confirms that in God everything is one where there are no relations of opposition. Therefore, God's activity *ad extra* emanates from One and the same God but is accomplished by Three different Divine Persons within that Oneness of nature. *Pastores Dabo Vobis*, 35, illustrates a clear example of how John Paul constantly envisions the work of the Three Divine Persons as emanating from the same God: "In truth, the Church... carries within her the mystery of the Father, who, being neither called nor sent by anyone (cf. Rom 11:33–35), calls all to hallow his name and do his will; she guards within herself the mystery of the Son, who is called by the father and sent to proclaim the kingdom of God to all and calls all to follow him; and she is the trustee of the mystery of the Holy Spirit, who consecrates for mission those whom the Father calls through his Son Jesus Christ." *Vita Consecrata*'s theology constitutes another approach to the work of the trinitarian God. Here, in the context of the formation of candidates for consecrated life, the Pope says that "God the Father, through the unceasing gift of Christ and the Spirit, is the educator par excellence of those who consecrate themselves to him... Formation then is a sharing in the work of the Father who, through the Spirit, fashions the inner attitudes of the Son in the hearts of young men and women."[84] This text clearly manifests the Pope's awareness of the danger of false monopolization that trinitarian thought sometimes attributes to one of the Three Divine Persons: on the contrary, the Father is now at work, through the Spirit, in order to fashion the Son in the hearts of the consecrated. Whereas in the common consciousness of the Church, the Son and the Holy Spirit constitute the Father's arms in the world,[85] in *Vita Consecrata* the Father Himself is working and the Son, if we may use the expression, is somehow passive.

Immanent Trinity

Pope John Paul II faces two major questions when he develops his thought on the *Immanent Trinity*. The first question, old as the controversies of the early Church, deals with the unity of the divinity of the Godhead and the distinction of the Three Divine Persons. St. Augustine, although not directly involved like St. Athanasius and the Cappadocians in the Arian controversy,

---

[83] J. Honoré, "Christ the Redeemer, Core of John Paul's Teaching," in *John Paul II. A Panorama of his Teachings*, New York: New City Press, 1989, 20.

[84] Pope John Paul II, *Vita Consecrata*, 66.

[85] See also Pope John Paul II, *Gift and Mystery. On the Fiftieth Anniversary of my Priestly Ordination*, New York: Doubleday, 1996, 44.

admitted that distinction of Persons within the unity of Divinity causes the trinitarian enigma.[86] As the writings of John Paul unfold throughout his Pontificate, that same trinitarian question persists. His trinitarian writings, implicitly and explicitly, invite the Church to be aware of that very problem as it lurks in many currents of contemporary theology.

The second question that John Paul treats, although implicitly without mentioning the contemporary trinitarian terminology usually heared in debates, is the relationship between Immanent and Economic Trinity. He does specifically use the term *Immanent*. Expressions such as *intra–trinitarian life*, *interpersonal communion* or similar concepts designate the Immanent Trinity. The term *economy* is a concept he often employs to describe God's involvement in the world, although he does not apply it to the Trinity. What was developed above in the section on the Economic Trinity is essential to understanding the thought of Pope John Paul II on the Immanent Trinity. In several ways, the Pope shows that what the Church knows about the Triune God in the Scripture and in the Tradition is an exact reflection of what God is in his very life and in His relationship to the world.

In *Dives in Misericordia*, 8, Pope John Paul II presents a well–rounded meditation on God's mercy with all its theological implications on His relationship to the world. The *admirabile commercium*, the wonderful exchange, is the law of the very plan of salvation: receiving God's mercy, man, in a sense, 'shows mercy' to the Crucified Son of God. The human heart's capacity to be merciful "reveal(s) in the same perspective the deep mystery of God: that inscrutable unity of Father, Son, and Holy Spirit, in which love, containing justice, sets in motion mercy, which in its turn reveals the perfection of justice."[87] The action of the Triune God *ad extra* reveals nothing but what this God is in Himself. In this context, the Immanent Trinity is the fundamental basis of God's expression to the world.

In an excerpt from his meditations on the Blessed Trinity, Pope John Paul II recalls the mystery of the Three Divine Persons within the One of divine unity:

> He is at the same time Father, Son and Holy Spirit. But it is not a matter of three separate Gods — that would be blasphemy — nor of simply diverse and impersonal modes of presenting himself on the part of one Divine person. This would be radically impoverishing the richness of his interpersonal communion.[88]

---

[86]See St. Augustine, *De Civ. Dei* XI, 10; *De Trin.* I, 2, 4; 3, 5; 5, 8; VI, 6, 8; *En. In Ps.* 68; *Epist.* 170, 238.

[87]Pope John Paul II, *Dives in Misericordia*, 8.

[88]*Prayers and Devotions from Pope John Paul II*, Edited and with an Introduction by Bishop Peter Canisius Johannes Van Lierde, Translated by Firman O'Sullivan, New York: Viking, A

In these simple words that are not from an Encyclical but from a meditation, John Paul displays the faith of the Church in the mystery of the Trinity. He repeats the same theological concept in *Familiaris Consortio*, 11: "God is love and in Himself He lives a mystery of personal loving communion." Both texts implicitly reject *Tritheism* and *Sabellianism* as erroneous approaches to the relations among the Divine Persons.

As far as *Tritheism* is concerned, in the cited document the emphasis on the self–subsistence of each of the Divine Persons, should not threaten the Oneness of nature:[89] God is still one God as He revealed Himself in the Old Testament, although the core of the New Testament's faith is the Revelation of the mystery of God as a Trinity of Persons. Revelation implies that within the Oneness of the Divine Nature, God is Three different Divine Persons. Since they share an everlasting "interpersonal communion," the Church affirms the self–subsistence of each one of them: they are not "diverse and impersonal modes" of presenting One and the same Divine Person. Indirectly, Pope John Paul II seems to refute Karl Rahner's way of indicating the Divine Person as *mode of subsistence.*

As far as *Sabellianism* is concerned, John Paul II detects many implicit theological tendencies that emphasize the unity of the Divinity to the point of dissolving the Trinity. In the document above cited from his prayers and devotions, John Paul II recurs to the expression *interpersonal communion* in order to defeat Sabellianism. This places him in the long Tradition of the Church in respect to the existence of a Trinity of different Divine Persons within the Oneness of the Divine Nature.[90]

In his pre–papal work on the theology of the Second Vatican Council, *Sources of Renewal*, he incorporates the classic Thomist metaphysics into his theological approach to the Divine Persons. Yet he goes beyond the metaphysics of universal nature in order to reach a further dimension in the notion of Person: within the Triune God, the infinite *communio* between the Three Divine Persons is built by the self–offering which each Divine Person made of Himself to the others: In the Trinity then, to be a Person means to give oneself completely to other Persons. This offering of oneself to the others explains the nature of *communio* among the Three of them: In the Tri–unity of

---

Giniger Book, 1984, 445.

[89]See also Pope John Paul II, *Dominum et Vivificantem*, 9, where he relates Jesus' words during the Last Supper as found in St. John's and the trinitarian formula of baptism according to St. Matthew: "The formula reflects the intimate mystery of God, of the divine life, which is the Father, the Son, and the Holy Spirit, the divine unity of the Trinity."

[90]See Fabio Giardini, "Trinitarian Communion and Christian Mission in *Redemptoris Missio*," in *Euntes* 47 (1994): 165–66.

God, the Three Divine Persons are a *communio* of loving circumincession.[91] In *Mulieris Dignitatem*, 6, Pope John Paul analyzes the meaning of image and likeness from a philosophical and theological point of view proceeding from the copy to the prototype. If person means a rational being (Boethius and Aquinas) that exists in relationship with another human person (metaphysics of concrete subjectivity), each Divine Person individualizes the whole Divine Nature in His personality and exists as a Person, thanks to the relations of origin between that Person and the others: "Being a person in the image and likeness of God thus also involves existing in a relationship, in relation to the other 'I.' This is a prelude to the definitive self–revelation of the Triune God: a living unity in the communion of the Father, Son and Holy Spirit."[92]

One also detects in John Paul's approach the influence of St. Augustine's concept of relations of origins: the expressions Father and Son imply separateness and therefore stand in relation to each other. *Father* and *Son* are terms that express an "ad aliquid," "relative dicuntur ad invicem": they express the Divine Persons relative to each other. The Father is not the Son and the Son is not the Father, although the term Father implies from all eternity the existence of a Son and the term Son implies from all eternity the existence of a Father. For Augustine that is a relative diversity because the distinction between the Persons happens within the same framework of a One and Unique divine essence. Absolute terms designate the unique essence of God: goodness, omnipotence, perfection... They are applied to the Divine Persons without multiplying the divine essence: the Father is God, Goodness, Perfection; the Son and the Holy Spirit are the same. But what makes the Divine Person a Person is the relation of opposition: the Son is Son in His relation to the Father and according to the relation of origin whether it is generation or procession. Augustine then considers the Divine Persons' characteristics relational and absolute, depending on the aspect according to which they are considered: the substance of the Father results from the fact that He is God, not of the fact that He is Father; His property as Father results from His relation to the Son (*ad Filium*). From these considerations derive the identity of divine essence despite the multiplicity of relations; at the same time, relations without divine essence cannot exist. Compared to one another, the divine Persons are another *subject*,

---

[91]See Karol Wojtyla, *Sources of Renewal: The Implementation of the Second Vatican Council*, San Francisco: Harper and Row, 1980, 61–62 and 133–138; Pope John Paul II, *Christifideles Laici*, 8; Gerald A. McCool, "The Theology of John Paul II," in *The Thought of Pope John Paul II*, John M. McDermott (ed.), Rome: Gregorian University Press, 1993, 46; Fabio Giardini, "Trinitarian Communion and Christian Mission in *Redemptoris Missio*," in *Euntes* 47 (1994): 165–166.

[92]See also Pope John Paul II, *Mulieris Dignitatem*, 7; *Christifideles Laici*, 8.

not another substance, an *alius*, not an *aliud*.[93] This entire idea of Augustine found in Aquinas a very precise terminology: what define the Divine Persons are *subsistent relations*.[94]

The teaching of St. Augustine permeates the writings of John Paul II, and especially in this instance of *Mulieris Dignitatem*, 6, where it seems to be geared towards the key point: *subject*. If for John Paul II being a person means existing in a relation to an "I," a fact that reveals the ultimate face of God, that relationship among Divine Subjects determines their properties as Father, Son and Holy Spirit: it is a living unity in the communion of Father, Son and Holy Spirit.[95] This unity founds and presupposes the communion among Three Subjects standing in relations of origin: the interpersonal communion between Father, Son, and Holy Spirit is possible because of the identity of nature. The originality of John Paul II lies in his emphasis on interpersonal communion. This aspect brings to life the trinitarian aspect of God from the point of view of its subjective dimensions, although the unity of the divinity will always be for John Paul the fundamental basis for the interpersonal communion. His personalism, however, augments the Thomistic and the Augustinian theology on the subjectivity of God: this subjectivity helps John Paul to develop a lively theology concerning the economy of each of the Divine Persons. This is clear from the very beginning of his Pontificate in the three major trinitarian Encyclicals: *Redemptor Hominis*, *Dives in Misericordia*, and *Dominum et Vivificantem*.

The *communion* among Divine Persons is not only a communion of love, but also and primarily a communion of nature. It is an eternal communion based on the Oneness of the Divine Nature. Even if the Pope has already confirmed that "the Father is the first source and the giver of life from the beginning,"[96] he still esteems the Divine Nature over the Person of the Father as the point of departure for the interpersonal communion of the Triune God and as "the divine and Trinitarian unity of the source:"[97] the Triune God reveals himself as "a living unity in the communion of the Father, Son and Holy Spirit," as *Mulieris Dignitatem*, 7 reads. *Orientale Lumen* alludes to the

---

[93]See St. Augustine, *De Trin.* VII, 11; *En. in Ps* 68, 5; Yves Congar, *Credo nello Spirito Santo*, vol. 3, Brescia: Queriniana 1987, 90.

[94]See St. Thomas Aquinas, *De Potentia*, q. 9, a. 1 and 2; *Summa Theologiae* I, q. 29, a. 4.

[95]See Pope John Paul II, *Mulieris Dignitatem*, 6.

[96]Pope John Paul II, *Redemptor Hominis*, 20. See also Ibid., *Sollicitudo Rei Socialis*, 49; *Tertio Millennio Adveniente*, 6; *Vita Consecrata*, 111.

[97]Pope John Paul II, *Dominum et Vivificantem*, 7 and 59; *Mulieris Dignitatem*, 7; Fabio Giardini, "Trinitarian Communion and Christian Mission in *Redemptoris Missio*," in *Euntes* 47 (1994): 165–166.

trinitarian realism that shapes the trinitarian theology of the East, although the faith in the unity of the Divine Nature is still rapt in the mystery. The divine essence in itself is unknowable because it is impossible to know what God is. The divine category is and will always be transcendent beyond the human mind and knowledge. One can only know that God is, "since he revealed himself in the history of salvation as Father, Son and Holy Spirit.[98]

Pope John Paul's preference of the Divine Nature over the Person of the Father[99] as the source of unity in the Godhead has a Scriptural background. One senses that the Pope is following the chronological momentum of God's self–revelation and self–communication in salvation history. The unity and the oneness of God is the central message of the Old Testament and is therefore chosen as the point of departure of the trinitarian communion, although the Trinity of Persons constitutes the culminating point of God's self–revelation and the essence of faith in the New Testament. As John Paul shows in *Mulieris Dignitatem*, 7, while the Old Testament was still concerned with the Oneness and unity of God, "within this fundamental truth about God the New Testament will reveal the inscrutable mystery of God's inner life. God, who allows himself to be known by human beings through Christ, is the unity of the Trinity: unity in communion."[100]

In the opinion of Yves Congar, St. Thomas Aquinas maintained a very balanced approach in his considerations of the Divine Essence of God and the Divine Persons. Aquinas did not blindly consider the common Essence as a primary dimension and then place within it the Three Divine Persons. In his necessary and absolute mystery, God is transcendent, independent, perfect, and self–sufficient. With an incomparable divine initiative He communicates His goodness in the very mystery of creation through the divine missions of Three Divine Persons. Through the Word of God revealed in the Church, God manifests Himself as Three Persons in the unity of Divine Substance. Since God stooped to ways common to human knowledge, it is logical, says St. Thomas that human beings ascend to Him using the same means.[101]

The approach of John Paul II is very close to that of Aquinas when it comes to the relationship between unity and diversity in the Godhead. His balance in approaching the question is identical to Aquinas, although John Paul clearly

[98]See Pope John Paul II, *Orientaale Lumen*, 6.

[99]The Father's 'monarchy' and his being the "principle of communion in love," is strongly underlined especially in the Eastern outlook on the trinitarian mystery. Such an approach has been presented especially by St. Irenaeus and the Cappadocian Fathers (see Pope John Paul II, *Orientale Lumen*, 6 and 15).

[100]See also Pope John Paul II, *Vita Consecrata*, 21.

[101]See St. Thomas Aquinas, *C. Gent.* IV, 1.

attempts to keep the unity of the divinity as a point of departure for his trinitarian theology. This explains the reason one feels that the consubstantiality of the Three Divine Persons constantly appears in the background when the economy of any of the Persons is being studied. An approach in which the Divine Nature is seen as the principle of communion, does not weaken the distinction of properties of the Persons or the strong personalistic approach of John Paul. The personalistic approach to God is rather strengthened because the Pope's focus is still to develop a trinitarian theology based on the economy of the Persons, even if he is looking at Them through the background of the unity of Nature. That is what Aquinas has done when he looks at God in His absolute mystery realizing that only through a divine initiative of love was that mystery revealed through the divine missions in order to be known and loved. The mystery of the transcendent unity makes the distinction of Persons more vibrant.

One understands that John Paul would prefer the expression *There are Three Divine Persons in God*[102] (personified nature) over the expression *The Three Divine Persons are One God* (a person possesses a nature). In *Mulieris Dignitatem*, 7, one reads: "The Father, Son and Holy Spirit, one God through the unity of the divinity, exist as persons through the inscrutable divine relationship."[103] And in *Christifideles Laici*, 18, where the Pope, meditating on the communion between the faithful and Christ underlines the fact that "in this communion is the wonderful reflection and participation in the mystery of the intimate life of love in God as Trinity, Father, Son and Holy Spirit as revealed by the Lord Jesus." The preference of the personified nature places his approach within the main Western tradition of looking at the Triune God.[104] The reason behind this approach is concern about preserving the consubstantiality between the Divine Persons. In fact, when the relations of origin that differentiate the Three Divine Persons from each other happen within the One, Unchanging Divine Nature, there is no risk of perceiving the Son or the Holy Spirit as less than the Father:[105] the Triune God "'exists' in himself as a transcendent reality of interpersonal gift."[106] It is very interesting to notice that throughout all his writings Pope John Paul II, when describing any activity of the Son or of the Holy Spirit, keeps going back to principle of consubstantiality with the Father within the Divine Nature as the basis for these

---

[102]See Pope John Paul II, *Mulieris Dignitatem*, 7; *Christifideles Laici*, 18.

[103]See also Pope John Paul II, *Christifideles Laici*, 18.

[104]See Yves Congar, *Credo nello Spirito Santo*, Vol. III, Brescia: Queriniana, 1987, 8–9.

[105]See Pope John Paul II, *Tertio Millennio Adveniente*, 6; *Christifideles Laici*, 18.

[106]Pope John Paul II, *Dominum et Vivificantem*, 59; *Christifideles Laici*, 18.

activities.[107] It is interesting because the Pope looks at the Divine Nature *in recto* and at each of the Divine Persons *in obliquo*, although, as a strong personalist, he showed from the very beginning of his Pontificate a noticeable interest in the identity and role of each of the Three Divine Persons. Perhaps the three different Encyclicals dedicated to the Son (*Redemptor Hominis*, 1979), to the Father (*Dives in Misericordia*, 1980), and to the Holy Spirit (*Dominum et Vivificantem*, 1986) is the Pope's way of coming closer to the Greek approach to the theology of the Triune God.

It has been stated in the section on the Christian personalism of John Paul II that his interest in the individual human person over the universality of nature places him in the tradition of the Cappadocians. Does this contradict what was just said about how he looks at the Divine Nature *in recto* and at the Divine Persons *in obliquo*? If one considers John Paul II's concept of 'nature' as applied on creatures, one discovers two trends. From a *phenomenological* point of view, 'nature' refers directly to a set of traits common to all beings of a species. There is only an indirect reference to the actual and concrete subject that enjoys those traits. Such an approach to the concept of nature results in an abstraction from the concrete existence of the subject in which alone it is real. At the same time, nature becomes a general term because "it refers to all subjects in their generality, not to the concrete particularity of such subjects."[108] The human nature not only provides the constitutive elements of the subject, but is also made by the subject. At birth nature gives man all the necessary conditions for a dynamism with regard to which man is still passive; however, that nature is not the principle of that specifically human dynamism of which the human person is the active source. Nature is an essential dimension of the concrete subjectivity of the human person "but from which it should not be separated and reified as an independent power."[109] In the *metaphysical sense*, nature is the constitutive principle of existing subjectivity and the source of all actions that take place in any concrete human subject, "responsible for all its dynamism, not just its passivity." Nature enables every concrete individual to become human as a person, or as a subject. However, even in this metaphysical sense of nature, this nature awaits an actualization that is possible only through the personal subject as the actual principle of transforming passivity into dynamism. Person becomes not a sample of nature,

---

[107]See Pope John Paul II, *Tertio Millennio Adveniente*, 3–4.

[108]See Karol Wojtyla, "Participation and Alienation," *Analecta Husserliana* 6 (1977): 65; Anselm K. Min, "John Paul II's Anthropology of Concrete Totality," in *Proceedings of the American Catholic Philosophical Association* 58 (1984): 122.

[109]Anselm K. Min, "John Paul II's Anthropology of Concrete Totality," in *Proceedings of the American Catholic Philosophical Association* 58 (1984): 122; Karol Wojtyla, *The Acting Person*, 77–81 and 182–183.

not an individualized humanity that is concretized in that specific human subject, but "the mode of individual being that pertains to mankind alone."[110]

Pope John Paul II does not arbitrarily apply to the Divine Nature and Persons the concepts of nature and person that he usually applies to human beings. He respects the *analogia esse* and the necessary *quantum leap* that exists between the philosophical concepts of person and nature in themselves and their attribution to the transcendental Nature of the Three Divine Persons. When it comes to the notion of human persons, he recurs to the notion according to which every person is in the mode of individual being that pertains to mankind thus making sure that a universal concept of person exists only in an individualized manner. Taking that individuality as a point of departure, the Pope is able to generalize and extend the understanding of the structure of that specific person to all human beings and to human nature in general.

In the case of the Divine Persons, however, the situation is analogous, yet still essentially different. The reason lies in the fact that the Three Persons share in One and the Same Divine Nature, essentially and numerically. The Three of them actualize the Divinity differently: the Father, the Son and the Holy Spirit individualize that Nature each according to His own properties. Since the Person of the Father is different from the Person of the Son and from the Person of the Holy Spirit, the personal actualization of the One Nature of God occurs in three different Persons. Since man must still be distinguished from the divine "supposits" because human individuality does not mean being an individual of just any rational nature, it should be clear that to be a 'subject' of existence and action in the metaphysical sense can be applied to God. Hence the analogy between human subjects that exist in a rational nature each as a mode of individual being pertaining only to human nature in general, and the Divine Subjects who exist in One and the same Divine Nature, essentially and numerically. That the principle of unity of the Three Persons lies in the Nature should not therefore be surprising, even in a philosophy like that of John Paul II. From the beginning of the Church's theology, debates were formed around the relationship between the Father and the Son, the Holy Spirit and the Father, and the Holy Spirit and the Son. In order to avoid creating a difference of nature between the Persons while one is theologizing about their own specific properties, the Thomistic approach to the understanding of the divine unity as adapted by John Paul II seems the securest way. That unity sheds light on the being of every Divine Person and allows an analogy to be applied to them, as long as that analogy respects both the likeness and essential difference between

---

[110]See Karol Wojtyla, *The Acting Person*, 73–74 and 83; Anselm K. Min, "John Paul II's Anthropology of Concrete Totality," in *Proceedings of the American Catholic Philosophical Association* 58 (1984): 122.

a human person and the Divine Persons.

It is important also to analyze the concept of *love* within the trinitarian theology of Pope John Paul II. Even though God is designated as *love*, love, as well as any other attribute, cannot exhaust the reality of the Divine Nature.[111] Love cannot make up the nature of God, although it is at the basis of the divine processions: love is the principle and power of that communion.[112] The love between human persons, whether it is in the context of marriage or not, reflects, as *Mulieris Dignitatem*, 7, puts it, the "communion of love that is in God through which the Three Persons love each other in the intimate mystery of the one divine life. The Father, Son and Holy Spirit, one God through the unity of the divinity, exist as persons through the inscrutable divine relationship. Only in this way can we understand the truth that God in himself is love (cf. 1 Jn 4:16)." This divine life will always be a mystery that can never be exhausted by the dimension of love, although love, as is shown in this text, is at the basis of the relations of origin between the Divine Persons.

Love is the basic principle for God's action *ad extra* the Divine Nature. Love relates the Immanent Trinity to history and this, for Pope John Paul II, is the Christian novelty: "the Father loved us so much as to give us his Only Begotten Son; through love, the Son poured out his blood for our sake; and the Holy Spirit was actually 'given to us' in such a way as to bring into us that same love with which God loves us (Rom 5:5)."[113]

Conclusion

In the trinitarian thought of Pope John Paul II, there are three stages of the economy of salvation: creation, Incarnation and sanctification. In creation, the Father creates the visible and the invisible world through the Son in the Holy Spirit and the diagram for that stage would be: Father⇨Son⇨Holy Spirit.[114] Through the Incarnation, the Son redeems creation by the will of the Father

---

[111]See Pope John Paul II, *Dives in Misericordia*, 13; *Christifideles Laici*, 18; Paul L. Peeters, "*Dominum et Vivificantem*: The Conscience and the Heart," in *Communio* 15 (1988): 149.

[112]See Pope John Paul II, *Familiaris Consortio*, 18; *Mulieris Dignitatem*, 7; *Vita Consecrata*, 21; *Celebrate 2000! Reflections on Jesus, the Holy Spirit, and the Father*, Ann Arbor, Michigan: Servant Publications, 1996, 41; Paul L. Peeters, "*Dominum et Vivificantem*: The Conscience and the Heart," in *Communio* 15 (1988): 149.

[113]*Prayers and Devotions from Pope John Paul II*, Edited and with an Introduction by Bishop Peter Canisius Johannes Van Lierde, Translated by Firman O'Sullivan, New York: Viking, A Giniger Book, 1984, 446.

[114]See Karol Wojtyla, *Sources of Renewal: The Implementation of the Second Vatican Council*, San Francisco: Harper and Row, 1980, 45–65 and 86–97; Pope John Paul II, *Vita Consecrata*, 1; Fabio Giardini, "Trinitarian Communion and Christian Mission in *Redemptoris Missio*," in *Euntes* 47 (1994): 165.

and sends forth the Holy Spirit of the Father. The diagram for Incarnation would be: Son⇨Father⇨Holy Spirit.[115] In sanctification, the Holy Spirit leads all creation through the Son to the Father and the diagram would be: Holy Spirit⇨Son⇨Father.[116]

If we join all three stages together we will obtain a closed circle which is the image of eternity: the creation *ex nihilo* that starts in the Triune God will be led back to its fountain after its Redemption. The diagram resulting from combining the three stages would be:

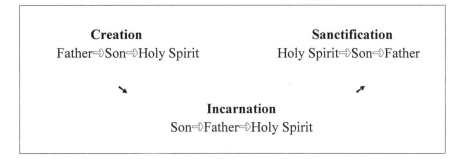

or in a form of a circle:

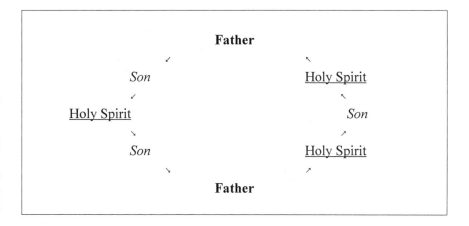

[115]See Karol Wojtyla, *Ibid.*; Pope John Paul II, *Redemptoris Missio*, 12 and 45; *Christifideles Laici*, 19; *Vita Consecrata*, 20 and 66; *Celebrate 2000! Reflections on Jesus, the Holy Spirit, and the Father*, Ann Arbor, Michigan: Servant Publications, 1996, 44; Fabio Giardini, "Trinitarian Communion and Christian Mission in *Redemptoris Missio*," in *Euntes* 47 (1994): 165.

[116]See Karol Wojtyla, *Ibid.*; Pope John Paul II, *Dominum et Vivificantem*, 32; *Redemptoris Missio*, 44; *Christifideles Laici*, 18; *Pastores Dabo Vobis*, 15; *Ut Unum Sint*, 100; Robert Morneau, "*Redemptor Hominis*: Themes and Theses," in *Review for Religious* 39 (1980): 248; Fabio Giardini, "Trinitarian Communion and Christian Mission in *Redemptoris Missio*," in *Euntes* 47 (1994): 165.

Notice that the three stages are an inseparable unity in which the creation was accomplished in vision of the Incarnation and the Incarnation in vision of the final sanctification of all creation.[117] The Father is the beginning and the end. The Son and the Holy Spirit work symmetrically in the economy of salvation.

---

[117]See Pope John Paul II, *Dominum et Vivificantem*, 52–53.

CHAPTER SEVEN

THE PROCESSION OF THE HOLY SPIRIT IN THE THOUGHT OF POPE JOHN PAUL II: THEOLOGICAL CONSIDERATIONS

Introduction

Giacomo Cardinal Biffi rightly states that "the large number of quotable expressions from the varied contexts would make it difficult to present the reader with a synthesized version of his (John Paul II's) teaching (on the Holy Spirit)." *Dominum et Vivificantem* provides the substantial and fundamental basis for the inquiry of the Pope's pneumatology, although a complete picture would be rather lacking if the other pontifical pronouncements were ignored.[1]

The study of the doctrine on the Holy Spirit as found in the writings of Pope John Paul II, is built on a very balanced framework. Being the successor of St. Peter and the visible sign of the unity of the Church,[2] Pope John Paul II, without compromising the truth of Divine Revelation,[3] shows an acute awareness of the sensitivity of the theological question of the procession of the Holy Spirit. He himself asserted that "the considerations that follow (the introduction of *Dominum et Vivificantem*) do not aim to explore exhaustively the extremely rich doctrine on the Holy Spirit, nor to favor any particular solution of questions which are still open."[4] This attitude affords the Pope the opportunity to treat the question of the Holy Spirit from a theological

---

[1]See Giacomo Cardinal Biffi, "The Action of the Holy Spirit in the Church and in the World," in *John Paul II. A Panorama of his Teachings*, New York: New City Press, 1989, 38.

[2]For John Paul's Petrine ministry for the unity of Christians, see Pope John Paul II, *Ut Unum Sint*, 4; Jan Cardinal Willebrands, "John Paul II and the search for full unity among Christians," in *John Paul II. A Panorama of his Teachings*, New York: New City Press, 1989, 48; Joseph Cardinal Cordeiro, "The religious sense of man," in *John Paul II. A Panorama of his Teachings*, New York: New City Press, 1989, 68–69.

[3]Pope John Paul II, *Ut Unum Sint*, 18.

[4]Pope John Paul II, *Dominum et Vivificantem*, 2. See also André Frossard, *Portrait of John Paul II*, San Francisco: Ignatius Press, 1990, 48–49.

perspective without siding with any specific contemporary pneumatological current and yet with full freedom to expound the wealthy patrimony of the Church's Tradition concerning the doctrine on the Holy Spirit.[5] His method of theologizing on the trinitarian mystery was very close to that of St. Augustine and St. Thomas Aquinas. Both of these Fathers took the scriptural data as their point of departure to provide the truth for their faith. Once the truth was provided, they put an extraordinary effort to understand that faith. John Paul's originality consists in his deep rethinking of the question, clearly presenting the tradition of the Church, and always starting from Scripture. That is why a theology of the procession of the Holy Spirit as it appears in the Gospel of St. John affords the Pope the opportunity to start again from Scripture without, however, neglecting the patrimony of the Church's Tradition. This approach is careful not to get caught up in the historical question of the *Filioque* in all its historical and doctrinal complexity with the theology on the Holy Spirit. It is no accident that *Dominum et Vivificantem*'s citations do not derive from previous ecumenical councils.[6]

The question of the procession of the Holy Spirit within the Immanent Trinity cannot be identified within the theological problem of the *Filioque*. All references to the procession of the Holy Spirit in the documents of Pope John Paul II are important on the theological level, but they do not explicitly treat the question of the *Filioque*. Such an intelligent politics, without compromising the truth of the Catholic faith, opens new doors for unity. An example to illustrate is John Paul's recommendation of St. Cyril and Methodius' teaching as "maintaining perfect orthodoxy." Knowing that the Apostles to the Slavic Nation refused to recite the Symbol of faith without the *Filioque*, the Pope's recommendation "can be read as yet another attempt by this pontiff to lessen the stature of the *Filioque* as a prime obstacle to the establishment of full Catholic–Orthodox communion."[7] This and many other implicit attempts afford John Paul II the occasion to use the theology of the Holy Spirit to encourage unity instead of division. The question of the *Filioque*

---

[5]See Pope John Paul II, *Ut Unum Sint*, 2; Terrence Prendergast, "'A Vision of Wholeness': A Reflection on the Use of Scripture in a Cross–section of Papal Writings," in *The Thought of Pope John Paul II*, Rome: Gregorian University, 1993, 87–88; George Every, "*Slavorum Apostoli*: A Note." In *One in Christ* 21 (1985): 272.

[6]See Terrence Prendergast, "'A Vision of Wholeness': A reflection on the use of Scripture in a cross–section of Papal writings," in *The Thought of Pope John Paul II*, Rome: Gregorian University, 1993, 72.

[7]See Joseph A. Loya, "John Paul II's Encyclical *Slavorum Apostoli*: An Ecumenical Assessment." In *Ecumenical Trends* 14 (1985): 168; Josef Kalvoda, "The Cyrilo–Methodian Idea." In *The Priest* 42 (February 1986): 19; George Every, "*Slavorum Apostoli*: A Note." In *One in Christ* 21 (1985): 272; "An Offer from the Pope," in *The Tablet* 249 (1995): 694; E. K. Bouboutsis, "Toward Unity with Diversity and Equality," in *Ecumenical Trends* 25 (1996): 10–12.

is still very complicated, especially because of all the dogmatico–historical and theological implications behind it.[8]

Pope John Paul II theologically reflects on the Scriptural references about the procession of the Holy Spirit within the framework of the Church's Tradition.[9] He follows exactly the line of thought of St. Augustine who draws his theology on the procession of the Holy Spirit from the New Testament and only afterwards brings the reasoning of faith into the study. St. Augustine, followed later on by St. Anselm and St. Thomas Aquinas, has pushed the Latin theology to search for the "intellectus fidei," the understanding of faith through reason and beyond Sacred Scripture.[10] The Pope also had recourse to the use of the reason in presenting the trinitarian mystery, and he did it very skillfully. John Paul, as it was seen in the course of analysis of his trinitarian texts, showed an extraordinary awareness of the main line in which Orthodox theology faced the trinitarian mystery. Because of the incomprehensibility of the divine Essence and the mystic knowledge that goes far beyond the Latin use of intellectual reasoning, Gregory Palamas (1296–1359), followed later on by Cabasilas (+1363), criticized the Latin Scholasticism of imposing created reason on the forbidden area of God's mystery.[11] Their influence has impregnated the whole history of Greek thinking concerning the procession of the Holy Spirit and the absolute limitations of the human reason in theologizing about the mystery of God. It is interesting to see what kind of approach the Pope will undertake when facing the diversity of theological thinking about this subject. It is sure, however, that with his treatment of the whole question of the procession of the Holy Spirit, he intends to ease the tensions between East and West and to avoid what Vladimir Lossky considered the essential cause of divergence between East and West. Yves Congar did not, by the way, share with Lossky that the *Filioque* poses insurmountable opposition and irreconcilable tensions.[12]

---

[8]Pope John Paul II, *Ut Unum Sint*, 2.

[9]See Pope John Paul II, *Dominum et Vivificantem*, 1–2.

[10]See Yves Congar, *Credo nello Spirito Santo*, Vol. III, Breascia: Queriniana, 1987, 11.

[11]See Em. Candal, *Nilus Cabasilas et theologia S. Thomae de Processione Spiritus Sancti, Novum e Vaticanis codicibus subsidium ad historiam theologiae Byzantinae saeculi XIV Plenius elucidandam*, Vatican, 1945.

[12]See Yves Congar, *Credo nello Spirito Santo*, Vol. III, Brescia: Queriniana, 1987, 7–8.

The Descent of the Holy Spirit as a Fundamental Truth of Faith

As confirmed in many of his documents,[13] the Pope is well aware of the renewal of the pneumatological dimension of salvation that was accomplished by the theology of Vatican II: "Since it pleased God not to manifest solemnly the mystery of the salvation of the human race until he poured forth the Spirit promised by Christ, we see the Apostles before the day of Pentecost 'continuing with one mind in prayer...'"[14] The Dogmatic Constitution *Lumen Gentium* compares the activity and the presence of the Holy Spirit in the Church "to the function which the soul as the principle of life fulfills in the human body."[15] Already Pope Paul VI, in his *Evangelii Nuntiandi*, confirmed the deep desire of the people of God to understand better the Spirit's identity and action at a time when "in the Church we are living an exceptionally favorable season of the Spirit."[16]

If the Incarnation of the Son is for John Paul II the *key truth of faith* and the *first fundamental truth*, the descent of the Holy Spirit is also a fundamental dimension in the economy of salvation because the Holy Spirit as "a divine person, he is at the center of the Christian faith."[17] Because of the Spirit's transcendental identity, there could be no reduction or minimizing of the indispensable role of the Holy Spirit in the economy of salvation. His role is as important as that of the Father and of the Son. As rightly expressed in *Redemptoris Missio*, the Spirit is "not an alternative to Christ, nor does he fill a sort of void which is sometimes suggested as existing between Christ and the Logos."[18]

Since John Paul II involves all Three Divine Persons in the Redemption each according to His own properties, he avoids reducing either the economy of the Father or that of the Holy Spirit to an appendix of the Incarnation. The sending of the Holy Spirit upon the Church during Pentecost is a *fundamental*

---

[13]See Karol Wojtyla, *Sources of Renewal: The Implementation of the Second Vatican Council*, San Francisco: Harper and Row, 1980, 45–65 and 86–97; Pope John Paul II, *Catechesi Tradendae*, 72; *Dominum et Vivificantem*, 2; *Redemptoris Missio*, 28–29.

[14]*Lumen Gentium*, 59. See also Pope John Paul II, *Redemptoris Mater*, 24; Terrence Prendergast, "'A Vision of Wholeness': A Reflection on the Use of Scripture in a Cross–section of Papal Writings," in *The Thought of Pope John Paul II*, Rome: Gregorian University, 1993, 87.

[15]*Lumen Gentium*, 7. Pope John Paul II, *Christifideles Laici*, 20.

[16]Pope Paul VI, *Evangelii Nuntiandi*, 75. See also Pope John Paul II, *Catechesi Tradendae*, 72.

[17]Pope John Paul II, *Dominum et Vivificantem*, 2.

[18]Pope John Paul II, *Redemptoris Missio*, 29; Giacomo Cardinal Biffi, "The Action of the Holy Spirit in the Church and in the World," in *John Paul II. A Panorama of his Teachings*, New York: New City Press, 1989, 39.

and key truth in the overall picture of the economy of salvation[19] because, as *Dominum Vivificantem* develops it (6–7), the Spirit is the full Revelation of the mystery of the Trinity: "built by Christ upon the Apostles, the Church became fully aware of these mighty works of God on the day of Pentecost, when those gathered together in the Upper Room 'were filled with the Holy Spirit'..."[20] *Veritatis Splendor* refers to the descent of the Holy Spirit as the fundamental event of salvation and places it in the context of moral law. It was St. Thomas Aquinas who, having summed up the great traditions of the Fathers of the East and the West, especially that of St. Augustine, reached the heart of the moral message of Jesus and the preaching of the Apostles. For Aquinas "the New Law is the grace of the Holy Spirit given through faith in Christ."[21]

Throughout all of Church life and existence, the Holy Spirit extends in the Church the presence of the Savior who "had to go away from us...in order that the Counselor should come to us and *should keep coming to us* as the Spirit of truth." That 'He should keep coming' indicates that Pentecost is a lasting happening by means of which God constantly forms people in Christ, as the Church, for their own salvation.[22] The risen crucified One gives the Spirit "as it were through the wounds of His crucifixion."[23] Christ promised and sent the Holy Spirit, the invisible Comforter (parákletos)[24] and the Spirit of truth,[25] once

---

[19]See Pope John Paul II, *Redemptor Hominis*, 18; *Dominum et Vivificantem*, 7; *Christifideles Laici*, 20; *Gift and Mystery. On the Fiftieth Anniversary of my Priestly Ordination*, New York: Doubleday, 1996, 44; Terrence Prendergast, "'A Vision of Wholeness': A Reflection on the Use of Scripture in a Cross–section of Papal Writings," in *The Thought of Pope John Paul II*, Rome: Gregorian University, 1993, 87–88; Angelo Scola, "'Claim' of Christ, 'Claim' of the World: On the Trinitarian Encyclicals of John Paul II," in *Communio* 18 (1991): 325; J. Honoré, "Christ the Redeemer, Core of John Paul's Teaching," in *John Paul II. A Panorama of his Teachings*, New York: New City Press, 1989, 18–19; Giacomo Cardinal Biffi, "The Action of the Holy Spirit in the Church and in the World," in *John Paul II. A Panorama of his Teachings*, New York: New City Press, 1989, 39.

[20]Pope John Paul II, *Redemptoris Mater*, 26.

[21]See St. Thomas Aquinas, *Summa Theologiae*, I–II, q. 106, a. 1 *corpus* and ad 2.; Pope John Paul II, *Veritatis Splendor*, 24; J. Honoré, "Christ the Redeemer, Core of John Paul's Teaching," in *John Paul II. A Panorama of his Teachings*, New York: New City Press, 1989, 18.

[22]Pope John Paul II, *Redemptor Hominis*, 7. See also Ibid., *Dives in Misericordia*, 2; *Dominum et Vivificantem*, 24; *Redemptoris Missio*, 6; *Pastores Dabo Vobis*, 14; *Veritatis Splendor*, 25; *Ut Unum Sint*, 14; *Homily at Christ the King Parish*, Rome, May 18, 1980; Giacomo Cardinal Biffi, "The Action of the Holy Spirit in the Church and in the World," in *John Paul II. A Panorama of his Teachings*, New York: New City Press, 1989, 40; Jan Cardinal Willebrands, "John Paul II and the search for full unity among Christians," in *John Paul II. A Panorama of his Teachings*, New York: New City Press, 1989, 52.

[23]Pope John Paul II, *Dominum et Vivificantem*, 24.

[24]Pope John Paul II, *Dominum et Vivificantem*, 3; *Redemptoris Mater*, 25; Giacomo Cardinal Biffi, "The Action of the Holy Spirit in the Church and in the World," in *John Paul II. A Panorama*

and for all to his Church.[26] The public revelation of the Church to the world is the fruit of the descent of the Holy Spirit. All of this is summarized by John Paul II's *Redemptor Hominis*, 18:

> This treasure of humanity enriched by the inexpressible mystery of divine filiation and by the grace of 'adoption as sons' in the only Son of God, through whom we call God 'Abba, Father' is also a powerful force unifying the Church above all inwardly and giving meaning to all her activity. Through this force the Church is united with the Spirit of Christ, that Holy Spirit promised and continually communicated by the Redeemer and whose descent, which was revealed on the day of Pentecost, endures for ever. Thus the powers of the Spirit, the gifts of the Spirit, and the fruits of the Holy Spirit are revealed in man.[27]

Pentecost is also a fundamental truth of faith in the sense that *the Holy Spirit fulfills Christ's salvific work* in the Church in the same exact way that Christ saves humanity: "the Redemption accomplished by the Son in the dimensions of the earthly history of humanity... is at the same time, in its entire salvific power, transmitted to the Holy Spirit..."[28] Salvation, as expressed in *Redemptoris Missio*, "always remains a gift of the Holy Spirit."[29] It is a gift of the Spirit because as the Pope explains later in *Tertio Millenio Adveniente*, 1, the mission of the Holy Spirit is the "continuation of the Son's mission."[30] If the Incarnation of the Word sums up all that God does to redeem a humanity

---

of his Teachings, New York: New City Press, 1989, 40.

[25]See Pope John Paul II, *Redemptor Hominis*, 3; *Dominum et Vivificantem*, 4.

[26]See Pope John Paul II, *Redemptor Hominis*, 2; *Christifideles Laici*, 20; Giacomo Cardinal Biffi, "The Action of the Holy Spirit in the Church and in the World," in *John Paul II. A Panorama of his Teachings*, New York: New City Press, 1989, 39; Jan Cardinal Willebrands, "John Paul II and the search for full unity among Christians," in *John Paul II. A Panorama of his Teachings*, New York: New City Press, 1989, 52; Josef Cardinal Tomko, "Mission and dialogue in the teaching of John Paul II," in *John Paul II. A Panorama of his Teachings*, New York: New City Press, 1989, 84.

[27]Pope John Paul II, *Redemptor Hominis*, 18; J. Honoré, "Christ the Redeemer, Core of John Paul's Teaching," in *John Paul II. A Panorama of his Teachings*, New York: New City Press, 1989, 18.

[28]Pope John Paul II, *Dominum et Vivificantem*, 11. See also Ibid., *Christifideles Laici*, 16; *Veritatis Splendor*, 27; *Gift and Mystery. On the Fiftieth Anniversary of my Priestly Ordination*, New York: Doubleday, 1996, 44; J. Honoré, "Christ the Redeemer, Core of John Paul's Teaching," in *John Paul II. A Panorama of his Teachings*, New York: New City Press, 1989, 18; Josef Cardinal Tomko, "Mission and dialogue in the teaching of John Paul II," in *John Paul II. A Panorama of his Teachings*, New York: New City Press, 1989, 84.

[29]Pope John Paul II, *Redemptoris Missio*, 9. See also Ibid., *Dominum et Vivificantem*, 3; Josef Cardinal Tomko, "Mission and dialogue in the teaching of John Paul II," in *John Paul II. A Panorama of his Teachings*, New York: New City Press, 1989, 84.

[30]See also Pope John Paul II, *Catechesi Tradendae*, 72.

he created out of nothing, the Holy Spirit enjoys a similar kind of 'incarnation' because He not only extends the Redemption of Christ in the life of the Church, but also enables her to "understand the correct meaning of the content of Christ's message." Saying that the Holy Spirit 'will teach' the Apostles means that "he will ensure continuity and identity of understanding in the midst of changing conditions and circumstances."[31] The coming of the Holy Spirit as described in *Dominum et Vivificantem* is not reduced to an abstract consequence of Redemption because John Paul presents Redemption itself as incomprehensible except through that coming of the Spirit. The encyclical's ultimate message, in the last analysis, consists in showing that the 'incarnation' of the Spirit, i.e. Pentecost, reveals the redeeming event of Jesus Christ in its plenitude and leads it through history towards the *Parousia*.[32]

Does this mean that for John Paul II the Redemption of Christ is incomplete or imperfect without the descent of the Holy Spirit? The answer has a paradoxical character. The Redemption of Christ is perfect and complete in the sense that Christ has done everything necessary in order to accomplish the Redemption in both divine and human dimensions. Christ has paid the necessary price to the Father, a price that counterbalanced the human evil in all its dimensions and bought back the human race to the Father. Yet without the Holy Spirit there could be no application of that Redemption to any human being in all history. The Holy Spirit, without monopolizing, possesses His own economy like the Father who plans and the Son who redeems.[33] The 'incarnation' of the Holy Spirit, although it enjoys its own identity since the Holy Spirit is a Divine Person different than the Son and since in Him there a is new salvific self–giving of God,[34] is still connected straightly to the Incarnation of the Word: every gift of the Holy Spirit is granted in order to bear fruit for the Lord. The 'incarnation' of the Holy Spirit is always hidden behind

---

[31]Pope John Paul II, *Dominum et Vivificantem*, 4. See also Ibid., *Christifideles Laici*, 16; *Vita Consecrata*, 4; *Celebrate 2000! Reflections on Jesus, the Holy Spirit, and the Father*, Ann Arbor, Michigan: Servant Publications, 1996, 74–75; Jan Cardinal Willebrands, "John Paul II and the search for full unity among Christians," in *John Paul II. A Panorama of his Teachings*, New York: New City Press, 1989, 52.

[32]See Pope John Paul II, *Ut Unum Sint*, 14; Josef Cardinal Tomko, "Mission and dialogue in the teaching of John Paul II," in *John Paul II. A Panorama of his Teachings*, New York: New City Press, 1989, 84.

[33]See J. Honoré, "Christ the Redeemer, Core of John Paul's Teaching," in *John Paul II. A Panorama of his Teachings*, New York: New City Press, 1989, 18; Giacomo Cardinal Biffi, "The Action of the Holy Spirit in the Church and in the World," in *John Paul II. A Panorama of his Teachings*, New York: New City Press, 1989, 41.

[34]Pope John Paul II, *Dominum et Vivificantem*, 11 and 14; J. Honoré, "Christ the Redeemer, Core of John Paul's Teaching," in *John Paul II. A Panorama of his Teachings*, New York: New City Press, 1989, 18.

and constantly oriented to the Incarnation of Christ. This hiddenness of the Holy Spirit behind the work of the Father and the Son is the reason for the long time it took Church tradition to attribute personal traits to the Spirit. He is often referred to as '*Ignoto Deo*.' In addition, St. Augustine's complaint about the lack of investigation of the mystery of the Holy Spirit is well known.[35] The style of John Paul respects the development of dogma and indicates a fine awareness of the theology of the Holy Spirit which is taking place in the Catholic Church. One senses that in *Redemptor Hominis*, 18 — as well as throughout *Dominum et Vivificantem* — the difficulty of the Pope's theology on the Holy Spirit in the economy of salvation results from his constant awareness of the enigma of the Spirit's peculiar identity within the Immanent Trinity: the 'spiration.' In his knowledge of St. Thomas Aquinas and St. Augustine, he acknowledges the theological dilemma of the Spirit's 'spiration' which is not a constitutive relation like 'Fatherhood' and 'Sonship.' In other words the name *Holy Spirit* is not a relative but an absolute name that could also be applied to the Father and the Son. Yet because of the 'authorized accommodation by the Scripture,' as Congar calls it, the name *Holy Spirit* is attributed as a proper name to the Third Person of the Trinity.[36]

The relationship of interdependence between the mission of the Son and the mission of the Holy Spirit could be called *causal*. Not only *after*, but *because* of the Redemption and the departure of Christ, the Holy Spirit came down on the Church.[37] This causality implies that "the Pentecostal event started on the day of the Resurrection."[38] A sound pneumatology, in the Pope's opinion, should never be deprived of its christological dimension: the Spirit makes ever present in the Church and in the world, in time and space, the mystery of Christ, because the christological mystery includes and reveals the mystery of the Holy Spirit. This is described beautifully in *Redemptoris Missio*:

---

[35]See *De fide et symbolo* 9, 19: PL 40, 191. For the theology of the Holy Spirit as treated from that specific point of view in the last hundred years, see the Mr Gaume's work in 1879; M. Landrieux's *Le divin Méconnu* in 1921; P. Victor Dillard's *Au Dieu inconnu* in 1938; Pastore A. Garnier's *Le Saint–Esprit, ce méconnu* in 1965; E. H. Palmer's *The Holy Spirit* in 1958; L. Wunderlich's *The Halfknown God: The Lord and Giver of Life* in 1963; Yves Congar's *Je Croit en l'Esprit Saint* in 1980; John J. O'Donnell's *Il Mistero della Trinità* in 1989.

[36]See St. Augustine, *De Trinitate* V, 14 and XV, 19; St. Thomas Aquinas, *Summa Theologiae* I, q. 36, a. 1 c e ad 1 and I, q. 40, a. 4; Yves Congar, *Credo nello Spirito Santo*, Vol. 3, Brescia: Queriniana, 1987, 18–19.

[37]See Pope John Paul II, *Dominum et Vivificantem*, 8 and 11. See also Ibid., *Vita Consecrata*, 4; J. Honoré, "Christ the Redeemer, Core of John Paul's Teaching," in *John Paul II. A Panorama of his Teachings*, New York: New City Press, 1989, 18.

[38]See Pope John Paul II, *Homily at Pentecost*, May 17, 1986; Giacomo Cardinal Biffi, "The Action of the Holy Spirit in the Church and in the World," in *John Paul II. A Panorama of his Teachings*, New York: New City Press, 1989, 40.

Whatever the Spirit brings about in human hearts and in the history of peoples, in cultures and religions serves as a preparation for the Gospel and can only be understood in reference to Christ, the Word who took flesh by the power of the Spirit 'so that as perfectly human he would save all human beings and sum up all things' (*Gaudium et Spes*, 45).[39]

The Holy Spirit extends in the life of the Church the salvific work of Christ because He is the divine agent who links Incarnation to Pentecost,[40] Mary being the human agent for that task: "And so, in the redemptive economy of grace, brought about through the action of the Holy Spirit, there is a unique correspondence between the moment of the Incarnation of the Word and the moment of the birth of the Church. The person who links these two moments is Mary."[41]

In the *pneumatology* of Pope John Paul II, the presence of the Holy Spirit in the Church does not limit the *Spirit's action outside the boundaries of the visible Body of Christ*. The Gospel of St. John (Jn 3:8) and some documents of Vatican II constitute the fundamental basis for the Pope to see the activity of the Holy Spirit as unlimited by space and time.[42] The Spirit "blows where he wills" sowing "the seeds of the Word" in the heart of every person, in various customs and cultures, "preparing them for full maturity in Christ" and supplying their efforts "to attain truth, goodness and God himself."[43] The Spirit of God is not only continually stirring humanity to search for the meaning of existence, He also, as Vatican II already asserted, "offers everyone the possibility of sharing in the Paschal Mystery in a manner known to God."[44] Man's existential and religious questioning stirred by the Spirit is a result of an activity *ad intra*: it is a questioning "which is occasioned not only by

---

[39]Pope John Paul II, *Redemptoris Missio*, 29. See also Ibid., *Dominum et Vivificantem*, 54; *Vita Consecrata*, 5; J. Honoré, "Christ the Redeemer, Core of John Paul's Teaching," in *John Paul II. A Panorama of his Teachings*, New York: New City Press, 1989, 19; Giacomo Cardinal Biffi, "The Action of the Holy Spirit in the Church and in the World," in *John Paul II. A Panorama of his Teachings*, New York: New City Press, 1989, 41.

[40]See Pope John Paul II, *Dominum et Vivificantem*, 42 and 64; *Redemptoris Missio*, 21.

[41]Pope John Paul II, *Redemptoris Mater*, 24.

[42]See Pope John Paul II, *Dominum et Vivificantem*, 53; *Redemptoris Missio*, 28–29; Giacomo Cardinal Biffi, "The Action of the Holy Spirit in the Church and in the World," in *John Paul II. A Panorama of his Teachings*, New York: New City Press, 1989, 45–46; Jan Cardinal Willebrands, "John Paul II and the search for full unity among Christians," in *John Paul II. A Panorama of his Teachings*, New York: New City Press, 1989, 50.

[43]See Jn 3:8; Pope John Paul II, *Redemptoris Missio*, 28–29; Vatican II, *Ad Gentes*, 3, 11, 15; *Gaudium et Spes*, 10–11, 22, 26, 38, 41, 92–93; *Lumen Gentium*, 17.

[44]*Gaudium et Spes*, 10, 15, 22; Pope John Paul II, *Redemptoris Missio*, 28; *Dominum et Vivificantem*, 53.

contingent situations but by the very structure of his (human person's) being."[45]

Pope John Paul II perceives the Holy Spirit as the divine agent who links every human person to the reality of the Church. In this way, if we may say, the Spirit reveals the impartiality of God in offering salvation to the whole human race without exception, although each according to his or her own status. Since this specific activity of the Holy Spirit guarantees a mysterious relationship of non–believers with the Church and particularly with the Paschal Mystery, the Spirit becomes the fundamental agent of unity and ecumenism, an aspect that frequently emerges in the pneumatology of the Pope.[46]

If Pope John Paul II has followed and developed the theology of Vatican II concerning the activity of the Holy Spirit outside the visible boundaries of the Church, he nonetheless does not allow the discernment of the Spirit's presence to become an exclusively subjective question with subjective criteria. The reason lies in the fact that it is the same Holy Spirit Who works within and outside of the visible Body of Christ. It should be kept in mind that, although the Spirit works everywhere without being restricted either by space or time, Pentecost is still a fundamental event that, parallel to the Incarnation of the Word, makes the Spirit being 'incarnate' in the Church: "the Holy Spirit accompanies the Church along her way and associates her with the witness he gives to Christ (cf. Jn 15: 26–27)."[47] The fullness of time that results from the entrance of the Word into history is also a result of the sending of the Spirit into history. In the same way the Church has the ultimate responsibility of discerning the presence of Christ outside its visible boundaries, so "every form of the Spirit's presence is to be welcomed with respect and gratitude, but the discernment of this presence is the responsibility of the Church, to which Christ gave his Spirit in order to guide her into all the truth (cf. Jn 16:13)."[48] This type of pneumatological ecclesiology affords John Paul II the opportunity to clarify many misconceptions regarding the relationship between believers and non–believers as far as conversion to Catholicism is concerned. The fact that people from outside the visible boundaries of the Catholic Church possess

---

[45]Pope John Paul II, *Dominum et Vivificantem*, 54; *Redemptoris Missio*, 28.

[46]See Address to Representatives of Non–Christian Religions, Madras (February 5, 1986): *AAS* 78 (1986): 767; Message to the Peoples of Asia, Manila (February 21, 1981), 2–4: *AAS* 73 (1981): 392–393: Address to Representatives of Other Religions, Tokyo (February 24, 1981, 3–4: *Insegnamenti* IV/1 (1981): 507–508; Pope John Paul II, *Dominum et Vivificantem*, 2; *Redemptoris Missio*, 30 and 36; *Familiaris Consortio*, 21.

[47]Pope John Paul II, *Redemptoris Missio*, 42; Giacomo Cardinal Biffi, "The Action of the Holy Spirit in the Church and in the World," in *John Paul II. A Panorama of his Teachings*, New York: New City Press, 1989, 41.

[48]Pope John Paul II, *Redemptoris Missio*, 29.

certain elements of truth is part of the fullness of means of salvation (sacramentum), and should not hinder the Church from leading all people to the whole truth. This is primarily because of the importance of the truth itself about God and man and, on the other hand, because it is the right of every human person to hear the Good News in its entirety. Therefore, the eminent place that the theological idea of *truth* occupies in the thought of the Pope[49] implies an explicit refusal of the idea that claims

> ...that it is enough to help people become more human or more faithful to their own religion, that it is enough to build communities capable of working for justice, freedom, peace and solidarity. What is overlooked is that every person has the right to hear the 'Good News' of the God who reveals and gives himself in Christ, so that each one can live out in its fullness his or her proper calling.[50]

In *Dominum et Vivificantem*, 52, Pope John Paul II, displays the action of the Holy Spirit called the divine adoption. Here the indispensable presence of the Holy Spirit in the economy of salvation explains one of the fundamental truths of the Church's faith. Because of the Incarnation, "there opens in a new way the source of this divine life in the history of mankind: the Holy Spirit." Although the filiation of divine adoption is born in man on the basis of the mystery of Incarnation, this rebirth *happens* only when the Father sends the Holy Spirit of His Son into our hearts: "Hence the divine filiation planted in the human soul through sanctifying grace is the work of the Holy Spirit."[51] It is this sanctifying grace of the Incarnation that, put in motion by the Holy Spirit, gives man the supernatural life as child of God. This kind of pneumatology affords the Pope the opportunity to look at the mystery of creation and the mystery of the Incarnation as a unity. Although John Paul does not ignore the fact that creation and grace are two levels that can and must be cultivated distinctly, in the order of divine Providence the whole economy of salvation must be viewed in the unity of God's design, without juxtaposition of levels, or extrinsic exclusiveness.[52] If Christ is the content of the

---

[49]See John Paul II, *Dominum et Vivificantem*, 4; Giacomo Cardinal Biffi, "The Action of the Holy Spirit in the Church and in the World," in *John Paul II. A Panorama of his Teachings*, New York: New City Press, 1989, 41.

[50]Pope John Paul II, *Redemptoris Missio*, 46.

[51]Pope John Paul II, *Dominum et Vivificantem*, 52. See also Paul L. Peeters, "*Dominum et Vivificantem*: The Conscience and the Heart," in *Communio* 15 (1988): 148.

[52]See Giacomo Cardinal Biffi, "The Action of the Holy Spirit in the Church and in the World," in *John Paul II. A Panorama of his Teachings*, New York: New City Press, 1989, 41 and 44; Josef Cardinal Tomko, "Mission and dialogue in the teaching of John Paul II," in *John Paul II. A Panorama of his Teachings*, New York: New City Press, 1989, 84; Paul L. Peeters, "*Dominum et Vivificantem*: The Conscience and the Heart," in *Communio* 15 (1988): 148.

supernatural adoption, the Spirit becomes this content in action. The influence of St. Thomas Aquinas is very relevant : what happened in the mystery of creation, that is the giving of life, is being elevated by participation to share in the divine life when the Holy Spirit puts in motion the content of Christ's adoption. This elevation by the Holy Spirit gives the human life a supernatural and a divine dimension. The action of the Holy Spirit in giving life (mystery of creation) and in giving sanctifying grace (mystery of the Incarnation), bestows on man a "supernatural vitality": the Uncreated Spirit and the created human spirit are in direct contact through the mystery of Incarnation.

In that context, John Paul reports the famous words of St. Augustine who says of God that He is "closer than my inmost being."[53] The Pope builds a bridge between these words and Jn 4:24, "God is spirit." This connection allows him to meditate on the mystery of God's presence in the world: being wholly transcendent with regard to the world, "he is not only close to this world but present in it, and in a sense immanent, penetrating it and giving it life from within. This is especially true in relation to man: God is present in the intimacy of man's being, in his mind, conscience and heart: an ontological and psychological reality..."[54] This does not mean that God could be identified with the world, because He is and will always be essentially different from all creatures. John Paul does not take his sight off of the *major similitudo in major dissimilitudo* of Vatican I.[55] Rather, the two expressions, connected together, explain how God, as transcendental as He in Himself is, can be present in the visible world. The answer is pneumatological: only because God is spirit, God can approach the visible creation: "only the Spirit can be 'closer than my inmost being,' both in my existence and in my spiritual experience. Only the Spirit can be so immanent in man and in the world, while remaining inviolable and immutable in his absolute transcendence."[56]

John Paul's approach to the divine adoption from the pneumatological point of view is quite original: it recuperates in the christological dimension its vitality and avoids a christomonistic approach to Redemption and to its anthropological implications. It confirms the trinitarian character of the Incarnation and sheds a new light on the operation of the Trinity in the economy of salvation. Nobody before Pope John Paul II connected the divine

---

[53]St. Augustine, *Confessiones*, III, 6, 11: CCL 27, 33; Pope John Paul II, *Dominum et Vivificantem*, 54.

[54]Pope John Paul II, *Dominum et Vivificantem*, 54. See also Pope John Paul II, *Celebrate 2000! Reflections on Jesus, the Holy Spirit, and the Father*, Ann Arbor, Michigan: Servant Publications, 1996, 74–76; Paul L. Peeters, "*Dominum et Vivificantem*: The Conscience and the Heart," in *Communio* 15 (1988): 148.

[55]See Pope John Paul II, *Mulieris Dignitatem*, 25.

[56]Pope John Paul II, *Dominum et Vivificantem*, 54.

adoption in Jn 1:12–14 and Rom 8:15 to a pneumatological dimension. This pneumatological dimension of anthropology demonstrates that man is not wrapped up in an exclusive christological box: the Holy Spirit not only leads to completion of the work of Christ, but reveals the trinitarian character of man's relationship with God. It is and always will be "to the Father through Christ in the Holy Spirit": each of the Divine Persons has His own unique role in the one plan of salvation.

The Paschal Mystery as a Trinitarian Event: The Cross of Christ and the Pouring Out of the Holy Spirit

Dying on the cross, Christ gave man the possibility to become the child of God. In its turn, the Church, through the power of the Holy Spirit, communicates this Spirit to all people in order to be introduced into the mystery of divine adoption fulfilled by Christ: every human being is "the living image of God the Father, redeemed by the blood of Jesus Christ and placed under the permanent action of the Holy Spirit."[57] The Holy Spirit ensures the sharing in Christ's mystery to individuals as well as to a whole community of the children of God.[58] He is one in many and therefore He brings the many to one, since "unity, after all, is a gift of the Holy Spirit."[59] In this regard, the Pope quotes Basil the Great in *Dominum et Vivificantem*, 59: the Holy Spirit "while simple in essence and manifold in his virtues,... extends himself without undergoing any diminishing, is present in each subject capable of receiving him as if he were the only one, and gives grace which is sufficient for all."[60]

In *Redemptoris Missio*, 6, Pope John Paul II draws a clear parallel between the christological and pneumatological dimension of Redemption and bases it on *Gaudium et Spes*, 22. Just as Christ, by His Incarnation, has united himself in some sense to every human being, so too "we are obliged to hold that the Holy Spirit offers everyone the possibility of sharing in the Paschal Mystery in manner known to God."[61] Not only the Incarnation is universal, but also Pentecost.

The action of the Holy Spirit, who breathes when and wherever he wills,[62]

---

[57]Pope John Paul II, *Sollicitudo Rei Socialis*, 40. See also Ibid., *Tertio Millennio Adveniente*, 8.

[58]See Pope John Paul II, *Dominum et Vivificantem*, 22; *Slavorum Apostoli*, 29; *Redemptoris Mater*, 5; *Tertio Millennio Adveniente*, 8.

[59]Pope John Paul II, *Tertio Millennio Adveniente*, 34. See also Ibid., *Dominum et Vivificantem*, 62; *Slavorum Apostoli*, 27.

[60]Saint Basil the Great, *De Spiritu Sancto*, IX, 22: PG 32, 110.

[61]*Gaudium et Spes*, 22. See Pope John Paul II, *Redemptoris Missio*, 6.

[62]Jn 3:8; Pope John Paul II, *Redemptoris Missio*, 20.

mysteriously reaches every human person because of the Paschal Mystery. Beside his creational function as Lord and Giver of life, in the order of salvation, the Holy Spirit possesses an entirely 'incarnational' function, a function that is different as much as the function of the Word after the Incarnation is different from before.

The moment of the Paschal Mystery, at least in the text of *Redemptoris Missio*, 6, seems to be the link between the Son and the Holy Spirit in their relationship to the Father.[63] That link happens through the Paschal Mystery because, as the Pope continues to quote and explains *Gaudium et Spes* in *Redemptoris Missio*, the ultimate and universal calling of each of us comes from God. Since this calling is realized in and through the Paschal Mystery, we are obliged to hold that the Holy Spirit offers everyone the possibility of sharing in this Paschal Mystery in a manner known to God.[64]

The cross of Christ is a trinitarian event, obviously not in the sense that the Father or the Holy Spirit died for us in the flesh. Rather, in the sense that the Father and the Holy Spirit were involved in the redemptive sacrifice of Christ.[65] The first and fundamental consequence of the cross of Calvary is the establishment of a relationship between the Three Divine Persons and humanity. In *Redemptor Hominis*, 9, John Paul II says:

> The cross on Calvary, through which Jesus Christ — a Man, the Son of the Virgin Mary, thought to be the son of Joseph of Nazareth — "leaves" this world, is also a fresh manifestation of the eternal fatherhood of God, who in him draws near again to humanity, to each human being, giving him the thrice holy "Spirit of truth (Jn 16:13)."[66]

In the new economy of salvation, the cross reveals the fatherhood of the Father, a fatherhood that was rejected through sin after the economy of creation. The Father now again approaches human beings but from a christic perspective and, through the cross, He gives His Holy Spirit. The Father gives the Holy Spirit because of the Cross of the Son: the linear tradition *Father→Son→Holy Spirit* of the Church is here very relevant.[67] In this specific text of *Redemptor Hominis*, 9, John Paul does not specify whether the Son is

---

[63]See also Pope John Paul II, *Dominum et Vivificantem*, 22; *Dominicae Cenae*, 3.

[64]See *Gaudium et Spes*, 22; Pope John Paul II, *Redemptoris Missio*, 10.

[65]See Pope John Paul II, *Redemptor Hominis*, 20; *Dominum et Vivificantem*, 23; *Salvifici Doloris*, 18.

[66]Pope John Paul II, *Redemptor Hominis*, 9.

[67]See also Pope John Paul II, *Dominum et Vivificantem*, 23; *Redemptoris Missio*, 22; *Veritatis Splendor*, 8; Josef Cardinal Tomko, "Mission and dialogue in the teaching of John Paul II," in *John Paul II. A Panorama of his Teachings*, New York: New City Press, 1989, 84.

a direct agent of spiration or not. It is sure, however, that the redemption of Christ is not only a condition, but also a direct cause of the procession of the Holy Spirit in the economy of salvation.[68] The redemption of Christ is a direct cause of the procession of the Holy Spirit because the cross connects the original event of creation with the new event of re–creation of humankind. It is One and the same Triune God who is involved in both the creation and the Redemption of humankind. As *Redemptor Hominis*, 9, reads:

> This revelation of the Father and outpouring of the Holy Spirit, which stamp an indelible seal on the mystery of the Redemption, explain the meaning of the Cross and death of Christ. The God of creation is revealed as the God of Redemption, as the God who is "faithful to himself" (1 Thess 5:24), and faithful to his love for man and the world, which he revealed on the day of creation.[69]

When God created the world through His Word, the Spirit was moving on the water; when God recreated the world through His Word, the Spirit was outpoured upon humanity. The procession of the Spirit is therefore always connected to the work of the Word, in creation as well as in salvation. It can be confirmed therefore that, as in *Redemptor Hominis*, 9, Pope John Paul II considers the Holy Spirit as proceeding from the Son as far as the economy of salvation is concerned.[70]

Redemptor Hominis, 18, proclaims that the descent of the Person of the Holy Spirit on the Church during Pentecost and His continual presence in the life of the Church, are the direct results of the Paschal Mystery. Once again Pope John Paul II confirms beyond all doubt that in the context of the *Economic Trinity*, the Holy Spirit proceeds from the Son:

> In this way, turning to man and his real problems, his hopes and sufferings, his achievements and falls — this too also makes the Church as a body, an organism, a social unit perceive the same divine influences, the light and strength of the Spirit that come from the crucified and risen Christ, and it is for this very reason that she lives her life. The Church has only one life: that which is given her by her Spouse and Lord.[71]

This life of the Church is described in *Slavorum Apostoli*: Pope John Paul II affirms the pneumatological dimension of the Church's act in extending the Divine Revelation of the Triune God accomplished by Christ. What Christ

---

[68]See also Pope John Paul II, *Dominum et Vivificantem*, 23; *Tertio Millennio Adveniente*, 8.

[69]Pope John Paul II, *Redemptor Hominis*, 9.

[70]See Pope John Paul II, *Sollicitudo Rei Socialis*, 40; *Tertio Millennio Adveniente*, 8; Robert Morneau, "*Redemptor Hominis*: Themes and Theses," in *Review for Religious* 39 (1980): 248.

[71]Pope John Paul II, *Redemptor Hominis*, 18. See also Ibid., *Redemptoris Missio*, 22.

revealed to humanity concerning the nature of God, a Trinity of Persons, is being proclaimed every day by the Church through the Holy Spirit. The procession of the Holy Spirit from the Son in the economy of salvation assures the continuity of God's plan of salvation in history. Pope John Paul II says:

> The concrete dimension of catholicity, inscribed by Christ the Lord in the very make–up of the Church, is not something static, outside history and flatly uniform. In a certain sense it wells up and develops every day as something new from the unanimous faith of all those who believe in God, One and Three, revealed by Jesus Christ and preached by the Church through the power of the Holy Spirit.[72]

In *Dominum et Vivificantem*, 39–41, Pope John Paul II recurs to the Letter to the Hebrews (Heb 9:13–14) in order to explain how Christ "offered himself without blemish to God," and how he did this "through the eternal Spirit."[73] The Spirit was present and active in the sacrifice of Jesus in the same way He was present and active in all of the stages of Jesus' life. This Anointing of Christ by the Holy Spirit found its ultimate expression in the suffering and death of Christ, where He opened himself totally to the action of the Spirit: The Spirit transforms suffering into eternal salvific love.

This is the manner of transformation of Christ's humanity into a perfect sacrifice: "Proceeding from the Father, He (the Spirit) directs toward the Father the sacrifice of the Son, bringing it into the divine reality of the Trinitarian communion."[74] Thus the sacrifice of Christ has an infinite value because it is trinitarian. What the Pope is constantly referring to is the hypostatic union of the humanity of Christ with His Person and the divine subjectivity of the Holy Spirit that is being revealed as present and active in the sacrifice of Christ. These two dimensions constitute the fundamental basis for the trinitarian character of Christ's sacrifice. As 'fire from heaven,' the Spirit consumes this sacrifice with the fire of the love which unites the Son to the Father in the trinitarian communion. We are not dealing with a sacrifice that is supposed to please the Father just because of Christ's obedience to him. Rather than an adoptionistic approach to Christ in His relationship with the Father regarding His sacrifice, the Pope recurs to a high christology: the sacrifice of Christ pleases the Father because, being united to Him in the trinitarian communion, Christ's humanity receives the action of the Holy Spirit that confirms the trinitarian character of the sacrifice. This receiving of the Holy Spirit enables

---

[72]*Slavorum Apostoli*, 18.

[73]See Pope John Paul II, *Dominum et Vivificantem*, 40; J. Honoré, "Christ the Redeemer, Core of John Paul's Teaching," in *John Paul II. A Panorama of his Teachings*, New York: New City Press, 1989, 18.

[74]Pope John Paul II, *Dominum et Vivificantem*, 41.

Christ, in the economy of salvation, to give the Spirit. He received "the Holy Spirit in such a way that afterwards — and he alone with God the Father — can 'give him' to the Apostles, to the Church to humanity."[75] This is the reason why in *Redemptionis Donum* Pope John Paul, referring to Pope Paul VI's *Evangelica Testificatio*, affirms that the Holy Spirit "is at work above all in the Church."[76] The trinitarian character of the sacrifice of Christ with the special emphasis on its pneumatological dimension, affords the pope the opportunity to speak of a procession of the Holy Spirit from the Son.

The Spirit "works in the depth of the mystery of the Cross," manifesting the "paradoxical mystery of love." The paradoxical character of the cross reveals the manner of the Spirit's transformation of suffering into a salvific love: on the one hand, God suffers in Christ who meets the rejection of "those who do not believe in him;" on the other hand, "from the depth of this suffering... the Spirit draws a new measure of the gift made to man and to creation from the beginning."[77]

As a result of the Spirit's action, a new humanity has been regenerated, a humanity that has returned to the love that was betrayed by the sin of Adam.[78] Here the Pope draws a parallel between what Christ has accomplished in His humanity through the action of the Holy Spirit, and the sin of the first man, Adam.[79] What shines as original in this parallel is its pneumatological dimension: the Holy Spirit is considered the link between the humanity of Adam and the humanity of Christ. Humanity that was subjected to sin in the descendants of Adam was restored in Jesus Christ and became subjected to God. It is as if a new humanity was molded by God. This reshaping happenes, however, through the suffering of Christ and the outpouring of the Holy Spirit Who not only anointed the humanity of Jesus, but also the humanity of all descendants of Adam.

Two remarks are necessary about the Adam/Christ parallel:

First of all, this parallel takes place in the context of Christ's sacrifice on the cross, not only in the familiar contrast found in the Church Fathers, such as disobedience/obedience, sin/righteousness, punishment/salvation. It is here presented as the new humanity of Christ which by the action of the Holy Spirit restores the corrupted humanity of Adam.

---

[75]Pope John Paul II, *Dominum et Vivificantem*, 41; J. Honoré, "Christ the Redeemer, Core of John Paul's Teaching," in *John Paul II. A Panorama of his Teachings*, New York: New City Press, 1989, 18–19.

[76]Pope Paul VI, *Evangelica Testificatio*, 6; Pope John Paul II, *Redemptionis Donum*, 13.

[77]Pope John Paul II, *Dominum et Vivificantem*, 41.

[78]See Pope John Paul II, *Dominum et Vivificantem*, 40.

[79]See Pope John Paul II, *Dominum et Vivificantem*, 40.

Secondly, in this presentation by John Paul II, the new humanity of Christ causes the regeneration of humanity in the descendants of Adam not so much because of the hypostatic union of Christ's humanity with the Word, as by the anointing by the Holy Spirit. The hypostatic union of the human nature of Christ with the Person of the Logos, is the regular context that usually frameworks the regeneration of the new humanity. Such a pneumatological dimension is an original concept introduced by the Pope.

The Holy Spirit as the Person–Love and the Person–Uncreated Gift: Procession of the Holy Spirit

The previous section considered the Paschal Mystery from a trinitarian point of view. In this specific event of the economy of salvation, the Holy Spirit is seen as a Divine Person Who necessarily proceeds from the Father and the Son. Now it is time to investigate the nature of that procession from a different angle. The opening key text for that purpose is *Redemptor Hominis*, 18:

> For by Christ's will there is in this sacrament (Eucharist) a continual renewing of the mystery of the sacrifice of himself that Christ offered to the Father on the altar of the Cross, a sacrifice that the Father accepted, giving, in return for this total self–giving by his Son, who 'became obedient unto death,' his own paternal gift, that is to say the grant of new immortal life in the Resurrection, since the Father is the first source and the giver of life from the beginning. That new life, which involves the bodily glorification of the crucified Christ, became an efficacious sign of the new gift granted to humanity, the gift that is the Holy Spirit, through whom the divine life that the Father has in himself and gives to his Son is communicated to all men who are united with Christ.[80]

In this text the Pope explains in more detail what he began in *Redemptor Hominis*, 9. The cross is a trinitarian event that involves all Three Divine Persons in the act of Redemption, each according to His own properties. In return for the sacrifice of Christ, the Father gives his own paternal gift, that is a new life to the world. Redemption is again displayed as an ontological recreation that stands parallel to the original creation given by the Father, who is first source and giver of life from the beginning. This new life is a sign of the new gift to humanity: the Holy Spirit.[81] It is a new gift because the Incarnation

---

[80]Pope John Paul II, *Redemptor Hominis*, 20. See also Ibid., *Celebrate 2000! Reflections on Jesus, the Holy Spirit, and the Father*, Ann Arbor, Michigan: Servant Publications, 1996, 41.

[81]The Holy Spirit as Gift belongs to a long standing tradition in the Church of which St. Augustine and St. Thomas were the champions (See St. Thomas Aquinas, *Summa Theologiae*, I, q. 38; Yves Congar, *Credo nello Spirito Santo*, Vol. 3, Brescia: Queriniana, 1983, 17; Pope John Paul II, *Evangelium Vitae*, 1). For studying John Paul II's understanding of the Holy Spirit as a gift, see J. Honoré, "Christ the Redeemer, Core of John Paul's Teaching," in *John Paul II. A Panorama of his Teachings*, New York: New City Press, 1989, 18.

of the Son is already the Father's gift to humanity. Since this gift must be trinitarian because God is a Trinity of Persons, the Holy Spirit becomes the gift of the Father to the world. This new gift, the Holy Spirit, communicates the life of the Father and the Son to all men redeemed by Christ. Since the divine life of the Father which He gave to the Son (Jn 5:26) is communicated in itself to the world through the Holy Spirit, this same Spirit communicates, at the same time, what is the Father's and what is the Son's. He communicates what He had received from the Father and what is already in the possession of the Son, because the Father gave it to the Son. Here, when Pope John Paul speaks of the divine life that the Father gave to the Son, he clearly indicates that event to be happening on the level of the Immanent Trinity. Since the Holy Spirit, "in whom the inscrutable God communicates himself to human beings,"[82] communicates that same life to the world, He had to possess it first. It follows that on the level of the Immanent Trinity, the Holy Spirit possesses what the Father and the Son possess: the divine life that He communicates to all men united with Christ. Therefore God exists in the Spirit in the mode of a Gift, gift in the most absolute sense of the term.[83] It is in the same sense that John Paul said in his 1994 document *Celebrate 2000!*: "The Church implores (from the Holy Spirit) the grace of the virtues that merit heavenly glory, implores eternal salvation, in the full communication of the divine life, to which the Father has eternally 'predestined' human beings, created through love in the image and likeness of the Most Holy Trinity."[84]

In *Redemptor Hominis*, 18, there is a significant theology of the procession of the Holy Spirit from the Father and the Son: its source is the divine life of the Father and the Son, a source that was outpoured upon the world. The relationship between the Son and the Holy Spirit in the framework of the intratrinitarian life is authentically reflected in the relationship between the work of both of them in the economy of salvation. This idea occurs also in *Christifideles Laici*, 12, where John Paul's trinitarian background is evidently Augustinian: the union between Christ and His disciples and the disciples among each other, is a sign of that eternal bond, "of that mystical communion

---

[82]Pope John Paul II, *Dominum et Vivificantem*, 1. See also Pope John Paul II, *Celebrate 2000! Reflections on Jesus, the Holy Spirit, and the Father*, Ann Arbor, Michigan: Servant Publications, 1996, 73; *Evangelium Vitae*, 1; Paul L. Peeters, "*Dominum et Vivificantem*: The Conscience and the Heart," in *Communio* 15 (1988): 148–150.

[83]See Pope John Paul II, *Celebrate 2000! Reflections on Jesus, the Holy Spirit, and the Father*, Ann Arbor, Michigan: Servant Publications, 1996, 73; J. Honoré, "Christ the Redeemer, Core of John Paul's Teaching," in *John Paul II. A Panorama of his Teachings*, New York: New City Press, 1989, 18.

[84]Pope John Paul II, *Celebrate 2000! Reflections on Jesus, the Holy Spirit, and the Father*, Ann Arbor, Michigan: Servant Publications, 1996, 76.

that binds the Father to the Son and the Son to the Father in the bond of love, the Holy Spirit (cf. Jn 17:21)."[85] Even clearer is this identification between Immanent and Economic Trinity in John Paul's *Celebrate 2000!*: "The Holy Spirit, in His mysterious bond of divine communion with the Redeemer of man, is the One who brings about the continuity of His work. He takes from Christ and transmits to all, unceasingly entering into the history of the world through the heart of man."[86]

It is most relevant, as far as the total self–giving of the person to others is concerned, that Pope John Paul II applies to the Divine Persons what he philosophically applies to human persons. In the context of the conscious self–determination of man through a total self–giving, the concrete intelligibility of the concrete acting person is revealed. On the level of the Divine Nature, the total self–giving love of the Father is necessary for self–fulfilling his own characteristic as Father. The total self–giving love of the Son, received from the Father, is returned to the Father but is still necessary for the self–fulfillment of the identity of the Son as Son. This essential and mutual love that unites them in tri–unity of God and which is the Holy Spirit, determines their personal properties and emphasizes, always with the Oneness of Nature, how each participates in the life of the other in a mysterious *perichoresis*. It is not a matter of a pure consciousness, but of a total and concrete divine subjectivity that is present differently in each of them. It is not possible to separate the notion of total self–giving of love presented in *Redemptor Hominis*, 18, from the strong Thomistic personalism of John Paul II that was studied in the first section of this volume.[87]

Notice how in the text of *Redemptor Hominis*, 18, Pope John Paul II keeps from confusing the Holy Spirit's operations in the order of creation with His operations in the order of salvation. His operations in time are kept distinct from His operations in eternity. While the Father is the first Source of life from the very beginning of creation, the Holy Spirit is the Giver of that life from the very beginning.[88] The Son, through His redeeming activity of recreation, made the Father the source of new immortal life and the Holy Spirit the new gift of that same immortal life. But this new immortal life that originates from the Father, although it is the direct result of the Resurrection of Christ, is communicated to the world through the Holy Spirit. It follows that the Holy Spirit is the gift of the divine life of the Father and the Son to men: the Holy

---

[85]See Pope John Paul II, *Vita Consecrata*, 21.

[86]Pope John Paul II, *Celebrate 2000! Reflections on Jesus, the Holy Spirit, and the Father*, Ann Arbor, Michigan: Servant Publications, 1996, 74.

[87]See also Pope John Paul II, *Veritatis Splendor*, 22.

[88]See also Pope John Paul II, *Dominum et Vivificantem*, 1.

Spirit is the Person–Uncreated Gift. And, as a Person–Uncreated gift, He necessarily proceeds from the Father and the Son because, at least in the Pope's context, the Holy Spirit makes humanity a sharer in the very *eternal* gift of Father–Son, a gift that is communicated in the context of *created* categories. A perfect example is found in a 1982 address to young people, John Paul says: "Who is the Holy Spirit? He is God himself; he is the Third Person of the Most Holy Trinity. He was sent to each one of us by the Father and the Son. He is the supreme gift, and remains constantly in us."[89] John Paul voices the same idea again in 1994: "He, the Spirit of the Son (see Galatians 4:6), configures us to Christ Jesus and makes us sharers in His life as Son — that is, sharers in His life of love for the Father..." And, again, in the same document, *Celebrate 2000!*, "...the Church unceasingly professes her faith that there exists in our created world a Spirit who is an uncreated gift. He is the Spirit of the Father and of the Son: like the Father and the Son He is uncreated, without limit, eternal, omnipotent, God, Lord."[90]

The conclusion is clear: we know the Immanent Trinity because the Father, Son, and Spirit reveal this most holy mystery. Both the Greek and Latin Fathers insist upon our knowledge in faith since faith is a true knowledge born of the love poured forth in our hearts by the Spirit (Rom. 5:5).[91] The analogy of being is protecting the objectivity of such knowledge, for if we only love our concepts or ideas we have of someone, we do not love them as they are in themselves. But we truly love the Father, Son, and Spirit as they are in themselves. We do not just love our ideas of them. So theologians who claim that the Immanent Trinity is unknowable to us, that we only know "God for us" end in a Trinitarian agnosticism that then justifies such terms as Mother and

---

[89]See Pope John Paul II, *To young people*, Murrayfield (Great Britain), May 31, 1982; *Celebrate 2000! Reflections on Jesus, the Holy Spirit, and the Father*, Ann Arbor, Michigan: Servant Publications, 1996, 41; Giacomo Cardinal Biffi, "The Action of the Holy Spirit in the Church and in the World," in *John Paul II. A Panorama of his Teachings*, New York: New City Press, 1989, 38.

[90]Pope John Paul II, *Celebrate 2000! Reflections on Jesus, the Holy Spirit, and the Father*, Ann Arbor, Michigan: Servant Publications, 1996, 74 and 75.

[91]In *Veritatis Splendor*, 22, John Paul transmits the intratrinitarian love between the Father and the Son to creational categories: the same love that the Father has given to the Son from all eternity is now being given to the Apostles. But that same love which is the Holy Spirit in Person when contemplated in the immanent Trinity, is itself communicated to the Apostles in the Economic Trinity: "As the Lord Jesus receives the love of his Father, so he in turn freely communicates that love to his disciples: 'As the Father has loved me, so have I loved you; abide in my love.' (Jn 15:9). Christ's gift is his Spirit, whose first 'fruit' (cf. Gal 5:22) is charity..." That same identification between the Immanent and Economic Trinity is brought up again by *Vita Consecrata* within the context of evangelical counsels. Here, the poverty of Christ "becomes expression of that total gift of self which the three Divine Persons make to one another. This gift overflows into creation and is fully revealed in the Incarnation of the Word and in his redemptive death." (Pope John Paul II, *Vita Consecrata*, 21.

Daughter rather than Father and Son. Because our love of God is the absolutely supernatural love of charity we love with God's own love, the Spirit, and so we love Father, Son, and Spirit as they are in themselves, that is, the Immanent Trinity. I believe that the text from *Redemptor Hominis*,18 can be understood within the traditional theology of Saint Thomas Aquinas. When St. Thomas writes of the "incomprehensibility" of God, he is not speaking of God's "unknowability" as Karl Rahner does. For St. Thomas we know by true judgments (the second operation of the mind). So by the light of faith we know the Father, Son, and Spirit truly. But what we know we do not comprehend (the understanding or first act of the mind). Indeed, in all eternity we shall know and love God within the Inner Trinitarian Processions, but our finite minds will never comprehend God. This distinction is, I believe, preserved in the theology of John Paul II in ways it is not in that of Karl Rahner, Karl Barth, and Walter Kasper.[92]

If *Redemptor Hominis*, 18, presents the Immanent Trinity as the Economic Trinity, the sending of the Holy Spirit in the context of economy coincides with the procession of the Holy Spirit in the context of the Immanent Trinity. John Paul uses the theology of the Holy Spirit as reported by St. John the Evangelist to present his idea of the Spirit's procession by the Father and the Son. Giacomo Cardinal Biffi rightly thinks that the Pope does not show a preference for any particular systematic approach to the 'properties' or 'appropriations' of the Holy Spirit within the trinitarian life. For Biffi, however, the problem is still open as to whether the "mission" of the Holy Spirit, or His sending, "also presupposes a 'procession' from the Father and the Son within the mystery of trinitarian life." Biffi is of the opinion that the Pope reiterates this doctrine, "while stressing at the same time the substantial identity of this formula with the Greek formula: 'from the Father, by the Son'."[93] I add to Cardinal Biffi's remark that John Paul, in *Redemptor Hominis*, 18, does present a theology on the Holy Spirit that deals with His procession in the intratrinitarian life. As said in the introduction about the procession of the Holy Spirit, the historical and complex question of the *Filioque* and the theology of the Holy Spirit as found in the Gospel of St. John, although related

[92]See K. Rahner, *Quelques remarques sur le traité dogmatique "De Trinitate"*, Frensh translation H. Bourboulon, in *Ecrits théologiques*, Vol. 8, DDB 1967, 107–140; Ibid., *Il Dio trino come fondamento originario e trascendente della storia della salvezza*, in *Mysterium Salutis*, Italian edition, Vol. 3, Brescia: Queriniana, 1977, 401–502; Karl Barth, *Church Dogmatics*, I, 479; Walter Kasper, *Il Dio di Gesù Cristo*, Brescia: Queriniana, 1984, 360; Yves Congar, *Credo nello Spirito Santo*, Vol. III, Brescia: Queriniana, 1987, 23–25; John J. O'Donnel, *Il Mistero della Trinità*, Roma: Editrice Pontificia Università Gregoriana–Edizioni Piemme, 1989, 40–41.

[93]Giacomo Cardinal Biffi, "The Action of the Holy Spirit in the Church and in the World," in *John Paul II. A Panorama of his Teachings*, New York: New City Press, 1989, 38–39; Pope John Paul II, *General Audience*, May 20, 1985.

by the fact that both deal with the sending of the Holy Spirit, are and will always be two separate issues for John Paul II. It seems as if he is allowing the Spirit Himself to work on history in order to lead it to the truth. No one could help noticing the perfect balance in the pneumatology of a Pope who, being very concerned about the unity of Christianity throughout his Pontificate,[94] would never do anything to compromise the truth of faith: John Paul's catechism reminds the Church that the Third Person "proceeds by way of the will and in the mode of love," a "commonly accepted doctrine in the teaching of the Church, and hence is something sure and binding."[95]

The identification between the Immanent and the Economic Trinity in *Redemptor Hominis*, 18, does not contradict the theological principle of the incomprehensibility of the essence of God in itself. What is confirmed by that identity is an unchangeableness of God when He reveals himself *ad extra*: whatever God is, He has revealed it in and through Jesus Christ, although the very categories of God's being are and will always be His own secret. Not even after death will any creature comprehend the essence of God, a question that St. Thomas Aquinas had already treated and was happily seconded by John Paul II. When St. Bernard said that "I know what God is for me; *quod ad se, ipse novit* (what He is in Himself, only He knows),"[96] his statement was refuted by St. Thomas, because God's exclusive knowledge of the mystery of Godhead does not imply that He revealed himself in a different way than what He really is.

This is not all about *Redemptor Hominis*, 18: the Holy Spirit is the Person–Relationality between eternity and time. In this regard, a very significant passage of *Dominum et Vivificantem* reads: "and in the superabundance of the uncreated gift there begins in the heart of all human beings that particular created gift whereby they 'become partakers of the divine nature'."[97] The dilemma of how the Uncreated Divine is present in history

---

[94]Pope John Paul II's Letter to Patriarch Dimitrios dated June 4, 1980, emphasizes that the *Filioque* "is one of the points which can and must be resolved in the dialogue between the two Churches." See also Giacomo Cardinal Biffi, "The Action of the Holy Spirit in the Church and in the World," in *John Paul II. A Panorama of his Teachings*, New York: New City Press, 1989, 39.

[95]Pope John Paul II, *General Audience*, November 20, 1985; Giacomo Cardinal Biffi, "The Action of the Holy Spirit in the Church and in the World," in *John Paul II. A Panorama of his Teachings*, New York: New City Press, 1989, 39.

[96]See St. Bernard, *De consideratione* V, 11, 24; *PL* 182, 802 B. A parallel consideration is found in Yves Congar who states:"questo fatto di una rivelazione della 'teologia', cioè del mistero eterno ed intimo di Dio, nella 'economia', cioè in quello che Dio ha fatto per noi nella sua opera di creazione e di grazia, fonda la tesi...sulla identità della Trinità economica e della Trinitàimmanente."(Yves Congar, *Credo nello Spirito Santo*, Vol. III, Brescia: Queriniana, 1987, 18)

[97]Pope John Paul II, *Dominum et Vivificantem*, 52.

could be better understood in the light of the identity–operation of the Holy Spirit, however only in His relation to the Father and the Son. The Holy Spirit assures the contact of the Father and the Son with the redeemed humanity and vice versa. This explains the reason why the Holy Spirit is the crowning event of the New Testament and the beginning point of the *Parousia*.[98]

One more paragraph of *Redemptor Hominis*, 18 is worthy of investigation. Here the Pope picks up once again the procession of the Holy Spirit in the economy of salvation, but places it clearly in a trinitarian context:

> This invocation addressed to the Spirit to obtain the Spirit is really a constant self–insertion into the full magnitude of the mystery of the Redemption, in which Christ, united with the Father and with each man, continually communicates to us the Spirit who places within us the sentiments of the Son and directs us toward the Father.[99]

In this text, Christ gives the Holy Spirit to humanity in order to welcome it into His own mystery. Because Christ is united with the Father and with each man, the Holy Spirit, when bestowed on humanity, fulfills the Christological dimension of Redemption in each man leading him to the Father. The content of the Holy Spirit's action within the framework of the economy of salvation is christological, although the first contact of God with man happens through the Holy Spirit: every human person redeemed by Christ is "placed under the permanent action of the Holy Spirit."[100] Both Divine Persons, the Son and the Holy Spirit, complete each other's work in the New Testament and during the age of the Church: the Holy Spirit proceeds from the Son as the culminating moment of Redemption, and the Son is the content of that Redemption when it is fulfilled by the contact of the Holy Spirit with humanity. In other words, the Holy Spirit extends the salvific work of the Son in history and the Son constitutes the content of that salvific work in eschatology for the eternal

---

[98]In *Veritatis Splendor*, 23, the activity of the Holy Spirit in history is linked to the *Parousia* when the Pope shed light on the connection between the life of grace that a person earns through his or her actions and the eternal life as the Spirit's gift of sanctification resulting from the value of the person's action. It is hard for John Paul to imagine an eternal life that stands just in a discontinuity with an earthly life shaped with vice. The metaphysical existence surely has a continuity with the present life, "the promise of eternal life is thus linked to the gift of grace, and the gift of the Spirit which we have received is even now the 'guarantee of our inheritance' (Eph 1:14)." (See also Pope John Paul II, *Vita Consecrata*, 42).

[99]Pope John Paul II, *Redemptor Hominis*, 18.

[100]Pope John Paul II, *Sollicitudo Rei Socialis*, 40. See also Ibid., *Redemptoris Missio*, 28; *Tertio Millennio Adveniente*, 8.

sanctification of man.[101] The Holy Spirit, then, proceeds from the Son, in order to come back to the Son, and through Him to the Father, along with that man who was redeemed by the Son. The originality of John Paul's thinking in this instance lies in the fact that he restores to the Western Tradition the pneumatological dimension of salvation: the Holy Spirit connects the man redeemed by Christ and Christ to the Father.

Whereas in *Redemptor Hominis*, 18, Pope John Paul II speaks of the divine life that the Father gave to the Son which was communicated to the world by the Holy Spirit, in *Redemptoris Mater*, 8, a text similar to *Dominum et Vivificantem*, 10 and 50, the Pope speaks of the Holy Spirit as the Person–love that unites the Father and the Son in the Immanent Trinity. The text reads:

> And if after the announcement of the heavenly messenger the Virgin of Nazareth is also called 'blessed among women' (cf. Lk 1:42), it is because of that blessing with which 'God the Father' has filled us 'in the heavenly places, in Christ.' It is a spiritual blessing which is meant for all people and which bears in itself fullness and universality ('every blessing'). *It flows from that love which, in the Holy Spirit, unites the consubstantial Son to the Father.*[102]

In this text, John Paul applies Ephesians 1:3 to the Virgin Mary: the blessing that God the Father bestowed on humanity in Christ reaches the Virgin Mary in a very special and unique way because she is 'blessed among women'. This spiritual blessing flows from the eternal and mutual love between the consubstantial Persons of the Father and the Son, that is the Holy Spirit. 'Spiritual blessing' is identified with 'grace' "which according to the New Testament has its source precisely in the Trinitarian life of God himself, God who is love (cf. 1 Jn 4:8)."[103] Dealt with in *Redemptoris Mater*, 8, is the procession of the Holy Spirit in the context of the Immanent Trinity. The Pope follows the trinitarian theology of St. Augustine and St. Thomas Aquinas who used the pattern of love to describe the nature of the intratrinitarian relations.[104] Both Father and Son relate to each other through an eternal bond of mutual love: it is an eternal love that explains an eternal generation of a begotten God

---

[101]I think that Cardinal Joseph Ratzinger meant to underline the christological content of Redemption when saying: "Heaven...must first and foremost be determined Christologically." (Joseph Ratzinger, *Eschatology*. Death and Eternal Life, Washington, 1988, 234) See also Pope John Paul II, *Dominum et Vivificantem*, 24; *Tertio Millennio Adveniente*, 44–45.

[102]Pope John Paul II, *Redemptoris Mater*, 8.

[103]Pope John Paul II, *Redemptoris Mater*, 8. See also Ibid., *Tertio Millennio Adveniente*, 49.

[104]See St. Thomas Aquinas, *Summa Contra Gentiles* IV, 19; *Summa Theologiae*, I, q. 37. St. Berbard compares the Holy Spirit with the kiss that the Father and the Son give to each other mutually (Yves Congar, *Credo nello Spirito Santo*, Vol. 3, Brescia: Queriniana, 1987, 17).

from an unbegotten God.[105]

In the theology of Pope John Paul II, the Holy Spirit achieves the very first redeeming contact with man in the context of Mary's intercession. The maternity of Mary in the order of grace, as *Redemptoris Mater* relates, "implores the gift of the Spirit who raises up the new children of God, redeemed through the sacrifice of Christ."[106] The mediation of the Redeemer's Mother intercedes with the Holy Spirit to accomplish the divine Sonship of the people of God. In a Tradition where Mary usually intercedes with her Son, the intercession with the Holy Spirit introduces an original aspect in the pneumatological Mariology of Pope John Paul II.

The Procession of the Holy Spirit in *Dominum et Vivificantem*

In the Encyclical Letter *Dominum et Vivificantem* there emerges more clearly than ever the teaching of Pope John Paul II on the doctrine of the Holy Spirit. It is very interesting to study at length the different aspects of pneumatology underlying the theology of this document.

The starting point of the pneumatology of *Dominum et Vivificantem* is the mystery of the Trinity.[107] Therefore, from the very beginning of his considerations, Pope John Paul II connects the famous exhortation of St. Paul's 2 Cor 13:13:"The grace of our Lord Jesus Christ and the love of God and the fellowship of the Holy Spirit be with you all" with the Nicene–Constantinople Creed: "from this exhortation (St. Paul's) now comes the present Encyclical on the Holy Spirit, who proceeds from the Father and the Son; with the Father and the Son he is adored and glorified."[108] The reference to the procession of the Holy Spirit from *both the Divine Persons of the Father and the Son*[109] is very clear and is taken from the conciliar framework of the Nicene–Constantinopolitan Creed. Does Pope John Paul II give a theological foundation to the procession of the Holy Spirit from the Father and the Son in *Dominum et Vivificantem*? In reflecting on "the mystery of the Father, Son and Holy Spirit, which perhaps in no passage of Sacred Scripture finds so emphatic an expression as here (in the Gospel of John),"[110] what other aspects are to be

---

[105]This aspect of mutual love between the Father and the Son will be more clarified when the text of *Dominum et Vivificantem*, 10, will be thoroughly analyzed.

[106]Pope John Paul II, *Redemptoris Mater*, 44.

[107]See Michael O'Carroll, "Dominum et Vivificantem," in *Veni Creator Spiritus: A Theological Encyclopedia of the Holy Spirit*, Collegeville: Liturgical Press, 1990, 70.

[108]Pope John Paul II, *Dominum et Vivificantem*, 2.

[109]See also Pope John Paul II, *Catechesi Tradendae*, 72.

[110]Pope John Paul II, *Dominum et Vivificantem*, 3.

found concerning the doctrine on the Holy Spirit?

Beyond doubt, John Paul's preference of the term *person* to designate the Father, the Son and the Holy Spirit, shines clearly in *Dominum et Vivificantem*.[111] The basis for this usage is the Gospel of St. John who calls each of them *person*, "the first distinct from the second and the third, and each of them from one another."[112] In these simple words the Pope confirms the long standing tradition of the Church concerning the distinction of Divine Persons within the Oneness of God. This distinction is real because Jesus refers to the Holy Spirit as 'he': this reference strengthens the personal identity of the Holy Spirit as different from the Father and the Son. At the same time, this distinction between the Divine Persons should not become a separation because, since "each of them are from one another," Jesus reveal the bonds which unite them to one another.[113] John Paul does not refer here to a specific contemporary pneumatology that develops its own understanding of the *perichoresis*; he rather bases this *perichoresis* on biblical data coming specifically from the Gospel of St. John.

The words of the Last Supper as found in the Gospel of St. John are the fundamental source for Pope John Paul II's trinitarian theology in *Dominum et Vivificantem*. He himself attested that "in the farewell discourse at the Last Supper, we can say that the highest point of the revelation of the Trinity is reached."[114] Commenting on these words the Pope explains in *Dominum et Vivificantem*, 8, how the Divine Persons are from one another:

> The Father 'sends' the Spirit in the name of the Son, the Spirit 'bears witness' to the Son. The Son asks the Father to send the Spirit–Counselor, but likewise affirms and promises, in relation to his own 'departure' through the Cross: 'if I go, I will send him to you.' Thus the father sends the Holy Spirit in the power of his fatherhood, as he has sent the Son; but at the same time he sends him in the power of the Redemption accomplished by Christ — and in this sense the Holy Spirit is sent also by the Son: 'I will send him to you'."[115]

This text deserves special attention if one intends to get closer to understanding the Pope's thought on the procession of the Holy Spirit. Notice

---

[111]See Pope John Paul II, *Dominum et Vivificantem*, 9.

[112]Pope John Paul II, *Dominum et Vivificantem*, 8.

[113]Pope John Paul II, *Dominum et Vivificantem*, 8.

[114]Pope John Paul II, *Dominum et Vivificantem*, 9. See also Michael O'Carroll, "Dominum et Vivificantem," in *Veni Creator Spiritus: A Theological Encyclopedia of the Holy Spirit*, Collegeville: Liturgical Press, 1990, 70.

[115]Pope John Paul II, *Dominum et Vivificantem*, 8. See also Josef Cardinal Tomko, "Mission and dialogue in the teaching of John Paul II," in *John Paul II. A Panorama of his Teachings*, New York: New City Press, 1989, 84.

that the identification between the Economic and the Immanent Trinity is clear in this text. It does not even pass through the Pope's mind that the Triune God in history could in any way be different from what God is in Himself. This identification affords the Pope the opportunity to construct the theological basis for the procession of the Holy Spirit from the Father and the Son, and not from the Father alone. Based on that identification, the *procession* of the Holy Spirit from the Father and his *sending* by the Father to the Church are synonyms.[116] The same is valid for the *begottenness* and the *sending* of the Son.

John Paul II does not deny the biblical data reporting that "the Holy Spirit... proceeds from the Father."[117] This procession of the Holy Spirit from the Father is parallel yet distinct from the begottenness of the Son; yet both begottenness and procession originate from the Father: the particular communion between the Holy Spirit and Christ has its original source in the Father.[118] By the power of His fatherhood, the Father has sent the Holy Spirit in the same way He sent the Son. These two processions from the Father explain, in the Pope's opinion, why the Holy Spirit is said to be proceeding from the Father: coming from the Father the Holy Spirit is sent by the Father.[119] Yet, if the Holy Spirit proceeds from the Father, this does not exclude the fact that He also proceeds from the Son, because He comes at the price of Christ's departure.[120] The procession from the Father is necessary because of the fatherhood of the Father, but, since it is a procession in the Augustinian sense of *principaliter*, it cannot be exclusive: Christ told the Apostles in the same Gospel of John and in the same context that "I will send him to you."[121] Consequently, the identification between the Economic and the Immanent Trinity allows the Pope to conclude that "in this sense the Holy Spirit is sent also by the Son."

In this text of *Dominum et Vivificantem*, 8, one notices the influence of St. Augustine who, as a first step affirmed that the Holy Spirit is the Spirit of the Father and of the Son. He bases his argument on the scriptural fact that the

---

[116]See Giacomo Cardinal Biffi, "The Action of the Holy Spirit in the Church and in the World," in *John Paul II. A Panorama of his Teachings*, New York: New City Press, 1989, 38.

[117]Jn 15:26; Pope John Paul II, *Dominum et Vivificantem*, 8. See also Ibid., *Dominum et Vivificantem*, 14.

[118]See also Pope John Paul II, *Dominum et Vivificantem*, 22; *Redemptoris Custos*, 7.

[119]See Jn 14:26 and 15:26; Pope John Paul II, *Dominum et Vivificantem*, 22 and 30.

[120]See Pope John Paul II, *Dominum et Vivificantem*, 48 and 67; Michael O'Carroll, "Dominum et Vivificantem," in *Veni Creator Spiritus: A Theological Encyclopedia of the Holy Spirit*, Collegeville: Liturgical Press, 1990, 70.

[121]Jn 16:7.

Holy Spirit is called Spirit of the Father (Mt 10:28; Jn 15:26) and Spirit of the Son (Gal 4:6; Jn 14:26; 20:22; Lk 6:19). Therefore, since the Holy Spirit is the Spirit of the Father and of the Son and Scripture asserts that He proceeds from the Father, it is obvious that He proceeds from the Son. However, for Augustine, the Son's faculty of being active in the procession of the Holy Spirit, derives entirely from the Father. In that sense, the Holy Spirit proceeds from the Father *principaliter*.[122] John Paul says that the Father sends the Holy Spirit in the power of His fatherhood, as He sends the Son. But the Father sends the Spirit in the power of Redemption and so, in that specific sense, the Son sends the Spirit. This is the way John Paul understands the active faculty of the Son in the procession of the Spirit: the sending of the Holy Spirit depends entirely on the power of the Father's fatherhood, but it happens at the point of the Son's Redemption.[123] It is only in the context of an identification between the Immanent and the Economic Trinity that John Paul states that the Holy Spirit clearly proceeds from the Father and the Son.

The sending of the Son and the procession of the Holy Spirit assume a closed circular pattern. Because of "the will and action of the Father,"[124] the Son accomplished the Redemption of humankind through the Incarnation. Because of the Redemption of humankind that Christ fulfilled, the Holy Spirit was sent to sanctify humanity. Because of the sanctification of humanity by the Holy Spirit, the Father receives back the people He created in His own image and likeness. If the *Son* and the *Holy Spirit* perform *ad extra* the will of the Father and if the *Holy Spirit* and the *Father* respectively sanctify and receive the humanity redeemed by the Son through the Holy Spirit to be led back to the Father, then the *Father* and the *Son* should be both involved in the mission of the Holy Spirit Who proceeds from the Father and the Son to bring to the Father through the Son redeemed humanity. In the Pope's approach in *Dominum et Vivificantem*, 8, he never confuses the different properties of the Divine Persons, since none of the Persons takes the place of the other Two in the economy of salvation. At the same time, they cannot be separated because the salvific work is still being accomplished by the One and the same God. Therefore, the closed circle of the Blessed Trinity as pictured by Pope John Paul II, is a natural argument against *Tritheism* as well as against *modalism*.

Insofar as he envisions the Holy Spirit as Person–Gift and Person–Love, Pope John Paul II dedicates *Dominum et Vivificantem*, 10, for that purpose:

---

[122]See St. Augustine, *De Trin.* XV, 17, 29 and 26, 47; *Sermo* 71, 26.

[123]See again Pope John Paul II, *Dominum et Vivificantem*, 8.

[124]Pope John Paul II, *Dominum et Vivificantem*, 8.

In his intimate life, God "is love," the essential love shared by the three divine Persons: personal love is the Holy Spirit as the Spirit of the Father and the Son. Therefore he "searches even the depths of God," as uncreated Love–Gift. It can be said that in the Holy Spirit the intimate life of the Triune God becomes totally gift, an exchange of mutual love between the divine Persons and that through the Holy Spirit God exists in the mode of gift. It is the Holy Spirit who is the personal expression of this self–giving, of this being–love. He is Person–Love. He is Person–Gift. Here we have an inexhaustible treasure of the reality and an inexpressible deepening of the concept of person in God, which only divine revelation makes known to us.[125]

This text leads to the completion of the theology on the Holy Spirit that John Paul started in *Redemptor Hominis*, 18, a text that has been extensively studied. It is an extremely rich document in many pneumatological aspects that are worthy of presentation.

Pope John Paul II uses the Letter of St. John (1 Jn 4:8 and 16) and the *Summa Theologiae* of St. Thomas Aquinas (I, qq. 37–38) to address the theological idea of love within the intratrinitarian life.[126] God, in his intimate life, is love, but not in the sense of an emotional movement that proceeds from the Divine Persons, and not from a decision on their part to be united in One Nature. Love, nevertheless, like any category that does not exhaust the very essence of God, is at the basis of the trinitarian unity.[127] This essential love shared by the Three Divine Persons explains the divine processions within the Trinity: God is love because the Father begets a Son and exists in Him completely as the Other, because the Son is in the Father in an eternal bond of mutual self–giving, and because this bond brings about the Otherness of the Father, and of the Son, and of the Holy Spirit. The Holy Spirit is therefore the personification of the essential love which God is in His intimate life. Because He is the Spirit of the Father and of the Son, the Holy Spirit is then the personification of the Love. The procession of the Holy Spirit from the Son is based, in St. John and Aquinas, on the personification of the mutual love between the Father and the Son.

Since the Father and the Son offer themselves mutually to each other, God in His very mystery becomes a Gift or, in the words of John Paul II, 'God exists in the mode of gift.' But this gift is based on the eternal mutual love between the Father and the Son, which is the Holy Spirit. Therefore the Holy Spirit is the eternal *Uncreated Love–Gift in Person*, and in Him 'the intimate life of the Triune God becomes totally gift.' Love explains why the Holy Spirit

---

[125]Pope John Paul II, *Dominum et Vivificantem*, 10.

[126]See also St. Thomas Aquinas, *Summa Contra Gentiles*, IV, 19; Yves Congar, *Credo nello Spirito Santo*, Vol. 3, Breascia: Queriniana, 1987, 17.

[127]See also Pope John Paul II, *Dominum et Vivificantem*, 21 and 67.

is a Gift; Gift expresses the very mystery of the divine processions within God; the personification of Love and of Gift is the Person of the Holy Spirit. Since He is Otherness from the mutual Love between the Father and the Son and, at the same time, He, in His Person, is their eternal gift to each other, He is the personal expression of God's self–giving, of this being–love. Being the personal expression of God's self giving, the Holy Spirit is Person–Gift.[128]

With this insight, Pope John Paul II presents the 'inexhaustible treasure of the reality and an inexpressible deepening of the concept of person in God, which only divine revelation makes known to us.' The reflection of the Pope on the notion of person in the Triune God affords him the opportunity to confirm the theology of St. Thomas Aquinas concerning the definition of person in God: each divine person is a subsistent relation. Subsistent relation means that the Father is not the Son and the Son is not the Father, although the Father is God and the Son is God. This means each of them is everything that the other is, except for that character which qualifies One of them in reference to the other, thus making Him distinct from the other within the unity of the Divinity. What characterizes the Divine Person then is the relation that unites Him and at the same time sets Him apart from the other. The opposition is that opposition of relation: whoever pronounces the name Father includes the Son and vice versa. But the unity derives from the communication of the whole Divine Nature that takes place through the mechanism of One Person being at the origin of the other. Therefore, what makes the Divine Person a Person is that relation of origin that makes each Person really different from the Person that stands at its origin. But in God, continues Aquinas, these relations of origin are in a real manner identical with the divine Essence, a fact that makes them subsistent relations. Each Divine Person is a divine subsistent relation considered as a distinct subsistence: relation of origin enjoys in God the prerogatives of the absolute divine essence, although maintaining its intratrinitarian incomunicability.[129]

The Pope goes beyond Aquinas to affirm that God Himself, within the mystery of Three Persons, exists in the mode of a gift. The relations of origin between the Divine Persons are not the product of a decision on their part; rather they constitute the reality of their being Three different Persons within One Divine Nature. In other words the relations of origin determine the mode of God's existence as a gift. Projected on the level of human person,

---

[128]See also Pope John Paul II, *Mulieris Dignitatem*, 29; Giacomo Cardinal Biffi, "The Action of the Holy Spirit in the Church and in the World," in *John Paul II. A Panorama of his Teachings*, New York: New City Press, 1989, 44–45.

[129]See St. Thomas Aquinas, *De Potentia* q. 8, a. 1 ad 4; a. 2; a. 3 ad 7 and 9; a. 4; q. 9, a. 4; a. 5 ad 13; q. 10, a.1 ad 12; a. 2 ad 1; *Summa Theologiae* Ia, q. 40; Ia, q. 28, a. 2; q. 29, a.3; q. 40, a.1; q. 42, a. 5; *I Sent.* d. 23, a. 3.

individualism, subjectivism, and any other approach that defines the person as an individual endowed with either conscience or freedom, cannot adequately describe the deep reality of the human person.

In *Dominum et Vivificantem*, 10, one should not overlook the influence of St. Augustine. As a starting point for the theology on the procession of the Holy Spirit, the Bishop of Hippo considered the Holy Spirit as the Spirit of the Father and of the Son. From there he orients his thoughts to the Holy Spirit as Love, *charitas*; the Divine Persons are Three: the First who loves the Second who was generated by Him, the Second who loves the One Who generated, and the Third who is Love. It is Augustine who demonstrated that, in God, that Love, *charitas*, is essential because God is Love (1 Jn 4:16). It is essential because the Holy Spirit, in the context of the economy of salvation, communicates God's love and because, on the intratrinitarian level, the Spirit is the substantial communion between the Father and the Son. Since He is common to the Father and the Son, He receives as His own the names that are common to the Father and to the Son, that is Love.[130]   The Holy Spirit is not only a Person–Gift in the context of the Immanent Trinity, but also in the economy of salvation. Being a Person–Gift is not reserved only for the intratrinitarian life: the Holy Spirit is the *fons vivus*, the living source vis-à-vis creatures. The idea of the Holy Spirit as living source of water is present in St. John the Evangelist, St. Irenaeus, St. Athanasius, St. Cyrill of Jerusalem and in Dydimus.[131]

As a parallel to *Redemptor Hominis*, 18, and *Dominum et Vivificantem*, 10, the following text of *Dominum et Vivificantem*, 50, quoted in *Tertio Millennio Adveniente*, 44, throws light on the Pope's trinitarian thinking about the Holy Spirit as a Person–Love and Person–Uncreated Gift:

> The great Jubilee at the close of the second Millennium...has a pneumatological aspect, since the mystery of the Incarnation was accomplished 'by the power of the Holy Spirit.' It was 'brought about' by that Spirit consubstantial—with the Father and the Son—who, in the absolute mystery of the Triune God, is the Person–Love, the uncreated gift, who is the eternal source of every gift that comes from God in the order of creation, the direct principle and, in a certain sense, the subject of God's self–communication in the order of grace. The mystery of the Incarnation constitutes

---

[130]See St. Augustine, *De quantitate animae* 34, 77; *De musica* VI, 17, 56; *De fide et symbolo* 9, 19–20; *De Trinitate*, VI, 5, 7; XV, 17, 27 f and XV, 19, 36 f; Yves Congar, *Credo nello Spirito Santo*, Vol. 3, Breascia: Queriniana, 1987, 97–98.

[131]See also Pope John Paul II, *Dominum et Vivificantem*, 34; *Mulieris Dignitatem*, 29; *Vita Consecrata*, 96; Paul L. Peeters, "*Dominum et Vivificantem*: The Conscience and the Heart," in *Communio* 15 (1988): 148; John 4:10 and 7:37–39; St. Irenaeus, *Adv. Haer.* III, 17, 2–3; IV, 14, 2; St. Athanasius, *First Letter to Serapion*, 19; St. Cyrill of Jerusalem, *Catech.* XVI, 11 and 12; Dydimus, *De Trin.* II, 6, 22; Th. De Régnon, *Etudes de Théologie Positive sur la Ste Trinité*, Vol. 4, 389 ff.

the climax of this giving, this divine self–communication.[132]

This text is very similar to *Redemptor Hominis*, 18, as to its terminology and theological content. Here the Pope recurs to the concept of *Person–Gift* which indicates the identity of the Holy Spirit within the context of the Immanent Trinity. The Holy Spirit is not only, as *Redemptor Hominis*, 18 describes it, a gift of the divine life of the Father and the Son communicated to the world. He is the Person–Love or the mutual love of the Father and the Son in Person. In this theological approach to the identity of the Holy Spirit, the Pope follows the path of St. Augustine, St. Thomas Aquinas and Hans Urs von Balthasar: in the intimate life of God, the Holy Spirit is the personal hypostasis of love.[133] All three have contributed to that aspect of Pneumatology in a very definitive way. The love between the Father and the Son, as Pope John Paul II understands it, is not something that is performed *ad extra*, outside the Divine nature. In other words, since everything in God is one where there are no relations of opposition, a mutual love between Father and Son cannot but be a substantial personality, the Holy Spirit.[134] This 'substantial' love between the Father and the Son is the eternal and mutual offering of themselves to each other.

This mutual offering of Father and Son to each other is the basis for understanding the Holy Spirit as the Person–Uncreated Gift. However, for John Paul this Person–Uncreated gift is the principle of relationality of the Father and the Son to creation: He is the source of every gift of God in the order of creation and the subject of God's self–communication in the order of salvation.[135] In this context of His operation in the world, the Holy Spirit works in the order of creation as well as in the order of salvation. His activity in the order of creation consists in being the source of what could be called 'natural' existence and in His power to maintain all creatures in existence. Through creation, the Spirit also expresses the beginning of God's salvific self–communication to the things he created.[136] This is the original beginning of God's salvific self–giving in the mystery of creation: man is created out of nothing in the image and likeness of God. Such a mystery, I mean that of

[132]Pope John Paul II, *Dominum et Vivificantem*, 50.

[133]See also Pope John Paul II, *Mulieris Dignitatem*, 29; Paul L. Peeters, "*Dominum et Vivificantem*: The Conscience and the Heart," in *Communio* 15 (1988): 150.

[134]See also Pope John Paul II, *Christifideles Laici*, 19.

[135]See Paul L. Peeters, "*Dominum et Vivificantem*: The Conscience and the Heart," in *Communio* 15 (1988): 150.

[136]See Giacomo Cardinal Biffi, "The Action of the Holy Spirit in the Church and in the World," in *John Paul II. A Panorama of his Teachings*, New York: New City Press, 1989, 44–45.

creation, should always be looked at as an essential dimension in the whole picture of the economy of salvation, because, without the original step of God's plan, the Incarnation of the Son and the descent of the Holy Spirit would lose their meaning. By detaching the mystery of creation from that of the Redemption, an implicit *manicheism* with dangerous opposition between the act of creation and the act of Redemption could imply an evil connotation in the mystery of creation. It could also suggest a divergence into two original mysteries prefigured together in the eternal will of the Creator.[137] Therefore, God's original beginning of His salvific self–giving is the first beginning, whereas His self–communication through Pentecost is a new beginning. It is new in relation to the first beginning and it is new because between the first and the new, sin intervened in the history of humanity, as a contradiction to the presence of the Holy Spirit of God in creation and as a contradiction to God's salvific self–communication to man.[138]

This salvific self–communication of God in the Holy Spirit took place when, because of the Incarnation of the Son,[139] the Holy Spirit came down on the Apostles on the day of Pentecost bringing to fulfillment the new era of the history of salvation. In the order of grace, "He gives the gift of grace to human beings through the whole economy of salvation."[140] The continuity in the identity of the Holy Spirit as the personal expression of God's self–giving within Himself and to the world, constitutes one more proof of the Pope's equating of the Immanent and the Economic Trinity. It is that continuity in the personal identity of the Three Divine Persons in the context of *divine processions* and in their *involvement in creation* that guarantees an absolute identity between the Immanent and the Economic Trinity:[141] the mutual Love and Gift of self between the Father and the Son, which is the Holy Spirit, is expressed in creating the world and saving humanity. "In John's Gospel," says John Paul, "we have as it were the revelation of the most profound 'logic' of the saving mystery contained in God's eternal plan, as an extension of the

---

[137]See Pope John Paul II, *Dominum et Vivificantem*, 12.

[138]See Pope John Paul II, *Dominum et Vivificantem*, 13.

[139]See Giacomo Cardinal Biffi, "The Action of the Holy Spirit in the Church and in the World," in *John Paul II. A Panorama of his Teachings*, New York: New City Press, 1989, 45.

[140]Pope John Paul II, *Dominum et Vivificantem*, 10; Paul L. Peeters, *"Dominum et Vivificantem:* The Conscience and the Heart," in *Communio* 15 (1988): 148; Giacomo Cardinal Biffi, "The Action of the Holy Spirit in the Church and in the World," in *John Paul II. A Panorama of his Teachings*, New York: New City Press, 1989, 45.

[141]In *Christifideles Laici*, 19, Pope John Paul II says: "In fact, that same Spirit is the One who from eternity unites the one and undivided Trinity, that Spirit who 'in the fullness of time' (Gal 4:4) forever unites human nature to the Son of God, that same identical Spirit who in the course of Christian generations is the constant and never–ending source of communion in the Church."

ineffable communion of the Father, Son and Holy Spirit. This is the divine 'logic' which from the mystery of the Trinity leads to the mystery of Redemption of the world in Jesus Christ."[142]

---

[142]Pope John Paul II, *Dominum et Vivificantem*, 11.

BIBLIOGRAPHY

Karol Wojtyla

Wojtyla, Karol. *Abe Chrystus sie Nami Postugiwal.* Kraków: Wydawnictwo Znak, 1979.

———. *The Acting Person.* Trans. Andrzej Potocki. Holland: R. Reidel Publishing Company, 1979.

———. *Amore e Responsabilità.* Milan: Marietti, 1978.

———. *Aux Sources du Renouveau.* Trans. M. Louette. éd. du Centurion, 1981.

———. *Brat Naszego Boga: Tekst i Rezyseria.* Prapremiera Swiatowa 13 grudina 1980. Kraków: Teatr Imienia J. Slowackiego w Krakowie, 1980.

———. *La Bottega Dell'orefice.* Vatican City: Libreria Editrice Vaticana, 1979.

———. *Collected Poems.* trans. J. Peterkiewicz. New York: Random House, 1979.

———. *The Collected Plays and Writings on Theatre.* Berkely: University California Press, 1987.

———. *Czlowiek Droga Koscióla.* Rome: Fundacja Jana Pawla II—Osrodek Dokumentacji Pontyficatu, 1992.

———. *Czlowiek w Polu Odpowiedzialnosci.* Rzym–Lublin, Poland: Instytut Jana Pawla II, KUL, 1991.

———. *Easter Vigil and Other Poems.* Trans. Jerzy Peterkiewics. London: Hutchinson and New York: Random House, 1979.

———. *En Esprit et en Vérité.* Trans. G. Jarczyk. éd. du Centurion, 1980.

———. *Evaluation of the Possibility of Constructing a Christian Ethics in the Assumptions of Max Scheler's System of Philosophy.* Lublin, 1959.

———. *Faith According to St. John of the Cross.* San Francisco: Ignatius Press, 1981.

———. *La Fede della Chiesa.* Milano: Editzioni Ares, 1978.

————. *Fruitful and Responsible Love.* New York: Seabury, 1979.

————. *The Jeweler's Shop.* New York: Random House, 1980.

————. *Kazania: 1962–1978.* Kraków: Wydawnictwo Znak, 1979.

————. *Milosc i Odpowiedzialnosc.* Lublin, Poland: Wydawnictwo Towarzystwa Naukowego Katolickiego Uniwersytetu Lubelskiego, 1985.

————. *Obecnosc: Karol Wojtyla w Katolickim Uniwersytecie Lubleskim.* Lublin, Poland: Redakcja Wydawnictwo, KUL, 1989.

————. *Opere Letterarie: Poesie e Drammi.* Vatican City: Libreria Editrice Vaticana, 1993.

————. *Pietra di luce: Poesie.* Vatican City: Libreria Editrice Vaticana, 1979.

————. *Persona e atto.* Rome: Libreria Editrice Vaticana, 1982.

————. *Person: Subjekt und Gemeinschaft.* Der Streit um den Menschen. Kevelær: Butzon and Bercker, 1970.

————. "The Person: Subject and Community." *Review of Metaphysics* 33 (1979): 273–308.

————. *Poezje i Dramaty.* Kraków: Wydawnictwo Znak, 1987.

————. *Przemówienia i Wywiady w Radio Watykanskim.* Rome: Fundacja Jana Pawla II—Osrodek Dokumentacji Pontyficatu.

————. *Questio de Fide apud S. Johannem a Cruce* (1948). San Francisco: Ignatius Press, 1981.

————. *Segno di contraddizione.* Milan: Vita e Pensiero, 1977.

————. *Sign of Contradiction.* New York: Seabury Press, 1979.

————. "Slowo konkowe." *Analecta Cracoviesia* n. 5–6, (1973–1974): 243–263.

————. *Sources of Renewal: The Implementation of the Second Vatican Council.* San Francisco: Harper and Row, 1980.

————. "The Task of Christian Philosophy Today." *Proceedings of the American Catholic Philosophical Association* 53 (1979): 3–4.

————. *Wyklady Lubelski: Czlowiek i Moralnosc.* Lublin, Poland: Wydawnictwo Towarzystwa Naukowego Katolickiego Uniwersytetu Lubelskiego, 1986.

————. *Zagadnienie Wiary w Dzielach Sw. Jana od Krzyza.* Kraków: Wydawnictwo O. O. Karmelitów Bosych, 1990.

Pope John Paul II

John Paul II. *Address to Presidents of Catholic Colleges and Universities* (at Catholic University*).* (October 7, 1979): 163–167.

————. *Address to the General Assembly of the United Nations,* October 2, 1980, 16–30.

————. *Address to the Youth of Paris.* (June 1, 1980), *L'Osservatore Romano* (English Edition), (June 16, 1980): 13.

————. *Affido a Te, O Maria.* Ed. Sergio Trassati and Arturo Mari. Bergamo: Editrice Velar, 1982.

————. *Africa: Apostolic Pilgrimage.* Boston: St. Paul Editions, 1980.

————. *Africa: Land of Promise, Land of Hope.* Boston: St. Paul Editions, 1982.

————. *Amantissima Providentia,* Apostolic Letter, 1980.

————. *The Apostles of the Slavs (Commemorating Sts. Cyril and Methodius): Fourth Encyclical Letter, June 2, 1985.* Washington D. C.: Office for Publishing and Promotion Services. United States Catholic Conference, 1985.

————. *Augustinum Hipponensem.* August 28, 1986. Boston: St. Paul Editions, 1986.

————. "Behold Your Mother," *Holy Thursday Letter of John Paul II,* Boston: St. Paul Editions, 1988.

————. *Brazil: Journey in the Light of the Eucharist.* Boston: St. Paul Editions, 1980.

————. Il Buon Pastore: *Scritti, Disorsi e Lettere Pastorali.* Trans. Elzbieta Cywiak and Renzo Panzone. Rome Edizioni Logos, 1978.

————. *Catechesi Tradendae, on Catechesis in Our Time.* Boston: St. Paul Editions, 1979.

————. *Centesimus Annus (Commemorating the Centenary of Rerum Novarum by Leo XIII): Ninth Encyclical Letter, May 1, 1991.* Washington D. C.: Office for Publishing and Promotion Services, United States Catholic Conference, 1991.

238   *The Mystery of the Trinity*

———. *Charter of the Rights of the Family. The Wanderer* Vol. 116, no 52 (December 29, 1983): 6.

———. *Chiamati all'Amore: Itinerari di Santità.* Trans. Aldo Cantarini. Rome: Edizioni Logos, 1980.

———. *Crossing the Threshold of Hope.* New York: Alfred A. Knopf, 1994.

———. *Dilecti Amici*, Apostolic Letter, 1985.

———. "A Discipline That Ennobles Human Love." *L'Osservatore Romano* (English Edition) Vol. 17, no. 36 (September 3, 1984): 1–6.

———. *Dives in Misericordia, On the Mercy of God.* Boston: St. Paul Editions, 1980.

———. *Divini Amoris Scientia*, Apostolic Letter, 1997.

———. *Divinus Perfectionis Magister*, Apostolic Constitution, 1983.

———. *Dominum et Vivificantem, On the Holy Spirit in the Life of the Church and the World.* Boston: St. Paul Editions, 1986.

———. *Dominicae Cenae*, The Mystery and Worship of the Eucharist, Boston, Daughters of St. Paul, 1980.

———. *Ecclesia in Africa, Apostolic Exhortation*, 1995.

———. *Ecclesia in Urbe*, Apostolic Constitutions, 1998.

———. *Egreggiae Virtutis*, Apostolic Letter, 1980.

———. *Epistle To The Council of Constantinople I. March 25, 1981* .

———. *The Encyclicals of John Paul II*, Edited with Introductions by Michael Miller, Indiana: Our Sunday Visitor, Inc., 1996.

———. *Euntes in Mundum*, Apostolic Letter, 1988.

———. *Evangelium Vitae*, Encyclical Letter, 1995.

———. *Ex Corde Ecclesiae*, Apostolic Constitution, 1990.

———. *Familiaris Consortio, Apostolic Exhortation, The Role of the Christian Family in the Modern World.* Boston: Daughters of Saint Paul, 1981.

———. *The Far East: Journey of Peace and Brotherhood.* Boston: St. Paul Editions, 1981.

———. *Fidei Depositum*, Apostolic Constitution, 1992.

————. *Fifth Centenary of Evangelization of the New World*, Apostolic Letter, 1990.

————. *Fiftieth Anniversary of Beginning of World War II*, Apostolic Letter, 1989.

————. *For the 1600th Anniversary of the First Council of Constantinople and the 1550th Anniversary of the Council of Ephesus*. Boston: St. Paul Editions, 1981.

————. *Fourth Centenary of the Union of Brest*, Apostolic Letter, 1995.

————. *France: Message Peace, Trust, Love and Faith*. Boston: St. Paul Editions, 1980.

————. *The Freedom of Conscience and of Religion*. Boston: St. Paul Editions, 1980.

————. *Germany: Pilgrimage of Unity and Peace*. Boston, St. Paul Editions, 1981.

————. *Gift and Mystery, On the fiftieth Anniversary of my Priestly Ordination*, Doubleday: New York, December, 1996.

————. *Insegnamenti di Giovanni Paolo II* (1978–). Vatican City: Libreria Editrice Vaticana, 1979–.

————. *Ireland "In the Footsteps of St. Patrick."* Boston: St. Paul Editions, 1979.

————. "Jesus Christ, Living Peace and Living Justice." (Homily of His Holiness at Mass in Yankee Stadium On October 2, 1979). *The Pope In America*. St. Paul: Wanderer Press, 1979, 25–27.

————. *John Paul II in America: Talks Given on the Papal Tour, September 1987*. Compiled and Indexed by the Daughters of St. Paul. Boston: St. Paul Editions, 1987.

————. *John Paul II, Pilgrimage of Faith: The First Year of the New Pope and the Story of His Visit to the United States*. Edited and illustrated by National Catholic News Service. New York: Seabury Press, 1979.

————. *Laborem Exercens. On Human Work*. Boston: St. Paul Editions, 1981.

————. *Laborem Exercens, On Human Work*. *L'Osservatore Romano* (English Edition) Vol. 14, no. 38 (September 21, 1981): 1–13.

————. *Laetamur Magnopere*, Apostolic Letter, 1997.

————. *Les Grands Mystères*, Apostolic Letter, 1984.

————. *Letter of His Holiness John Paul II to the Bishops of The United States*. Boston: St. Paul Editions, 1983.

————. *Letter of Pope John Paul II to Women*, Boston: St. Paul Editions, 1995.

————. *Letter of the Pope to Children in the Year of the Family*, Boston: St. Paul Editions, 1994.

————. *Letter To Families From Pope John Paul II*, 1994 Year of the Family, Boston: St. Paul Editions, 1994.

————. "Letter to German Episcopal Conference, May 15, 1980." *L'Osservatore Romano* (June 30, 1980): 8–9,

————. *Love and Responsibility*. Trans. H. T. Willetts. New York: Farrar, Straus, Giroux, 1981.

————. *Magnum Matrimonii Sacramentum*, Apostolic Constitution, 1982.

————. *Maria: Omelie*. Preface by Stefan Cardinal Wyszynski. Trans. Janina Korzeniewska. Vatican City: Libreria Editrice Vaticana, 1982.

————. *Maximilien Kolbe, Patron de notre siècle difficile*. Paris: Lethielleux, 1982.

————. *Messages of John Paul II: Servant of Truth*. Boston: St. Paul Editions, 1979.

————. *Message for World Peace Day*. London: Catholic Truth Society, 1979.

————. *Na Dalekim Wschodzie: Homilie i Przemówienia: 2 V 1984–11 V 1984*. Warsaw: Instytut Wydawniczy Pax, 1988.

————. *Negotiation: the Only Realistic Solution to the Continuing Threat of War, an Address to Men of Science*. Boston: St. Paul Editions, 1982.

————. *On the Christian Meaning of Human Suffering* [Salvifici Doloris]. Office of Publishing Services: Washington, D.C., 1984.

————. *On the Dignity and Vocation of Women. Mulieris Dignitatem*. Boston: St. Paul Editions, 1988.

————. *On the Dignity and Vocation of Women: Apostolic Letter, August 15, 1988*. Washington D. C.: Office for Publishing and Promotion Services. United States Catholic Conference, 1988.

————. *On the Holy Spirit in the Life of the Church and the World: Fifth Encyclical Letter, May 18, 1986*. Washington D. C.: Office for

Publishing and Promotion Services. United States Catholic Conference, 1986.

———. *On Human Work: Third Encyclical Letter, September 14, 1981.* Washington D. C.: Office for Publishing and Promotion Services. United States Catholic Conference, 1981.

———. *On the Mercy of God: Second Encyclical Letter, November 30, 1980.* Washington D. C.: Office for Publishing and Promotion Services. United States Catholic Conference, 1980.

———. *On the Mystery and Worship of the Eucharist Dominicae Cenae.* Boston: St. Paul Editions, 1980.

———. *On the Occasion of the Marian Year.* Letter May 22, 1988. Washington D. C.: Office of Publishing and Promotion Services, United States Catholic Conference, 1988.

———. *On the Permanent Validity of the Church's Missionary Mandate: Eighth Encyclical Letter, January 22, 1991.* Washington D. C.: Office of Publishing and Promotion Services, United States Catholic Conference, 1991.

———. *On the Role of Mary in the Mystery of Christ: Sixth Encyclical Letter, March 25, 1987.* Washington D. C.: Office of Publishing and Promotion Services, United States Catholic Conference, 1987.

———. *On Social Concerns: Seventh Encyclical Letter, December 30, 1987.* Washington D. C.: Office of Publishing and Promotion Services, United States Catholic Conference, 1987.

———. *Operosam Diem*, Apostolic Letter, 1996.

———. *Orientale Lumen, The Light of the East*, Apostolic Letter, Boston: St. Paul Editions, 1995.

———. *Ordinatio Sacerdotalis, On Preserving Priestly Ordination to Men Alone*, Boston: St. Paul Editions, 1994.

———. *L'Osservatore Romano*, weekly edition in English.

———. *Pastor Bonus*, Apostolic Constitution, 1988.

———. *Pastores Dabo Vobis, I Will Give You Shepherds*, Post–Synodal Apostolic Exhortation of John Paul II, Boston: St. Paul Editions, 1992.

———. *Patres Ecclesiae*, Apostolic Letter, 1980.

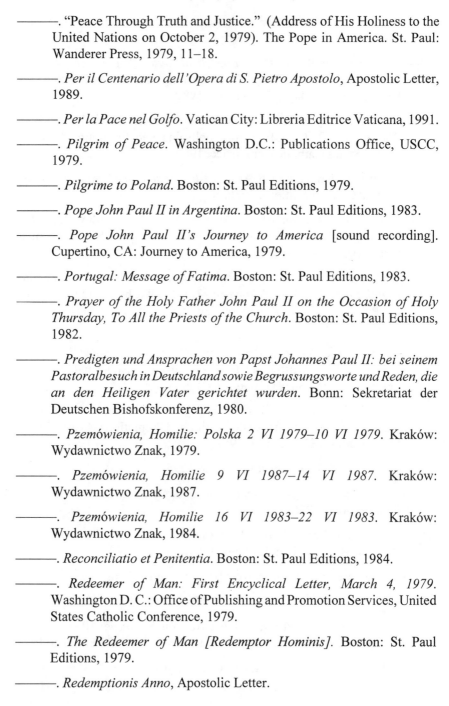

————. "Peace Through Truth and Justice." (Address of His Holiness to the United Nations on October 2, 1979). *The Pope in America*. St. Paul: Wanderer Press, 1979, 11–18.

————. *Per il Centenario dell'Opera di S. Pietro Apostolo*, Apostolic Letter, 1989.

————. *Per la Pace nel Golfo*. Vatican City: Libreria Editrice Vaticana, 1991.

————. *Pilgrim of Peace*. Washington D.C.: Publications Office, USCC, 1979.

————. *Pilgrime to Poland*. Boston: St. Paul Editions, 1979.

————. *Pope John Paul II in Argentina*. Boston: St. Paul Editions, 1983.

————. *Pope John Paul II's Journey to America* [sound recording]. Cupertino, CA: Journey to America, 1979.

————. *Portugal: Message of Fatima*. Boston: St. Paul Editions, 1983.

————. *Prayer of the Holy Father John Paul II on the Occasion of Holy Thursday, To All the Priests of the Church*. Boston: St. Paul Editions, 1982.

————. *Predigten und Ansprachen von Papst Johannes Paul II: bei seinem Pastoralbesuch in Deutschland sowie Begrussungsworte und Reden, die an den Heiligen Vater gerichtet wurden*. Bonn: Sekretariat der Deutschen Bishofskonferenz, 1980.

————. *Pzemówienia, Homilie: Polska 2 VI 1979–10 VI 1979*. Kraków: Wydawnictwo Znak, 1979.

————. *Pzemówienia, Homilie 9 VI 1987–14 VI 1987*. Kraków: Wydawnictwo Znak, 1987.

————. *Pzemówienia, Homilie 16 VI 1983–22 VI 1983*. Kraków: Wydawnictwo Znak, 1984.

————. *Reconciliatio et Penitentia*. Boston: St. Paul Editions, 1984.

————. *Redeemer of Man: First Encyclical Letter, March 4, 1979*. Washington D. C.: Office of Publishing and Promotion Services, United States Catholic Conference, 1979.

————. *The Redeemer of Man [Redemptor Hominis]*. Boston: St. Paul Editions, 1979.

————. *Redemptionis Anno*, Apostolic Letter.

————. *Redemptionis Donum. To Men and Women Religious on Their Consecration in the Light of the Mystery of the Redemption*. Boston: St. Paul Editions, 1984.

————. *Redemptor Hominis, The Redeemer of Man. L'Osservatore Romano* (English Edition) Vol. 12, no. 12 (March 19, 1979): 3–14.

————. *Redemptoris Custos, On the Person and Mission of Saint Joseph in the Life of Christ and of the Church*, Boston: St. Paul Editions, 1989.

————. *Redemptoris Mater. Mary: God's Yes to Man, Introduction by Joseph Cardinal Ratzinger, Commentary by Hans Urs von Balthasar*. San Francisco: Ignatius Press, 1988.

————. *Redemptoris Missio*, Encyclical Letter, 1990.

————. "Remain Faithful to the Universal Magisterium." (Address of His Holiness Delivered in Chicago to a Plenary Assembly of the Bishops of the United States on October 5, 1979). *The Pope in America*. St. Paul: Wanderer Press, 1979, 53–58.

————. *Rutilans Agmen*, Apostolic Letter, 1979.

————. *Sacrae Disciplinae Leges. Apostolic Constitution for the Promulgation of the New Code of Canon Law*. Boston: St. Paul Editions, 1983.

————. *Salvifici Doloris, The Christian Meaning of Human Suffering. Origins* Vol. 13, no. 37 (February 23, 1984): 609 , 610–624.

————. *Sanctorum Altrix*, Apostolic Letter, 1980.

————. *Sapientia Christiana* (April 15, 1979). English Text. Washington D. C.: USCC, 1979.

————. *Sescentesima Anniversaria*, Apostolic Letter, 1987.

————. *Situation in Lebanon*, Apostolic Letter, 1989.

————. *Slavorum Apostoli. In Commemoration of the Eleventh Centenary of the Evangelizing Work of Saints Cyril and Methodius*. Boston: St. Paul Editions, 1985.

————. *The Splendor of Truth [Veritatis Splendor]*. Boston: St. Paul Editions, 1993.

————. *Sollicitudo Rei Socialis*. Boston: St. Paul Editions, 1987.

————. *Sources of Renewal: The Implementation of the Second Vatican Council*. Trans. P. S. Falla. San Francisco: Harper & Row, 1980.

————. *Spiritus Domini*, Apostolic Letter.

————. *Talks of John Paul II*. Boston: St. Paul Editions, 1979.

————. *Tertio Millennio Adveniente: Apostolic Letter on Preparation for the Jubilee of the Year 2000, November 10, 1994*. Vatican City: Libreria Editrice Vaticana, 1994.

————. *Theology of the Body* (A series of sixty–three addresses at the Wednesday audiences.) *L'Osservatore Romano*. (English Edition). Vol. 12, nos. 37–40, 42, 44–48, 51–53, (September 10, 17, 24, October 1, 15, 29, November 5, 12, 19, 26, December 17, 24, 1979). Vol. 13, nos. 1–3, 5–8, 10–11, 13–14, 16–18, 20, 22–23, 25–26, 30–46, 49–50, 52, (January 7, 14, 21, February 4, 11, 18, 25, March 10, 17, 31, April 8, 21, 28, May 5, 19, June 2, 9, 23, 30, July 28, August 4, 11, 25, September 1, 8, 15, 22, 29, October 6, 13, 20, 27, November 3, 10, 17, December 9, 15, 29m 1980). Vol. 14, nos. 2–3, 5–7, 12, 14–19 (January 12, 19, February 2, 9, 16, March 23, April 6, 13, 21, 27. May 4, 11, 1981). This series can also be found in the two–volume series: *Original Unity of Man and Woman: Catechesis on the Book of Genesis* and *Blessed Are the Pure of Heart: Catechesis on the Sermon on the Mount and Writings of Saint Paul*. Boston: Saint Paul Editions, 1981, 1983.

————. *To The Youth of the World*. Boston: St. Paul Editions, 1985.

————. *Three Hundred Fifty Years of Union of Uzhorod*, Apostolic Letter, 1996.

————. *Truth's Splendor: Tenth Encyclical Letter, August 6, 1993*. Washington D. C.: Office for Publishing and Promotion Services, United States Catholic Conference, 1993.

————. *Turkey—Ecumenical Pilgrimage*. Boston: St. Paul Editions, 1980.

————. *Unity in the Work of Service: On the Occasion of His Second Pastoral Visit to the United States*. Washington D. C.: National Catholic Conference of Catholic Bishops, United States Catholic Conference, 1987.

————. *Universi Dominici Gregis*, Apostolic Constitution, 1996.

————. *U.S.A.—The Message of Justice, Peace and Love*. Boston: St. Paul Editions, 1979.

————. *Ut Unum Sint*, Encyclical Letter, 1995.

————. *The Word Made Flesh: The Meaning of the Christmas Season*. Trans. Leslie Wearne, San Francisco: Harper & Row, 1985.

————. *Veritatis Splendor*, Encyclical Letter, 1993.

————. *Vicesimus Quintus Annus*, Apostolic Letter, 1988.

————. *Vita Consecrata, Consecrated Life, Post–Synodal Apostolic Exhortation of the Holy Father John Paul II*, Boston: St. Paul Editions, 1996.

————. *Words of Certitude: Excerpts From His Talks and Writings As Bishop and Pope*. New York: Paulist Press, 1980.

————. *W Polsce: Przemówienia i Homilie 1979, 1983, 1987*. Warsaw: Instytut Wydawniczy Pax, 1991.

————. *W Indiach: Homilie i Przemówienia: 31–11 II 1986*. Warsaw: Instytut Wydawniczy Pax, 1990.

————. *W Weilkiej Brytanii 28 V 1982–2 VI 1982 i Argentynie 11 VI 1982–12 Vi 1982: Homilie i Przemówienia*. Warsaw: Instytut Wydawniczy Pax, 1989.

Trinitarian Theology

Biffi, Giacomo. "The Action of the Holy Sprit in the Church and the World." in *JohnPaul II: A Panorama of His Teachings*. Preface by Joseph Bernardin. New York: New York City Press, 1989, 38–47.

"Encyclical: *Dives in Misericordia*." Editorial. *The Tablet* 234 (1980): 1210.

Every, George. "*Slavorum Apostoli*: A Note." *One in Christ* 21 (1985): 271–273.

Ferraro, Giuseppe. "The Pneumatological Dimension." *L'Osservatore Romano* 37 (1981): 5.

Galichon, Alain. "The First Encyclical." *L'Osservatore Romano* 33 (1979): 6–7.

Hamer, Jerome. Presentation at the Press Conference for the Publication *of Dominum et Vivificantem*. *L'Osservatore Romano* 23 (1986): 16–17.

Lapide, Pinchas. "*Dives in Misericordia*: An Encyclical for Christians and Jews." *Journal of Ecumenical Studies* 18 (1981): 140–142.

Martin, Ralph. "Rich in Mercy." *New Covenant* 11 (July 1981): 20–22.

McDermott, John M. ed. *The Thought of Pope John Paul II*. Rome: Gregorian University, 1993.

Mondin, Battista. "A Monumental Comment on *Dives in Misericodia.*" *L'Osservatore Romano* 36 (1981): 5.

Morneau, Robert F. "*Dives in Misericordia*: Themes and Theses." *Review for Religious* 40 (1981): 670–683.

———. *Themes and Theses of Six Recent Papal Documents: A Commentary*. New York: Alba House, 1985, 111–135.

O'Carroll, Michael. "*Dominum et Vivificantem.*" in *Veni Creator Spiritus: A Theological Encyclopedia of the Holy Spirit*. Collegeville: Liturgical Press, 1990, 70–72.

O'Hare, Joseph. "Mercy Appears." *America* 143 (1980): 402.

Peeters, Paul L. "*Dominum et Vivificantem:* The Conscience and the Heart." *Communio: International Catholic Review 15* (1988): 148–155.

Scola, Angelo. "'Claim' of Christ, 'Claim' of the World: On the Trinitarian Encyclicals of John Paul II." *Communio* 18 (1991): 331–332.

Various Authors. *John Paul II: A Panorama of His Teachings*. New York: New York City Press, 1989.

Christology

"All Ways Lead to Man." Editorial. *America* 140 (1979): 249.

Baum, Gregory. "The First Papal Encyclical." *The Ecumenist* 17 (1979): 55–59.

Buttiglione, Rocco. *Il Pensiero Di Karol Wojtyla*. Milano: Editoriale Jaca Book, 1982.

———. *Karol Wojtyla: The Thought of the Man Who Became Pope John Paul II*. Grand Rapids: William B. Eerdmans Publishing Company, 1997.

Galichon, Alain. "The First Encyclical." *L'Osservatore Romano* 33 (1979): 6–7.

Gawronski, Raymond, T. "*Redemptor Hominis.*" in *The Thought of Pope John Paul II*. Edited by John M. McDermott. Rome: Gregorian University Press, 1993.

Honoré, Jean. "Christ the Redeemer, Core of John Paul II's Teaching." in *John Paul II: A Panorama of His Teachings*. Preface by Joseph Bernardin. New York, NY: New York City Press, 1989.

McCabe , Herbert. "Manuals and Rule Books." *The Tablet* 247 (1993): 1583–1585.

———. *"Redemptor Hominis."* New Blackfriars 60 (1979): 146–147.

McDermott, John M. ed. *The Thought of Pope John Paul II*. Rome: Gregorian University, 1993.

McDonagh, Edna. *"Redemptor Hominis* and Ireland." *The Furrow* 30 (1979): 624–640.

Morneau, Robert F. *"Redemptor Hominis*: Themes and Theses." *Review for Religious* 390 (1980): 247–262.

———. *Themes and Theses of Six Recent Papal Documents: A Commentary.* New York: Alba House, 1985, 111–135.

Richards, Michael. "Mankind Redeemed." *Clergy Review* 64 (1979): 194–195.

Saward, John. *Christ is the Answer: The Christ–Centered Teaching of Pope John Paul II*. Edinburgh: T & T Clark, 1995.

Schall, James. *"Redemptor Hominis*: The Amazement of God." *Homiletic and Pastoral Review* 80 (October 1979): 11–19.

Stevens, M. *"Redemptor Hominis."* in *The New Dictionary of Catholic Social Thought*. Edited by Judith A. Dwyer. Collegeville: Liturgical Press, 1994, 817–822.

Various Authors. *John Paul II: A Panorama of His Teachings*. New York: New York City Press, 1989.

Williams, George Huntston. *The Mind of John Paul II: Origins of His Thought and Action*. New York: Seabury Press, 1981.

Mariology

Alchrin, Arthur MacDonal. *"Redemptoris Mater*: An Anglican Response." *One in Christ* 23 (1988): 324–329.

Aristide Serra, OSM. "Le fonte bibliche della 'Redemptoris Mater'." in *Redemptoris Mater: Contenuti e Prospettive Dottrinali e Pastorali*, 71–78. Rome: Pontificia Accademia Mariana Internazionale, 1988.

Bertetto, Domenico, S.D.B., ed. *Maria nel Magistero di Giovanni Paolo II; Primo Anno di Pontificato, 16 ottobre 1978–21 ottobre 1979.* Rome: Libreria Ateneo Salesiano, 1980.

―――. *Maria nel Magistero di Giovanni Paolo II; Secondo Anno di Pontificato, 22 ottobre 1979–21 ottobre 1980.* Rome: Libreria Ateneo Salesiano, 1981.

―――. *Maria nel Magistero di Giovanni Paolo II; Terzo Anno di Pontificato, 22 ottobre 1980–21 ottobre 1981.* Rome: Libreria Ateneo Salesiano, 1983.

―――. *Maria nel Magistero di Giovanni Paolo II; Quarto Anno di Pontificato, 22 ottobre 1981–21 ottobre 1982.* Rome: Libreria Ateneo Salesiano, 1984.

―――. *Maria nel Magistero di Giovanni Paolo II; Quinto Anno di Pontificato, 22 ottobre 1982–21 ottobre 1983.* Rome: Libreria Ateneo Salesiano, 1986.

―――. *Maria nel Magistero di Giovanni Paolo II; Sesto Anno di Pontificato, 22 ottobre 1983–21 ottobre 1984.* Rome: Libreria Ateneo Salesiano, 1986.

Calkins, Arthur Burton. "John Paul II's Consecration to the Immaculate Heart of Mary: Christological Foundation." *Miles Immaculatae 23* (1987): 88–116, 364–417.

―――. *Totus Tuus. John Paul II's Program of Marian Consecration and Entrustment.* Academy of the Immaculate, U.S.A., 1992.

De Fiores, Stefano, S.N.M. "La 'Redemptoris Mater' e la spiritualità mariana." in *Redemptoris Mater: Contenuti e Prospettive Dottrinali e Pastorali,* 55–70. Rome: Ponteficia Accademia Mariana Internazionale, 1988.

Fehlner, Peter Damian, O.F.M. "Mulieris Dignitatem." *Miles Immaculatae 25* (1989): 6–9.

Galot, Jean. "Prospettive Metodologiche e Dottrinali dell' Enciclica 'Redemptoris Mater'." in *Redemptoris Mater: Contenuti e Prospettive Dottrinali e Pastorali,* 37–52. Rome: Ponteficia Accademia Mariana Internazionale, 1988.

Gomez, Felipe. "A New Encyclical Letter: The Mother of the Redeemer." *East Asian Pastoral Review* 24 (1987): 108–118.

Heft, James L. "*Redemptoris Mater*: Mary's Journey of Faith." *Catechist* 21 (September 1987): 4–5.

Joseph de Sainte–Marie, O. C. D. "Reflexions sur un acte de consecration: Fatima, 13 mai 1982." *Marianum 44* (1982): 88–142.

Little, Joyce A. "*Redemptoris Mater*: The Significance of Mary for Women." *Marian Studies 39* (1988): 136–158.

Luis, Angel, C. S. S. R. "La consagracion a Maria en la vida y doctrina de Juan Pablo II." *Estudios Marianos 51* (1986): 77–112.

Luneau, René. *Le rêve de Compostelle*. Paris: Centurion, 1989.

McDermott, John M. ed. *The Thought of Pope John Paul II*. Rome: Gregorian University, 1993.

Meo, Salvatore, O.S.M. "La 'Mediazione materna' di Maria nella Enciclica 'Redmptoris Mater'." in *Redemptoris Mater: Contenuti e Prospettive Dottrinali e Pastorali*, 131–57. Rome: Pontificia Accademia Mariana Internazionale, 1988.

O'Connor, Edward D., C. S. C. "The Roots of Pope John Paul II's Devotion to Mary." *Marian Studies 39* (1988): 78–114.

Ratzinger, Joseph Cardinal. Presentation at the Press Conference for the Publication of *Redemptoris Mater*. *L'Osservatore Romano* 13 (1987): 21, 23.

Solesmes, Benedictine Monks of., eds. *Our Lady's Papal Teachings*. Trans. Daughters of St. Paul. Boston: St. Paul Editions, 1961.

Stahel, Thomas H. "*Redemptoris Mater*." *America* 156 (1987): 353–354.

Suro, Roberto. "The Writing of *Sollicitudo Rei Socialis*: A Behind–the–Scenes Account." *Critic* 6 (May 1988): 13–18.

"Symposium on *Redemptoris Mater*: Report on the 1988 Convention." *Marian Studies* 39 (1988): 34–162.

Taylor, Richard J. "*Redemptoris Mater*: Pope John Paul II's Encyclical for the Marian Year: Some Reflections." *Priest & People* 2 (1988): 133–136.

Winowska, Maria. "Le Culte Mariale en Poplogne." in *Maria: Etudes sur la Sainte Vierge*, ed. Hubert du Manoir, S.J., 4: 684–709. Paris: Beauchesne et ses Fils, 1956.

Zalecki, Marian, O. S. P. *Theology of a Marian Shrine: Our Lady of Czestochowa*. Marian Library Studies, n.s., 8. Dayton, OH: University of Dayton, 1976.

Ecclesiology

Casaroli, Agostino. *Nella Chiesa per il Mondo: Omelie e Discorsi*. Milan: Rusconi Libri, 1987.

Del Rio, Domenico. *Memoria del Concilio*. Rome: Borla, 1985.

Dionne, Robert J. *The Papacy and the Church*. New York: Philosophical Library, 1987.

Dunn, Joseph. *No Lions in the Hierarchy*. Dublin: Columbia Press, 1994.

Evangelisti, David. *Joannes Paulus II: Light in the Church*. Vatican City: Libreria Editrice Vaticana, 1980.

Faulhaber, Robert William. "The Church and Culture—John Paul II's 'On Human Work'." *Listening* 18 (1983): 103–118.

Guasco, Maurilo, Elio Guerriero and Francesco Traianiello. *La chiesa del Vaticano II*. Milan: San Paolo, 1994.

Kelly, George A. *Keeping the Church Catholic with John Paul II*. San Francisco: Ignatius Press, 1993.

Kilmartin, Edward J., *Church, Eucharist and Priesthood: A Theological Commentary on "The Mystery and Worship of the Most Holy Eucharist"*. New York: Paulist Press, 1981.

McDermott, John M. ed. *The Thought of Pope John Paul II*. Rome: Gregorian University, 1993.

Williams, George Huntston. *The Mind of John Paul II: Origins of His Thought and Action*. New York: Seabury Press, 1981.

Missiology–Evangelization

Alazraki, Valentina. *Juan Pablo II El Viajero De Dios*. Mexico: Editorial Diana, 1990.

Balducci, Ernesto. *L'uomo planetario*. Milan: Camunia, 1985.

Bland, Joan, ed. *The Pastoral Vision of John Paul II*. Chicago: Franciscan Herald Press, 1982.

Boyaxhiu, Mother Theresa. "Charity: The Soul of Missionary Activity." *L'Osservatore Romano* 14 (1991): 5.

Braaten, Carl E. "A Papal Letter on the Church's Missionary Mandate." *Dialog* 30 (1991): 182–183.

Burrows, William R., ed. *Redemption and Dialogue: Reading "Redemptoris Missio" and Dialogue and Proclamation*. Maryknoll: Orbis, 1993.

Caggiano, Pietro, Hilary Ngweno and M. Amin. *John Paul II in Kenya: Karibu Kenya Babe Mtakatifu*. Nairobi: Kenya Catholic Secratariat: Catholic Bookshop, 1980.

Colombo, Domenico. "Mission and the Kingdom." *L'Osservatore Romano* 17 (1991): 6.

De Montclos, Christine. *Les voyages de Jean Paul II*. Paris: Centurion, 1990.

Del Rio, Domenico. *Wojtyla: Un Pontificato Itinerante*. Bologne: Edizioni Dehoniane, 1994.

Del Rio, Domenico and Luigi Accatoli. *Wojtyla, The New Moses*. Milan: Mondadori, 1988.

———. *Wojtyla: Il nuovo Mosè*. Milan: Mondadori, 1988.

Dominic, A. Paul. "Mission before Mission: God's Mission within Us." *Review for Religious* 52 (1992): 119–130.

Dorr, Donal. "*Redemptoris Missio*: Reflections on the Encyclical." *The Furrow* 42 (1991): 339–347.

D'Souza, Henry Sebastian. "Pope John Paul's New Challenge to Asia." *L'Osservatore Romano* 14 (1991): 6.

Every, George. "*Slavorum Apostoli*: A Note." *One in Christ* 21 (1985): 271–273.

Gheddo, Piero. "Gospel and Development." *L'Osservatore Romano* 11 (1991): 5.

Giardini, F. "Trinitarian Communion and Christian Mission in *Redemptoris Missio*." *Euntes* 47 (1994): 151–166.

John Paul II and the New Evangelization. Laurence J, McGulley Lecture by Avery Dulles, S. J., New York: Fordham University, 1991.

Kaiser, Philip M. *Journeying Far and Wide: A Political and Diplomatic Memoir*. New York: Charles Scribner and Sons, 1992.

Kalvoda, Josef. "The Cyrilo–Methodian Idea." *The Priest* 42 (February 1986): 18–19.

Kroeger, James H. "Rekindling Mission Enthusiasm." *The Priest* 48 (January 1992): 32–36.

Lopez–Gay, Jesus. "Spirit, Salvation and Mission." *L'Osservatore Romano* 9 (1991): 6.

Loya, Joseph A. "John Paul II's Encyclical *Slavorum Apostoli*: An Ecumenical Assessment." *Ecumenical Trends* 14 (1985): 167–168.

Major Adresses of Pope John Paul II on His Pastoral Visits to Various Countries. Boston: Daughters of St. Paul.

McDermott, John M. ed. *The Thought of Pope John Paul II*. Rome: Gregorian University, 1993.

Montclos, Christine de. *Les Voyages de Jean–Paul II*. Paris: Centurion, 1990.

Morneau, Robert F. *Themes and Theses of Six Recent Papal Documents: A Commentary*. New York: Alba House, 1985, 111–135.

Murphy, Francis Xavier. *The Pilgrim Pope, A Man For All People: John Paul II's visits to the U.S.A., Mexico, Poland and Ireland*. South Hackensack, N. J.: Shepherd Press, 1979.

Neuhaus, Richard John. "Reviving the Missionary Mandate." *First Things* 16 (1991): 61–64.

O'Donnell, Timothy. "The Crisis of Faith and the Theology of Mission: A Reflection on *Redemptoris Missio*." *Faith and Reason* 18:3 (1992): 5–13.

Offredo, Jean. *Jean Paul II: L'aventurier de Dieu*. Paris: Carrere–Michel Lafon, 1986.

St. John–Stevas, Norman. *Pope John Paul II: His Travels and Mission*. London, Boston: Faber and Faber, 1982.

Stransky, Thomas F. "From Vatican II to *Redemptoris Missio*: A Development in the Theology of Mission." in *The Good News of the Kingdom: Mission Theology for the Third Millennium*. Edited by Charles Van Engen, Dean S. Gillilan, and Paul E. Pierson. Maryknoll: Orbis, 1993, 137–147.

Teissier, Henri. "Ours is Not a Silent Witness to Muslims." *L'Osservatore Romano* 38 (1992): 7.

Tomko, Josef. Presentation at the Press Conference for the Publication of *Redemptoris Missio*. *L'Osservatore Romano* 4 (1991): 1, 21.

Ureña, Manuel. "The Missionary Impulse in the Church According to *Redemptoris Missio*." *Communio* 19 (1992): 94–102.

Zago, Marcello. "Church's Mission: Is It One or Many?" *L'Osservatore Romano* 9 (1991): 7, 9.

Philosophical Anthropology–Morality

Albacete, Lorenzo. "The Pope against Moralism and Legalism." *Anthropos* 10 (1994): 81–86.

"Alcune forme di fondamentalismo." *La Civilitá Cattolica* (April 1994).

Allsopp, Michael E. and John J. O'Keefe, eds. *Veritatis Splendor: American Responses*. Kansas City: Sheed & Ward, 1995.

Anderson, Carl A. "*Veritatis Splendor* and the New Evangelization." *Anthropos* 10 (1994): 61–74.

Anderson, Carl A. "Gospel Offers Man the Opportunity to Regain His Authentic Personhood." *L'Osservatore Romano* 26 (1995): 10.

Basso, Domingo. "Encyclical is Meant Vigorously to Arouse the Conscience of Society." *L'Osservatore Romano* 36 (1995): 6.

Bennet, J. "Whatever the Consequences." *Analysis* 26 (1996): 83–102.

Bergonzoni, Luciano. *Sessualità E Amore: Catechesi di Papa Wojtyla Sulla Teologia Del Corpo*. Padova: Edizioni Messaggero Padova, 1981.

Bernardin, J. *Consistent Ethic of Life*. Kansas City: Sheed and Ward, 1988.

Brugués, Jean–Louis. "Man Comes from beyond Himself Since He is Created in God's Image." *L'Osservatore Romano* 15 (1994): 10–11.

Buttiglione, Rocco. *Il Pensiero Di Karol Wojtyla*. Milano: Editoriale Jaca Book, 1982.

———. *Karol Wojtyla: The Thought of the Man Who Became Pope John Paul II*. Grand Rapids: William B. Eerdmans Publishing Company, 1997.

Caffarra, Carlo. "Death of God's Only Son Revealed Dignity and Value of All Human Life." *L'Osservatore Romano* 21 (1995): 10.

Cahill, Lisa Sowle. "The Lasting Contribution of *Veritatis Splendor*." *Commonweal* 120 (1993): 15–16.

Callam, Daniel. "The Gospel of Life." *The Canadian Catholic Review* 13 (June 1995): 2–3.

Carrasco de Paula, Ignacio. "Church's Moral Teaching Shows Man the Way to Eternal Salvation." *L'Osservatore Romano* 32/33 (1995): 6.

Casini, Carlo. "When Sense of God is Lost, There is Tendency to Lose Sense of Man." *L'Osservatore Romano* 18 (1995): 6.

Cessario, Romanus. "Moral Absolutes in the Civilization of Love." *Crisis* 13 (May 1995): 18–23.

Chapelle, A. "Les enjeux de 'Veritatis Splendor'." *Nouvelle Revue Theologique* (Nov.–Dec. 1993): 801–817.

Chappelle, Albert. "Encyclical's Clarifications Develop Catechism's Treatment of Morality." *L'Osservatore Romano* 18 (1994): 21–22.

"The Christian Humanism and Adequate Personalism of Karol Wojtyla." *Pope John Paul II Lecture Series* (1985): 36–40.

Ciccione, Lino. "Acceptance of Contraception Leads to Promotion of Abortion." *L'Osservatore Romano* 24 (1995): 10.

Clément, Oliver. "Some Orthodox Reflections on Recent Papal Encyclicals." *One in Christ* 31 (1995): 237–280.

Cole, Basil. "The New Sins against Faith and *Evangelium Vitae*." *Angelicum* 73 (1996): 3–19.

Colombo, Roberto. "Discoveries of Science Support Prohibition of Killing Human Embryo." *L'Osservatore Romano* 42 (1995): 10–11.

Cottier, Georges. "Distorted Concept of Subjectivity Contradicts Dignity of the Person." *L'Osservatore Romano* 43 (1995): 10.

———. "Morality of a Human Act Depends Primarily on Object Chosen by Will." *L'Osservatore Romano* 6 (1994): 11.

"A Coup for the Pope." Editorial. *The Tablet* 247 (1993): 1251–1252.

Curley, Terence P. "*Evangelium Vitae* and Our Culture." *The Priest* 51 (October 1995): 18–20.

Curran, Charles E. *The Living Tradition of Catholic Moral Theology*. Notre Dame, Indiana: University of Notre Dame Press, 1992.

Curran, Charles and Richard A. McCormick, S. J. eds. *Readings in Moral Theology No. 5: Official Catholic Social Teachings*. New York: Paulist Press, 1986.

Devaux, Michaël. "The Truth of Love, The Lie of Death." *Communio* 23 (1996): 110–121.

Drane, J. F. "The Philosophical Roots of John Paul II." *America* (May 26, 1975): 426–29.

Dulles, Avery. "John Paul II and the Truth about Freedom." *First Things* 55 (1995): 36–41.

Durkin, Mary G. *Feast of Love: Pope John Paul II on Human Intimacy.* Chicago: Loyola University Press, 1983.

Ernst, Wilhelm. "Theology is Essentially an Ecclesiastical Science That Must Serve the Church." *L'Osservatore Romano* 16 (1994): 6.

Fedoryka, Damian P. "The Gift of *Veritatis Splendor.* " *Social Justice Review* 85 (1994): 140–150.

Figueiredo, Fernando A. "Human Beings Are Merely Stewards and Not Lords Who Can Dispose of Life at Will." *L'Osservatore Romano* 46 (1995): 10.

Finnis, J. *Natural Law and Natural Rights.* Oxford: Oxford University Press, 1980.

Finnis, John. "Beyond the Encyclical." *The Tablet* 248 (1994): 9–10.

———. "Goods are Meant for Everyone." *L'Osservatore Romano* 12 (1988): 11.

Finnis, John and Germain Grisez. "Negative Moral Precepts Protect the Dignity of the Human Person." *L'Osservatore Romano* 8 (1994): 6–7.

Ford, John C. and Germain Grisez. "Contraception and the Infallibility of the Ordinary Magisterium." *Theological Studies* Vol. 39, no. 2 (June 1978): 258–312.

Fraling, Bernhard. "Freedom is Not Abolished by God's Law, but is Protected and Promoted." *L'Osservatore Romano* 3 (1994): 9–10.

Fuchs, Joseph. "Good Acts and Good Persons." *The Tablet* 247 (1993): 1444–1445.

Greeley, Andrew M. *The Young Catholic Family: Religious Images and Marriage Fulfillment.* Chicago: Thomas More Press, 1980.

Grisez, G. "Against Consequentialism." *American Journal of Jurisprudence* 23 (1978).

———. *Contraception and the Natural Law.* Milwaukee: Bruce, 1964.

Grisez, G. and J. Boyle. *Life and Death with Liberty and Justice.* Notre Dame: University of Notre Dame, 1979.

Grisez, Germain. "*Veritatis Splendor:* Revealed Truth versus Dissent." *Homiletic and Pastoral Review* 94 (March 1994): 8–17.

Grootaers, Jan and Joseph A. Selling. *The 1980 Synod of Bishops 'On the Role of the Family'*. Louvain: Leuven University Press, 1983.

Guggenheim, Antoine. "Liberté et verité selon K. Wojtyla." *Nouvelle Revue Theologique* 115 (March/April 1993): 194–210.

Haas, John. "'The Gospel of Life' and the Death of Penalty." *Crisis* 13 (July/August 1995): 20–23.

Hamlon, John S., *A Call to Families: Study Guide and Commentary for Familaris Consortio*. Forward by Archbishop Edourd Gagnon. Collegeville, MN: Human Life Center, St. Johns University, 1984.

Hauerwas, Stanley Martin. "*Veritatis Splendor* is Unique." *Commonweal* 120 (1993): 16–18.

Hausman, Noëlle. "Moral Theologians are Obliged to Teach Authentic Church Doctrine." *L'Osservatore Romano* 12 (1994): 8–17.

Healy, Jack. "*Veritatis Splendor* and the Human Person." *The Linacre Quarterly* 61 (November 1994): 16–36.

Hellman, John. "John Paul II and the Personalist Movement." *Cross Currents* XXX, 4 (1981).

Herranz, Gonzalo. "The Respect and Care of All Human Beings is Part of Doctor's Charism." *L'Osservatore Romano* 30 (1995): 10.

Herranz, Julián. "Conversion of the Offender is Goal of Canonical Sanction for Abortion." *L'Osservatore Romano* 25 (1995): 10.

Hickey, James A. "The Path to Spiritual Healing After Abortion is through Reconciliation." *L'Osservatore Romano* 40 (1995): 6.

Hittinger, Russell. "Law and Liberty in *Veritatis Splendor*." *Crisis* 13 (May 1995): 13–17.

———. "The Pope and the Theorists: The Oneness of Truth." *Crisis* 11 (December 1993): 31–36.

Hogan, Richard. "A Commentary on 'Familiaris Consortio'." *The Wanderer*. Vol. 115, no. 10 (March 11, 1982): Supplement, 1–3.

———. "A Theology of the Body: A Commentary on the Audiences of Pope John Paul II from September 5, 1979 to May 6, 1981." *Fidelity* Vol. 1, no. 1 (December, 1981): 10–15, 24–27.

Hogan, Richard M. and John M. LeVoir. *Covenant of Love, Pope John Paul II on Sexuality, Marriage, and Family in the Modern World.* San Francisco: Ignatius Press, 1985.

Horkhiemer, M. "Materialismo e morale." *Teoria critica* Vol. I, 75.

Hume, Basil. "Introducing the Encyclical *Evangelium Vitae.*" *Briefing* 25 (April 1995): 3–8.

Janssens, Louis and Joseph A. Selling. "Theology and Proportionality: Thoughts about the Encyclical *Veritatis Splendor.*" *Bijdragen* 55 (1994): 118–132.

Johnstone, Brian V. "The Catholic Moral Tradition and *Veritatis Splendor.*" *Studia Moralia* 31 (1993): 283–306.

———. "The Encyclical *Veritatis Splendor.*" *The Ecumenical Review* 48 (1994): 345–350.

———. "Life in a Culture of Death." *Priests & People* 9 (November 1995): 409–413.

———. "Sin is Healed by Grace, but Church Must Help Sinner Acknowledge Guilt." *L'Osservatore Romano* 5 (1994): 10.

Keating, James. "An Ethic of Prayerful Listening: *Veritatis Splendor.*" *Emmanuel* 100 (1994): 345–350.

Kennedy, Terrence. "'Fundamental Option' Can Radically Change as Result of Popular Acts." *L'Osservatore Romano* 5 (1994): 10.

Kiely, Bartholomew. "Humble Admission of Limitations Allows Person to Grow in Freedom." *L'Osservatore Romano* 4 (1994): 11.

Kmiec, Douglas W. "Behind the 'Empty Cloud' of Autonomous Reason—Or Why It Doesn't Matter if Natural Law of *Veritatis Splendor* is 'Real Law'." *The American Journal of Jurisprudence* 39 (1995): 37–46.

Krapiec, Mieczylaw. *I—Man.* Trans. Marie Lescoe, Andrew Woznicki, Theresa Sandok, et al. New Britain, Conn.: Mariel Publications, 1983.

Lake, Frank. *With Respect: A Doctor's Response to a Healing Pope.* London: Darton, Longman and Todd, 1982.

Lauer, Q. Review of *The Acting Person. America* 140 (1979) 337.

Law, Bernard Cardinal. *Christian Marriage—A Covenant of Love and Life.* Boston: Daughters of St. Paul, 1998.

Lawler, Ronald D., O.F.M., Cap. *The Christian Personalism of John Paul II.* Chicago: Franciscan Herald Press. 1982

Lecomte, Bernard. *La Verité l'emportera toujours sur le mensonge.* Paris: J. C. Lattes, 1991.

Lescoe, F. *Philosophy Serving Contemporary Needs of the Church.* New Britain, CT: Marial Publications, 1979.

Letter to the Bishops of the Catholic Church on the Pastoral Care of Homosexual Persons. Vatican City: Congregation for the Doctrine of the Faith, 1986.

Lobato, Abelardo. "Technological Man Has Neglected Moral Sense That Underlies Culture." *L'Osservatore Romano* 20 (1995): 10–11.

López Trujillo, Alfonso. "Church Believes That Human Life, However Weak, Is Gift from God." *L'Osservatore Romano* 17 (1995): 9–10.

MacIntyre, Alsadair. "How Can We Learn What *Veritatis Splendor* Has To Teach?" *The Thomist* 58 (1994): 171–195.

Maestri, William F. *A Guide for the Study of "Veritatis Splendor."* Boston: *St. Paul Books and Media,* 1993.

Marthaler, Berard L. "The Gospel of Life." *Living Light* 32 (Fall 1995): 6–45.

Martin, Francis X. "The Integrity of Christian Moral Activity: The First Letter of John and *Veritatis Splendor*." *Communio* 21 (1994): 265–285.

Martini, Marco. "Gospel is Basis for Action." *L'Osservatore Romano* 29 (1991): 9.

Maritain, J. "The End of Machiavellianism" *The Range of Reason.* London: G. Bles, 1953.

———. "Truth and Tolerance." *Commonweal* 66 (1957): 631–633.

May, William. *Sex, Marriage and Chastity: Reflection of a Catholic Layman, Spouse and Parent.* Chicago: Franciscan Herald Press, 1981.

May, William E. "Evangelium Vitae." *Linacre Quarterly* (February 1995): 87–96.

———. "Moral Theologians and *Veritatis Splendor*." *Homiletic and Pastoral Review* 95 (December 1994): 7–16.

———. "The Splendor of Accuracy: How Accurate?" *Anthropos* 10 (1994): 465–483.

————. "Theologians and Theologies in the Encyclical." *Anthropos* 10 (1994): 39–60.

McCartney, James J., *Unborn Persons: Pope John Paul II and the Abortion Debate*. New York: P. Lang, 1987.

McCormick, Richard A. "The Gospel of Life." *America*, 172 (1995): 10–17.

————. "Some Early Reactions to *Veritatis Splendor*." *Theological Studies* 55 (1994): 481–506. Reply by John Neuhaus. "Moral Theology and its Pique." *First Things* 49 (1985): 88–92.

————. "*Veritatis Splendor* and Moral Theology." *America* 169 (October 30, 1993): 8–11.

McDermott, John M. ed. *The Thought of Pope John Paul II*. Rome: Gregorian University, 1993.

McHugh, James T. "Bishops Must See that the Church's Moral Doctrine is Faithfully Taught." *L'Osservatore Romano* 17 (1994): 22.

McInerny, Ralph. "Locating Right and Wrong: *Veritatis Splendor* versus Muddled Moralizing." *Crisis* 11 (December 1993): 37–40.

McQuillen, Michael P. "The Tarnished Splendor of Autonomy." *Linacre Quarterly* 62 (Fall 1995): 49–51.

Medina Estévez, Jorge. "Communion with God Gives Truth and Joy to Every Expression of Life." *L'Osservatore Romano* 23 (1995): 10–11.

Melady, Thomas. "Public Catholicism and *Evangelium Vitae*." *Crisis* 13 (June 1995): 16.

Melina, Livio. "Conscience Witnesses to a Truth that Precedes It and Surpasses It." *L'Osservatore Romano* 2 (1994): 10–11.

————. "Lack of Objective Moral Anchor Leads to Abuse of Political Power." *L'Osservatore Romano* 19 (1995): 10–11.

Merecki, Jaroslaw and Tadeusz Styczen. "Denying Legal Protection to Weakest Undermines the State Itself." *L'Osservatore Romano* 44 (1995): 10.

————. "The Splendor of Human Freedom Must Be Seen in Relation to Truth." *L'Osservatore Romano* 49 (1993): 10–11.

Moynihan, Robert. "Truth is Ecumenical, Says Ratzinger: Letter from Rome." *Crisis* 11 (November 1993): 25–27.

The Mystery of the Trinity

Mudge, Lewis S. "*Veritatis Splendor* and Today's Ecumenical Conversation." *The Ecumenical Review* 48 (1996): 158–163.

Mumford, Stephen D. *The Pope and the New Apocalypse: The Holy War Against Family Planning*. North Carolina: Center for Research on Population and Security, 1986.

Nash, Nicholas. "Teaching in Crisis." *The Tablet* 247 (1993): 1480–1482.

Negri, L. *L'uomo e la cultura nel magistero di Giovanni Paolo II*. Bologna: CSEO, 1983.

Neuhaus, Richard John. "The Prophetic Humanism of *Evangelium Vitae*." *Crisis* 14 (May 1996): 22–24.

————. "The Splendor of Truth: A Symposium." *First Things* 39 (1994): 14–29.

"The New Encyclical." Editorial. *America* 169 (October 23, 1993): 3.

Novak, Michael. "The Gospel of Life." *Crisis* 13 (June 1995): 6–7.

————. "The Hope of Splendor." *Crisis* 11 (December 1993): 4–5.

————. "The Pope Strikes Again." *Crisis* 11 (November 1993): 5–7.

O'Connor, John J. "Holy Father Warns Us That We Face an Objective 'Conspiracy Against Life'." *L'Osservatore Romano* 27 (1995): 10.

Petrà, B. "God's Laws Are Not Impossible, for Divine Grace Enables Man to Obey." *L'Osservatore Romano* 11 (1994): 10–11.

Pinckaers, Servais. "The Use of Scripture and the Renewal of Moral Theology: The Catechism and *Veritatis Splendor*." *The Thomist* 59 (1995): 1–19.

————. "We Are Capable of Living Christ's Love By Saving Grace of His Spirit." *L'Osservatore Romano* 47 (1993): 11.

Porter, Jean. "Moral Reasoning, Authority and Community in *Veritatis Splendor*." *Annual of the Society of Christian Ethics* 15 (1995): 201–209.

Potterie, Ignace de la. "Believers Should Live and Act in Light of Christ's Life and Example." *L'Osservatore Romano* 46 (1993): 10.

Propati, Giuseppe. "L'affermazione dei valori umani negli studi di Karol Wojtyla." *Rassegna di Teologia* (Jan. Feb. 1979): 6–18.

Ratzinger, Joseph Cardinal. "Christian Faith as 'the Way': An Introduction to *Veritatis Splendor*." *Communio* 21 (1994): 109–207.

———. "Glaube als Weg Hinführung zur Enzyklika des Papstes uber die Grudlagen der Moral." *Internationale Katholische Zeitschrift* 6/93 (November 1993): 564–570.

———. Presentation at the Press Conference for the Publication of *Evangelium Vitae. L'Osservatore Romano* 14 (1995): 1–2.

"The Resplendence of Truth." Editorial, *The Tablet* 247 (1993): 999–1000.

Rhonheimer, Martin. "Given His Creaturely Status, Man's Autonomy is Essentially Theonomy." *L'Osservatore Romano* 51/52 (1993): 8–9.

———. "Intrinsically Evil Acts and the Moral Viewpoint: Clarifying a Central Teaching of *Veritatis Splendor*." *The Thomist* 58 (1994): 1–39.

Rodriquez Luño, Angel. "Decisions Contrary to the Law of God Are Not Justified by 'Good Intention'." *L'Osservatore Romano* 7 (1994): 10 –11.

Roth, Gottfried. "Life Must Awaken in the Physician a Reverential Awe of the Lord's Gift." *L'Osservatore Romano* 37 (1995): 6.

"The Sacredness of Human Life." Editorial. *The Tablet* 249 (1995): 411.

Schindler, David I. "Christological Aesthetics and *Evangelium Vitae*." *Communio* 22 (1995): 193–224.

Schmitz, Kenneth L. *At the Center of the Human Drama: The Philosophical Anthropology of Karol Wojtyla/Pope John Paul II*. Washington D. C.: Catholic University of America Press, 1993.

Schooyans, Michel. "Man Can Misuse His Will, Claiming a Sovereignty That is Not His Own." *L'Osservatore Romano* 10 (1994): 10–11.

Scola, Angelo. "Following Christ: On John Paul II's Encyclical *Veritatis Splendor*." *Communio* 20 (1993): 724–727.

———. "In Christ Man Learns That Freedom and Moral Law Are Not Opposed." *L'Osservatore Romano* 44 (1993): 10.

Segalla, Giuseppi. "In His Life and Teaching Jesus Fulfills the law and Reveals the Will of God." *L'Osservatore Romano* 48 (1993): 10–11.

Seifert, Josef. "Karol Cardinal Wojtyla (Pope John Paul II) as Philosopher and the Cracow/Lublin School of Philosophy." *Aletheia* Vol. 2 (1981): 130–199.

Selling, Joseph A. and Jan Jans, eds. *The Splendor of Accuracy: An Examination of the Assertions Made by Veritatis Splendor.*" Grand Rapids: Eerdmans, 1994.

Sgreccia, Elio. "New Connection Emerges between Safeguarding Life and Environment." *L'Osservatore Romano* 29 (1995): 10–11.

Shaw, R. "Contraception, Infallibility and the Ordinary Magisterium." *Homiletic and Pastoral Review* 78 (July 1978): 9–19.

Smith, Janet. "Natural Law is a Guide to Morality for Christians and Non–Christians." *L'Osservatore Romano* 1 (1994): 10.

Smith, Russell E. "*Veritatis Splendor* Teaches the Splendor of Truth." *Faith & Reason* 21 (1995): 55–75.

Smith, William. "The Role of the Christian Family, Articles 28–35.*" Pope John Paul and the Family*. Edited by Michael J. Wrenn. Chicago: Franciscan Herald Press, 1983, 73–107.

Smith, William B. "*Veritatis Splendor* is a Moral Masterpiece: No Truth, No Freedom." *Crisis* 11 (November 1993): 28–31.

Spaemann, Robert. "Even the Best of Intentions Does Not Justify the Use of Evil Means." *L'Osservatore Romano* 50 (1993): 11.

Stafford, Jame Francis. "Reflections on *Veritatis Splendor.*" *Communio* 21 (1994): 363–366.

Stravopoulos, Alexandre M. "*Veritatis Splendor*: An Orthodox Reaction." *The Ecumenical Review* 48 (1996): 155–157.

Sullivan, Francis A. "The Doctrinal Weight of *Evangelium Vitae.*" *Theological Studies* 56 (1995): 560–565.

Suro, Roberto. "The Writing of *Sollicitudo Rei Socialis*: A Behind–the–Scenes Account." *Critic* 6 (May 1988): 13–18.

"Symposium on *Evangelium Vitae.*" *The Human Life Review* 21 (Summer 1995): 25–72.

Szostek, Andrzej. "Man's Fundamental Option Can Be Radically Altered by Individual Acts." *L'Osservatore Romano* 16 (1994): 14.

"Teen Fertility Awareness/Billings Method Study." *Fellowship of Catholic Scholars Newsletter* Vol. 7, no. 2 (March, 1984): 11, 15.

Tettamanzi, Dionigi. "The Call to Freedom Lived in Truth is Heart of the New Evangelization." *L'Osservatore Romano* 13 (1994): 9–10.

Torre, Joseph M. de la. "John Paul's Stubborn Humanism." *Homiletic and Pastoral Review* 92 (February 1992): 56–59.

Tremblay, Réal. "Grace of Christ's Presence Heals and Transforms the Human Heart." *L'Osservatore Romano* 45 (1993): 10.

Tuck, Mary. "A Message in Season." *The Tablet* 247 (1993): 1583–1585.

Tymieniecka, Anna–Teresa. "The Origins of the Philosophy of John Paul II." *Proceedings of The American Catholic Philosophical Association Meeting.* (1979). Washington: Catholic University, 1979, 16–27.

Various Authors. *La Filosofia Di Karol Wojtyla.* Bologna, Italy: Centro Studi Europa Orientale, 1983.

"The Vatican's Summary of *Evangelium Vitae*." *Origins* 24 (1995): 728–730.

Vial Correra, Juan de Dios. "Objective Forms of Evil Aimed at Weakest Have No Justification." *L'Osservatore Romano* 31 (1995): 6.

Vree, Dale. "The Splendor of Truth and the Squalor of Sin." *New Oxford Review* 60 (December 1993): 2–8.

Wilkins, John, ed. *Considering Veritatis Splendor.* Cleveland: The Pilgrims Press, 1994.

Williams, B. *Consequentialism: For and Against.* Cambridge: Cambridge University Press, 1973.

Williams, George Huntston. *The Mind of John Paul II: Origins of His Thought and Action.* New York: Seabury Press, 1981.

Woznicki, Andrew A. *A Christian Humanism: Karol Wojtyla's Existential Personalism.* New Britain, CT, Marial Publications, 1980.

———. "Dialogistic Thomism and Dialectical Marxism." *The New Scholasticism* 52 (1978): 214–35.

———. "The Influence of Maritain in Poland." Lecture at the International Maritain Congress, Niagra University, May 28, 1937.

Wren, Michael ed. *Pope John Paul II and the Family.* Chicago: Franciscan Herald Press, 1983.

———. "Wyszynski, Wojtyla and the Woman: A True Love Story." *Mater Fidei Et Fidelium* 17–23: 445–452. Collected Essays to Honor Theodore Koehler on his 80th Birthday, Marian Library Studies, University of Dayton, Dayton, Ohio 1985–1991.

Zieba, Maciej. "Truth and Freedom in the Thought of Pope John Paul." *The Tablet* 247 (1993): 1510–1512.

Social Teaching

Acts of the United Nations Seminar on *Centesimus Annus*: John Paul's Latest Social Encyclical. *L'Osservatore Romano* 47 (1991): Supplement, i–xii.

After 1991: Capitalism and Ethics. A Colloquium in the Vatican 1992. Vatican City: Pontifical Council for Justice and Peace, 1992.

Andrè –Vincent, I. (Phillipe). *Les Droits de L'Homme Dans L'Enseignement de Jean Paul II.* Paris: Librairie Générale de Droit et de Jurisprudence, 1983.

Aristide, Jean–Bertrand. *Théologie et Politique.* Montréal: Les Éditions du CIDIHCA, 1992.

Aubert, Robert, *et al. The Christian Centuries, vol. 5: The Church in a Secularized Society.* New York: Paulist Press and London: Darton, Longman and Todd, 1978.

Barta, Russel. "Work: In Search of New Meanings." *Chicago Studies* 23 (August 1984): 155–168.

Baum, Gregory. "The Anti–Cold War Encyclical." *The Ecumenist* 26 (1988): 65–74.

———. "Capitalism *ex cathedra.*" *Health Progress* 73 (April 1992): 44–48.

———. "*Laborem Exercens.*" in *The New Dictionary of Catholic Social Thought.* Edited by Judith A. Dwyer: Collegeville: Liturgical Press, 1994, 527–535

———. *The Priority of Labor: A Commentary on Laborem Exercens: Encyclical Letter of Pope John Paul II.* New York: Paulist Press, 1982.

Baum, Gregory and Robert Ellsberg, eds. *The Logic of Solidarity: Commentaries on Pope John Paul II's Encyclical on Social Concern.* Maryknoll, New York: Orbis Books, 1990.

Bayer, Richard C. "Christian Personalism and Democratic Capitalism." *Horizons* 21 (1994): 313–331.

Bedoyere, Quentin de la. "Man and His Work." *The Tablet* 235 (1981): 1192–1194.

Bianchi, Eugene C. and Rosemary Radford Reuther, eds. *A Democratic Catholic Church and the Reconstruction of Roman Catholicism*. New York: Crossroad, 1992.

Boff, Leonardo. *Church, Charism and Power*. London: SCM Press, 1985.

———. *Liberation Theology: from Confrontation to Dialogue*. New York: Harper & Row, 1986.

Bowe, Paul. "*Centesimus Annus.*" *Doctrine and Life* 41 (1991): 312–318, 324–331.

———. "*Sollicitudo Rei Socialis*: A Commentary on the Encyclical." *Doctrine and Life* 38 (1988): 227–233.

Brovedani, E. "Giovanni Paolo II e la scienza." *Aggiornamenti sociali* 24 (1984): 9–10.

Brown, Lester R. *Our Democratically Divided World*. Washington, D.C.: Worldwatch Institute, 1986.

Brzezínski, Zbigniew. *Power and Principle*. New York: Farrar, Straus and Giroux, 1983.

Burns, Gene. *The Frontiers of Catholicism*. Berkeley: Univerisity of California Press, 1992.

Buttiglione, Rocco. "Behind *Centesimus Annus.*" *Crisis* 9 (June 1991): 8–9.

———. "Christian Economics 101." *Crisis* (July–August 1991): 8–9.

Byron, William J. "Solidarity, Path to Development and Peace." *America* 158 (1988): 445–446.

Caldecott, Stratford. "Cosmology, Eschatology, Ecology: Some Reflections on *Sollicitudo Rei Socialis.*" *Cummunio* 15 (1988): 305–318.

Calvez, Jean–Yves. "*Solllicitudo Rei Socialis.*" in *The New Dictionary of Catholic Social Thought*. Edited by Judith A. Dwyer. Collegeville: Liturgical Press, 1994, 912–917.

Carrier, Hervè, S. J. *The Social Doctrine of the Church Revisited*. Vatican City: Vatican Polyglot Press, 1990.

Cassin, R. *Religions et Droits de l'Homme. Amicorum discipulorumque Liber.* (1972): 97.

———. "Le Droits de l'Homme." *RCADI* 140 (1974): 330.

Charrier, Fernando. "Labor and Capital." *L'Osservatore Romano* 42 (1981): 8.

Cox, Harvey. *The Secular City*. New York: Collier Books, Macmillan, 1990.

———. *The Silencing of Leonardo Boff*. Oak Park, Illinois: Meyer–Stone Books, 1988.

D'Amato, Al. *Power, Pasta and Politics*. New York: Hyperion, 1995.

de La Chappelle, P. *La Déclaration Universelle des Droits de l'Homme et le Catholicisme*. Paris: L.G.D.J., 1967.

de Laubier, Patrick. *La Pensée Sociale de L'Église Catholique: Un Idéal Historique de Léon XIII à Jean Paul II*. Paris: Editions Albatros, 1980.

Desto, Robert A. "*Laborem Exercens*." in *A Century of Catholic Social Thought*. Edited by George Weigel and Robert Royal. Lanham: University Press of America 1991. 145–161.

Donahue, Thomas R. *Trade Union Perspective of Laborem Exercens*. Washington: American Federation of Labor and Congress of Industrial Organizations, 1982.

d'Onorio, J. B., ed. *Le Saint–Siège dans les relations internationales*. Paris: Cerf, 1989.

Dorr, Donal. "The New Social Encyclical." *The Furrow* 32 (1981): 700–712.

Duncan, Roger. "On Reading *Laborem Exercens*." *Homiletic and Pastoral Review* 86 (July 1986): 11–19.

Etchegary, Roger. "Presentation at the Press Conference for the Presentation of *Centesimus Annus*." *L'Osservatore Romano* 18 (1991): 1, 4.

———. "Presentation at the Press Conference for the Publication of *Sollicitudo Rei Socialis*." *L'Osservatore Romano* 9 (1988): 14.

Ethical and Pastoral Dimensions of Population Trends. Vatican City: Pontifical Council for the Family, Libreria Editrice Vaticana, 1994.

Faley, Roland James. "Pope as Prophet: The New Social Encyclical." *America* 158 (1988): 447–450.

Fantoli, Annibale. *Galileo: per il Copernicanesimo e per la Chiesa*. Vatican City: Libreria Editrice Vaticana, 1993.

"Fasting and Solidarity": Pontifical Messages for Lent. Vatican City: Pontifical Council Cor Unum. 1991.

Faulhaber, Robert William. "The Church and Culture—John Paul II's 'On Human Work'." *Listening* 18 (1983): 103–118.

Filibeck, Giorgio. *Les Droits de l'Homme dans l'Enseignement de l'Église: De Jean XXIII à Jean–Paul II.* Vatican City: Libreria Editrice Vaticana, 1992.

———. *The Social Teaching of John Paul II: Human Rights* . Vatican City Press, 1980.

Fiore, Benjamin. "*Laborem Exercens.*" in *The Thought of John Paul II: A Collection of Essays and Studies.* Edited by John M. McDermott. Rome: Gregorian University Press, 1983, 231–236.

Fonseca, Aloysius J. "Reflections on the Encyclical Letter *Sollicitudo Rei Socialis.*" *Gregorianum* 70 (1989): 5–24.

Fortin, Ernest L. "Free Markets Have Their Limits: Three Cheers For Capitalism." *Crisis* 10 (November 1992): 20–25.

Gargantini, Mario. *I Papi E La Scienza: Antologia del magistero della Chiesa sulla questione scientifica da Leone XIII a Giovanni Paolo II.* Milano: Jaca Book, 1985.

Gini, Al. "Meaningful Work and the Rights of the Worker: A Commentary on *Rerum Novarum* and *Laborem Exercens.*" *Thought* 67 (1992): 225–239.

Ginsburg, Helen. "Teachings of John Paul II on Work and Rights of Workers." *Social Thought* 13 (Spring/Summer 1987): 46–59.

Glemp, Jozef. "Human Work in the Teaching of Our Holy Father John Paul II." in *John Paul II: A Panorama of His Teachings.* Preface by Joseph Bernardin. New York: New City Press, 1989, 144–160.

Guttierrez, Gustavo. *The Pope and Revolution: John Paul II Confronts Liberation Theology.* Washington, D. C.: Ethics and Public Policy Center, 1982.

Guttierrez, Gustavo, Francis McDonagh, Cândido Padin O. S. B. and John Sobrino, S. J. *Santo Domingo and After: The Challenges for the Latin American Church.* London: Catholic Institute for International Relations, 1993.

Haas, Richard: "The Market Place." *Living Prayer* 27 (July/August 1994): 10–11.

Habiger, Matthew. *Papal Teaching on Private Property 1891–1981.* Lanham: University Press of America, 1990.

————. "Reflections on *Centesimus Annus.*" *Social Justice Review* 82 (1991): 139–142.

————. "Situating *Sollicitudo Rei Socialis* in Catholic Social Teaching." *Social Justice Review* 79 (1988): 138–144.

Hanson, Eric O. *The Catholic Church in World Politics*. Princeton, NJ: Princeton University Press, 1987.

Hauerwas, Stanley. "In Praise of *Centesimus Annus.*" in *To Do Justice and Right Upon Earth*. Edited by Mary E. Stamps. Collegeville: Liturgical Press, 1993. 63–83.

Hebblethwaite, Margaret. *Basic is Beautiful: Base Ecclesial Communities from Third World to First World*. London: HaperCollins, 1993.

Heckel, Roger. *The Social Teaching of John Paul II: Basis for Motivations and Ways of the Church's Intervention on Socio–Political Issues*. Vatican City Press, 1981.

————. "Continuity and Renewal." *L'Osservatore Romano* 40 (1981): 4–5.

————. *The Social Teaching of John Paul II: General Aspects of the Social Catechesis of John Paul II—The Use of the Expression 'Social Doctrine' of the Church*. Vatican City Press, 1980.

————. *The Social Teaching of John Paul II: The Human Person and Social Structures*. Vatican City Press, 1980.

————. *The Social Teaching of John Paul II: Religious Freedom*. Vatican City Press, 1980.

————. *The Social Teaching of John Paul II: The Theme of Liberation*. Vatican City Press, 1980.

————. *The Struggle Against Racism: Some Contributions of the Church*. Vatican City Press, 1979.

Hehir, J. Bryan. "Challenge to a Tradition." *Commonweal* 108 (1981): 522.

————. "Papal Foreign Policy." *Foreign Policy* (Spring 1990).

————. "Reordering the World." *Commonweal* (June 14, 1991): 393–394.

————. "Taking on the Super–Rivals: Reactions to the Pope's Latest Encyclical." *Commonweal* 115 (1988): 169–170.

Hennelly, Alfred T. "Pope John Paul's Spirituality of Work." *America* 146 (1982): 31–33.

Higgins, George G. with William Bole. *Organized Labor and the Church.* Mahweh, NJ: Paulist Press, 1993.

Hittinger, Russell. "The Pope and the Liberal State." *First Things* 28 (1992): 33–41.

Hoffe, Otfried. *Jean Paul II et les Droits de l'Homme.* Fribourg: Édition Saint–Paul, 1980.

Hollenbach, David. "Christian Social Ethics After the Cold War." *Theological Studies* 53 (1992): 75–95.

———. "The Pope and Capitalism." *America* 164 (1991): 590–591.

The Holy See at the Service of Peace: Pope John Paul II's Addresses to the Diplomatic Corps (1978– 1988). Vatican City: Pontifical Council for Justice and Peace, 1988.

Houck, John W. and Oliver F. Williams, eds. *Co–creation and Capitalism: John Paul II's Laborem Exercens.* Washington D.C.: University Press of America, 1983.

Human Rights and the Church: Historical and Theological Reflections. Vatican City: Pontifical Council for Justice and Peace, 1990.

International Economics: Interdependence and Dialogue. Vatican City: Pontifical Council for Justice and Peace, 1984.

Joblin, Joseph, S.J. "Doctrine et action sociale: Reflexion Sur l'Évolution du Movement Social Chrétien Avant et Après *Rerum Novarum.*" *Rerum Novarum Laborem Exercens 2000: Symposium* (1982): 89–114.

Johnson, Paul. *Pope John Paul II and the Catholic Restoration.* New York: St. Martin's Press, 1981.

Kaiser, R. B. *The Politics of Sex and Religion.* Kansas City, MO: Leaven Press, 1985.

Kelley, John J. "The Silence about Subsidiarity." *America* 145 (1981): 382–383.

Kennedy, Robert G. *Dignity of Work: John Paul II Speaks to Managers and Workers.* Lanham, Maryland: University Press of America, 1994.

Keston College. *Religion in Communist Lands*, Vol. 9 Nos. 1 – 2.

Kiliroor, Matthew. "Social Doctrine in *Sollicitudo Rei Socialis.*" *The Month* 21 (1988): 711–714.

Krys, Roman. "Collective Political Human Rights According to Pope John Paul II." *Revue Belge de Droit International* (1981).

———. "Individual Human Rights According to Pope John Paul II." *Revue de Droit International de Sciences Diplomatiques et Politiques* 3.

Kuzcynski, Janusz. "To Elevate the World: The Potential of Pope John Paul II's Pontificate." *Dialectics and Humanism, The Polish Philosophical Quarterly* Vol. 6 (1979): 3–27.

Lader, Lawrence. *Politics, Power and the Church: The Catholic Crisis and Its Challenge to American Pluralism.* New York: Macmillan, 1987.

Langan, Thomas. "The Strained Theology of Gregory Baum." *This World* 6 (Fall 1983): 71–84.

Lawler, Philip F., ed. *Papal Economics.* Washington: Heritage Foundation, 1981.

Loades, Anne L., ed. "On *Centesimus Annus.*" *Theology* 95 (1992): 405–432.

Lopinski, Maciej, Marcin Moskit and Mariusz Wilk. *Konspira: Solidarity Underground.* Berkeley: University of Berkeley Press, 1990.

Lynn, Thomas D. "Of Politics, Catholics and the Social Doctrine." *Social Justice Review* 84 (1993): 18–21.

Mahoney, Roger M. "Perspectives for Viewing the Social Concerns Encyclical." *Origins* 18 (1988): 69–72.

McCormick, Patrick. "*Centesimus Annus.*" in *The New Dictionary of Catholic Social Thought.* Edited by Judith A. Dwyer. Collegeville: *Liturgical Press*, 1994. 132–143.

———. "That They May Converse: Voices of Catholic Social Thought." *Cross Currents* 42 (Winter 1992): 521–527.

McDermott, John M. ed. *The Thought of Pope John Paul II.* Rome: Gregorian University, 1993.

McGurn, William. "*Sollicitudo Rei Socialis.*" in *A Century of Catholic Social Thought.* Edited by George Weigel and Robert Royal. Lanham: University Press of America, 1991, 163–176.

Morneau, Robert F. "The Church's Social Concerns: Ten Lessons." *Emmanuel* 95 (1989): 70–73.

———. *Themes and Theses of Six Recent Papal Documents: A Commentary.* New York: Alba House, 1985, 111–135.

Mourgeon, J. *Les Droits de l'Homme*. Paris: PUF, 1978.

Murphy, William, Msgr. *The Social Teaching of John Paul II: The Person, the Nation and the State*. Vatican City Press, 1980.

Myers, Kenneth A., ed. *Aspiring to Freedom: Commentaries on John Paul II's Encyclical "The Social Concerns of the Church."* Grand Rapids: Eerdmans, 1988.

Naughton, Michael J. "The Virtuous Manager and *Centesimus Annus*." *Social Justice Review* 85 (1994): 150–152.

Nell–Breuning , Oswald V. *Soziallehre der Kirche: Erlauterungen der lehramtlichen Dokumente*. Zurich: Eropaverlag, 1983.

———. *Arbeit vor Kapital: Kommentar zur Enzyklika Laborem Exercens von Johannes Paul II*. Zurich: Europaverlag, 1983.

Neuhaus, Richard John. *Doing Well and Doing Good: The Challenge to the Christian Capitalist*. New York: Doubleday, 1992.

———. "John Paul's 'Second Thoughts' on Capitalism." *First Things* 41 (1994): 65–67.

Novak, Michael. *The Catholic Ethic and the Spirit of Capitalism*. New York: The Free Press, 1993.

———. *Catholic Social Thought and Liberal Institutions*. New Brunswick, New Jersey: Transaction Publishers, 2nd.

———. *The Spirit of Democratic Capitalism*. New York: Simon and Schuster, 1992.

Preston R. H. "*Centesimus Annus*: An Appraisal." *Theology* 95 (1992): 405–416.

Preston, Ronald. "Twenty Years After *Populorum Progressio*: An Appraisal of Pope John Paul's Commemorative Encyclical." *Theology* 92 (1989): 519–525.

Preston, Ronald H. "Pope John Paul II on Work." *Theology* 86 (January 1983): 19–24.

Przetacznik, Frank. *The Catholic Concept of Genuine and Just Peace as a Basic Collective Human Right*. Lewiston, New York: The Edwin Mellen Press, 1991.

Quade, Quentin, ed. *The Pope and the Revolution: John Paul II Confronts Liberation Theology*. Washington, D. C.: Ethics and Public Policy Center, 1982.

Rauscher, Anton. "Laborem Exercens Within the Context of the Church's Commitment to the Work of Peace and Justice." *Rerum Novarum Laborem Exercens 2000: Symposium* (1982): 179.

Refugees: A Challenge to Solidarity. Vatican City: Pontifical Council for the Care of Migrants and Itinerant People, Libraria Editrice Vaticana, 1992.

Romero, Oscar Archbishop. "La Liberación Integral en América Latina." *Opiniones Latinoamericanas* (June 1979).

Roos, Lothar. "On Theology and Ethics of Work." *Communio* 11 (1984): 136–144.

Rossi, Romano, Msgr. *The Social Teaching of John Paul II: Human Labor*. Vatican City Press, 1981.

Schall, James. "The Teaching of *Centesimus Annus*." *Gregorianum* 74 (1993): 17–43.

Schall, James V., S. J. , ed. "Capitalism, Business and Human Priorities." in J. W. Houck and O. F. Williams, eds. *The Judeo–Christian Vision of the Modern Corporation*. Notre Dame, IN: University of Notre Dame Press, 1982.

———. *The Church, the State and Society in the Thought of John Paul II*. Chicago: Franciscan Herald Press, 1982.

———. *Sacred in All its Forms*. Boston: St. Paul Editions, 1984.

———. "The Unexpected Encyclical." *Social Justice Review* (September/ October 1991): 143–147.

Schambeck, Herbert. "State Cannot Create Human Values but Only Respect and Promote Them." *L'Osservatore Romano* 35 (1995): 6.

Schotte, Jan. "The Social Teaching of the Church: *Laborem Exercens*, A New Challenge." *Review of Social Economy* 40 (1982): 340–357.

Schotte, Jan, C. I. C. M. and the Pontificia Commissio Justitia et Pax , eds. *Rerum Novarum Laborem Exercens 2000: Symposium*. Rome: Instituto Pio XI, 1982.

Selling, Joseph A. "The Theological Presuppositions of *Centesimus Annus*." *Louvain Studies* 17 (Spring 1192): 35–47.

Seminar on Pope John Paul II's Encyclical *Sollicitudo Rei Socialis*. *L'Osservatore Romano* 45 (1988): Supplement, i–viii.

Six, Jean–François. *Church and Human Rights*. United Kingdom: Saint Paul Publications, 1992.

"Socialism and Antheism." *Dialectics and Humanism, The Polish Philosophical Quarterly* (January 1987).

"The Solidarity Encyclical." Editorial. *America* 158 (1988): 251.

"*Sollicitudo Rei Socialis*." Editorial. *Commonweal* 115 (1988): 131–132.

Sorge, Bartolome. "*Laborem Exercens*: Toward a New Solidarity." in *Official Catholic Social Teaching: Readings in Moral Theology*. Edited by Charles Curran and Richard McCormick. Vol. 5. New York: Paulist Press, 1986, 241–246.

Spasowski, Romuald. *The Liberation of One*. Orlando, Florida: Harcourt Brace Jovanovich, 1986.

Spiazzi, Raimondo. *I documenti sociali della Chiesa. Da Pio IX a Giovanni Paolo II (1864–1982)*. Milan: Massimo, 1983.

———. "Gospel of Work and Dignity of Man." *L'Osservatore Romano* 41 (1981): 9–10.

Suro, Roberto. "The Writing of *Sollicitudo Rei Socialis*: A Behind–the–Scenes Account." *Critic* 6 (May 1988): 13–18.

"Symposium on *Centesimus Annus*." *The Pope Speaks* 37 (1992): 80–82.

Traffas, John R. "The Spirit of Community and the Spirituality of Work: A Note on *Laborem Exercens*." *Communio* 10 (1983): 407–411.

Tucker, Jeffrey A. "Papal Economics 101: The Catholic Ethic and the Spirit of Capitalism." *Crisis* 9 (June 1991): 16–21.

Turner, Frank. "John Paul II's Social Analysis." *The Month* 24 (1991): 344–349.

Utz, Arthur F. "*Centesimus Annus* Gives Us a Profoundly Ethical View of Social and Economic Politics." *L'Osservatore Romano* 28 (1991): 8, 10.

Vasak, K. *Les Dimensions Internationales des Droits de l'Homme*. UNESCO, 1978.

Villey, M. *Philosophie du Droit*. Paris: Dalloz, 1979.

Volf, Miroslav. "On Human Work: An Evaluation of the Key Ideas of the Encyclical *Laborem Exercens.*" *Scottish Journal of Theology* 37 (1984): 65–67.

Walsh, Michael and Brian Davies, eds. *Proclaiming Justice and Peace.* Mystic CT: Twenty–Third Publications, 1991.

Weigel, George, ed. *A New Worldly Order: John Paul II and Human Freedom.* Washington, D. C.: Ethics and Public Policy Center, 1991.

White, Robert Edward. "Blaming the Villians, not the Victim: John Paul II and the Superpowers." *Commonweal* 115 (1988): 555–559.

Williams, George Huntston. *The Contours of the Church and State in Thought of John Paul II.* Waco, Texas: Baylor University Press, 1983.

———. *The Law of Nations and the Book of Nature.* Collegeville, Minnesota: St. John's University Press, 1984.

———.*The Mind of John Paul II: Origins of His Thought and Action.* New York: Seabury Press, 1981.

Williams, Oliver F. and John W. Houck, eds. *The Making of an Economic Vision: John Paul II's "On Social Concern."* Lanham: University Press of America, 1991.

Williams, Paul L., ed. *Catholic Social Thought and the Teaching of John Paul II.* Scranton, PA: Northeast Books, 1983.

Wood, Jr., James E. and Derek Davis, eds. *The Role of Religion in the Making of Public Policy.* Waco, Texas: Baylor University Press, 1991.

Woodrow, Alain. "The Pope's Challenge to Western Democracy." *The Tablet* 249 (1995): 448–449.

Wright, Clive. "Work, Life–style and Gospel." *The Way* 34 (April 1994): 126–137.

History–Biography–Spirituality

Accattoli, Luigi. *Io ho Avuto Paura a Ricevere Questa Nomina.* Torino: Società Editrice Internazionale, 1993.

Actes et Documents du Saint Siège relatifs à la seconde guerre mondiale, II, La Sainte Siège et la situation religieuse en Polonge et dans les pays baltes. 2 Vols. Rome: Vatican Press, 1967.

Andreotti, Giulio. *Ad ogni morte di Papa.* Milan: Rizzoli, 1980.

Andrews, T. *The Polish National Catholic Church in America and Poland.* London: SPCK, 1953.

Annuario Pontifico 1994. Vatican City: Libreria Editrice Vaticana, 1994.

Arias, Juan. *El Enigma Wojtyla.* Madrid: Ediciones El Pais, 1985.

―――. *L'enigma Wojtyla.* Rome: Borla, 1986.

Ash, Timothy Garton. *Polish Revolution: Solidarity.* New York: Scribners, 1983.

―――. *The Magic Lantern.* New York: Random House, 1990.

―――. *The Uses of Adversity.* New York: Vintage, 1990.

―――. *We the People.* Cambridge: Granta Books, 1990.

Ascherson, Neal. *The Struggles for Poland.* London: M. Joseph, 1987.

Asherson, Newl. *The Polish August: The Self Limiting Revolution.* New York: Viking Press, 1982.

Baker, K., "John Paul II in the United States of America." *Homiletic and Pastoral Review* 80 (January 1980): 21–27.

Bergonzoni, Luciano. *Emilia Kaczorowska in Wojtyla.* Edizioni Carroccio, Vigodarzere, 1998.

―――. *Edmondo Wojtyla.* Padova: Centro Editoriale Cattolico Carroccio, 1992.

Bernstein, Carl and Marco Politi. *His Holiness.* New York: Doubleday, 1996.

Blazynski, George. *John Paul II: A Man From Krakow.* London: Weidenfeld & Nicolson, 1979.

―――. *Pope John Paul II: A Biography.* London: Weidenfeld & Nicolson, and New York: William Morrow, 1979.

Briggs, Kenneth. *Holy Siege: The Year That Shook Catholic America.* San Francisco: Harper San–Francisco, 1992.

Brumberg, Abraham, ed. *Poland: Genesis of a Revolution.* New York: Random House, 1983.

Cannon, Lou. *President Reagan: The Role of a Lifetime.* New York: Simon and Schuster, 1991.

Chelini, Jean. *La vita quotidiana in Vaticano sotto Giovanni Paolo II.* Milan: Rizzoli, 1986.

Comas, José. *Polonia y Solidaridad*. Madrid: Ediciones El País, 1985.

Conway, Ronald. "Papal Obsessions." *World Press Review* (December 1993): 45.

Cooney, John. *The American Pope: The Life and Times of Francis Cardinal Spellman*. New York: Times Books, 1984.

Craig, Mary. *The Crystal Spirit*. London: Hodder & Stoughton, 1986.

————. *Man from a Far Country: A Portrait of Pope John Paul II*. New York: Morrow, 1979.

Davies, Norman. *God's Playground: A History of Poland*. Vols. 1 and 2. New York: Columbia University Press, 1982.

Davis, Raymond, trans. And ed. *The Book of Pontiffs (Liber Pontificalis)*. Liverpool: Liverpool University Press, 1989.

Della Rocca, Fernando. *Papi di Questo Secolo*. Padova, Italy: Cedam, 1981.

de Roeck, Jef. *The Man from Poland*. Trans. Jack Reide. Methuen.

Dobrowski, Tadeusz. *Polish Painting from the Enlightenment to Recent Times*. Warsaw: Ossolineum, 1981.

Dostoevski, F. M. *Memorie dal sottosuolo*. Torino, 1980.

Finke, Roger and Rodney Stark. *The Churching of America: 1776–1990*. New Brunswick, New Jersey: Rutgers University Press, 1992.

Fisher, Loren, ed. *Pope John Paul II An American Celebration*. Somerville, New Jersey: Elf Publishing, 1995.

Frossard, André. *"Be Not Afraid!": Pope John Paul II speaks out on His Life, His Beliefs, and His Inspiring Vision for Humanity*. Trans. J. R. Foster. New York: St. Martin's Press, 1984.

————. *Diálogo con Juan Pablo II*. Milan: Rusconi, 1983.

————. *Portrait de Jean–Paul II*. Paris: Éditions Robert Laffont, 1988.

————. *Portrait of John Paul II*. San Francisco: Ignatius Press, 1988.

————. *Portret Jan Pawla II*. Kraków: Wydawnictwo Znak, 1988.

Gawronski, Jas. *Il Mondo di Giovanni Paolo II*. Milan: Mondadori, 1994.

Gelmi, Josef. *Die Päpste in Lebensbildern*. Vienna: Verlag Styria, 1989.

Ginsborg, Paul. *A History of Contemporary Italy*. New York: Penguin, 1990.

Gligora, Francesco, and Biagia Catanzaro. *Storia dei Papi e degli Antipapi da San Pietro a Giovanni Paolo II*, 2 Vols. Rome: Panda Edizioni, 1989.

Gorbachev, Mikhail. *Erinnerungen*. Berlin: Siedler Verlag, 1995.

———. *Perestroika: New Thinking for Our Country and the World*. New York: Haper and Row, 1987.

Greeley, Andrew M. *A Catholic Myth: The Behavior and Beliefs of American Catholics*. New York: Collier Books, Macmillan, 1990.

———. *The Making of the Popes*. London: Futura, 1979.

———. *The Making of the Popes 1978: The Politics of Intrigue in the Vatican*. Kansas City, Kansas: Andrews and McMeel, 1979.

Grygiel, Stanislaw. *L'uomo vista della Vistola*. Bologna: CSEO, 1978.

Haig, Alexander. *Caveat: Realism, Reagan and Foreign Policy*. New York: Macmillan, 1984.

Hebblethwaite, Peter. *In The Vatican*. New York: Oxford Univerisity Press, 1987.

———. *The Papal Year*. London: Cassell, Ltd., 1981.

———. *Paul VI*. London: HarperCollins, 1993.

———. *Paul VI: The First Modern Pope*. New York: Paulist Press, 1993.

———. "Pope John Paul II as Philosopher and Poet." *The Heythrop Journal* XXI (1980).

———. *Synod Extraordinary*. London: Darton, Longman & Todd, 1985.

———. *The Year of Three Popes*. Cleveland: William Collins, 1979.

Hebblethwaite, Peter and Ludwig Kaufmann. *John Paul II: A Pictorial Biography*. Maidenhead, England: McGraw–Hill Book Company, 1979.

Herman, Edward S. and Frank Brodhead. *The Rise and Fall of the Bulgarian Connection*. New York: Sheridan Square Publications, 1986.

Hitchcock, James. *Pope John Paul II & American Catholicism*. New York: The National Committee of Catholic Laymen, Inc.

Honea, Charles H., ed. *A Reader's Companion to Crossing the Threshold of Hope*. Brewster, MA: Paraclete Press, 1996.

Jaruzelski, Wojciech. *Erinnerungen*. Munchen: Piper, 1993.

Jennings, Peter and Eamonn McCabe. *The Pope in Britain: Pope John Paul II British Visit, 1982.* London: Bodley Head, 1982.

Johnson Paul. *Pope John Paul II.* London, 1982.

Karolek, Tadeusz. *John Paul II: The Pope from Poland.* Trans. David Evans. Warsaw: Interpress Publishers, 1979.

Kreutz, Andej. *Vatican Policy on the Palestinian–Israeli Conflict.* New York: Greenwood Press, 1990.

"La biographie du nouveau pape." *Documentation Catholique* 75 (November 5, 1978): 906–907.

Lapide, P. *The Last Three Popes and the Jews.* London, 1967.

Le Corre, Dominique and Mark Sabotka. *John Paul II in Poland: 2–10 June 1979.* Bagnolet, France: Le Corre, 1979.

Lernoux, Penny. *People of God: The Struggle for World Catholicism.* New York: Viking Press, 1989.

Levillain, Phillipe and Francois–Charles Uginet. *Il Vaticano o le frontiere della grazia.* Milan: Rizzoli, 1985.

Libanio, Christo and Carlos Alberto. *Diaro di Puebla.* Brescia: Ed. Queriniana, 1979.

Licheri, Gianni. *Quel conclave e poi Wojtyla jet.* Brescia: Queriniana, 1979.

Longford, Lord. *Pope John Paul II: An Authorized Biography.* New York: William Morrow and Company, 1982.

Macciocchi, M. A. *Di là dalle Porte di Bronzo.* Milan: Mondadori, 1987.

MacDowell, Bart. *Inside the Vatican.* Washington: National Geographic Society, 1991.

MacEoin, Gary. *The Inner Elite.* Kansas City: Sheed, Andrews and McMeel, 1978.

Maffeo, Sabino, S. J. *In the Service of Nine Popes: 100 Years of the Vatican Observatory.* Vatican City: The Vatican Observatory and the Pontifical Academy of Sciences, 1991.

Malinski, Mieczyslaw. *Il mio vecchio amico Karol.* Rome: Ed. Paoline, 1980.

———. *The Life of Karol Wojtyla.* Trans. P. S. Falla. New York: Doubleday, 1979.

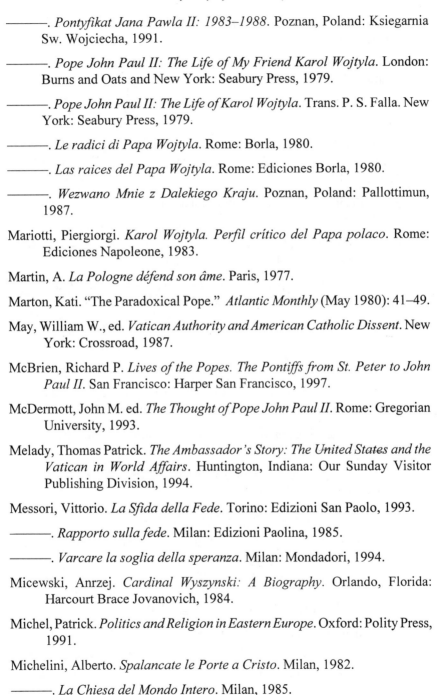

———. *Pontyfikat Jana Pawla II: 1983–1988*. Poznan, Poland: Ksiegarnia Sw. Wojciecha, 1991.

———. *Pope John Paul II: The Life of My Friend Karol Wojtyla*. London: Burns and Oats and New York: Seabury Press, 1979.

———. *Pope John Paul II: The Life of Karol Wojtyla*. Trans. P. S. Falla. New York: Seabury Press, 1979.

———. *Le radici di Papa Wojtyla*. Rome: Borla, 1980.

———. *Las raices del Papa Wojtyla*. Rome: Ediciones Borla, 1980.

———. *Wezwano Mnie z Dalekiego Kraju*. Poznan, Poland: Pallottimun, 1987.

Mariotti, Piergiorgi. *Karol Wojtyla. Perfil crítico del Papa polaco*. Rome: Ediciones Napoleone, 1983.

Martin, A. *La Pologne défend son âme*. Paris, 1977.

Marton, Kati. "The Paradoxical Pope." *Atlantic Monthly* (May 1980): 41–49.

May, William W., ed. *Vatican Authority and American Catholic Dissent*. New York: Crossroad, 1987.

McBrien, Richard P. *Lives of the Popes. The Pontiffs from St. Peter to John Paul II*. San Francisco: Harper San Francisco, 1997.

McDermott, John M. ed. *The Thought of Pope John Paul II*. Rome: Gregorian University, 1993.

Melady, Thomas Patrick. *The Ambassador's Story: The United States and the Vatican in World Affairs*. Huntington, Indiana: Our Sunday Visitor Publishing Division, 1994.

Messori, Vittorio. *La Sfida della Fede*. Torino: Edizioni San Paolo, 1993.

———. *Rapporto sulla fede*. Milan: Edizioni Paolina, 1985.

———. *Varcare la soglia della speranza*. Milan: Mondadori, 1994.

Micewski, Anrzej. *Cardinal Wyszynski: A Biography*. Orlando, Florida: Harcourt Brace Jovanovich, 1984.

Michel, Patrick. *Politics and Religion in Eastern Europe*. Oxford: Polity Press, 1991.

Michelini, Alberto. *Spalancate le Porte a Cristo*. Milan, 1982.

———. *La Chiesa del Mondo Intero*. Milan, 1985.

Michnik, Adam. *The Church and the Left*. Chicago: University of Chicago Press, 1993.

————. *Letters from Prison and Other Essays*. Berkeley: University of California Press, 1985.

Murphey, Francis X. *The Papacy Today*. London: Weidenfeld and Nicolson, 1981.

National Catholic News Service. *Nights of Sorrow, Days of Joy: Papal Transition, Paul VI, John Paul I, John Paul II*. Washington: The Service, 1978.

Naughton, Michael. *The Good Stewards*. Lanham, Maryland: University Press of America, 1992.

Nemic, L. *John Paul II. A Festive Profile*. New York: Catholic Book Publishing Co., 1979.

Nichols, Bruce. *The Uneasy Alliance: Religion, Refugee Work and U. S. Foreign Policy*. New York: Oxford University Press, 1988.

Nichols, Peter. *The Pope's Divisions: the Roman Catholic Church Today*. Faber and Faber.

O'Brien, Darcy. *The Hidden Pope*. New York: DayBreak Books, 1998.

O'Byrne, Seamus, ed. *Challange or Crisis?: Texts by Pope John Paull II on Religious Life*. Dublin, Ireland: Veritas Publications, 1987.

O'Carroll, Michael. *Poland and John Paul II*. Dublin: Veritas Publications, 1979.

Ockrent, Christine and Alexandre De Marenches. *Dans le secret des princes*. Paris: Edition Stock, 1986.

Oram, James. *The People's Pope*. Sydney: Bay Books.

Parker, Michael. *Priest of the World's Destiny: John Paul II*. Milford, Ohio: Faith Publishing Company, 1995.

Perea, Francisco J. *El Papa en México*. México: Editorial Diana, 1979.

Persico, Joseph E. *Casey*. New York: Viking, 1990.

Piekarski, Adam. *The Church in Poland*. Warsaw: Interpress Publishers, 1978.

Pope John Paul II on Jews and Judaism: 1979–1986. Washington, D.C.: Office for Publishing and Promotion Services, United States Catholic Conference, 1987.

Priesthood In the Third Millennium: Adresses of Pope John Paul II—1993. Compiled by Rev. James P. Socias. New Jersey: Scepter Publishers, 1994.

Quinn, J. "An Open Moment for Faith." *Origins* 9 (November 22, 1979): 365.

Ramet, Pedro, ed. *Catholicism and Politics in Communist Societies.* Durham, NC: Duke University Press, 1990.

Reese, Thomas J., S. J. *Archbishop: Inside the Power Structure of the American Catholic Church.* New York: Harper and Row, 1989.

————. *A Flock of Shepherds: The National Conference of Catholic Bishops.* Kansas City: Sheed and Ward, 1992.

Rendina, Claudio. *I Papi.* Rome: Newton Compton Editori, 1983.

Rhynne, Xavier. *John Paul's Extraordinary Synod.* Wilmington, Del.: Michael Glazier, 1986.

Ricciardi, Andrea E. *Il Potere del Papa: da Pio XII a Giovanni–Paolo II.* Rome: Editori Laterza, 1993.

————. *Il Vaticano e Mosca 1940–1990.* Rome: Editori Laterza, 1993.

Richard, Lucien, O. M. I., Daniel Harrington, S. J. and John W. O'Malley, S. J., eds. *Vatican II: The Unfinished Agenda: A Look to the Future.* Mahweh, NJ: Paulist Press, 1987.

Roeck, Jefd. *Juan Pablo II: El Hombre Que Vino de Polonia.* Averbode, Belgium: Verlag Altiora, 1978.

Romero, Oscar Archbishop. *A Shepherd's Diary.* Cincinnati: St. Anthony Messenger Press, 1986.

Rosenberg, Tina. *The Haunted Land.* New York: Random House, 1995.

Ruiz, José María González. *Memoria del concilio.* Rome: Borla, 1985.

Rynne, Catherine. *Knock 1879–1979.* Dublin: Veritatas, 1979.

Schopflin, George. *Politics in Eastern Europe 1945–92.* Oxford: Blackwell, 1993.

Svidercoschi, Gianfranco. *Lettera a un amico ebreo.* Milan: Mondadori, 1993.

————. *Letter To A Jewish Friend.* New York: Crossroad Publishing Company. 1994.

Synod of 1985. Extraordinary. Boston: St. Paul Editions, 1986

Synodus Extraordinaria. Relatio Finalis. L'Osservatore Romano (December 10, 1985): Supplement.

Szajkowski, Bogdan. *Next to God . . . Poland: Politics and Religion in Contemporary Poland.* New York: St. Martin's, 1983.

Szoldrski, O. W., C.S.S.R., *Martyrologium Cleri Polonici sub occupatione Germanica, 1939–1945.* Rome, 1965.

Szostak. John M. and Frances Spatz Leighton. *In the Footsteps of Pope John Paul II: An Intimate Personal Portrait.* Englewood Cliffs, NJ: Prentice Hall, 1980.

Szulc, Tad. *Pope John Paul II: The Biography.* New York: Scribner, 1995.

Tajne Dokumenty, Panstwo Kosciól: 1980–1989. London: Aneks Publishers, 1993.

Talks of John Paul II. Boston: Daughters of St. Paul, 1979.

Thatcher, Margaret. *The Downing Street Years.* London: HarperCollins, 1993.

Thomas, Gordon and Max Morgan–Witts. *Averting Armageddon.* New York: Doubleday, 1984.

———. *Pontiff.* Garden City, NJ: Doubleday, 1983.

Tulat, Jean. *Le Pape Contre le Guerre du Golfe.* Paris: Oeil, 1991.

Uboldi, Rafaello. *Vita di Papa Wojtyla.* Milan: Rizzoli, 1983.

Vircondelet, Alain. *Jean–Paul II: Biographie.* Paris: Édition Juilliard, 1994.

Von Rauch, Georg. *A History of Soviet Russia.* Trans. Peter and Annette Jacobsohn. New York: Frederick A. Praeger.

Wahle, Hedwig. *Das Gemeinsame Erbe Judentum und Christentum in Heilsgeschichtlichem Zusammenhang.* Innsbruck, Austria, 1980.

Walesa, Lech. *The Struggle and The Triumph: An Autobiography.* New York: Arcade, 1992.

Vree, Dale. *Un Chemin d'Espoir: Autobiographie.* Paris: Fayard, 1987.

———. *A Way of Hope: An Autobiography.* New York: Henry Holt, 1987.

Walsh, Michael. *John Paul II.* London: Harper Collins, 1994.

Wandycsz, Piotr. *A History of East Central Europe, Volume VII (The Lands of Partitioned Poland, 1795 –1918).* University of Washington Press.

Weschler, Lawrence. *The Passion of Poland.* New York: Pantheon Books, 1984.

Whale, John (ed.). *The Pope from Poland: An Assessment.* London: Collins, 1980.

Whale John, ed. and Peter Hebblethwaite. *The Man Who Leads the Church: An Assessment of Pope John Paul II.* San Francisco: Harper & Row, 1980.

Will, George. "A Pope with Authority." *Newsweek* (June 23, 1980): 92.

Willebrands, Johannes Cardinal. *The Church and Jewish People: New Considerations.* Mahweh, New Jersey: Paulist Press, 1992.

Willey, David. *God's Politician: Pope John Paul II, the Catholic Church and the New World Order.* New York: Saint Martin's Press, 1992.

Wills, Garry. *Under God: Religion and American Politics.* New York: Simon and Schuster, 1990.

Winn, Wilton. *Keepers of the Keys: John XXIII, Paul VI and John Paul II: Three Who Changed the Church.* New York: Random House, 1988.

Woodward, Bob. *Veil.* New York: Simon and Schuster, 1987.

Wynn, Wilton. *Keeper of the Keys.* New York: Random House, 1988.

Wyszynski, Stefan Cardinal. *Work.* London, 1966.

———. *A Strong Man Armed.* London, 1966.

Zizola, Giancarlo. *Il Conclave: Storia i segreti, L'elezione papale da San Pietro a Giovanni Paolo II.* Rome: Newtown Compton Editori, 1993.

———. *Le restaurazioni di papa Wojtyla.* Bari: Laterza, 1985.

———. *Le successeur.* Paris: Desclèe de Brouwer, 1995.

Ecumenism

"An Offer from the Pope." *The Tablet* 249 (1995): 694–695.

"Applause for the Pope's Unity Call—with Reservations." *The Tablet* 249 (1995): 714.

Bouboutsis, E. K. "Toward Unity with Diversity and Equality." *Ecumenical Trends* 25 (1996): 10–12.

Cassidy, Edward Idris. "*Ut Unum Sint* and the Great Jubilee Year 2000." *Bulletin* [Centro Pro Unione] 49 (Spring 1996): 3–8.

Cassidy, Edward Idris and Eleuterio F. Fortino. "Comment on the Encyclical Letter *Ut Unum Sint* of the Holy Father Pope John Paul II on Commitment to Ecumenism." *Information Service* [Pontifical Council for Promoting Christian Unity] 89 (1995): 83–87.

Crow, P. A. "One of the Most Powerful Witnesses in Recent Time." *Inside the Oikoumene* 9 (1995): 6–8.

Directory for the Application of Principles and Norms on Ecumenism. Vatican City: Pontifical Council for Christian Unity, 1993.

McDermott, John M. ed. *The Thought of Pope John Paul II*. Rome: Gregorian University, 1993.

Mcfarlane, R. "An Aglican Response to the Encyclical *Ut Unum Sint*." *Ecumenical Trends* 25 (1996): 12–14.

Neuhaus, Richard John. "'That They May All Be One': The Pope's Twelfth Encyclical." *Crisis* 13 (September 1995): 25–27.

Nilson, J. "The Challenges of *Ut Unum Sint*." *Ecumenical Trends* 25 (1996): 8–10.

"Reactions to *Ut Unum Sint* from Protestant Churches Around the World." *Catholic International* 6 (1995): 397–398.

Reardon, Ruth. "'A Source of Joy': *Ut Unum Sint* and Interchurch Families." *One in Christ* 31 (1995): 397–398.

Stron, R. "An Aglican Response to the Papal Encyclical *Ut Unum Sint*." *Unity Digest* 13 (1995): 7–12.

Suenenes, Léon Joseph Cardinal. *Ecumenism and Charismatic Renewal*. London: Darton, Longman and Todd, 1978.

Zago, Marcello. "The Missionary Importance of the Encyclical *Ut Unum Sint*." *Omnis Terra* 29 (1995): 488–494.

Indispensable Bibliography for Understanding Pope John Paul II

Acta Apostolocae Sedis (1909–).

Acta Sanctae Sedis (1865–1908).

Acta Synodalia Sacrosancti Concilii Oecumenici Vaticana Secundi. Vatican Press, 1970.

Aquinas, Thomas. *In librium Aristotelis de caelo et mundo commentarium*. I, 1.22 (Parma edition, 1865, t. XIX, 58)

———. *Summa Theologica*. New York: Benziger Brothers, Inc., 1947

Augustine, St. *The Confessions*. New York: Collier Books, 1961.

———. *Contra Academicos (Against the Sceptics)*. *Fathers of the Church: Writings of St. Augustine* (Vol. 1). New York: Gima, 1948.

Bertetto, Domenico, S.D.B., ed. *La Madonna nella Parola di Paolo VI*. 2nd Edition. Rome: Libreria Ateneo Salesiano, 1980.

Bokenknotter, Thomas. *A Concise History of the Catholic Church*. New York: Doubleday, 1990.

Borghi, C. "Mentalità scientifica e religione." *Cristiani e società* (1980).

Bosco, Father Teresio. *Saint Maximilian Kolbe*. Melbourne: A.C.T.S. Publications.

Caprile, Giovanni. *Il Concilio Vaticano II*. Rome: La Civiltà Cattolica.

———. *Il sinodo straordinario, 1985*. Rome: La Civiltà Cattolica, 1986.

Catechism of the Catholic Church. English Translation. United States Catholic Conference, Libreria Editrice Vaticana. Mahwah, NJ, 1994.

Catholic Almanac. Huntington, Indiana: Our Sunday Visitor Publishing Division, 1994.

Christian Social Association. *Information Bulletin*, monthly. Warsaw.

Clissold, Kenneth. *The Wisdom of Spanish Mystics*. New York: New Directions, 1997.

Congar, Yves. *Je Croit en l'Esprit Saint*. vol. III. Paris: Les Editions du Cerf, 1980.

———. *La Parole et le Souffle*. Collection 'Jesus et Jesus Christ', no. 20. Paris: Desclèe, 1984.

Crosson, F. J. "Phenomenology." *New Catholic Encyclopedia*. New York: McGraw–Hill, 1967.

"Cultura impregno per l'uomo. Atti del IV convegno sul Magistero Pontificio." *La Traccia* 4 (1984).

De Fiores, Stefano, S.N.M. *Itenerario spirituale di S. Luigi Maria de Montfort (1673–1716) nel periodo fino al sacerdozio (5 giugno 1700)*. Marian Library Studies, n.s. 6. Dayton, OH: University of Dayton, 1974.

De Fiores, Stefano, S. M. M. and Salvatore Meo, O.S.M., eds. *Nuovo Dizionario di Mariologia*. Milan: Edizioni Paoline, 1985.

De Montfort, St. Louis–Marie Grignion, *Oeuvres completes de saint Louis–Marie Grignion de Montfort*. Paris: Editions du Seuill, 1982.

———. *God Alone: The Collected Writings of St. Louis Mary de Montfort*. Bay Shore, NY: Montfort Publications, 1987.

Denziger, Henricus, and Adlofus Schonmetzer, S.J., eds. *Enchiridion Symbolorum Definitionum et Declarationum de Rebus Fidei et Morum*. 32nd ed. Frieburg–im–Breisgau: Herder, 1963.

Dewar, Diana. *Saint of Auschwitz, the Story of Maksymillian Kolbe*. London: Darton, Longman and Todd.

Documentos de la Conferencia del Episcopado Dominicano: 1955–1990. República Dominicana: Colección Qunito Centenario, Santo Domingo, 1990.

Dolan, Jay P. *The American Catholic Experience: A History from Colonial Times to the Present*. Notre Dame, Indiana: University of Notre Dame Press, 1992.

Du Roy, O. J. B. "Augustine, St." *New Catholic Encyclopedia* 1: 1041–1058. New York: McGraw Hill, 1967.

Flannery, Austin, O. P. *Vatican II: The Conciliar and Post Conciliar Documents*. Boston: St. Paul Editions, 1992.

Flannery, Austin, ed. *Dignitatis Humanae, Declaration on Religious Liberty*. *Documents of Vatican II*. (December 7, 1965). Grand Rapids: William B. Eerdmans Publishing, 1975.

———. *Gaudium et Spes, Pastoral Constitution on the Church. Documents of Vatican II*. (November 21, 1964). Grand Rapids, MI: William B. Eerdmans Publishing, 1975.

———. *Lumen Gentium, Dogmatic Constitution on the Church. Documents of Vatican II*. (November 21, 1964). Grand Rapids, MI: William B. Eerdmans Publishing, 1975.

———. *Presbyterorum Ordinis, Decree on the Ministry and Life of Priests. Documents of Vatican II*. (December 7, 1965). Grand Rapids, MI: William B. Eerdmans Publishing, 1975.

Galot, Jean. *Christ De Notre Foi*. Louvain: Editions Sintal, 1986.

———. *Christ, Qui Es–Tu?* Louvain: Editions Sintal, 1985.

Garaudy, Roger. *Marxism in the 20th Century*. Trans. Rene Hague. Collins.

Garrigou–Lagrange, Reginald. *Christian Perfection and Contemplation According to St. Thomas and St. John of the Cross*. St. Louis: Herder, 1937.

————. *The Theological Virtues*. St. Louis: Herder, 1964.

Gramatowski, Wiktor and Zofia Wilinska. *Jan Pawel II: Bibiligrafia Polska 1978–1983*. Rome: Fundacja Jana Pawla II, Osrodek Dokumentacji Pontyficatu, 1987.

Gramatowski, Wiktor, Zofia Wilinska and Danuta Guzajewska. *Jan Pawel II: Bibliografia Polska 1984–1986*. Rome: Fundacja Jana Pawla II, Osrodek Dokumentacji Pontyficatu, 1991.

Grenet, Paul. *Thomism, An Introduction*, Trans. James F. Ross. Harper and Row.

Ingarden, R. *Sulla responsabilità*. Bologna, 1982.

Insegnamenti di Giovanni Paolo II. Vatican City: Libreria Editrice Vaticana, 1979–.

Insegnamenti di Paolo VI (1963–1978). 15 vols. Vatican City: Libreria Editrice Vaticana, 1965–1979.

Kalser, Robert. *The Encyclical That Never Was*. London: Sheed & Ward, 1989.

Kant, I. *Critica della Ragion patrica*. Bari: 1966, 152.

————. *Critique of Practical Reason*, I, i, 3, Chicago: University of Chicago Press, 1949.

————. *Fondazione della metafisica dei costumi*. Milano: 1982, 74

————. *Foundations of the Metaphysics of Morals*, II, Chicago: University of Chicago Press, 1949.

Kelly, J. N. D. *The Oxford Dictionary of Popes*. Oxford University Press, 1986.

Koehler, Theodore, S. M. "Mary's Spiritual Maternity after the Second Vatican Council." *Marian Studies 23* (1972): 39–68.

Kolbe, St. Maximilian, O. F. M. Conv. *Gli Scritti di Massimiliano Kolbe: eroe di Oswiecim e Beato della Chiesa*. 3 vols. Trans. Cristoforo Zambelli. Florence: Citta di Vita, 1975–1978.

Laurentin, Rene. "The Magisterium of the Church on the Alliance of the Hearts of Jesus and May." Trans. Srs. Edita Telan, M.I.C., and Rachel de Mars, M.I.C., in *The Alliance of the Hearts of Jesus and Mary: The International Theological/Pastoral Conference, Manila Phillipines, 30 November–3 December 1987, Texts and Documents*, 158–187. Manila: Bahay Maria, 1988.

———. "Mary and Womanhood in the Renewal of Christian Anthropology." *Marian Library Studies* 1: 77–95. Dayton, OH: University of Dayton, 1969.

———. *A Short Treatise on the Virgin Mary*. New Jersey: AMI Press Washington, 1991.

———. *A Year of Grace with Mary: Rediscovering Her Presence and Her Role in Our Consecration*. Trans. Msgr. Michael J. Wrenn. Dublin: Veritas, 1987.

Mahoney, Roger. "The Teaching of Revelation." *L'Osservatore Romano* 32/33 (1991): 9.

Neuner, J., S.J., and J. Dupuis, S.J., eds. *The Christian Faith in the Doctrinal Documents of the Catholic Church*. New York: Alba House, 1982.

Papfava, Francesco, ed. *The Sistine Chapel*. Vatican City: Musei Vaticani, 1992.

Paul VI. *Humanae Vitae, On Human Life*. Washington: United States Catholic Conference, 1968.

———. *Mary—God's Mother and Ours*. Boston: St. Paul Editions, 1979.

Pieper, Josef. *Introduction to Thomas Aquinas*. Trans. Richard and Clara Winston. Faber and Faber.

Pius IX. *The Bull 'Ineffabilis'*. Translated and Edited by U. J. Bourke, Printed and Published by John Mullany, 1868.

Pius XII. "Munificentissimus Deus." *Selected Documents of His Holiness Pope Pius XII 1939–1958*. National Catholic Welfare Conference, Washington, D.C.

———. *Mystici Coporis. The Mystical Body of Christ*. Washington: National Catholic Welfare Conference, 1943.

Pontifical Council for the Family. *Marriage and the Family*. San Francisco: Ignatius Press, 1987.

Poupard, Paul. *Il Concilio Vaticano II*. Edizioni Piemme, 1987.

Ratzinger, Joseph Cardinal. *Dogma y predicación.* Brescia: Queriniana, 1974.

———. *Turning Point for Europe?* San Francisco: Ignatius Press, 1994.

Ratzinger, Joseph Cardinal with Vittorio Messori. *The Ratzinger Report.* San Francisco: Ignatius Press, 1985.

Roschini, Gabriele M., O.S.M. *Maria Santissima nella Storia della Salvezza.* 4 vols. Isola del Liri: Tipografia Editrice M. Pisani, 1969.

Sacrosanctum Oecumenicum Concilium Vaticanum II. *Constitutiones, Decreta, Declarationes.* Cura et studio Secretariae Generalis Concilii Oecumenici Vaticani II. Vatican City: Typis Polyglottis Vaticanis, 1974.

Santo Domingo Conclusions: New Evangelization, Human Development, Christian Culture. Fourth Conference of Latin American Bishops, October 12–28, 1992. Washington, D.C.: Secretariat, Bishop's Committee for the Church in Latin America, National Conference of Catholic Bishops, 1993.

Satini, Alceste. *Agostino Casaroli: Uomo del Dialogo.* Torino: Edizioni San Paolo, 1993.

Simon, Ulrich. *A Theology of Auschwitz.* London: SPCK, 1978.

Statistical Yearbook of the Church. Vatican City: Secretaria Status, Rationarium Generale Ecclesiae, 1991.

Styczen, Tadeusz, S. D. S, *Le encicliche di Giovanni Paolo II.* Milan: Mondadori, 1994.

Suenenes, Léon Joseph Cardinal. *Ecumenism and Charismatic Renewal.* London: Darton, Longman and Todd, 1978.

Terelya, Josyp and Michael H. Brown. *Witness.* Milford: Faith Publishing Company, 1992.

Thompson, Colin P. *The Poet and the Mystic: A Study of the Cantico Espiritual of San Juan de la Cruz.* Oxford University Press, 1997.

Trasatti, Sergio and Arturo Mari. *Journey in Suffering.* Bergamo, Italy: Editrice Velar, 1981.

Vatican Council II: The Conciliar and Post Conciliar Documents. Volumes 1 and 2. Northport, NY: Costello, 1992.